TRADE ISSUES, POLICIES AND LAWS

TRADE REFORMS, POVERTY AND INEQUALITY IN BANGLADESH

TRADE ISSUES, POLICIES AND LAWS

Additional books in this series can be found on Nova's website under the Series tab.

Additional e-books in this series can be found on Nova's website under the e-book tab.

TRADE ISSUES, POLICIES AND LAWS

TRADE REFORMS, POVERTY AND INEQUALITY IN BANGLADESH

BODRUN NAHAR
MAHINDA SIRIWARDANA
AND
MALCOLM TREADGOLD

nova publishers
New York

Library of Congress Cataloging-in-Publication Data

ISBN: 978-1-63117-505-3

Published by Nova Science Publishers, Inc. † New York

CONTENTS

Preface		**vii**
About the Authors		**ix**
List of Tables		**xi**
List of Figures		**xv**
List of Appendices		**xvii**
List of Abbreviations		**xix**
Chapter 1	Introduction	**1**
Chapter 2	The Bangladesh Economy: Policies and Performance	**9**
Chapter 3	An Overview of Poverty, Inequality and the Labour Market in Bangladesh	**25**
Chapter 4	A Survey of Literature	**37**
Chapter 5	The Bangladesh Model: Theoretical Structure	**57**
Chapter 6	The Database	**99**
Chapter 7	Eliminating Tariffs: Macroeconomic, Sectoral and Household Effects	**123**
Chapter 8	Eliminating Tariffs: Effects on Poverty and Inequality	**153**
Chapter 9	Conclusion	**177**
Appendices		**185**
References		**221**
Index		**235**

PREFACE

The primary concern of this study is to identify the impacts that the unilateral elimination of all import tariffs would have on poverty and inequality in Bangladesh. The study also explores the impacts on macroeconomic performance, on output and employment in individual industries, on employment by gender and skill category, and on the household income and consumption of various socio-economic groups.

A static multi-sectoral, multi-factor and multi-household computable general equilibrium (CGE) model is used to simulate the short run and long run effects of the unilateral removal of all tariffs, both with and without an endogenously determined uniform consumption tax to compensate for the loss of tariff revenue. Changes in poverty are assessed in terms of the head count index (a measure of the incidence of poverty), the poverty gap index (a measure of the average depth of poverty) and the squared poverty gap index (a measure of the severity of poverty). Changes in the inequality of household incomes are assessed in terms of the Gini index, the Atkinson index and the entropy index.

In the short run, the removal of tariffs without a compensatory consumption tax results in a marginal decline in poverty in rural areas according to all three poverty indices, while in urban areas fewer people experience poverty but the average depth and severity of poverty increase. Simultaneously, inequality increases slightly among households in both rural and urban areas according to all three measures of inequality. In the long run, however, there are significant reductions in poverty accompanied by declines in inequality in both rural and urban areas.

Combining the removal of tariffs with a compensatory consumption tax produces short run increases in all three poverty measures and decreases in all three inequality measures for both rural and urban areas. On the other hand, poverty falls in the long run, although the declines in the poverty measures are smaller than the long run declines that occur in the absence of a consumption tax. Inequality also falls in the long run, the declines in the inequality measures being larger than their short run declines, but smaller than their long run declines in the absence of a consumption tax.

The authors gratefully acknowledge the assistance of the Swinburne University of Technology Research Authority in facilitating the publication of this book.

ABOUT THE AUTHORS

Bodrun Nahar is a Senior Lecturer in Economics at the Faculty of Business and Design, Swinburne University of Technology, Sarawak Campus, Malaysia, and a former Associate Professor at the University of Chittagong in Bangladesh. She received her PhD in Economics from the University of New England, Australia. Her principal research areas are computable general equilibrium modelling, international trade policy analysis and the poverty and distributional impacts of trade policies in the South Asia region. She has more than 16 years of teaching and research experience in Economics. Her publications include a book and a number of articles on aspects of the Bangladesh economy. Journals in which she has published include *The Developing Economies*, *South Asia Economic Journal*, *Economic Affairs* and *Asian Profile*.

Mahinda Siriwardana is Professor of Economics at UNE Business School, University of New England, Armidale, Australia. He received his PhD from La Trobe University in Melbourne. His main research interests include computable general equilibrium modelling, trade policy analysis, and carbon price modelling. He has published several books, book chapters, and numerous journal articles in these fields. Some of his recent articles appeared in *South Asia: The Journal of South Asian Studies, The Journal of Developing Areas, The Global Economic Review, Forest Policy and Economics, Journal of the Asia Pacific Economy, South Asian Economic Journal, Journal of Economic Integration, The North American Journal of Economics and Finance, Academy of Taiwan Business Management Review, Tourism Analysis, Environmental and Resource Economics, Tourism Management, The Developing Economies, Journal of Asian Economics, and International Journal of Global Energy Issues.* He is also a recipient of several Australian Research Council (ARC) grants.

Malcolm Treadgold is an Emeritus Professor and former Professor of Economics at the University of New England, Australia. He received his PhD from the Australian National University. His principal research interests are development economics, macroeconomics and the history of economic thought. He is the author of *Bounteous Bestowal: The Economic History of Norfolk Island* and *The Economy of Fiji: Performance, Management and Prospects*, and co-author of *The Australian Economy: Your Guide*. Other publications include articles in *World Development*, *Financial History Review*, *History of Economics Review*, *Australian Economic History Review* and *International Journal of Economic Policy in Emerging Economies*.

LIST OF TABLES

Table 1.1. Percentage of people living on less than US $1 a day (1993 purchasing power parity), 1981-2004 .... **2**

Table 1.2. Income disparities between the lowest and highest quintile in Bangladesh, 1981-2004 .... **5**

Table 2.1. Evolution of import restrictions **14**

Table 2.2. Average exchange rate (taka per US $) **17**

Table 2.3. Trends in fiscal account, 1980-2005 (as percentage of GDP) **18**

Table 2.4. Annual exchange rates (TK per US $) and trade policy bias in Bangladesh, 1991-1998 .... **19**

Table 2.5. Macroeconomic indicators, 1973-2005 .... **20**

Table 3.1. Head count indices of poverty using the Cost of Basic Needs Method, 1983/84-2005 (percentage of population below the poverty line) **27**

Table 3.2. Regional trends in poverty (head-count ratio), 1991-2005 (using the upper poverty line) **28**

Table 3.3. Poverty incidence by labour force status of household head, 2000 (using the upper poverty line) **28**

Table 3.4. Trends of HDI in Bangladesh, 1975-2004 .... **30**

Table 3.5. Income distribution in Bangladesh (percentage share of income of households by quintile group), 1973-2005 .... **32**

Table 3.6. Population, labour force and employment, 1983/84-1999/2000 .... **34**

Table 3.7. Sectoral distribution of employment (per cent) **35**

Table 3.8. Real wages indices, 1990/91-1999/2000 (base 1969/70 =100) **36**

Table 5.1. Main sets of the Bangladesh model **59**

Table 5.2. Tally of variables and equations of the Bangladesh model (Standard closure) **95**

Table 6.1. Domestic Supply table at purchasers' prices 103

Table 6.2. Use Table at purchasers' prices 103

Table 6.3. Import duties by commodity 104

Table 6.4. Domestic taxes by commodity 104

Table 6.5. Contents of the RAWDATA.HAR 107

Table 6.6. Contents of the ORANI-G data files 107

Table 6.7. A simplified representation of the Bangladesh model SAM database (in Million Taka) 117

Table 6.8. Household income composition (per cent) 120

Table 6.9. Labour income composition by sex and occupation (per cent) 121

Table 6.10. Income Distribution among Household Groups 121

Table 7.1. Projected effects of a 100 per cent tariff cut in all sectors: Selected macro variables (percentage changes) 127

Table 7.2. Projected effects of a 100 per cent tariff cut: output and employment by industry (percentage changes) 132

Table 7.3. Percentage changes in nominal factor prices 141

Table 7.4. Employment by occupational group (percentage changes) 142

Table 7.5. Nominal and real disposable income of households (percentage changes) 143

Table 7.6. Household consumption effects in the long run (percentage changes) 145

Table 7.7. Macroeconomic effects of tariff liberalisation for different values of Armington elasticities in the short run (percentage changes) 146

Table 7.8. Macroeconomic effects of tariff liberalisation for different values of Armington elasticities in the long run (percentage changes) 147

Table 7.9. Macroeconomic effects of tariff liberalisation for different values of primary factor elasticities in the short run (percentage changes) 149

Table 7.10. Macroeconomic effects of tariff liberalisation for different values of primary factor elasticities in the long run (percentage changes) 150

Table 8.1. Base year estimates of FGT poverty indices (in percentages) 159

Table 8.2. FGT poverty indices (in percentages) for various policy experiments (short run) 160

Table 8.3. Percentage changes of poverty indices from the base year for various policy experiments (short run) 160

Table 8.4. FGT poverty indices (in percentages) for various policy experiments (long run) 161

Table 8.5. Percentage changes of poverty indices from the base year for various policy experiments (long run) **161**

Table 8.6. Other poverty indices under different policy scenarios (short run) **163**

Table 8.7. Percentage changes of other poverty indices from the base year (short run) **163**

Table 8.8. Other poverty indices under different policy scenarios (long run) **164**

Table 8.9. Percentage changes of other poverty indices from the base (long run) **164**

Table 8.10. Inequality measures for different policy simulations (short run) **167**

Table 8.11. Percentage changes of inequality indices from the base year (short run) **167**

Table 8.12. Inequality measures for different policy simulations (long run) **168**

Table 8.13. Percentage changes of inequality indices from the base year (long run) **168**

Table 8.14. Income inequality sensitivity to changes in elasticities (simulation 1) **174**

List of Figures

Figure 2.1. Unweighted average protective import duties for all tariff lines, 1991/92-2004/05. .... **11**

Figure 2.2. Unweighted average protective import duties for industrial tariff lines, 1991/92-2004/05. .... **12**

Figure 2.3. Unweighted average protective import duties for agricultural tariff lines, 1991/92-2004/05. .... **12**

Figure 2.4. Average protective tariffs by type of goods, FY 1996-FY2005. .... **13**

Figure 2.5. Import penetration, export orientation and trade–GDP ratios, 1973-2005 .... **19**

Source: Calculated from BBS, *Statistical Yearbook of Bangladesh* (various issues). **21**

Figure 2.6. Sectoral contributions to GDP, 1970-2005 (per cent) **21**

Figure 2.7. Commodity composition of exports (percentage shares), 1980-2003 .... **22**

Figure 2.8. Rates of domestic saving and investment, 1980-2005. .... **23**

Figure 3.1. Head count index by acres of land owned, 2005 (using upper poverty line). **29**

Figure 3.2. Incidence of poverty by educational statistics, 2005 (using upper poverty line). **29**

Figure 3.3. Long-term trends in inequality in Bangladesh, 1973-2005 .... **33**

Figure 5.1. Structure of production **64**

Figure 5.2. Structure of investment demand. **71**

Figure 5.3. Structure of consumer demand. **75**

Figure 5.3. From TAB to EXE file **96**

Figure 5.4. From EXE file to model solution. **97**

Figure 6.1. The Bangladesh model input-output database. **100**

Figure 6.2. Overview of data preparation steps **106**

Figure 7.1. The schematic representation of short run closure.. **125**

Figure 7.2. The schematic representation of the long run closure.. **126**

Figure 7.3. Short run effects of complete removal of tariffs on real incomes of household groups for different values of Armington elasticities (Simulation 1).. **147**

Figure 7.4. Long run effects of complete removal of tariffs on real incomes of household groups for different values of Armington elasticities (Simulation 1).. **148**

Figure 7.5. Short run effects of complete removal of tariffs on real incomes of household groups for different values of primary factor elasticities (percentage changes) (Simulation 1)... **151**

Figure 7.6. Long run effects of complete tariff reduction on real incomes of household groups for different values of primary factor elasticities (percentage changes) (Simulation 1).. **151**

Figure 8.1. Short run poverty effects of complete removal of tariffs under different sets of Armington elasticities.. **169**

Figure 8.2. Long run poverty effects of complete removal of tariffs under different sets of Armington elasticities.. **170**

Figure 8.3. Short run poverty effects of complete removal of tariffs under different sets of primary factor elasticities.. **171**

Figure 8.4. Long run poverty effects of complete removal of tariffs under different sets of primary factor elasticities.. **173**

LIST OF APPENDICES

Appendix A

Table A 2.1. Effective protection rates (EPRs) in 40 sectors in Bangladesh (percentages) **185**

Appendix B

Table B 5.1. List of variables in the Bangladesh model **186**

Table B 5.2. List of coefficients and parameters in the Bangladesh model **192**

Table B 5.3. Derivation of consumer demand for a composite commodity **195**

Appendix C

Table C 6.1. Commodity and industry classification in the Bangladesh model **197**

Table C 6.2. Sectoral mapping of I-O Table 2000 and SAM 2000 for Bangladesh **199**

Table C 6.3. Elasticities of substitution between domestic and imported commodities **201**

Table C 6.4. Household expenditure elasticities **202**

Appendix D

Table D 7.1. Base case tariff rates, import share and export share (expressed as ratios) **204**

Table D 7.2. Fan decomposition (simulation 1) (per cent) **207**

Table D 7.3. Short run changes in imports by usage (simulation 1) (in Million Taka) **210**

Table D 7.4. Ranked Fan decomposition (simulation 2) (per cent) **214**

Table D 7.5. Base year total wage payments by industry and occupational group (in Million Taka) **218**

List of Abbreviations

ADB	Asian Development Bank
APTA	Asia-Pacific Trade Agreement
AVAT	Advanced Value Added Tax
BBS	Bangladesh Bureau of Statistics
BOI	Board of Investment
CBN	Cost of Basic Needs
CES	Constant Elasticity of Substitution
CET	Constant Elasticity of Transformation
CGE	Computable General Equilibrium
DCI	Direct Calorie Intake
FDD	Foreign Direct Investment
FEI	Food Energy Intake
EPZ	Export Processing Zone
ERP	Effective Rate of Protection
GATT	General Agreement on Tariffs and Trade
GDP	Gross Domestic Product
GOB	Government of Bangladesh
GTAP	Global Trade Analysis Project
HDI	Human Development Index
HIES	Household Income and Expenditure Survey
HDR	Human Development Report
IPO	Import Policy Order
IFS	International Financial Statistics
IMF	International Monetary Fund
L/C	Letter of Credit
LES	Linear Expenditure System
MDGs	Millennium Development Goals
MFN	Most Favoured Nation
NCBs	Nationalised Commercial Banks
NIP	New Industrial Policy
PRSP	Poverty Reduction Strategy Paper
QRs	Quantitative Restrictions
REER	Real Effective Exchange Rate

RIP	Revised Industrial Policy
RMG	Ready-made Garments
SAFTA	South Asian Free Trade Area
SAM	Social Accounting Matrix
SAP	Structural Adjustment Program
SAPTA	South Asian Preferential Trade Agreement
VAT	Value Added Tax
WB	World Bank
WTO	World Trade Organization
XPB	Export Performance Benefit
XPL	Export Performance Licensing

Chapter 1

INTRODUCTION

1.1. BACKGROUND TO THE STUDY

Since the early 1980s, the liberalisation of domestic markets and their integration into the global economy have become an important development strategy for developing countries. The strategy has been pursued in various ways, including reductions in quantitative restrictions, tariff reductions, and simplification of tariff structures. While some of these trade reforms have been implemented unilaterally, most have been initiated through the structural adjustment reform programs of the World Bank and the IMF, or through regional trade agreements. The insistence of the IMF and the World Bank on trade reform is based on the belief that liberalisation will bring important welfare gains to these countries.

According to mainstream economic theory, trade reform leads to greater allocative efficiency and hence greater aggregate income. In addition, mainstream economic theory recognises that trade reform affects the distribution of aggregate income. For example, the Stolper-Samuelson theorem (Stolper and Samuelson, 1941) suggests that in developing countries with abundant supplies of unskilled labour, trade liberalisation will increase the real wages of unskilled labour and thus its share of the functional distribution of income. In so far as it is the poorer groups who rely upon unskilled labour for their livelihoods, it can therefore be argued that trade liberalisation is particularly beneficial for the poor in unskilled-labour-abundant developing countries.

Contrary to this theoretical argument, critics of globalisation claim that closer integration of developing countries with the world economy means that in developing countries the rich get richer and the poor get poorer. The critics also claim that the World Trade Organization (WTO), whose members account for nearly 90 per cent of international trade, reinforces the asymmetry of economic and political power among nations, despite developing countries making up three quarters of its membership. Public protests during recent WTO, IMF, World Bank and World Economic Forum (WEF) meetings have drawn attention to the current uneven character of the global trade regime. The Doha Round of the WTO was named the 'Development Round' to indicate a focus on reform of the global trading system in favour of the development of the poor countries. By 2012, however, a lack of progress in negotiations had left the interests of poor countries unsatisfied.

Within this context, and accepting the importance of the "Millennium Development Goals", which seek to halve world poverty by 2015, the IMF and the World Bank are now imposing poverty reduction policies as a condition of their funding to developing countries.[1] To meet World Bank funding conditions, a developing country needs to prepare a Poverty Reduction Strategy Paper (PRSP) in assessing the impacts of its economic policies on the poor.

There has been considerable debate in the empirical literature about the impacts of trade liberalisation on poverty and inequality. The majority of the recent empirical literature exploring the impact of trade liberalisation has concluded that trade liberalisation has a positive impact on poverty reduction (for example, Ben-David, Nordstrom and Winters (1999); Cline (2004); Collier and Dollar (2001); McCulloch, Winters, and Cirera (2001); Oxfam (2002); Winters (2002); and Winters, McCulloch, and McKay (2004)). On the other hand, critics of globalisation and trade liberalisation (for example, Cornia (2003) and Gunter and van der Hoeven (2004)) contend that in the majority of cases trade liberalisation has worsened inequality. Most studies have tried to correlate trade liberalisation and poverty via growth in the economy. For example, Cline (2004), World Bank (2004), Hertel and Reimer (2004) and Rajan and Bird (2002) have emphasised long-term growth as the primary vehicle for poverty reduction. In addition, Dollar and Kraay (2002) and Dollar and Kraay (2001) used a cross-country regression approach to examine growth performance in relation to trade policy and found no general trend in inequality among countries known as 'globalisers'.

Table 1.1. Percentage of people living on less than US $1 a day (1993 purchasing power parity), 1981-2004

Region	1981	1987	1993	1999	2004
East Asia and the Pacific	57.7	28.2	25.2	15.5	9.0
China	63.8	28.6	28.4	17.8	9.9
Europe and Central Asia	0.7	0.4	3.6	3.8	0.9
Middle East and North Africa	5.1	3.1	1.9	2.1	1.5
South Asia	51.6	44.9	37.1	35.8	32.0
Sub-Saharan Africa	42.3	47.2	45.5	45.8	41.1
Latin America and Caribbean	10.8	12.1	8.4	9.7	8.6
Total	40.6	28.7	25.6	22.3	18.4

Note: Figures for 2004 show preliminary estimates.
Source: World Bank (2007b).

Table 1.1 provides some indication of general trends in poverty in the developing world by tracing the share of population living on less than US $1 a day in developing countries during the period 1981-2004. It can be seen that except for Europe and Central Asia, this measure of the extent of poverty fell in all regions over the 24-year period. The greatest reductions occurred in China, where the proportion of people living on less than US $1 a day fell from 63.8 per cent to 9.9 per cent, and in East Asia and the Pacific, where the proportion fell from 57.7 per cent to 9.0 per cent. Sub-Saharan Africa showed a net increase until 1999,

[1] The Millennium Development Goals (MDGs) are the eight goals in the Millennium Declaration that was adopted by 189 nations and signed by 147 heads of states and governments during the UN Millennium summit in September 2000.The goals are: (1) to eradicate extreme poverty and hunger; (2) to achieve universal primary education; (3) to promote gender equality and empower women; (4) to reduce child mortality; (5) to improve maternal health; (6) to combat HIV/AIDS, Malaria, TB and other diseases; (7) to ensure environmental sustainability; and (8) to promote a global partnership for development. The member countries have agreed to achieve these goals by the year 2015.

but thereafter the proportion declined to 41.1 per cent in 2004. In South Asia the proportion fell substantially, but in 2004 its level of 32.0 per cent was still the second highest in the developing world after Sub-Saharan Africa.

Despite decreasing poverty trends, it is cause for concern that by 2008 about 2.5 billion people, i.e., 43 per cent of the total population of all developing countries, still lived on less than US $2 a day in terms of 2005 purchasing power parity, and about 1.3 billion people, i.e., 22 per cent, lived on less than US $1 a day. Among these, about 44 per cent lived in South Asia (World Bank, 2012).

It is also cause for concern that poverty reduction has been accompanied by rising inequality. In developing regions, the share of the poorest fifth of the population in national consumption fell from 4.6 per cent to 3.9 per cent between 1990 and 2004. The largest falls were in Eastern Asia, where the share of the poorest fifth fell from 7.1 per cent in 1990 to 4.5 per cent in 2004, and in the CIS (Commonwealth of Independent States), where it fell from 7.9 per cent in 1990 to 6.2 per cent in 2004.

In the context of on-going debate about the impacts of trade liberalisation on poverty and inequality, country case studies offer the opportunity for close and specific examination of the issues. Bangladesh, the subject of this case study, is an appropriate and readily justified choice. It was among the first of 35 countries that adopted Bretton Woods Institution-sponsored structural adjustment programs. As a contracting party to the GATT since 1972, and as an original member of the WTO, Bangladesh has initiated various policy reforms in order to integrate with the world economy. In the 1980s, it was the second country in the South Asian region after Sri Lanka to start opening up its economy. It has also become party to many regional trade agreements, including the South Asian Preferential Trade Agreement (SAPTA), the South Asian Free Trade Area (SAFTA), the Bay of Bengal Initiative for Multi-Sectoral Technical and Economic Cooperation (BIMSTEC)[2] and the Asia-Pacific Trade Agreement (APTA)[3] also known as the Bangkok Agreement. However, despite the implementation of various international programs and individual government efforts, poverty has remained widespread, especially in rural areas. According to a World Bank report in 2002 (World Bank, 2002), Bangladesh had the highest incidence of poverty in South Asia, the third highest absolute number of poor in the world after India and China, and one of the lowest per capita GDP figures (US $366 per annum in 2000) in the world. About 36 per cent of the population lived on less than US $1 per day (in 2000) and about 82.8 per cent lived on less than US $2 per day. Also, the distribution of income displayed severe inequality. In 2005 the top 20 per cent of households in terms of income received nearly 53 per cent of total household income, while the bottom 20 per cent received little more than 5 per cent.

---

[2] BIMSTEC, which came into effect in July 2006, offers co-operation in six areas: trade and investment, technology, transport and communication, energy, tourism and fisheries. The member countries are Bangladesh, India, Sri Lanka, Thailand, Myanmar, Nepal and Bhutan.

[3] ATPA was established in 1975. Current member countries are Bangladesh, India, Lao Peoples Democratic Republic, the Republic of Korea, Sri Lanka, and China.

1.2. Trade Liberalisation and the Bangladesh Economy

Following independence in 1971,[4] Bangladesh initially pursued a highly protectionist trade policy as part of an inward-looking development strategy that also involved nationalisation of major industrial enterprises, banking and infrastructure, price controls and control of agricultural inputs and marketing (Ahmed and Sattar 2004). The protectionist trade policy was implemented through quantitative controls on imports, exceptionally high tariff rates on imports, and strict exchange controls. In the early 1980s, however, there was a sharp change in policy direction, involving the adoption of market-oriented liberalising policy reforms under the guidelines of the IMF and the World Bank. Reforms launched in the 1980s were aimed mainly at privatisation of state-owned enterprises, financial liberalisation and some limited liberalisation of foreign trade. Major progress in trade policy reform occurred in the 1990s, with a substantial scaling down and rationalisation of tariffs, removal of most trade–related quantitative restrictions on imports (QRs), elimination of import licensing, unification of exchange rates and the move to a more flexible exchange rate system (Ahmed and Sattar, 2004).[5] On the export side, greater efforts were made to expand and diversify the export base. As well as, long-standing bonded warehouse and duty drawback schemes, export incentives now included income tax exemptions and tax holidays, concessional interest rates on bank loans, and export credit guarantee facilities. Finally, in 2003, Bangladesh adopted a floating exchange rate in place of the fixed exchange rate system dating from 1972. Although the initial response of the economy to the reforms was not promising, dramatic changes occurred during and after the 1990s.[6] Openness, measured by the ratio of trade (exports plus imports) to GDP, increased from 18 per cent in the 1980s to 23 per cent in the 1990s, and to over 30 per cent during the period 2000-05 (IFS). The growth of real GDP, which had averaged 3.5 per cent annually in 1980-85, increased to 5.2 per cent in 2000-05, while the average annual rate of growth of per capita real GDP rose from 1.3 per cent to 3.3 per cent (IFS). Also between 1980-85 and 2000-05, the average annual rate of inflation fell from 10.8 per cent to 3.4 per cent; the government budget deficit as a proportion of GDP fell from 9.3 per cent to 4.5 per cent; and the current account deficit in the balance of payments, expressed as a proportion of GDP, shrank from 3.2 per cent to only 0.1 per cent. Clearly, Bangladesh's more liberal trade policies were associated with faster economic growth and greater stability.

1.3. Research Problem

The acceleration in the growth of per capita income in Bangladesh was accompanied by considerable progress in poverty reduction. The overall incidence of poverty (as measured by the proportion of the population living below the Bangladesh Bureau of Statistics' 'upper' poverty line) fell from 59 per cent in 1991-92 to 40 per cent in 2005. Over the same period, the poverty gap (the average shortfall from the poverty line, counting the non-poor as having zero shortfall) fell from 17 per cent to 9 per cent. Notwithstanding the reduction in poverty,

---

[4] Before 1971, Bangladesh was the eastern part of Pakistan. It became an independent nation after a war of liberation.

[5] The nature and extent of economic reforms in Bangladesh are discussed in more detail in Chapter 2.

[6] Details on Bangladesh's post 1990 economic performance are to be found in Chapters 2 and 3 of this study. See also Hossain (2006), and Mujeri and Khondker (2002).

the faster rate of growth in incomes in Bangladesh was also accompanied by a substantial increase in household income inequality. As shown in Table 1.2, there was little net change in the ratio of the share of the top quintile of households in total income to the share of the bottom quintile between 1981-82 and 1991-92, but thereafter the ratio trended strongly upwards. Similarly, between 1983 and 1991 there was only a small increase in the Gini coefficient from 0.36 to 0.39, but thereafter it rose steeply to 0.47 in 2005.[7]

To what extent did trade liberalisation contribute to the combination of faster economic growth, reduced poverty and increased inequality observed in Bangladesh? This question has provided the motivation for the present study, which seeks to develop an analytical framework to explore the direct and indirect effects of trade policy reform on poverty and inequality, as well as on macroeconomic performance and economic structure.

Table 1.2. Income disparities between the lowest and highest quintile in Bangladesh, 1981-2004

Year	1981-82	1983-84	1985-86	1988-89	1991-92	1995-96	2000	2004
Ratio of top 20% to lowest 20%	6.8	6.0	6.0	7.0	6.9	8.8	11.0	11.1

Source: BBS (1988), BBS (2004a) and BBS (2006).

1.4. Objectives of the Study

The general aim of this study is to examine quantitatively how a change in trade policy involving the complete removal of all import tariffs affects poverty and household income distribution in Bangladesh, in both the short run and the long run. In addition, this study seeks to gain insight into how the elimination of tariffs affects various macroeconomic indicators, output and employment in individual industries, and households' welfare. Specifically, this study seeks to answer the following questions.

- What will be the impact of eliminating tariff protection on poverty and the distribution of income?
- Which industries will be most affected by the removal of tariffs?
- How will various socio-economic groups be affected by the removal of tariffs?
- How will various macroeconomic aggregates such as GDP, aggregate employment, exports, and imports be affected by the removal of tariffs?

In line with these questions, the specific objectives of the study are:

1. to provide an overview of trade liberalisation policies in Bangladesh and accompanying developments in macroeconomic performance, poverty, inequality and the labour market;

[7] In this context, the Gini coefficient measures the extent to which the distribution of income deviates from a perfectly equal distribution of income. It ranges in value from zero (everyone has the same income) to one (where all income accrues to one person).

2. to develop a static multi-sectoral, multi-factor and multi-household computable general equilibrium (CGE) model for Bangladesh, that incorporates an endogenous poverty line;
3. to link the CGE model to household income and expenditure survey data, using a top-down representative household approach; and
4. to assess the effects of the removal of tariffs (both with and without a consumption tax to compensate for the loss of tariff revenue) on macroeconomic performance, output and employment in individual industries, poverty and the distribution of income.

1.5. METHODOLOGY

The static multi-household, multi-sector computable general equilibrium model developed in this study to assess the effects of tariff liberalisation in Bangladesh follows IDC-GEM, a SAM-based computable general equilibrium model of the South African Economy (Horridge et al. 1995). IDC-GEM is, in turn, based on the Australian ORANI-F model (Horridge, Parmenter, and Pearson, 1993), which closely follows ORANI, a multi-sectoral CGE model for the Australian Economy (Dixon et al. 1997). Using the approach proposed by Decaluwé et al. (1999), poverty analysis is performed with income variations in combination with an endogenously determined poverty line in a representative household approach. By using a non-parametric representative household approach, income distribution functions are empirically estimated for each group of households from household survey data and are linked to the CGE model in a top-down fashion.

The Foster-Greer-Thorbecke (FGT) measure of poverty is used to quantify household poverty levels. It allows us to estimate three poverty indices: the head count ratio, poverty gap index and squared poverty gap index. We also employ three measures of inequality: the Gini index, the Atkinson index and the Entropy index.

1.6. OUTLINE OF THE STUDY

The rest of this study is structured as follows. Chapter 2 presents an overview of trade liberalisation policies in Bangladesh and accompanying macroeconomic developments. Chapter 3 examines trends in poverty, inequality and labour market conditions in Bangladesh. Chapter 4 explores the theoretical and empirical linkages between trade policy, inequality and poverty. In addressing the empirical linkages, this chapter highlights the CGE literature that has focused on poverty and income inequality. In addition, Chapter 4 surveys CGE models that have been used for analysing policies in Bangladesh. Chapter 5 develops a static multi-sectoral, multi-household CGE model for the Bangladesh economy. Chapter 6 describes the construction of the database for the Bangladesh model and the construction of the social accounting matrix (SAM) that is needed to implement the income distribution part of the model. Chapter 7 describes the closure of the model and presents the macroeconomic, sectoral (industry) level and household level results of alternative trade policy simulations. Chapter 8 presents the poverty and inequality results of the trade policy simulations. Finally,

Chapter 9 summarises the main findings of the study, briefly discusses their policy implications, notes some limitations of the study, and offers suggestions for future research.

Chapter 2

THE BANGLADESH ECONOMY: POLICIES AND PERFORMANCE

2.1. INTRODUCTION

Since gaining political independence from Pakistan in 1971, the Bangladesh economy has undergone numerous shifts in trade, fiscal, industrial and financial policies. Immediately after independence Bangladesh adopted a protectionist inward-oriented policy regime with rigid trade and exchange controls. In the 1980s and 1990s, the country experienced a radical shift to a more liberal policy regime under the structural adjustment programs (SAPs) suggested by the World Bank and the International Monetary Fund (IMF).[1] The biggest challenge within Bangladesh's economic reform program has been the liberalising of its trade sector. Other policy measures include reforms in the fiscal, financial and the industrial sectors.

This chapter presents an overview of the trade liberalisation policies pursued in Bangladesh and accompanying macroeconomic developments. Section 2.2 is a very brief outline of the historical context from which the trade policy reforms emerged. Section 2.3 describes their nature and extent and highlights the implementation of various import liberalisation and export promotion policies in Bangladesh. It also examines financial sector reforms (including reforms of the foreign exchange market), and fiscal reforms. Section 2.4 uses a variety of measures of trade openness to assess the progress achieved in trade liberalisation in Bangladesh. Section 2.5 evaluates the macroeconomic performance of the Bangladesh economy. Section 2.6 provides a brief conclusion.

2.2. ECONOMIC CONDITIONS IN THE 1970S

The war of liberation in 1971 that led to the independence of Bangladesh left the new nation with a badly damaged and dislocated economy. Transport, communication and power systems had been particularly hard hit. Real GDP in 1972-73 was 13 per cent below its 1969-

[1] Structural Adjustment Programs (SAP) are the policy changes the IMF and the World Bank require of developing countries in return for providing them with new loans or lower interest rates on existing loans. An SAP is implemented through a Structural Adjustment Facility (SAF), Enhanced Structural Adjustment Facility (ESAF), Structural Adjustment Loans (SALs), and Sectoral Adjustment Loans (SECALs). See Rashid (2000).

70 level, and real GDP per head was 17 per cent lower. Faced with the urgent investment requirements of reconstruction and rehabilitation and inadequate domestic and foreign resources, the government turned to deficit finance. As a result, there were large increases in the money supply and rapid inflation (Rashid, 2000). Inevitably, given the fixed exchange rate, the taka (the domestic currency) became severely overvalued, and with steeply rising imports and depressed exports, foreign exchange reserves fell to low levels. Despite a 58 per cent devaluation of the taka in 1975, trade deficits persisted, averaging over 8 per cent of GDP in the period 1973-1980.

Over the same period, prompted by the chronic balance of payments problem, policy makers pursued a highly protectionist trade policy. The tariff structure was characterised by very high tariffs on imports of final goods and lower tariffs on imports of intermediate and primary products. In addition, widespread quantitative restrictions (QRs) banned the import of luxury and non-essential commodities. This pattern of protection contributed to industry growing faster than agriculture (which failed to keep up with population growth) and to exports remaining highly concentrated on raw jute and jute goods.

By 1975-76, real GDP had recovered to its 1969-70 level (although because of population growth it would not be until the early 1980s that real GDP per head exceeded its 1969-70 level). Over the period 1973-1980 as a whole, real GDP recorded a compound annual rate of growth 5.6 per cent. This was substantially higher than the growth rates subsequently recorded in the 1980s (see Table 2.6). It was, however, growth from a much lower, war-devastated production base and it benefited from the relatively high productivity of gross investment focused largely on reconstruction and rehabilitation.

2.3. Nature and Extent of Economic Reforms

Economic liberalisation in Bangladesh can be divided into three phases: phase I (FY 1982-FY1986), phase II (FY 1987-FY 1991) and phase III (FY 1992-onwards) (Bayes & Muhammad, 1998). Phase I included the New Industrial Policy of 1982, which provided for denationalisation of public enterprises and simplification of investment sanctioning procedures. This policy was followed by some downward adjustment of tariffs and QRs. Phase II saw the introduction of the Revised Industrial Policy of 1986, which was aimed at promoting private enterprise and providing incentives and opportunities for private investment. Phase III brought a significant intensification of the trade liberalisation program. In addition, the Industrial Policy of 1991 (revised in 1992), which was based on the philosophy of market economy,[2] offered greater incentives for private investment through provisions such as tax holidays, and accelerated depreciation allowances. The following sections examine key aspects of these phases in more detail.

2.3.1. Import Policy Changes

Under this heading we deal first tariff reform and then the phasing-out of quantitative restrictions.

[2] See Ahmed (2001).

2.3.1.1. Tariff Reform

During the 1980s, in addition to some downward adjustment of tariff levels, there were several attempts to reform the tariff structure through reducing the variance of tariffs. The number of statutory rates was cut from 24 to 11 in 1986, and then in 1988 the government adopted a three-year program to cut maximum tariffs on imports of most final goods to 100 per cent, on intermediate products to 75 per cent, and on raw materials to 20 per cent (Ahammad, 1995).

The overall situation, however, did not begin to show substantial improvement until the early 1990s. Thereafter, operative tariff rates and statutory tariff rates were equalized. The number of tariff bands was gradually reduced from 15 in 1992-93 to 5 (0 per cent, 7.5 per cent, 15 per cent, 22.5 per cent and 30 per cent) in 2004-05. The maximum tariff rate was lowered from 300 per cent in 1990-91 to 37.5 per cent in 1999-2000. Most favoured nation (MFN) tariffs fell from an average of 58 per cent to 22 per cent over the same period (WTO, 2006), and the share of duty-free tariff lines increased from 4 per cent in 1992 to 30 per cent in 2003.

The unweighted average protective rate of all tariff lines, which includes para-tariffs as well as customs duties, provides a useful summary measure of nominal tariff protection.[3] This rate fell from 73.6 per cent in 1991-92 to 32.0 per cent in 1995-96 and then to 26.6 per cent in 2004-05. The much slower pace of liberalisation after 1995-96 reflected a combination of smaller cuts in import duties and an increased use of para-tariffs (Figure 2.1). This combination meant that for industrial tariff lines the average protective rate fell only modestly from 31.9 per cent to 25.4 per cent between 1995-96 and 2004-05 (Figure 2.2), while for agricultural goods it meant that over the same period the average protective rate actually rose slightly from 32.4 per cent to 32.7 per cent (Figure 2.3).

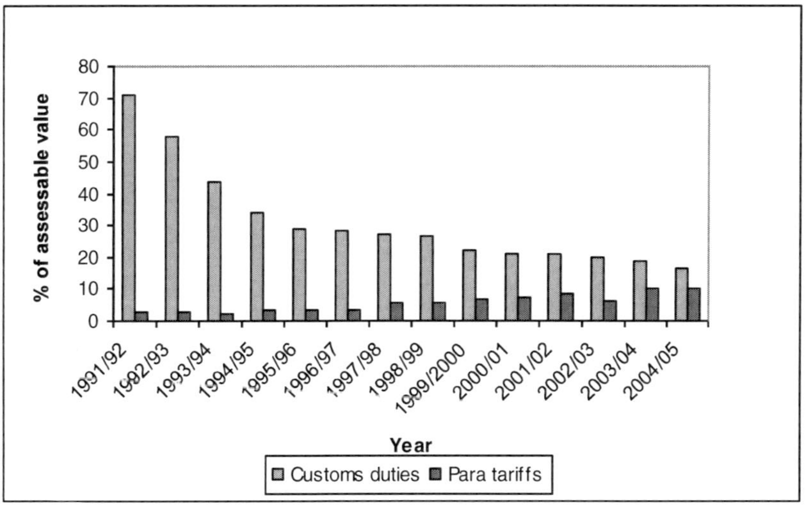

Source: World Bank (2006b).

Figure 2.1. Unweighted average protective import duties for all tariff lines, 1991/92-2004/05.

[3] Para-tariffs are fees and charges that are imposed on imports in addition to, or in place of, tariffs. Since the early 1990s Bangladesh has used five different para-tariffs to raise revenue as well as provide extra protection for selected import competing industries. They are the Infrastructure Development Surcharge (IDSC), Supplementary Duties (SD), Regulatory Duties, protective VAT (Value Added Tax) and License Fee. See World Bank (2006b) for details.

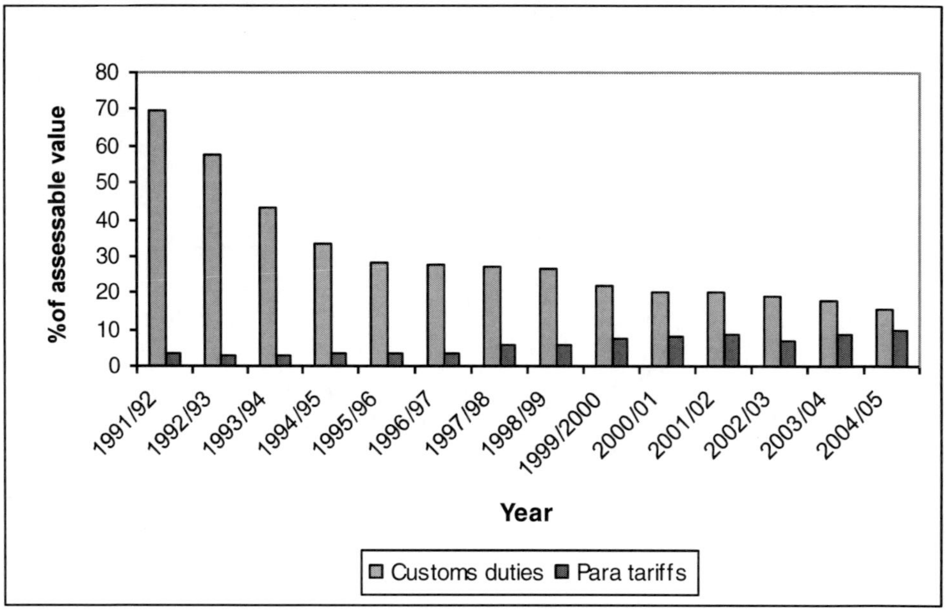

Source: World Bank (2006b).

Figure 2.2. Unweighted average protective import duties for industrial tariff lines, 1991/92-2004/05.

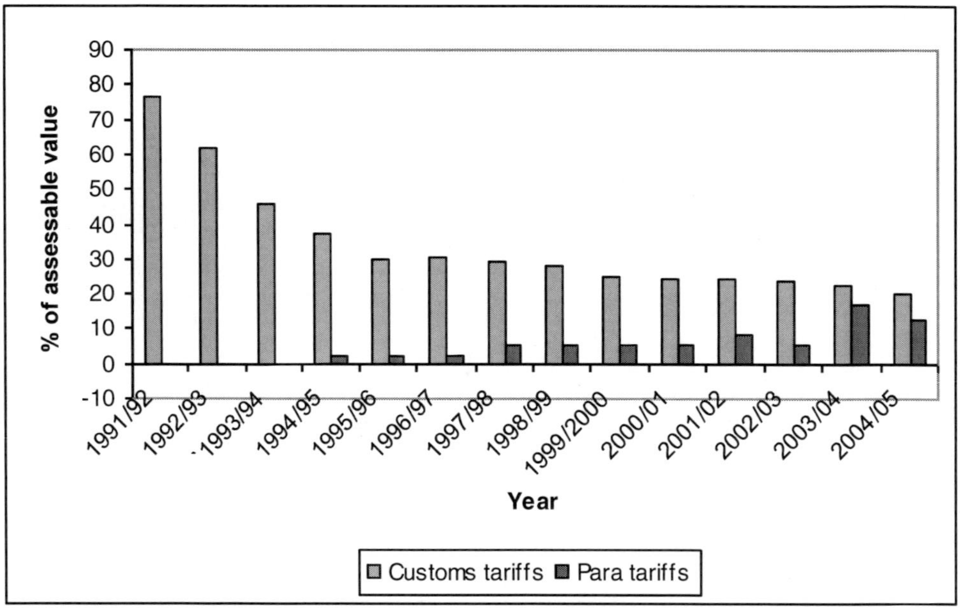

Source: World Bank (2006b).

Figure 2.3. Unweighted average protective import duties for agricultural tariff lines, 1991/92-2004/05.

As shown in Figure 2.4, between 1995-96 and 1004-05 the average protective rate for final consumer goods consistently exceeded the average protective rate for intermediate goods, and the latter consistently exceeded the average protective rate for raw materials. This escalation in the tariff system created distorting differences in effective rates of protection (ERPs), both within the import substitution sector and between import substitution activities and export activities.[4] Estimates of industry-wide ERPs by the Bangladesh Tariff Commission for the period 1992-93 to 1999-2000 indicate that between 1992-1993 and 1995-96 there were large declines in both the average industry ERP (from 75.7 per cent to 33.0 per cent) and in the coefficient of variation for the ERPs (from 111.5 per cent to 77.7 per cent). Over the subsequent four year to 1999-2000, however, there was a much smaller decline in the average ERP to 24.5 per cent, while the coefficient of variation actually rose slightly to 81.6 per cent.[5]

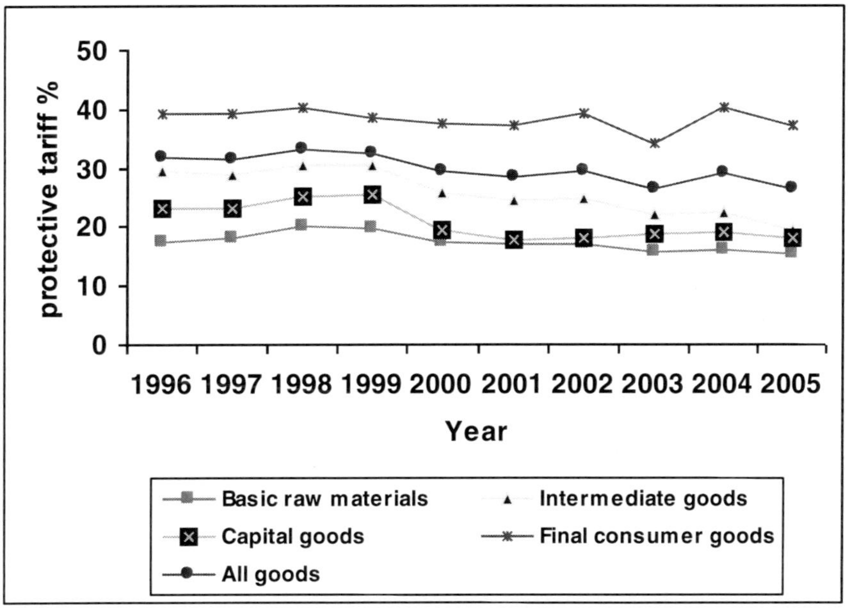

Source: Adapted from World Bank (2006b).

Figure 2.4. Average protective tariffs by type of goods, FY 1996-FY2005.

2.3.1.2. Elimination of Quantitative Restrictions

In the early 1980s Bangladesh had a very restricted import regime characterised by QRs under which imports of many products were effectively banned; only commodities included in the 'positive list' were allowed to be imported. In 1985 the 'positive list' was replaced by the 'negative list', which listed all banned items, and the 'restricted list', which listed items that were allowed to be imported under certain conditions. Items not included in these two lists could be imported freely. During the 1990s there were significant reductions in the number of commodities subject to quantitative restrictions. Major relaxations of QRs took place under the Import Policy Order (IPO) of 1991-93, which reduced the number of items on the import control list from 325 to 193, and IPO 1993-95, which further reduced the number to 111. Despite a limited and temporary reversal of the process of relaxation in the latter half

[4] The effective rate of protection is the percentage change in the value added per unit of output in an industry because of the imposition of tariffs. It takes into account the effects of tariffs on importable inputs to the industry as well as the effccts of tariffs on imports that compete with the output of the industry.

[5] See Appendix A, Table A 2.1.

of the 1990s, IPO 2003-2006 eventually reduced the number to 63, of which only 24 were listed for trade-related (protective) purposes (Table 2.1).

Table 2.1. Evolution of import restrictions

	IPO 1991-93	IPO 1993-95	IPO 1995-97	IPO 1997-02	IPO 2003-06
Number of items in the control list at the HS-4 digit level	193 (15.6%)	111 (9.0%)	120 (9.7%)	122 (9.8%)	62 (4.98%)
Number of trade related items in the control list at the HS-4 digit level	79 (6.4%)	19 (1.5%)	27 (1.9%)	27 (2.2%)	24 (1.9%)

Source: Ahmed and Sattar (2004), WTO (2006).

According to Ahmed and Sattar (2004), whereas in 1990 about 26 per cent of all HS-4 digit codes were subject to QRs,[6] by 2002 only 122 items (or 10 per cent of items) covering about 2 per cent of imports remained restricted for either trade or non-trade reasons. Furthermore, the number of banned items was sharply reduced from 135 in the fiscal year 1990 to only 5 in 2000 (Rashid, 2000). Under IPO 2003-06, trade related restrictions were limited to a few agricultural products, some packaging materials and textiles. Nearly 40 per cent of all QRs applied to textile products. However the ban on textile fabric imports for use in the domestic market was removed in January 2005 (World Bank, 2006b). Other remaining restrictions on the import of goods were on the grounds of health, safety, environment and other non-trade considerations.

2.3.2. Export Promotion Policies

Bangladesh's use of export promotion policies dates back to the late 1970s when, in the face of a chronic balance of payments problem, the government sought to expand and diversify exports through a range of measures to offset or reduce the costs of protection to exporters (Ahammad, 1995). Measures included:

1. the Export Performance Licensing (XPL) Scheme introduced in 1977. Under this scheme, exporters of non-traditional products obtained freely tradeable Import Entitlement Certificates equal in value to a certain percentage of their gross f.o.b export earnings, and freely tradeable. In 1986, the XPL scheme was renamed the Export Performance Benefit Scheme (XPB), with cash subsidies replacing the certificates at increased rates of entitlement (Ahammad, 1995; Ahmed, 2001).
2. the Special Bonded Warehouse Facility introduced for the ready-made garment industry in 1978, which allowed firms producing exclusively for export to import and stock duty free imports. Until 1993, this facility was available only for 100 per cent exporters in the garment industry using back-to-back letters of credit (L/C) and to suppliers that sold 100 per cent of their output to garment exporters (Ahmed, 2001).

[6] The Harmonized System (HS) is an internationally accepted system of classification of imports. The greater the number of digits, the greater is the level of detail in the description of the commodity.

After 1993, the special bonded warehouse facility was extended to all '100 per cent' exporters and 'deemed exporters'.[7]

3. Duty drawbacks. Under this system, exporters of manufactures who were not eligible under the Bonded Warehouse Facility could obtain a full or partial refund of the value of customs duties and sales taxes already paid on the importation of raw materials used in the production of export products. From 1980 a flat rate draw back scheme was introduced, under which it was paid on the basis of a rate determined on the f.o.b value of export products according to input-output coefficients.

By the time of Bangladesh's *Fifth Five year Plan 1997-2002* (GOB 1998), the government was committed to an export-led growth strategy involving a far wider range of an export promotion policies. Fiscal incentives now included (in addition to bonded warehouse facilities and duty drawback) income tax exemption for 50 per cent of income from exports (a provision introduced in 1995-96 to replace income tax rebates of up to 50 per cent); provision for tax holidays; and a continuation of duty-free import of capital machinery for export-oriented industries outside Export Processing Zones. Among other incentives were export credits at concessional interest rates, export credit guarantee facilities, and the entitlement of exporters to retain up to 40 per cent of their export earnings (7.5 per cent in the case of lower value added items such as ready-made garments) in their foreign currency accounts.

The impact that export promotion policies had on the growth of exports is uncertain. Although a relatively early study suggests that they did not have much positive effect (Ahammad, 1995: p. 27), there is some evidence to indicate that they at least contributed to a reduction in anti-export bias between 1991-92 and 1997-98.[8]

2.3.3. Financial Sector Reform Policies

Bangladesh inherited from Pakistan a repressed financial sector that featured interest rate controls, directed credit, and complex rules for money and capital markets. The degree of repression was almost immediately exacerbated by the nationalisation of all commercial banks and other financial institutions (Chowdhury, 2001). In 1982, a process of financial reform began with government decisions to privatise two nationalised commercial banks (NCBs) and to issue licences to a number of new private commercial banks (PCBs). The main aims of the government were to demonstrate a commitment to the private sector and to create competitive conditions in banking (Bhattacharya and Chowdhury, 2003).

In 1984, the government appointed the National Commission on Money, Banking and Credit to investigate problems in the banking sector. In response to the commission's report the government began a Financial Sector Reform Programme (FSRP) in 1990. This was supported by Financial Sector Adjustment Credit (FSAC) provided by the World Bank. The FSRP finished in 1996, but reforms continued to be pursued through the remainder of the decade and into the new century (Bhattacharya and Chowdhury, 2003).

[7] The local raw materials used for producing exportable products, and local products and raw materials used in foreign investment enterprises were deemed to be exports.

[8] See Table 2.4.

A key achievement was the liberalisation of interest rates on both loans and deposits. Starting in 1990, banks became free to set their own interest rates within prescribed bands. In 1992, the interest rate bands for loans were abolished for all sectors, except exports, agriculture, and small and cottage industries (Chowdhury 2000). In 1997, interest rate bands on deposits were eliminated and in 1999 the remaining bands for loans were withdrawn. (Chowdhury, 2001)

Significant progress was also made in the area of loan defaults, one of the biggest problems of the financial sector in Bangladesh. Measures included revisions to banks' loan classification and provisioning criteria and to legal provisions and procedures for enforcing recovery of loans by financial institutions. ('Money Loan Court' legislation was strengthened in 2003). In addition, efforts were made to improve the availability of information on credit risk. The Bangladesh Bank (the central bank) set up a Credit Information Bureau, and all newly sanctioned bank loans of more than10 million taka became subject to review by a Large Loan Review Cell (Chowdhury, 2001) As a result of these initiatives the level of bad loans gradually declined.

Other initiatives included improvements in the prudential supervision of financial institutions, a strengthening of the capital adequacy requirement for banks (brought up to the international standard of a minimum of 8 per cent of risk-weighted assets), and the introduction of central bank bills to facilitate indirect monetary management through open market operations (Chowdhury, 2000).

2.3.3.1. Reforms in Foreign Exchange Regime

Immediately after independence in 1971, Bangladesh's currency, the taka (TK), was pegged to the British pound sterling at £1=TK.18.97. However, due to existing expansionary fiscal and monetary policies, this system led to a crisis in the balance of payments (Hossain, 2000), and, as already noted, in 1975 the taka was devalued against the pound by 58 per cent. In 1979, the taka was pegged to a trade-weighted basket of the currencies of Bangladesh's major trading partners, but allowed to fluctuate within margins of 2.5 per cent on either side of the peg. In 1983, the intervention currency was changed from the pound to the US dollar, and after 1985 Bangladesh pursued a policy of frequent adjustment of the nominal official exchange rate peg to offset differences in the domestic and foreign inflation rates and thus keeps the real exchange rate constant.

From 1974 Bangladesh had operated a multiple exchange rate regime involving the official pegged rate and a secondary foreign exchange rate associated with the introduction of the Wage Earner's Scheme.[9] This scheme aimed to increase foreign currency remittances from the Bangladeshi workers employed abroad by providing an open market that offered a more favourable rate of exchange (determined by auction) than the official pegged rate. Importers facing shortages of foreign exchange allocations could buy foreign exchange in this market. Because of the increasing inflow of remittances, the Wage Earner's Scheme became in time an important medium for import liberalisation. It enabled importers to avoid the cumbersome and time-consuming process of import licensing (Bhuyan and Rashid, 1993). As the percentage difference between the official exchange rate and the secondary foreign

[9] The Wage earner's scheme aimed to increase foreign currency remittances from the Bangladeshi workers employed abroad by providing an open market that offered a more favourable rate of exchange (determined by auction) than the official pegged rate. Importers facing shortages of foreign exchange allocations could buy foreign exchange in this market.

exchange rate (known as the exchange rate premium) narrowed, more imports were shifted to the secondary market from the official market. Between 1983 and 1990, the percentage of total imports financed through the secondary market increased from 21 to 47 percent. Ultimately in 1992 the government unified the two exchange rates.

In 1994, Bangladesh accepted the Article VIII obligations of the IMF and thus committed to make the taka fully convertible on the current account. Under this obligation, authorised foreign exchange dealers were allowed, without any restrictions, to convert taka into foreign exchange for all trade and other current account transactions. The objectives of this measure were: i) to create confidence in the Bangladesh currency and thus in the management of the economy; ii) to facilitate international trade and support for the process of trade liberalisation; and iii) to link the economy with international markets, particularly financial markets (Alam, 1995).

Eventually, in May 2003 Bangladesh introduced a fully market-based exchange rate. Under this system, the Bangladesh Bank did not interfere in the determination of the exchange rate, except for occasional interventions to dampen excess volatility through the sale and purchase of foreign exchange (Younus and Chowdhury, 2006). Between 2002-03 and 2004-05 the taka depreciated by 22 per cent against the US dollar (Table 2.2)

Table 2.2. Average exchange rate (taka per US $)

Fiscal Year	1996-97	1997-98	1998-99	1999-00	2000-01	2001-02	2002-03	2003-04	2004-05
Average exchange rate	42.70	45.46	48.00	50.31	53.96	57.43	57.90	58.94	61.39

Source: GOB (2005).

2.3.4. Fiscal Policy Changes

The tax structure of Bangladesh can be divided into direct taxes and indirect taxes. Direct taxes include taxes on the income of individuals and corporations, and taxes on land and gifts. Indirect taxes include customs duty, VAT, taxes on motor vehicles, travel, electricity and turnover. In Bangladesh, over the entire period covering the 1990s and early twenty first century, indirect taxes accounted for about 75 per cent of total taxes, and around 50 per cent of indirect tax revenue came from taxation of imports in the form of custom duty, sales tax, development surcharge, license fees and regulatory duty (Chowdhury, 2005).

As part of structural adjustment, the government initiated a major reform of the tax system. The objective was to reduce the heavy dependence on trade taxes by moving more towards domestic taxes. Steps taken in this direction included the introduction of a VAT in 1991, in place of sales tax at the import stage and excise duty on domestically produced goods. The VAT was introduced at a uniform rate of 15 per cent at the manufacturer-cum-import level.[10]It was followed by an Advanced Value Added Tax (AVAT), introduced in

[10] At the initial stage, textiles, medicines, books, the output of cottage industries, capital goods, hand-made cigarettes, bank services, fertilizer, and other agricultural inputs were exempted from the VAT (World Bank, 1995).

2004 at a rate of 1.5 per cent and calculated on the assumption of a minimum 10 per cent value addition at the wholesale and retail levels (WTO, 2006).

With these reforms, total revenue of the government rose significantly. Table 2.3 shows the trends in revenue, expenditure and the budget deficit, relative to GDP, during the period 1980-2005. Total revenue, which had averaged about 9 per cent of GDP during the 1980s, grew to an average of more than 10 per cent over the next fifteen years, almost entirely as a result of an increase in the ratio of tax revenues to GDP. Meanwhile, a result of the government's better control of current expenditures, total expenditure as a proportion of GDP fell from 17.5 per cent to about 15 per cent. Reflecting these developments, the budget deficit as a proportion of GDP fell from an average of about 8 per cent in the 1980s to about 5 per cent over the next fifteen years.

Table 2.3. Trends in fiscal account, 1980-2005 (as percentage of GDP)

	1980-85	1985-90	1990-95	1995-00	2000-05
Total revenue	8.90	9.00	10.70	9.20	10.30
Tax revenue	7.20	7.20	8.60	7.40	8.20
Total expenditure	18.40	16.60	17.00	13.60	14.80
Overall budget deficit	9.30	7.50	6.60	4.50	4.50

Sources: World Bank (1995), GOB (2003a) and GOB (2006).

2.4. Measuring the Degree of Openness

As a result of the reform and liberalisation measures outlined in the previous section, Bangladesh became increasingly open to international market forces. This section provides some summary indicators of the changes in the degree of openness of the Bangladesh economy. They are (1) the import penetration ratio, (2) the export orientation ratio, (3) the trade-GDP ratio, and (4) the anti-export bias ratio.

Figure 2.5 shows the behaviour of the import penetration ratio (measured as the ratio of merchandise imports to GDP), the export orientation ratio (measured as the ratio of merchandise exports to GDP) and the trade-GDP ratio (measured as the ratio of the sum of merchandise imports and exports to GDP) over the period 1973-2003.

Starting from 17 per cent in 1973, the import penetration ratio trended downwards until the early 1990s, where upon it embarked on an upward trend to reach 22 per cent in 2005. The export penetration ratio, which was only 6 per cent of GDP in 1973, showed little net change until the early 1990s, but thereafter it also trended upwards to about 14 per cent in 2005. Finally, combining the two previous indicators, the ratio of trade (exports + imports) to GDP recorded a net increase from 23 per cent to 35 per cent over the period 1973-2005 as a whole. Reflecting the import penetration ratio, the trade-GDP ratio showed an initial downward trend to below 20 per cent, but from the early 1990s it displayed a strong upward trend, which resulted from the concurrent upward trends in both import and export ratios. Clearly, all three of these indicators show that as trade policy reform intensified in the 1990s, so did the importance of foreign trade to the economy.

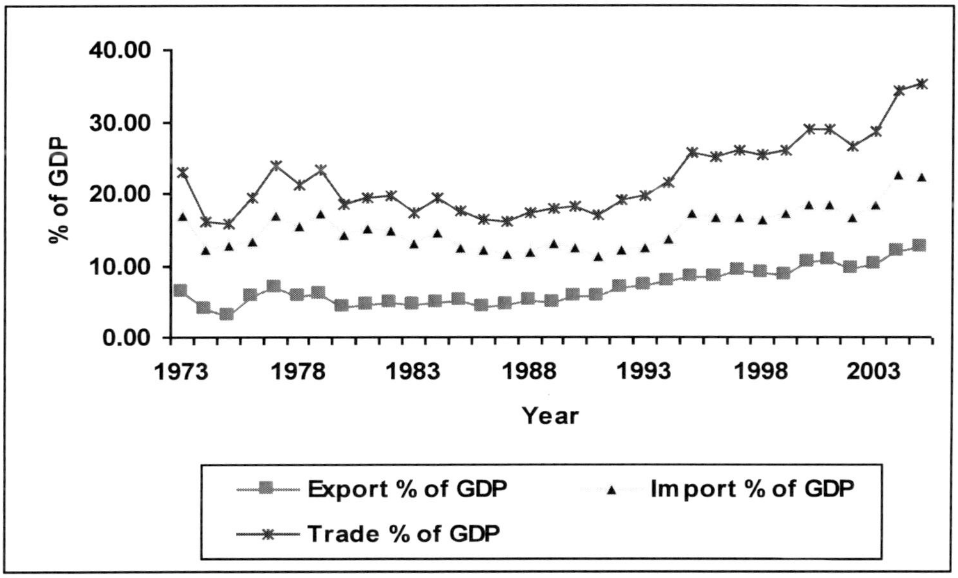

Source: Drawn from IMF, *International Financial Statistics* (various issues).

Figure 2.5. Import penetration, export orientation and trade–GDP ratios, 1973-2005.

The fourth indicator of openness, the anti-export bias ratio, measures the extent to which the structure of protection and incentives is biased against exports and in favour of import substitutes (Krueger, 1978, Bhagwati, 1988). It is estimated as the ratio of the effective exchange rate for imports (EERm) to the effective exchange rate for exports (EERx). EERm is the domestic market value of imports worth one unit of foreign currency, and is derived by adjusting the nominal exchange rate for protective import taxes and any scarcity premium arising from quantitative controls/restrictions. EERx is the domestic currency equivalent of proceeds from exports worth one unit of foreign currency, and is derived by adjusting the nominal exchange rate for subsidies and other export promotion schemes. A ratio of one indicates a neutral trade regime, a ratio above one indicates anti-export bias, and a ratio below one indicates pro-export bias.

Table 2.4. Annual exchange rates (TK per US $) and trade policy bias in Bangladesh, 1991-1998

Fiscal Year	Nominal exchange rate	EERm	EERx	EERm/EERx
1991-92	38.15	63.84	38.53	1.657
1992-93	39.14	60.81	39.72	1.531
1993-94	40.00	56.97	40.48	1.407
1994-95	40.20	52.79	40.53	1.302
1995-96	40.84	51.91	41.25	1.258
1996-97	42.70	54.16	43.22	1.253
1997-98	45.46	58.44	46.25	1.263

Source: World Bank (1999a).

World Bank estimates for Bangladesh show the anti-export bias ratio falling steadily from 1.66 to 1.26 between 1991-92 to1995-96, and then remaining essentially unchanged over the next two years, as a partial reversal of the earlier decline in the EERm counterbalanced a continuing decline in the EERx (Table 2.4). Nevertheless, over the period 1991-92 to 1997-98 as a whole, the anti-export bias ratio still recorded a net reduction of 24 per cent. This substantial shift in the structure of relative incentives for the production and consumption of exportables vis-à-vis importables is consistent with the upward movements in the export orientation and import penetration ratios over the same period.

2.5. Macroeconomic Performance and Structural Change

Following the reconstruction period of 1973-1980 when the Bangladesh economy expanded rapidly off a low war-devastated production base, the compound annual growth rate of real GDP slowed to a modest 3.5 per cent in the first half of the 1980s (Table 2.5). With the population growing at 2.4 per cent, the result was a growth rate for real GDP per head of less than 1.1 per cent.

The annual rate of growth of real GDP increased slightly to 3.8 per cent in the latter half of the 1980s, as the impact of early market-oriented policy reforms began to be felt, and then continued to accelerate in the 1990s as the trade liberalisation program intensified. By 1995-2000, it exceeded 5 per cent, a performance that was repeated in 2000-2005. Meanwhile, with the added impetus of a declining rate of increase of population, the annual rate of increase of GDP per head exceeded 3 per cent in 1995-2000 and again in 2000-05.

Table 2.5. Macroeconomic indicators, 1973-2005

Indicators	1973-80	1980-85	1985-90	1990-95	1995-2000	2000-05
Real GDP growth rate	5.61	3.50	3.81	4.34	5.06	5.17
Per capita real GDP growth rate	3.28	1.06	1.53	2.08	3.03	3.26
Trade balance–GDP ratio	-8.37	-8.46	-6.43	-4.76	-4.79	-4.63
Current account-GDP ratio	-4.56	-3.18	-2.18	-0.18	-1.18	-0.14
Inflation rate	19.30	10.80	8.30	4.20	3.80	3.40

Sources: Estimates derived from IMF, *International Financial Statistics* (various issues), BBS (Bangladesh Bureau of Statistics), *Statistical Yearbook of Bangladesh* (various issues), and Bangladesh Bank, *Economic Trends* (various issues).

Economic growth was associated with considerable structural change. Figure 2.6 shows sectoral contributions to GDP in terms of a broad three-way division of the economy into agriculture, industry and services. It can be seen that by 1980, when real GDP per head had been essentially restored to levels achieved before the War of Liberation, the share of agriculture in total GDP was, at 34 per cent, some seven percentage points below its pre-war (1970) level. On the other hand, the share of industry had increased two percentage points to 21 per cent, and the share of services had increased by five percentage points to about 45 per cent.

The share of agriculture continued to decline steadily through to 2005, when it amounted to about 22 per cent of GDP, a little over half its pre-war level. The share of industry stagnated between 1980 and 1990, but over the following 15 years rose by 2.6 percentage points to 24.2 per cent in 2005. The main driver of industrial growth was the export-oriented ready-made garments industry. During the 1990s, medium and large scale manufacturing as a whole grew at about 7 per cent annually, but at only about 4 per cent when the ready-made garments industry is excluded (Mahmud, Ahmed and Mahajan, 2008).

The services sector grew relatively rapidly during the 1980s, increasing its share of GDP to nearly 52 per cent in 1990. Thereafter its share stabilised, showing no significant net change through to 2005. Yet, despite the services sector having long been the largest contributor to GDP, it was the agricultural sector that remained the single largest employer of labour. Until the 1960s, agriculture had directly employed about 80 per cent of the labour force (Hossain, 1995). By the 1990s this share had declined to about 60 per cent (Hossain, 2006), and although it continued to decline along with the share of agriculture in GDP, the Bangladesh Labour Force Survey of 2002-03 found that 51.69 per cent of the labour force was still employed in agriculture, with the industry and service sectors accounting for 13.56 per cent and 34.75 per cent respectively (BBS, 2014b)

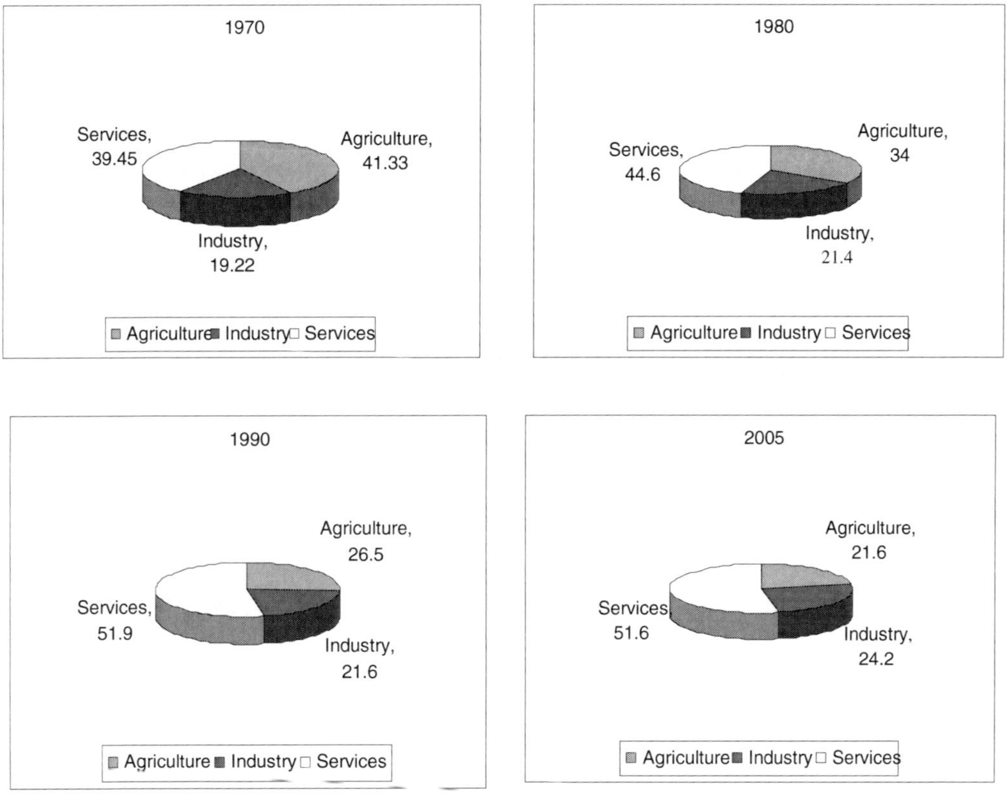

Source: Calculated from BBS, *Statistical Yearbook of Bangladesh* (various issues).

Figure 2.6. Sectoral contributions to GDP, 1970-2005 (per cent).

Exports played a key role in both economic growth and structural change. As implied by the behaviour of the export orientation ratio (Figure 2.5), merchandise export earnings increased more or less proportionately with nominal GDP between 1973 and 1990 before growing, on average, significantly faster than GDP through to 2005. In the early post-independence years, exports were dominated by Bangladesh's traditional export commodities, mainly jute and jute products (68 per cent of total exports), but also leather and leather products, and tea. Together they accounted for 82 per cent of exports in 1980. During the following decade, however, the rapid growth of hitherto minor, non-traditional exports transformed the commodity composition of Bangladesh's exports. By 1990, ready-made garments and knitwear formed the largest export category, accounting for 50 per cent of total exports; the share of jute and jute products had dropped to about 23 per cent; and frozen food (mainly shrimps), another non-traditional export, had moved into third place (8 per cent). The rapid growth of ready-made garments and knitwear exports continued through the 1990s, their share of total exports reaching 75 per cent in 2000 and remaining at this level up to 2003. Meanwhile, the share of jute and jute products fell to 6 per cent in 2000 and only 4 per cent in 2003 (Figure 2.7).

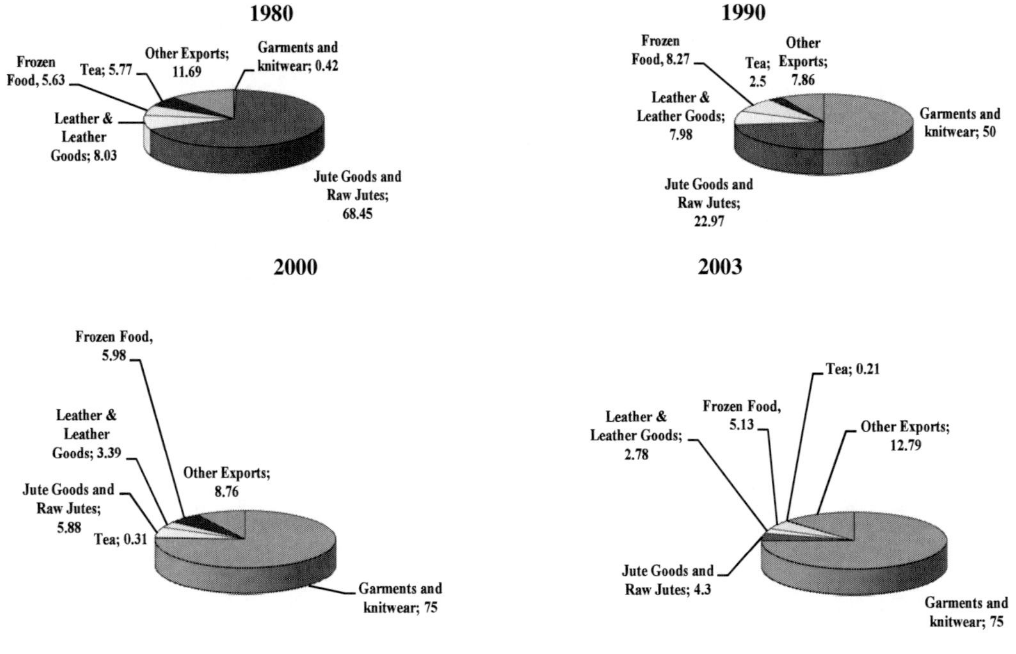

Source: Drawn from Ahmed (2005).

Figure 2.7. Commodity composition of exports (percentage shares), 1980-2003.

In contrast to exports, there were no remarkable structural changes in the commodity composition of total imports. Bangladesh's imports continued to consist mainly of capital goods, raw materials and intermediate goods for export-oriented products, and final consumer goods. One notable phenomenon, however, is the increase in the coverage of imports by exports. In 1999-2000, merchandise exports financed about 69 per cent of imports compared with only 35 per cent in the early 1980s (BBS, 2004a). This improvement was reflected in the balance of trade deficit expressed as a percentage of GDP, which declined from an average of over 8 per cent in the early 1980s to an average of less than 5 per cent in the period 1990-2005 (Table 2.5). In turn, the reduction in the trade balance as a percentage of GDP reinforced the impact of a rising inflow of remittances on the current account deficit, it fell from an average of more than 3 per cent of GDP in the first half of the 1980s to only 0.14 per cent in 2000-05.

There was remarkable success in reducing inflation and keeping it under control. The average annual rate of inflation declined continuously from 19 per cent in 1973-80 to 8 per cent the late 1980s, and then to less than 4 per cent in the late 1990s. By 2000-05, it was down to 3.4 per cent (Table 2.5). The average annual inflation rate for 2000-04 was 4.9 per cent, which was lower than in India, Pakistan and Sri Lanka, where the rates were 7.7, 7.9, and 10.4 per cent respectively (World Bank, 2006a).

There were also improvements in both the domestic saving- and investment rates (Figure 2.8). From a negligible level at the beginning of the 1980s, the ratio of domestic saving to GDP rose to around 10 per cent by the beginning of the 1990s and then continued to rise to a plateau of about 18 per cent in the early years of the twenty-first century. The ratio of investment to GDP had briefly reached this level two decades earlier, but then fell away during the mid-1980s before also trending upwards, in this case to reach about 25 per cent in 2005.

Foreign as well as local investors contributed to the increase in the investment rate. At the time of independence, the total volume of FDI (foreign direct investment) in Bangladesh was only US $27 million, and new inflows were slow to arrive. But starting from a trickle in the 1980s, the inflow of foreign direct investment rose to nearly US $400 million in 1997-98, (World Bank, 1999b), helped by private sector reforms and large export and investment incentives. In 2004, FDI in Bangladesh increased to about US $660.8 million (BOI, 2005), the bulk going into the gas, garment and textile sectors.

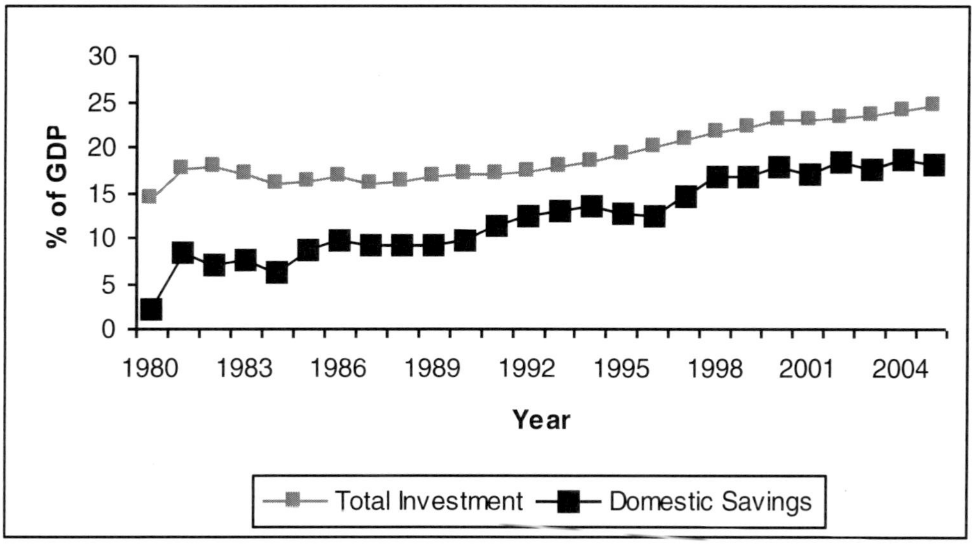

Source: World Bank (2007).

Figure 2.8. Rates of domestic saving and investment, 1980-2005.

2.6. SUMMING-UP

This chapter has described Bangladesh's reform policies and provided a brief account of economic development from independence until the early years of the present century.

Beginning in the 1980s, the government undertook a series of radical policy changes, including liberalisation of the trade and foreign investment regime, strengthening of the financial sector, closing or privatising some loss-making state-owned enterprises, and broadening the tax base by introducing a VAT. Macroeconomic indicators suggest a broadly positive relationship between the reform policies and economic performance. However, economic policies have to be judged not only in aggregate terms but also by their impacts on poverty and inequality. The next step is to examine these dimensions of economic performance in Bangladesh.

Chapter 3

AN OVERVIEW OF POVERTY, INEQUALITY AND THE LABOUR MARKET IN BANGLADESH

3.1. INTRODUCTION

The present chapter provides an historical overview of poverty, inequality and labour market developments in Bangladesh. Section 3.2 constructs a poverty profile of Bangladesh. Section 3.3 explores changes in income inequality in Bangladesh. Section 3.4 looks at labour force trends, structural changes in employment, and the behaviour of real wages. Section 3.5 summarises the key points.

3.2. A POVERTY PROFILE OF BANGLADESH

3.2.1. Trends in Poverty Incidence in Bangladesh

There have been numerous studies of the incidence of poverty in Bangladesh. Some have investigated the relationship between trade liberalisation and poverty incidence, and concluded that globalisation has contributed positively to poverty reduction. They include Osmani (2005), Mujeri and Khondker (2002), Roy (1996), World Bank (1998), Osmani et al. (2003), Sen et al. (2004) and Annabi et al. (2005). Other studies have measured the trends and determinants of poverty (for example, Hossain and Sen (1992), Khundker et al. (1994), Khan (1990), Osmani (1990) and Wodon (1999). Although all of the studies used data provided by the Household Expenditure Surveys (HES) conducted by the Bangladesh Bureau of Statistics (BBS), there remains much controversy about the extent of poverty, particularly in the 1970s and 1980s (Ravallion and Sen, 1996).

Most studies have measured the incidence of poverty by the head count ratio. This measure may be broadly defined as the percentage of the population with a level of consumption, income or some other indicator of welfare that is below the level of a specified poverty line. Three methods have been used in Bangladesh to set an absolute poverty line: the direct calorie intake (DCI) method, the food-energy-intake (FEI) method, and the cost of basic needs (CBN) method (World Bank 1998). The DCI method uses caloric intake as the welfare indicator, and equates the poverty line with a normatively defined minimum calorific intake per person per day. It is a time-consistent approach, but relies on a narrow indicator of welfare that is not representative of individuals' command (or lack of command) over basic goods and services. The FEI method uses consumption expenditure as the welfare indicator, and sets the poverty line by computing the consumption level at which households are expected to meet the normative nutritional requirement (Wodon, 1997). This approach uses a representative indicator, but its poverty lines are not necessarily consistent in terms of real purchasing power across time and space. Finally, the CBN method also uses consumption expenditure as the welfare indicator, but sets the poverty line at the level of expenditure at which households are able to satisfy pre-determined basic needs. It is an approach that is both representative and consistent across time and space (World Bank, 1998). In the mid-1990s, the Bangladesh Bureau of Statistics (BBS) abandoned the FEI method and replaced it with the CBN method. There were three steps involved in estimating CBN poverty lines (World Bank, 1998). The first was the definition and costing of a representative, fixed food bundle that provided minimal nutritional requirements of 2,122 kilocalories per person per day. Separate costings of the fixed bundle for 14 geographic areas, using area-specific food prices, yielded a so-called food poverty line for each area. The second step was the estimation of area-specific allowances for non-food consumption. Because of the difficulty of defining a fixed non-food bundle, 'lower' and 'upper' allowances for non-food basic needs were computed for each area from representative households' actual non-food expenditures.[1] The third step was simply to add the food poverty lines to the 'lower' and 'upper' non-food allowances, thus obtaining the total lower and upper poverty lines for each geographical area.

The World Bank/BBS estimates of the incidence of poverty, using the CBN method, are presented in Table 3.1. This table has several notable features. First, it shows that the national incidence of poverty declined between 1983-84 and 2005, as measured both by lower and upper poverty lines. Over this period, the proportion of Bangladesh's population identified as poor (per capita consumption below the upper poverty line) fell from 58.50 per cent to 40 per cent, and the proportion of the population identified as extremely poor (per capita consumption below the lower poverty line) fell from 40.91 per cent to 25.1 per cent.).

Second, the decline in poverty incidence was far from steady. For both poverty lines, the national head count ratio fell sharply between 1983-84 and 1985-86, but then increased in the years through to 1991-92, before again declining. Broadly similar patterns of short-run change can be observed in both rural and urban areas. The damaging effects of floods on agricultural output in 1987 and 1988 appear to have contributed to the fluctuations (Sen et al. 2004).

Third, if the period 1983/84 to 2005 is divided into just two sub-periods, pre-1991/92 (corresponding approximately to the initial phases of reform) and post-1991/92 (corresponding approximately to the intensive phase of reform), it can be seen that in terms of net changes the decline in the national incidence of poverty was confined to the later sub-period. For example, using the upper poverty line, the national incidence of poverty actually increased by 0.6 per cent between 1983/84 and 1991/92, as a 2.7 per cent increase in poverty in rural areas outweighed a 10.5 decrease in poverty in urban areas. On the other hand,

[1] The lower non-food allowance was estimated by taking the median per capita amount spent on non-food items by a group of households whose per capita total expenditure was close to the food poverty line. The upper non-food allowance was obtained by taking the median per capita amount spent on non-food items by a group of households whose per capita food expenditure is close to the food poverty line (BBS, 2006).

between 1991/92 and 2005, the national incidence of poverty fell by as much as 32.0 per cent, reflecting falls of 28.4 per cent and 36.7 per cent in rural and urban areas respectively. This evidence is not inconsistent with the hypothesis that trade liberalisation reduced the incidence of poverty in Bangladesh. It is also not inconsistent with acceleration in the rate of growth in per capita consumption expenditure at the national level. Per capita HIES (Household Income and Expenditure Survey) consumption expenditure grew at an annual rate of 0.6 per cent between 1983-84 and 1991-92. This increased to 2.7 per cent between 1991-92 and 2000 (Sen and Hulme, 2006).

Table 3.1. Head count indices of poverty using the Cost of Basic Needs Method, 1983/84-2005 (percentage of population below the poverty line)

Year	% of population under lower poverty line			% of population under upper poverty line		
	Rural	Urban	National	Rural	Urban	National
1983/84	42.62	28.03	40.91	59.61	50.15	58.50
1985/86	36.01	19.90	33.77	53.14	42.92	51.73
1988/89	44.30	21.99	41.32	59.18	43.88	57.13
1991/92	45.95	23.29	42.69	61.19	44.87	58.84
1995/96	39.76	14.32	35.55	56.65	35.04	53.08
2000	37.90	19.90	34.30	52.30	35.20	48.90
2005	28.60	14.60	25.10	43.00	28.40	40.00

Sources: World Bank (1998), BBS (2006).

A fourth notable feature of Table 3.1 is the difference in the incidences of poverty between rural and urban areas. For each year in the table, the incidence in rural areas was higher than the incidence in urban areas for both upper and lower poverty lines, with the difference being proportionately larger for the lower poverty line. In this case, the ratio of the rural head count index to the urban head count index rose from 1.5 in 1983/84 to 2.0 in 1991/92, but showed no net change between then and 2005, as both indices registered similar percentage declines. In the case of the upper poverty line, the ratio rose from about 1.2 in 1983/84 to 1.4 in 1991/92, and then showed a further net increase to 1.5 in 2005, as the percentage decline of the urban head count index outstripped the percentage decline of the rural head count index.

There were also considerable differences in the incidence of poverty among regions. Using the upper poverty line, Table 3.2 reveals that in 1991/92 the Rajshahi division had the highest incidence of poverty (71.9 per cent), followed by the Khulna division (59.6 per cent) and the Dhaka division (59.3 per cent). The Chittagong division, which then included the area that in 1995 became the Sylhet division, recorded the lowest incidence (46.6 per cent) Between 1991/92 and 2000 there were substantial reductions in the incidence of poverty in the Dhaka, Khulna and Rajshahi divisions, and from 2000 to 2005, the incidence of poverty declined in all divisions. By the latter year, the Dhaka division had the lowest incidence (32.0 per cent), while the Rajshahi division continued to have the highest (51.2 per cent).

Table 3.2. Regional trends in poverty (head-count ratio), 1991-2005 (using the upper poverty line)

Division	1991-92	2000	2005
Chittagong	46.60	47.70	34.00
Dhaka	59.30	44.80	32.00
Khulna*	59.60	47.00	45.70
Rajshahi	71.90	61.00	51.20
Sylhet	..	42.40	33.80
All Divisions	58.80	48.90	40.00

*Including Barisal division.

Sources: World Bank (2002), BBS (2006).

3.2.2. Incidence of Poverty by Labour Force Status of Head of Household

Table 3.3 shows how the incidence of poverty in 2000 varied according to the labour force status of the head of household. Persons residing in households where the head worked as a casual wage labourer experienced by far the highest incidences of poverty, 75 per cent in rural areas and 67 per cent in urban areas. Some 46 per cent of the poor in rural areas (equal to about a third of the rural population) and 36 per cent of the poor in urban areas (equal to about a fifth of the urban population) were included in this category. The next highest incidences of poverty were among persons residing in urban households where the head was self-employed in agriculture and among persons in rural households where the head was self-employed in the non-agricultural industries.

Table 3.3. Poverty incidence by labour force status of household head, 2000 (using the upper poverty line)

Labour force status	Rural			Urban		
	Headcount index (%)	Per cent of		Headcount index (%)	Per cent of	
		Population	Poor		Population	Poor
Casual wage labour	74.90	33	46	66.9	20	36
Salaried employment	35.10	9	6	24.1	30	20
Self-employment: non-agriculture	44.60	18	15	32.2	32	28
Self-employment: agriculture	43.30	31	25	47.9	5	7
Unemployed/not working	42.90	10	8	25.9	13	9
Total	53.00	100	100	36.6	100	100

Source: ADB and Government of Japan (2004).

3.2.3. Poverty and Landownership

In Bangladesh, where 80 per cent of the population lives in rural areas and 50 per cent still depend on agriculture, land ownership is a key determinant of poverty. Figure 3.1 provides evidence from 2005 that the incidence of poverty tends to increase as the size of land holdings owned by households decreases, with a national incidence of 56.4 per cent among households owning less than 0.05 acres of land. Earlier evidence for 1995/96 indicated that among the landless in rural areas, six out of ten were very poor and seven out of ten were poor, while among marginal landowners (those owning less than half an acre), six out of ten were very poor and eight out of ten were poor (World Bank, 1998).

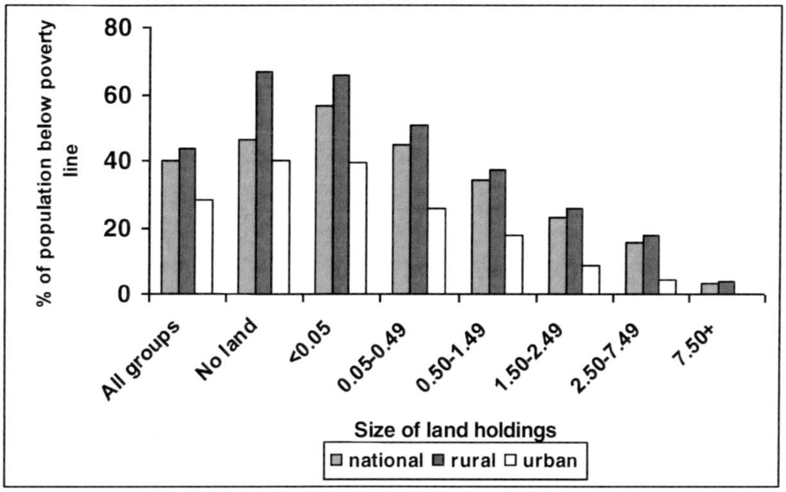

Source: BBS (2006).

Figure 3.1. Head count index by acres of land owned, 2005 (using upper poverty line).

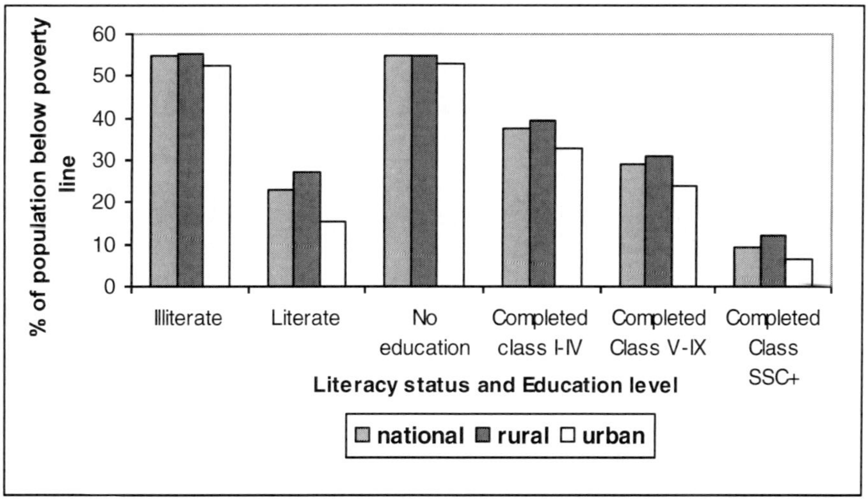

Source: BBS (2006).

Figure 3.2. Incidence of poverty by educational statistics, 2005 (using upper poverty line).

3.2.4. Poverty and Educational Attainment

Figure 3.2 reveals that for Bangladesh as a whole in 2005 households whose heads were illiterate had a probability of being poor of 54.7 per cent. The comparable figure for the literate was 31.7 percentage points lower. Figure 3.2 also shows that poverty declined as heads of households became more educated. Another notable feature was that with increasing education levels, urban poverty fell faster than rural poverty.

3.2.5. Human Development Index (HDI)

Since poverty is multidimensional (World Bank, 2002), it is important to define poverty in Bangladesh not only in terms of income or consumption but also in terms of the wider Human Development Index (HDI). The HDI is a composite index that measures the average achievements of a country in four basic dimensions of human development: life expectancy at birth; the adult literacy rate; the combined gross enrolment ratio for primary, secondary and tertiary schools; and gross domestic product per capita measured in terms of purchasing power parity. Bangladesh has made greater progress in terms of the HDI than in terms of income growth and poverty reduction narrowly defined. Indeed, its progress measured by the HDI compares favourably with most low-income countries. In 2004, it ranked 137 among 175 member countries, with an HDI of 0.51, a large improvement on its 0.347 in 1975 (Table 3.4). Bangladesh is one of the few countries amongst the least developed countries that increased its HDI score by 20 per cent between 1990 and 2004 (UNDP, 2006).

Table 3.4. Trends of HDI in Bangladesh, 1975-2004

Year	1975	1980	1985	1990	2000	2004	HDI rank in 2004
HDI	0.347	0.366	0.391	0.422	0.454	0.510	137

Source: UNDP (2006).

3.3. Trends in Income Inequality in Bangladesh

Although Bangladesh achieved substantial reductions in poverty over the 1990s and into the first half of the twenty first century, there has been concern that growing income inequality has limited the poverty-reducing effects of economic growth (Khan, 2006, Osmani et al. 2003, Sen et al. 2004, World Bank, 2002, Wodon, 1999). For instance, according to World Bank (2002) estimates, had the observed rate of growth during the period between 1991-92 and 2000 been distribution-neutral, poverty would have fallen by almost twice the actual observed rate.

Table 3.5 presents data on the distribution of household income over the period 1973-2005. The top half of the table shows the income shares of households ranked from lowest to highest quintile. Comparison of the end years, 1973/74 and 2005, for Bangladesh as a whole shows that at the national level in 2005 the income shares of all of the first four quintiles were lower than they had been in 1973/74 whereas the fifth (highest) quintile was nearly eight percentage points higher.

Most of this increase in inequality occurred from 1991/92 onwards, broadly coinciding with the intensification of trade reforms. In the 14 years from 1991/92 to 2005, the income share of the first (lowest) quintile fell from 6.5 per cent to 5.3 per cent; the share of the second quintile fell from 10.9 per cent to 9.1 per cent; the income share of the third quintile fell from 15.5 per cent to 13.1 per cent; and the share of the fourth quintile fell from 22.1 per cent to 19.8 per cent. Correspondingly, the fifth quintile increased its share from 44.9 per cent to 52.7 per cent. This meant that in 2005 the fifth quintile's income share was about ten times larger than the first quintile's share, whereas in 1991/92 it had been less than seven times larger.

Closer to the extremes of household income distribution, the share of income accruing to the top five per cent of households increased from 18.9 per cent in 1991/92 to 26.9 per cent in 2005, a 42 per cent increase. On the other hand, the share of the lowest five per cent fell from 1.03 per cent in 1991/92 to 0.77 per cent in 2005, a 25 per cent decrease. Thus, while in 1991/92 the ratio of the share of the top five per cent of households to the share of the lowest five per cent 18.3 by 2005, it had nearly doubled to 35.0.

Broadly similar patterns of change occurred in both rural and urban areas although inequality was higher in urban areas than in rural areas. In urban areas the share of each of the first four quintiles declined from 1991/92 to 2005, with a combined proportionate decrease of nearly 18 per cent. Correspondingly, the share of the fifth quintile increased by over 20 per cent. Closer to the extremes of the urban income distribution, the ratio of the share of the top five per cent of households to the share of the lowest five per cent rose from 17.8 in 1991 to 45.3 in 2005.

In rural areas the share of each of the first four quintiles also declined from 1991/92 to 2005, but with a smaller combined proportionate decrease of 10 per cent and a corresponding increase the share of the fifth quintile of about 13 per cent. The ratio of the share of the top five per cent of households to the share of the lowest five per cent rose from 16.6 in 1991/92 to 26.2 in 2005.

The Gini coefficient provides a summary indicator of the degree of inequality in the distribution of income. Figure 3.3 shows that, starting from an initial value of 0.36 in 1973/74, the national Gini coefficient increased to 0.39 in 1981/82, but then fell back to 0.36 in 1983/84, and did not again reach 0.39 until 1991/92. Thus, until 1991/92, the Gini coefficient provides little or no indication of an upward trend in the degree of inequality. Thereafter, however, the coefficient continued to rise, sharply at first and then more slowly, to reach 0.47 in 2005. The increase of more than 20 per cent between 1991/92 and 2005 represents a major increase in overall equality.

In the case of urban areas, the values of Gini coefficient were generally above those of the national coefficient. The urban coefficient rose from 0.38 in 1973/74 to 0.41 in 1981/82, before showing a small net decline to 0.40 in 1991/92. It then rose rapidly from 0.40 in 1991/92 to 0.44 in 1995/96 and to 0.50 in 2000 where it remained until 2005. In the case of rural areas, income inequality remained more or less stable until 1991/92, when the rural coefficient was 0.36, the same value as in 1973/74. It then increased to 0.38 in 1995/96 and 0.43 in 2005.

Table 3.5. Income distribution in Bangladesh (percentage share of income of households by quintile group), 1973-2005

Group	National					Urban					Rural				
	1973/74	1983/84	1991/92	1995/96	2005	1973/74	1983/84	1991/92	1995/96	2005	1973/74	1983/84	1991/92	1995/96	2005
1st Quintile	7.00	7.2 6	6.52	5.71	5.26	6.8	6.92	6.70	5.12	4.82	7.20	7.32	6.74	6.49	5.88
2nd Quintile	11.30	11.75	10.89	9.83	9.10	11.00	10.95	10.89	9.04	8.48	11.90	11.92	11.15	10.94	9.96
3rd Quintile	15.10	15.90	15.53	13.88	13.13	16.00	15.34	14.91	14.17	12.44	15.10	16.20	15.78	15.14	14.06
4th Quintile	22.80	21.73	22.10	20.50	19.79	22.00	22.57	21.43	20.33	18.71	23.30	21.86	22.58	21.62	20.76
5th Quintile	44.80	43.38	44.87	50.08	52.71	45.20	44.22	46.07	52.34	55.56	42.50	42.70	43.75	45.81	49.35
Gini Coefficient	0.36	0.36	0.39	0.43	0.47	0.38	0.41	0.40	0.44	0.50	0.36	0.35	0.36	0.38	0.43
Bottom 5%	1.20	1.17	1.03	0.88	0.77	-	1.18	1.09	0.74	0.67	-	1.19	1.07	1.00	0.88
Top 5%	16.40	18.30	18.85	23.62	26.93	18.60	16.93	19.42	24.30	30.37	16.00	18.14	17.80	19.73	23.03
Bottom 40%	18.30	19.01	17.41	15.54	14.36	17.80	17.87	17.59	14.16	13.30	19.10	19.24	17.89	17.43	15.84
Ratio of top 5% to bottom 5%	13.67	15.64	18.30	26.84	34.97	-	14.35	17.82	32.84	45.33	-	15.24	16.64	19.73	26.17

Source: Khan and Hossain (1989), BBS (2001) and BBS (2006).

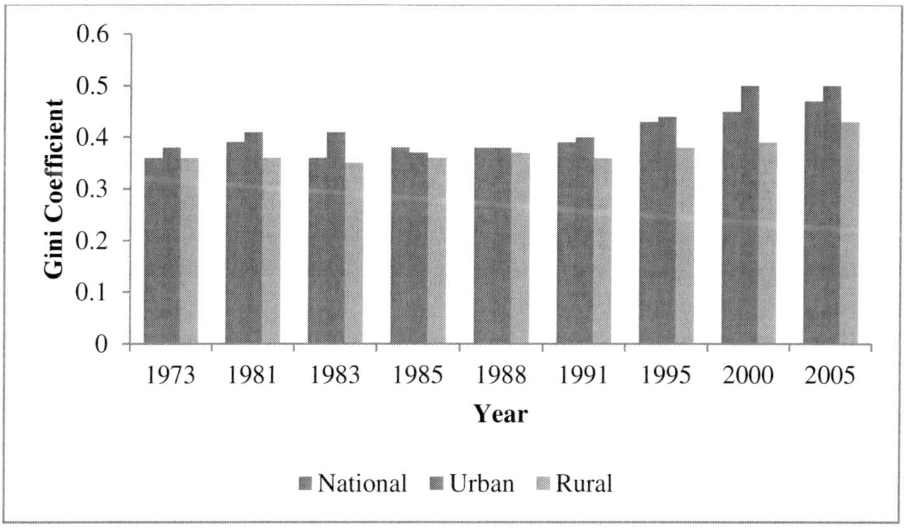

Source: Same as Table 3.5.

Figure 3.3. Long-term trends in inequality in Bangladesh, 1973-2005.

In general, it appears that whereas in the early phases of liberalisation policies in the 1980s the distribution of income was relatively stable, the intensification of trade reforms in the 1990s was accompanied by a substantial worsening of inequality.

3.4. Labour Market Developments in Bangladesh

The evidence provided in Chapter 2 and earlier parts of this chapter suggests at least broad correlations between trade liberalisation, faster economic growth, reductions in poverty and greater inequality. There are many possible interdependencies among these phenomena. For example, labour market behaviour in the form of increasing employment and/or real wages is potentially a key link between economic growth and the reduction of poverty. This section examines labour market trends in Bangladesh during the period of liberalisation and reform.

3.4.1. Demographic Changes and the Labour Market

Table 3.6 shows estimates of total population, labour force and employment from 1983/84 to 1999/2000.[1] Over the period as a whole, total population increased by about a third, although annual rates of growth trended downwards, reflecting a declining birth rate. Annual rates of growth of the labour force also trended downwards, but generally exceeded those of the total population. Between 1983/84 and 1999/2000, there was an overall increase in the labour force of 58 per cent, mainly as a result of growth in the working age population (Mujeri, 2004).

[1] Labour force and employment data refer to persons aged 10 years and above.

Table 3.6. Population, labour force and employment, 1983/84-1999/2000

Year	Population (million)	Civilian labour force (million)	Employed population (million)		
			Male	Female	Total
1983/84	95.21	28.49	25.55	2.43	27.98
1984/85	97.66	29.51	26.43	2.55	28.98
1990/91	109.02	35.90	30.44	4.47	34.91
1995/96	121.85	41.73	33.16	7.15	40.31
1999/2000	127.50	45.04	33.67	9.15	42.82

Sources: BBS Labour Force Surveys, as reported in Mujeri (2004).

Over the same period, employment grew by 53 per cent, also faster than the total population, with the proportion of the population in employment rising from about 29 per cent in 1983/84 to 32 per cent in 1990/91 and close to 34 per cent in 1999/2000. On the other hand, employment grew more slowly than the labour force. From 1983/84 to 1990/91, employment increased at an average annual rate of 3.2 per cent, compared with a corresponding labour force figure of 3.4 per cent. Subsequently, from 1990/91 to 1999/2000, the average annual rate of increase of employment declined to 2.3 per cent, while the corresponding labour force figure fell to 2.5 per cent. As a result of these differences between the rate of increase of employment and the rate of increase of the labour force, the national rate of unemployment rose from 1.8 per cent in 1983/84 to 2.8 per cent in 1990/91 and 4.9 per cent in 1999/2000.

Since the measurement of employment includes (and the measurement of unemployment excludes) any person who is in gainful employment for one or more hours a week, the unemployment rate is an inadequate guide to the underutilisation of labour. It needs to be supplemented by an indicator of the degree of underemployment within the employed population. The number of employed persons working less than 35 hours a week has been used as a rough measure of underemployment in Bangladesh (Mujeri, 2004). Expressed as a percentage of the labour force, this measure shows a net increase from 4.8 per cent in 1983/84 to 18.4 per cent in 1999/2000.

3.4.2. The Changing Structure of Employment

During the 1980s and 1990s the structure of employment underwent three major changes. Perhaps the most striking change was in the male/female composition of employment. Between 1983/84 and 1990/91, female employment grew at a rapid average annual rate of 9.1 per cent, while male employment grew at the much more modest rate of 2.5 per cent. This disparity in growth rates led to the female share of total employment increasing from 8.7 per cent to 12.8 per cent. Then, between 1990/91 and 1999/2000, the average annual rate of growth of female employment declined only slightly to 8.3 per cent, while the corresponding rate of growth for male employment fell as low as 1.2 per cent. As a result, the female share of total employment continued to increase, reaching 21.4 per cent in 1999/2000.

The second major change is found in the rural/urban composition of employment. Between 1983/84 and 1990/91, urban employment increased at an average annual rate of 9.8 per cent, while rural employment increased at an average annual rate of only 1.9 per cent, leading to the share of urban employment in total employment expanding from 13.5 per cent to 20.8 per cent. Over the following nine years to 1999/2000, the annual rate of growth of urban employment fell to only 3.3 per cent while the annual rate of growth of rural employment improved slightly to 2.1 per cent. With this much smaller disparity between the urban and rural growth rates, the share of urban employment in total employment continued to rise, but by less than two percentage points to 22.5 per cent. The third major change consisted of shifts in the distribution of employment among industrial sectors, as shown in Table 3.7. After allowing for inter-sectoral differences in labour productivity, the shifts in the sectoral distribution of employment are broadly consistent with the shifts in the sectoral contributions to GDP discussed in Chapter 2. In particular, between the 1980s and 1990s the share of agriculture in total employment declined (although it continued to employ more people than all the other sectors combined); the share of manufacturing increased, thanks in large part to the growth of the export-oriented ready-made garments industry; and the shares of both other industries (construction, power, etc.) and services also increased.

Table 3.7. Sectoral distribution of employment (per cent)

Year	Agriculture	Manufacturing	Other Industries	Services	Total
1983/84	58.8	8.9	2.1	30.2	100.0
1984/85	57.7	9.3	2.2	30.8	100.0
1995/96	51.1	9.9	2.8	36.1	100.0
1999/2000	50.8	10.0	3.5	35.7	100.0

Source: BBS Labour Force Surveys, as reported in Mujeri (2004).

3.4.3. Trends in Real Wages

Table 3.8 shows index numbers of real wage rates for the manufacturing, construction and agricultural sectors of the Bangladesh economy for the period 1990/91 to 1999/2000, on a base of 1969/70 = 100. Although the absence of index numbers between 1969/70 and 1990/91 precludes detailed analysis of this earlier period, it appears that real wages at the start of the 1990s had not changed greatly from their pre-independence levels of 21 years earlier. The 1990/91 index numbers for manufacturing and construction real wages were respectively only 14 and 7 per cent higher than their base values, and the index number for agricultural real wages was actually 5 per cent lower.

Over the next nine years, however, the real wage index for manufacturing rose in net terms by over 20.0 per cent or at an average annual rate of 2.1 per cent; the real wage index for construction rose by 8.4 per cent or at an average annual rate of 0.9 per cent; and the real wage index for agriculture rose by 10.5 per cent or at an average annual rate of 1.2 per cent. Although the upward time paths of the three indices were far from steady (indeed, the agricultural index peaked in 1996/97), it appears that the intensification of trade reforms in the 1990s broadly coincided with stronger growth in real wages.

Table 3.8. Real wages indices, 1990/91-1999/2000 (base 1969/70 =100)

Year	Manufacturing	Construction	Agriculture
1990/91	114	107	95
1991/92	113	104	98
1992/93	119	109	105
1993/94	121	106	106
1994/95	121	100	103
1995/96	123	105	104
1996/97	130	111	108
1997/98	137	114	107
1998/99	131	113	102
1999/2000	137	116	105

Source: Rahman and Islam (2003).

3.5. Concluding Remarks

This chapter has provided an overview of poverty, inequality and labour market developments in Bangladesh during the period of trade reforms. The national incidence of poverty, measured in relation to both the lower and upper poverty lines, declined substantially in the later, more intensive stages of these reforms when there was a marked acceleration in the rate of economic growth. Reductions in the incidence of poverty occurred in both rural and urban areas, although rural poverty remained consistently higher than urban poverty. On the other hand, income inequality increased in both rural and urban areas, with the degree of inequality remaining more severe in urban areas. The examination of labour market trends has revealed that between the mid-1980s and the end of the century there was substantial growth in aggregate employment. Nevertheless, as the trade liberalisation program intensified in the 1990s, the annual rate of increase of employment slowed, notwithstanding the acceleration in the rate of economic growth and indications of stronger growth in real wages. This slowing in the rate of increase of employment is likely to have contributed to the observed increase in inequality, but retarded the reduction in poverty, while real wage growth is likely to have had the opposite effects.

Chapter 4

A SURVEY OF LITERATURE

4.1. INTRODUCTION

The present chapter provides a survey of theoretical and methodological studies that analyse how trade policies affect poverty and inequality. The focus is mainly on studies that use a general equilibrium framework, an approach that can capture both the direct and indirect effects of trade policies within a constrained optimisation framework. Section 4.2 provides a brief overview of theoretical considerations relating to trade liberalisation, poverty and inequality. Section 4.3 reviews empirical research into the links between trade, poverty and income inequality. It highlights different methodological aspects of the computable general equilibrium models (CGE) that have been used in analysing trade policies within both developed and developing countries. Section 4.4 discusses the application of CGE models to the Bangladesh economy.

4.2. THEORETICAL APPROACHES

In the historical development of international economics and development economics, the effects of economic policy on the distribution of welfare among individuals and households were often neglected. As Corden (1997) pointed out, much of normative economic theory ignored distributional issues by concentrating on Pareto-optimality. A policy was justifiable provided that those that gained by it could (in principle, but not necessarily in practice) compensate those than lost by it, and still be better off. Both the classical theory of international trade and its neo-classical refinements showed how a country benefits from specialisation and trade, but they neglected to show how the gains of real income within each country were divided among labour, capital and land (Metzler, 1949). Heckscher and Ohlin were the first to analyse the influence of international trade on the distribution of national income. They argued that international trade, by increasing the demand for each country's abundant factors of production, tends to equalise the relative returns to the factors of production in different countries (Metzler, 1949). In an extension of Heckscher and Ohlin's work, Stolper and Samuelson (1941) provided a rigorous analysis of the income distribution effects of a tariff in a general equilibrium model (see below).

In development economics, the early theorising of the 1950s and 1960s was dominated by an aggregate growth point of view, with little concern for distribution. In the conventional view, growth in GDP per capita had little effect on the relative distribution of income among individuals, implying that poverty (defined in relation to a given level of real income) would eventually decline as the mean income of the population rose (Bourguignon et al. 2006). The 1970s saw the emergence of extensive support for the 'Kuznets inverted U' hypothesis that the relative distribution of income would become more unequal in the early stages of economic development, before becoming more equal in the later stages. However, this relatively optimistic long-run view was increasingly questioned as a result of the failure of rapid aggregate growth to improve employment opportunities. Empirical work by Adelman and Morris (1973), Paukert (1973), and Ahluwalia (1976) showed that for most developing countries, the distribution of income deteriorated as a consequence of growth. These findings increased concerns about distributional issues towards the end of the 1970s.

In the literature, there are three approaches to income distribution: (1) the functional distribution of income; (2) the extended functional distribution of income; and (3) the size distribution of income among households.[1] The functional distribution of income refers to the shares of the national income accruing to the primary factors of production, namely land, labour and capital. The extended functional distribution disaggregates the functional distribution by sectors and mode of production (Adelman and Robinson, 1989). It refers to the distribution of income among disaggregated factors as for example, labour differentiated by skills and education, capital by type or sector, and land by region or type. The size distribution of income refers to the shares of income accruing to households at different income levels or in different income ranges, as discussed in Chapter 3. International trade theory has long been concerned with the issue of how functional income distribution changes as a result of policy shocks. The well-known Stolper-Samuelson theorem predicts that the removal of a tariff barrier will increase the real return to the factor of production with which the country is abundantly endowed, and reduce the real return to the scarce factor, as relative product prices move in favour of the industry that uses the abundant factor more intensively. The theorem has attracted criticisms on the grounds of the many restrictive assumptions from which it was derived. They include only two commodities, both of which are produced even when there is no tariff; two factors of production, both in fixed supply, and both of which are needed in the production of each commodity; constant returns to scale; marginal productivity factor pricing; free mobility of both factors; and given world prices of exports and imports. However, subsequent analyses and refinements of the theorem by Metzler (1949), Bhagwati (1959), Jones (1965), Chipman (1969), Either (1974) and Jones and Scheinkman (1977) have shown that the essential features of the theorem hold much more generally than in the context of the model from which it was originally derived.[2]

While accepting that the the Stolper-Samuelson theorem is likely to be of broad relevance, Winters (2000) argued that by itself the theorem is not sufficient to answer questions of trade and poverty in the real world, and needs to be supplemented by further analysis to derive concrete conclusions. He also provided a conceptual framework identifying a range of trade-to-poverty links. In similar vein, Bannister and Thugge (2001) identified five

[1] See Adelman and Robinson (1989) for a detailed discussion of these concepts and their applications.

[2] See Deardorff and Stern (Eds.) (1994) for an overview of the Stolper-Samuelson theorem with its extensions, verifications and refinements.

channels through which trade liberalisation can affect the poor. The first channel is product markets. Trade liberalisation will affect the welfare of the poor through reducing prices of imports and import substitutes for poor consumers and producers, raising export prices for poor producers, and increasing the availability of new products. The second channel is factor markets, particularly labour markets. The Stolper-Samuelson theorem implies that, for a developing economy with abundant supplies of unskilled labour and a highly protected capital-intensive or skilled-labour-intensive import-competing sector, trade liberalisation will benefit the poor through increasing the real wages of the unskilled. However, Bannister and Thugge agree with Winters that the theorem is not sufficient for the analysis of trade/poverty relationships. Key variables that need to be taken into account include the elasticity of the supply of labour and the flexibility of labour markets; whole industries may disappear as a result of trade reform; and adjustment is more likely to occur through changes in employment than changes in wages.

The third channel is the public sector. Trade reforms have impacts on government revenue and expenditure. Lower tariffs reduce government revenue, which in turn could adversely affect the poor if public services on which they depend are cut back to preserve fiscal balance. Bannister and Thugge argue, however, that government revenue can increase in some instances through increased trade flows, reduced incentives for smuggling and corruption, simplification of the tariff regime and appropriate macroeconomic and exchange rate policies.

The fourth channel through which trade liberalisation can affect the poor is by their participation in economic growth. Bannister and Thugge recognise that, in addition to the one-off boost to aggregate income as a result of a more efficient allocation of resources, trade liberalisation may contribute positively to the long-term growth of an economy through improved incentives for investment and innovation, higher flows of foreign direct investment, technology transfers and new business practices that increase overall productivity. Finally, trade liberalisation can affect the poor by increasing the vulnerability of an economy to external shocks, such as sharp changes in the terms of trade. The effects of the shocks on the poor will be disproportionately large if the shocks impact directly on sectors such as agriculture, where the poor tend to be relatively heavily concentrated. As noted by Bannister and Thugge, an obvious prescription for dealing with external shocks is the use of a more flexible exchange rate policy as a complement to demand management policy.

4.3. Methods of Empirical Analysis

Empirical analysis of how trade reforms affect poverty and inequality has involved a variety of methodologies, reflecting in part differences in data availability among different countries has necessitated different approaches. Reimer (2002) has classified the literature into four broad methodological categories: cross-country regression analysis, partial equilibrium or cost-of-living analysis, general equilibrium simulation and micro-macro synthesis. The classification used in the present section differs from Reimer's by including the methodologies of his micro-macro synthesis category within a more broadly specified version of the general equilibrium simulation category. (See sub-section 4.3.3.2 below.)

4.3.1. Cross-Country Regression Analysis

This approach tests for relationships among trade (or trade policy), growth, poverty and income inequality variables measured at the national level (Reimer, 2002). For example, using cross-country regression analysis, Dollar and Kraay (2001) found a strong positive effect of trade on economic growth, but little systematic evidence of a relationship between changes in trade volumes and changes in the income share of the poor. They concluded that the increase in growth rates that accompanies expanded trade leads to proportionate increases in the incomes of the poor. (See also Dollar and Kraay 2002).

Rodriguez and Rodrik (2000) have criticised various studies that have used the cross-country approach to investigate the link between trade policy and economic growth, arguing that in large part their strong results stem from either misspecification or the use of measures of openness that are proxies for other policy or institutional variables that have independent effects on growth. More generally, Reimer (2002) has pointed out that successful estimation of relationships between trade policy, growth, and poverty is crucially dependent on appropriate measurement of these variables, and the careful sorting out of omitted variable and endogeneity problems, both of which are challenging tasks given the limited availability of data. Reimer has also observed, however, that the cross-country regression approach has some advantages over other approaches that rely on simulation methods (see below) to establish the links between trade and poverty. It uses statistical tools for testing hypotheses, rather than only making predictions; its results are more general than the country-specific results of many simulation models; and it may be able to account for some dynamic features of trade reform missed by static simulation models.

4.3.2. Partial Equilibrium Analysis/Cost-of-living Analysis

This approach seeks to estimate at the household level the welfare impacts of price changes arising directly from trade liberalisation. Generally the approach emphasises one or a limited number of markets, which are assumed not to have important linkages with other sectors of the economy. After identifying the new prices resulting from trade liberalisation (actual changes or simulated), the effects of the price changes on welfare, poverty and income distribution are assessed, using data from household surveys.

Case (1998) used the 1993 South African Living Standards to quantify the effects of trade reform on household wellbeing. She calculated the changes in welfare for Africans and Whites from household budget shares together with estimates of the demand system from a linear expenditure system and estimates of the changes in consumer prices expected from tariff reforms. Comparison of the cost of reaching a household's initial level of utility at the new (lower) prices after trade reform with the cost at original prices yielded a measure of the household welfare gain. Case's results show that a 75 per cent reduction in tariffs reduces the cost of reaching the household's initial level of utility by about 2 per cent for African households and by 1 per cent for White households. However, as Case recognises, her method ignores the potential effects of trade reform on employment and wages, not to mention other factor incomes accruing to households.

Levinsohn et al. (1999) investigated the impact of the Asian financial crisis on the Indonesian poor, using consumption data from the 1993 SUSENAS (National Economic

Survey of Indonesia) of 58,100 households. They computed a Laspeyres cost-of-living index for each household by combining the SUSENAS consumption data with price data for 1997-98. These were used to measure the impact of the crisis on households. The results showed that very low-income households in both urban and rural areas experienced disproportionately large cost-of-living increases from the international shocks, with the urban poor being most adversely affected by the crisis. An important drawback of the study is that in the absence of comprehensive information on the changes in household income over the course of the crisis, it fails to estimate the real effects of the crisis on households.

Minot and Goletti (2000) examined how liberalisation of both internal and external rice market affects food security and poverty in Vietnam. They developed an agricultural spatial equilibrium model with four staple food markets (rice, maize, sweet potatoes and cassava) in seven regions, where the supply of each crop in each region is a function of producers' prices for all four commodities. Demand is a function of per capita expenditure, consumer prices and a Stone's price index. The demand system was approximated by an Almost Ideal Demand System (AIDS). The model was simulated for: 1) removal of the rice export quota; 2) changing the quota level; 3) replacing the quota with tax; and 4) removal of restrictions on the internal movement of food. The effects on rice prices, production, consumption and income were then combined with household survey data to examine the impacts on real income and poverty among the regions. The results showed that export liberalisation would raise the rice price and thus be unfavourable for the urban poor, non-farm rural households and rice-deficit regions. However, higher prices would create positive effects for farmers, especially in rice exporting regions, and because poor households are mainly farming households, for Vietnam as a whole the poor would tend to be better off, both absolutely and relative to the non-poor. Overall, there would be a slight decline in the incidence of poverty. Porto (2003) estimated the poverty impacts of national trade reforms (tariff cuts) and foreign trade reforms (reductions in agricultural subsidies and tariffs on agricultural and manufactured goods in developing countries) on poverty in Argentina, in three steps. The first was an assessment of the impact of the trade reforms on the domestic prices of traded goods. The second was the estimation of wage-price elasticities that measured the responses of wages to changes in traded good prices. Finally, the elasticities were applied to the changes in traded good prices to derive changes in household labour income, which were used to estimate the changes in poverty. The results show that both national and foreign trade reforms would significantly alleviate poverty. National reforms would have the bigger marginal impact on poverty, but as the scope for foreign reforms were larger, the total impact of foreign reforms was potentially greater.

Nicita (2004) studied the effects of trade liberalisation in Mexico during the 1990s using a farm-household model in which the effects of trade liberalisation on household welfare operated through the movement of the prices of goods and factors of production. Econometric estimation yielded pass-through elasticities and price-wage elasticities that were then inserted into a household welfare function (a measure of the percentage change in money metric utility). The study found that trade liberalisation produced different outcomes for different household groups, as the effects of liberalisation on domestic prices and labour income varied among regions and income groups. Trade liberalisation benefited all income groups and reduced poverty, but richer households gained proportionately more than poorer households. In regional terms, households in states closest to the US border experienced proportionate gains three times greater than those in the less developed states in the south of the country.

4.3.3. Computable General Equilibrium Models

A comprehensive analysis of the effects of any policy shock on poverty and income inequality needs an economy-wide framework that captures the impact on the "extended" functional distribution of income and maps it through to the size distribution of income among households (Lofgren, Robinson, and El-Said, 2003). Because it meets these requirements, and has the added advantage of permitting counterfactual analysis, CGE modeling based on Social Accounting Matrices (SAMs) is the most widely used methodology for analysing the impact of trade liberalisation on poverty and inequality.[3]

CGE analysis of income distribution analysis began with the pioneering work of Adelman and Robinson (1978) on Korea, with other studies soon following, including further work on Korea by Dervis, Melo, and Robinson (1982). In the early 1990s there emerged another wave of income distribution analysis mainly sponsored by the OECD: Thorbecke (1991) on Indonesia, de Janvry et al.(1991) for Ecuador, Morrison (1991) for Morocco, Bourguignon et al. (1991) for two archetype Economies, Chia et al.(1994) for Cote d' Ivoire, and Lambert et al. (1991) for Cote d'Ivoire. Also, beginning in the 1990s, other SAM-based CGE models examined how a policy shock affected the welfare of households in various categories.[4] Examples are Dorosh et al.(1994) for Niger, Horridge et al.(1995) for South Africa, Chan et al. (1998) for Vietnam, Harris (1999) for Mexico, Bautista and Thomas (1997) for the Philippines, Dorosh and Sahn (2000) for Africa, and Kemal et al. (2001) for Pakistan.

These models focused on the impact of counterfactual policy scenarios on income distribution and welfare issues, using a representative household assumption. No information on poverty was used. In measuring the distribution of income among household groups, each of these studies developed a comprehensive SAM for each respective economy, which included a detailed disaggregation of households, factors, activities, and commodities. The SAM also provided a complete mapping of value added from factors of production to household income. Khan (2004) has termed these models first and second generation models for developing economies.

Decaluwé et al. (1999) were the first to establish that CGE models could also be used to address poverty. Their innovation was to endogenise a poverty line based on a unique and constant basket of basic needs commodities, which could be used to estimate poverty incidences among various socioeconomic household groups. Allowing for the fact that the poverty line changes following a variation in prices due to a policy shock, poverty levels in base periods were compared with the poverty levels in the after-shock period. Subsequently, following Decaluwé et al. (1999), a number of CGE modellers, for example Cockburn (2002), Bourguignon et al. (2003), Croser (2002) and Savard (2003) assessed poverty impact through CGE models. These models belonged to the third generation of CGE models for developing economies identified by Khan (2004).

Savard (2003) classified income distribution and poverty analysis in CGE modelling into three main categories: (1) the CGE model with traditional representative household (CGE-

[3]Cloutier et al. (2008) provide a comprehensive review of CGE literature on welfare, poverty and income distributional impacts of trade liberalisation. For an older, but wider review of the use of CGE models in development policy analysis in developing economies, see Bandara (1991).

[4] Income level and socio-economic group are two criteria commonly used to define household categories (Cloutier et al. 2008),

RH), (2) integrated multi-households CGE analysis (CGE-IMH), and (3) the micro-simulation approach. In considering them below, the second category is subsumed under an expanded version of the third category, following the example of Cloutier et al. (2008).

4.3.3.1. Traditional Representative Household Approach

In the traditional representative household approach, data from a household survey are classified into the categories of households contained in the model.[5] In less developed countries, these are commonly specified as rural or urban, skilled or unskilled and landed or landless, whereas in developed countries representative households are identified in terms of income and expenditure groups (Davies, 2004).

Following a policy shock, the CGE model provides growth rates of real disposable income or consumption for all categories of households. By applying these growth rates to disposable income or consumption expenditure of each household in each household group in the household survey, a vector of income or consumption for each household group is calculated. Various poverty indices (for example, the headcount ratio, poverty gap index and poverty severity index[6]) are then estimated with this new vector of income or consumption.

The representative household approach has been widely used in a large number of trade and poverty studies over the past decade. Lofgren et al. (2003) identified two methods of linking a CGE model with representative households to a household module to estimate poverty: (1) by specifying a distribution of income for each representative household type and (2) by using disaggregated household survey data where each survey observation is allocated to a representative household in the CGE model. The first method, known as the parametric approach, was pioneered by Adelman and Robinson (1978) in their model of the Republic of Korea. In this method, a specific parametric distribution (usually a log-normal distribution) is assumed to describe the dispersion of income within each group. However, it is further assumed that the mean of the income distributions changes endogenously, while the variances are fixed or determined exogenously. Usually, the parameters of these distributions are estimated from household survey data. These distributions are then used to evaluate the poverty incidences within each group in a general equilibrium framework. Following a shock, e.g., trade liberalisation, the mean income of each household group changes, which in turn shifts the income distribution proportionately. For an increase in income the fitted distribution shifts to the right, (for a decrease in income it shifts to the left), without modifying the shape of the distribution.

The overall distribution of income is then estimated empirically by summing the separate within-group distributions, and overall poverty and inequality measures are generated from it. Different authors used different functional forms in modelling households' income distribution. Adelman and Robinson (1978), Chia et al.(1994), Dervis, Melo, and Robinson (1982) used the log-normal distribution. De Janvry et al. (1991) used the Pareto distribution. Later Decaluwé et al. (1999) provided further refinements on this approach. They proposed a flexible beta distribution to model the within-group income distributions in preference to a log-normal or Pareto distribution, as beta distributions can be skewed to the right or to the left or be symmetric. The second method of linking a CGE model with representative households to a household module makes direct use of the household survey data to estimate intra-group

[5] See Lofgren et al. (2003) for a brief description of this approach.

[6] See Chapter 8.

distributions. With this method, changes in average household income are derived from the CGE model for each household category, and then applied to all corresponding households in the survey to estimate changes in poverty and inequality indices. This approach is known as the non-parametric approach.

An extensive literature has emerged on the impact of reform policies on poverty and inequality using either the parametric or non-parametric representative agent approach. Some of these studies are outlined briefly below.

Decaluwé et al. (1999) used a CGE model for an archetypal African economy with four areas of activity (agriculture, industry, marketable and non-marketable services) to analyse the impacts of a fall in the world price of an export crop and a cut in import tariffs on income distribution and poverty. Calibrated on an African SAM, their model sought to compare the poverty incidence before and after policy shocks. After aggregating the household groups into six representative groups, an income distribution (beta distribution) was formulated for each group, each distribution corresponding to the characteristics of its group. In addition, a poverty line consisting of a basket of basic needs commodities was endogenised in the CGE model. With each shock, households' average income level changed, so income distribution shifted proportionately. Poverty measures embodying the effects of the shock were calculated from the post-shock within-group income distributions and the new, endogenously determined poverty line.

Pradhan and Sahoo (2006) developed a 28-sector, 3-factor and 9-household group a SAM-based neo-classical CGE model to analyse the impacts of reductions in trade barriers on poverty and welfare in India. Households were divided into four rural and five urban occupational household groups, according to their principal sources of income. Pradhan and Sahoo undertook three policy simulations: complete removal of tariffs; complete removal of tariffs with an increase in indirect taxes on domestic demand to maintain constant government revenue; and a 40 per cent increase in the quota limits applying to imports of agricultural products (excluding food grains) and manufactured food and food articles. Results showed that removal of tariffs by itself led to a decline in overall welfare (measured in terms of equivalent variation), but also a decline in the incidence of poverty; that removal of tariffs accompanied by a compensatory increase in indirect taxes led to declines in overall welfare and an increase in poverty; and that partial relaxation of quotasled to an increase in overall welfare and a decline in poverty.

Following Decaluwé et al. (1999), Stifel and Thorbecke (2003) also examined the impact of trade liberalisation on poverty for an archetypal African economy. As in Thorbecke (1997), the economy was modelled in a dual-dual framework by assuming that the backward sector was rural and agricultural while the modern sector was urban and industrial. The model was calibrated to a SAM for an archetypal Sub-Saharan African economy with four production activities, four factors of production and nine socio-economic household groups. For income distribution and poverty analysis, a beta distribution function was formulated for each household group based on socio-economic characteristics, and allowed to vary systematically in response to exogenous shocks. It was then used with an endogenous nominal poverty line to estimate Foster-Greer-Thorbecke (FGT) poverty measures.[7] An important contribution of this study was the modelling of inter-group migration and its effects on poverty.

[7] See Chapter 8.

Naranpanawa (2005) developed a poverty focused multi-household CGE model for the Sri Lankan economy. To simulate intra-group distributions, empirically estimated beta distribution functional forms were linked with the model in a 'top-down' fashion. Following Decaluwé et al.(1999), a money metric poverty line was endogenised in the model. Simulations experiments were carried out both in the short run and long run for 100 per cent tariff cuts on manufactured imports, on agricultural imports and across the board. The results show that all three forms of trade liberalisation reduce poverty in both the short and long run. However, with the partial exception of agricultural tariff cuts, there is evidence of increases in inequality over both periods, with the increases being larger in the short run.

Unlike the studies described above, Aka (2004) quantified the poverty, inequality and welfare impacts of trade liberalisation and tax reform in Cote d'Ivoire by using the actual distributions from the household survey data. In Using a CGE model comprising four sectors (agriculture, industry, tradeable services and non-tradeable services) and nine groups of households, Aka (2004) separately simulated the elimination of taxes on agricultural exports, the elimination of taxes on agricultural imports, and the elimination of taxes on industrial exports. The results for all households showed that in each case poverty decreased, but inequality increased.

Cororaton et al. (2006) used a non-parametric approach with 12 household categories based on the 1994 family Income and Expenditure Survey of Philippine households to simulate the impacts of the Doha Round of WTO negotiations and other possible trade reforms on poverty in the Philippines. The simulations included additional indirect taxation to compensate for the loss of domestic tariff revenue. The study found that, both with and without Special and Differential Treatment (SDT) for developing countries, Doha would increase poverty slightly in the Philippines, especially among rural households.

Bussolo and Round (2002) and Boccanfuso et al. (2003) provided comparisons between the parametric and non-parametric representative household approaches. Bussolo and Round (2002) developed a SAM-based model for Ghana. In analysing the possible effects of a range of budget-neutral redistributive income transfers on poverty, they conducted simulations to compare parametric and non-parametric approaches to poverty calculations. Their simulation results produced changes in poverty indices that were the same in direction but different in magnitude. Boccanfuso et al.(2003) performed a similar test for Senegal. These authors used seven different continuous distribution functions and one non-parametric method to evaluate poverty with the Foster-Greer-Thorbecke poverty indices. The authors found some distributions produced quite different poverty indices from other functional forms, and the results did not follow a systematic pattern.

The main drawback of the representative household approach (whether parametric or non-parametric) is that following a policy shock, the approach is unable to capture the within-group variation of inequality because the relative dispersions of intra-group incomes are assumed constant. Thus, with given heterogeneity of income sources and consumption patterns of households, the assumption of fixed relative dispersion may well lead to biased results even when using highly disaggregated household categories. It is widely recognised that endogenising the relative distribution of income within each group would produce more satisfactory results, as its contribution to total inequality may be significant. This consideration led to the development of the micro-simulation approach.

4.3.3.2. Micro-simulation Approach[8]

Micro-simulation investigates the impact of any shock at the micro level by focusing on the economic behaviour of individual agents (usually households and firms). In the present context, the micro-simulation approach refers to the combining or joining of a module of household behaviour, estimated from household survey data, with a CGE model. Since this approach captures as many agents as there are in the household survey, it provides a better reflection of household heterogeneity in terms of household income sources, consumption preferences and demographic compositions than the representative household approach. More specifically, it becomes possible to endogenise intra-group distributions.

Micro-simulation modelling in the CGE context can be classified into three broad categories: integrated multi-household analysis, the sequential top-down approach, and the iterative top-down/bottom-up approach.

4.3.3.2.1. Integrated Multi-household CGE Analysis (CGE-IMH)

In the CGE-IMH approach, individual data usually found in household income and expenditure surveys is directly integrated in the general equilibrium model according to the principles of micro-simulation. This ensures households' heterogeneity with regard to their endowment and consumption patterns. Further, by taking as many households as possible into account, the model allows the modeller to avoid a pre-judgment about grouping households into categories. In addition, unlike the representative household approach, no prior assumption about any distribution parameter is needed.

Cogneau and Robilliard (2000) provided an early example of this approach. To evaluate the impacts of different growth strategies on income distribution and poverty in Madagascar, they built an econometrically estimated micro-simulation model of labour allocation, based on household survey data and representing 4,508 households, which they embedded in a general equilibrium framework. The combination of general equilibrium and micro-simulation yielded post-shock measures of poverty and inequality, without the need for any explicit or implicit assumptions about within-group distributions of income. In general, the effects of the growth shocks on poverty and inequality were relatively small, an outcome that Cogneau and Robilliard attributed to an initial diversification of household income sources, the scope for households to reallocate labour in response to shocks, and the unequal distribution of factors of production.

Cockburn (2002) integrated all the 3,373 households in a nationally representative survey directly in a CGE model for Nepal to analyse the impact of the elimination of import tariffs. Because of full household information on income from each factor of production, and on consumption, this model simulation predicts how each individual household is affected by trade liberalisation. An existing CGE model based on a 1986 Social Accounting Matrix of Nepal was used for the analysis. It consisted of five factors of production (skilled and unskilled labour, land, agricultural and non-agricultural capital), three household groups (small, large and non-farm) and fifteen production sectors. All sectors, factors of production and households were separated into the same three regions: urban, Terai and hills/mountains. To maintain government revenue neutrality, following the elimination of import tariffs, an endogenously determined uniform consumption tax was imposed. Poverty and income distribution analysis was undertaken with the software DAD. Model simulation results

[8] See Davies (2004) for a comprehensive discussion of this approach.

showed that trade liberalisation in Nepal favoured urban households as opposed to Terai and hill/mountain households. Urban poverty fell and rural poverty increased. Inequality increased in the urban areas as well as the hills and mountain areas.

Annabi et al. (2005) developed a sequential dynamic micro-simulation CGE model for Senegal to assess the effects of trade liberalisation on poverty and inequality.[9] Using an integrated micro-simulation approach, the model was calibrated to a 1996 Social Accounting Matrix and 1995 Household Survey data covering 3278 households. The study found that in the short run full removal of tariffs results in small increases in poverty and inequality. In the long run, the positive effects of trade liberalisation on capital accumulation lead to a substantial decrease in poverty, Inequality, however, increases by more than in the short run.

While the main advantages of the CGE-IMH analysis, compared with the representative household approach, are the capture of intra-group income distributional changes and the freeing of modellers from the need to pre-select household groups or aggregation (Savard, 2003), CGE-IMH is not without problems. It requires a large amount of statistical information and data reconciliation creates difficulties because of the size of the model. Thus there is doubt about its practical application, especially with respect to large countries, which require greater sectoral detail, and where survey data may exceed 100,000 households (Hertel and Reimer, 2004). To avoid these problems, while still making use of detailed household survey data, various analysts developed an approach whereby a CGE model is linked with a separate micro-simulation modelling framework, which is used to assess the effects of CGE simulations at the individual household level. Reimer (2002) termed this approach 'micro-macro synthesis', but it is also known by a longer and more specific name, 'the sequential top-down/layered micro-simulation approach'.

4.3.3.2.2. Sequential Top-down/ Layered Micro-simulation Approach

In this approach, a micro-simulation model is linked with a CGE model in two sequential steps. In the first step, the CGE model is simulated to generate a vector of factor and commodity prices and employment levels resulting from a policy shock. In the second step, the changes in variables in the CGE model are fed into the micro-simulation framework to analyse the income distribution and poverty impacts at the household level.

Top-down micro-simulation methodologies vary in complexity. The simplest is the pure accounting approach (Bourguignon et al. 2006; Bibi and Chatti, 2006), which is effectively an extension of the partial equilibrium or cost-of-living approach to include a complete vector of CGE-estimated commodity and factor prices (Hertel and Reimer, 2004). Examples of this type of analysis are Chen and Ravallion (2004), Ianchovichina et al.(2002) and Bibi and Chatti (2006). Chen and Ravallion used Chinese household survey data to assess the impacts of changes in goods and factor prices induced by China's accession to the WTO, as simulated by a CGE model, on the welfare of individual households. Their results suggested negligible overall changes in inequality and poverty.

Ianchovichina et al. (2002) assessed the impact of potential elimination of all tariffs on poverty and inequality in Mexico, using household survey data for 1996. Their two-step approach first involved employing the CGE model of the Global Trade Analysis Project (GTAP) to simulate the changes in prices of both product and factor services that would result

[9] Unlike a static model, a dynamic model includes accumulation effects, i.e., the capital stock is updated endogenously with a capital accumulation equation.

from the change in policy. Secondly, they applied the changes in prices to the household survey data to estimate the effects of the policy change on poverty and inequality. The results indicate a slight fall in poverty and a negligible rise in inequality. They also indicate that welfare increases in general for all expenditure deciles, but the poor benefit proportionately more than the rich.

Bibi and Chatti (2006) used a recursive dynamic CGE model of the Tunisian economy to obtain simulations of the prices of consumer goods and the average nominal income of each household group over the period 1998-2015, under both protection and free trade assumptions. These results were then used to assess the effects on the real income of each household in a sample of 2,500. Since households within the same group did not have the same budgetary share for each good, simulated real income varied between households within the same group. The simulation results showed that in the short run poverty fell more slowly under free trade than under protection. In the long run, however, this outcome was reversed: poverty fell more rapidly under free trade than under protection.

A significant shortcoming of pure accounting analysis is that it abstracts from the responses of households to price changes, particularly in terms of labour market, consumption and income behaviours. This shortcoming is addressed in an alternative micro-simulation methodology that uses household survey data to estimate a reduced form behavioural model of household real income generation. In a classic paper, Robilliard et al. (2001) linked the post-simulation outputs of a CGE model to a household income micro-simulation model for Indonesia, to simulate the effects of the 1997 financial crisis on poverty and inequality. The CGE model, which contained thirty eight sectors and fifteen factors of production, was solved to provide required inputs for the micro-simulation model in the form of prices, wages and employment levels. The latter model was based on econometrically estimated reduced form equations for individual earnings, household income from self-employment, and the occupational choice of all household members of working age. Simulation of the financial crisis shock, using the full modelling framework, resulted in a 92.5 per cent increase in the head count index of poverty and a 5.5 per cent increase in the Gini coefficient of inequality.

In a related study, Bourguignon et al. (2003) used essentially the same pair of linked models to analyse the impacts of a two external shocks on the Indonesian economy, a 50 per cent drop in the foreign prices of oil and processed oil exports, and a 30 per cent drop in exogenous foreign savings (capital inflow). Their simulation results provided quite different distributional effects from those they obtained with a representative household approach. For example, whereas the representative household approach predicted that a reduction in foreign savings would reduce inequality in the distribution of real household income, the micro-simulation approach predicted that the effect would be a rise in inequality. Similarly, the micro-simulation approach showed much larger adverse effects on poverty. According to Bourguignon et al. the main reasons for the differences are that, unlike the representative household approach, the micro-simulation approach takes into account changes in occupations, thereby recognising an important source of actual changes in income distribution, and in addition it takes into account the heterogeneity of consumption behavior.

Later work in the same vein by Robilliard and Robinson (2005) sought to explore ways in which the Doha Development Agenda might contribute to poverty reduction in Indonesia. In particular, the impact of trade liberalisation was examined through three simulations: (1) unilateral liberalisation by Indonesia; (2) full liberalisation excluding Indonesia; and (3) full liberalisation including Indonesia. Among these scenarios, (3) produced the largest reduction in poverty. Further investigation of (3) indicated that alternative, less flexible specifications of the labour market would still result in significant reductions in the incidence of poverty. Robilliard and Robinson also compared, in the context of scenario (3), two alternative proposals for replacing revenue lost as a result of the removal of tariffs: an increase in direct taxes on household income and an increase in VAT. Although the direct tax replacement was found to be more effective in terms of efficiency gains and poverty reduction, it was recognised that political and practical considerations could lead to a government preference for the VAT option.

Also following Robilliard et al. (2001), Bussolo and Lay (2003) estimated the impacts of 1990s tariff cuts on poverty in Columbia. Their simulation results showed that in rural areas the movement of workers from the informal to formal sector, and the subsequent rise in unskilled wages, reduced poverty substantially. In comparing their micro-simulation results with representative household results, it was found that the representative household approach (RH) underestimated rural poverty reduction, and overestimated urban poverty reduction.

Vos and de Jong (2003) combined a CGE model analysis with a micro-simulation approach in a top-down fashion to analyse the effects of trade liberalisation on poverty and income distribution in Ecuador. Based on a neoclassical structuralist tradition, the CGE model was calibrated to the 1993 Social Accounting Matrix for Ecuador. In the micro-simulation approach, labour market adjustment was the central transmission mechanism through which the policy shocks affected poverty and income distribution at the household level. However, instead of specifying a full income and labour choice model, Vos and de Jong adopted a more rudimentary approach involving a randomised process to estimate the effects of labour market changes on the incomes of individuals. They then explored various counterfactual policy scenarios, including implementation of the Free Trade Agreement for the Americas (FTAA). Simulation results suggested that this form of trade liberalisation would induce only small gains in real GDP and total employment, while widening the wage gap between skilled and unskilled workers. Both poverty and inequality would increase slightly.

Herault (2007) combined a SAM-based CGE model with a micro-simulation model to assess the effects of trade liberalisation on South African households. His approach extended that of Robilliard et al. (2001) to take into consideration changes in capital returns and transfers at the household level. In the first stage, the CGE model was used to simulate the effects of a complete removal of import tariffs. In the second stage, the changes in prices, direct tax rates, returns from capital and labour and employment levels generated by the CGE model were transmitted to the micro-simulation model based on household survey data. In the micro-simulation model, the labour market was divided into five segments: inactive, unemployed, subsistence agricultural workers, informal workers and formal workers. A multinomial logit specification was used for an underlying selection model that estimated the probabilities of each individual of working age being in one of the five segments, with a regression model used to predict individual gross earnings in each segment. Herault's simulation results showed a significant reduction in poverty, mainly driven by an expansion in formal sector employment, especially for low-skilled and skilled workers. Blacks, who accounted for about 95 per cent of the poor, benefited most from this expansion. Overall, there was also a slight reduction in inequality. To some extent, the reduction reflected a higher rate of growth in real income per capita for Blacks (the poorest racial group) than for Coloureds, Asians and Whites (the richest racial group), but mainly it was the result of declines in intra-group inequalities for Blacks, Coloureds and Asians.

While the sequential top-down micro-simulation approach, like integrated multi-household analysis, can capture within-group variations in inequality, it has the advantage that there is no need for full reconciling of micro and macro data. However, a major problem with the behavioural version of the sequential top-down approach is that the responses of households to commodity and factor price changes in the micro-simulation analysis are not transmitted or fed back to the CGE model, i.e., the feedback effects of household behaviours are not taken into account in the CGE model, so that consistency between the macro and micro model is not assured.

4.3.3.2.3. Iterative Top-down/Bottom-up Approach

Savard (2003) proposed another approach, the top-down/bottom-up approach that takes into account the above problem. By introducing a bi-directional link between the household model and the CGE model, a convergent solution between the two models is obtained. The simulation process begins by using the CGE model to generate a vector of goods and factor prices. The vector is then transmitted to the household micro-simulation model, which identifies the behavioural responses of households to the price changes. Next, household consumption and labour supply responses are aggregated and fed back into the CGE model as exogenous variables, where upon the above procedures are repeated. This iterative process continues until there is complete consistency between the results of the two models.

Savard (2003) argued that, compared with the integrated micro-simulation approach, this method has three advantages: it does not need to scale the household data to national data; there is no limit to the level of disaggregation in terms of the number of households and the production sectors; and (3) there is more choice of functional forms to present microeconomic household behaviour. On the other hand, as Savard recognised, there is no guarantee a converging solution will be found.

Savard applied his approach to the Philippines, using data from a 1997 family income and expenditure survey, a labour force survey for 1997 to 1998, and a 1990 SAM. Results for a simulated 30 per cut in tariffs included, at the national level, a very small increase in inequality (a 0.12 per cent increase in the Gini index) and a more substantial fall in the incidence of poverty (a 1.77 per cent fall in the head count ratio).

In a later study using a 1997 SAM, Savard (2005) compared the top-down/bottom-up micro-simulation approach with the representative household approach for the case of the Philippines. Three versions of a standard CGE model were used for each of the two approaches: first, full factor mobility with the consumption expenditure function derived from a Cobb-Douglas utility function; second, full factor mobility with a linear expenditure system; and third, capital immobility, labour market segmentation and a linear expenditure system. For each of the versions, Savard (2005) simulated the effects of a uniform 50 per cent reduction in customs duties with a representative household approach and with a top-down micro-simulation approach. The two approaches yielded similar macroeconomic and sectoral results, but very different results for poverty and inequality. At the national level, the two approaches showed the same direction of change in the incidence of poverty in each of the three CGE-versions, but the changes were proportionately much larger for the top-down approach. On the other hand, the two approaches showed opposite directions of change in the national degree of inequality in each of the CGE-versions. On the basis of his results, Savard suggests that in the analysis of poverty and inequality the representative agent approach is likely to lead to biased conclusions.

4.3.4. Multi-Country Analysis

Multi-country CGE models, such as the Global Trade Analysis Project (GTAP) model, have proved helpful in capturing the impacts of bilateral and multilateral trade agreements on poverty and income inequality at the national level.[10] A common approach (see Hertel and Ivanic 2006) is to begin by using a multi-country or global model to simulate, for a target country, the shifts in export demand schedules and changes in import prices that result from trade liberalisation policies in other countries. This information is then passed as inputs to the target country's national CGE model, which is linked to a household micro-simulation framework.

Ferreira-Filho and Horridge (2005) followed this approach in assessing the potential effects of the Doha Round trade negotiations on poverty and income distribution in Brazil. The focus was on two trade liberalisation scenarios, the central Doha scenario of partial liberalisation and a full liberalisation scenario. In each case, the starting point was a set of GTAP model simulations of the effects of the scenario, excluding a reduction in Brazil's tariffs, in changing Brazilian import prices and shifting Brazilian export demand schedules. These effects, together with the Brazilian tariff shock were applied to a static inter-regional CGE model of Brazil, and its results were then used to update a household micro-simulation model containing 112,055 Brazilian households and 263,938 adults spread across 27 regions. For each scenario, the simulated outcomes revealed relatively small overall declines in inequality and poverty, although they were absolutely larger in the case of full liberalisation.

Zhai and Hertel (2006) combined the results of a global model with a national CGE model in order to investigate the effects of multilateral trade reform policies on poverty in China.[11] Within the national model, the rural and urban household sectors were disaggregated into 60 urban and 40 rural representative households, according to their primary sources of income and relative income levels. Zhai and Hertel undertook four simulations: (1) elimination of all import tariffs and agricultural export subsidies in the rest of the world, plus elimination of domestic agricultural production subsidies in OECD countries; (2) unilateral trade liberalisation by China, involving elimination of all its import tariffs and non-tariff barriers; (3) global free trade, involving the first and second scenarios combined; and (4) the standard Doha scenario, which in the case of China included tariff cuts mainly in the range of 25 to 33 per cent. Multilateral trade liberalisation effects were incorporated into the CGE model by exogenous shifts in import prices and export demand schedules obtained from global simulations (GTAP simulations). The results suggested that multilateral trade reforms would reduce poverty in China, especially in rural areas. For China as a whole, the overall headcount ratio fell by 1.3 per cent under the Doha scenario and by 2.6 per cent under global free trade.

Cicowiez et al. (2009) analysed the impacts of global and domestic trade reforms on poverty and inequality in Argentina, with particular attention given to export taxes. A global economy-wide model (the World Bank's global LINKAGE model, with the GTAP 7 data base) was used to estimate the terms-of-trade and export demand effects arising from possible

[10] The GTAP model is a standard global applied general equilibrium model with specific features of perfectly competitive markets, and constant returns to scale technology. See Hertel (1997) for details of the GTAP model structure and data base.

[11] They also investigated the effects of increased spending on rural education in the context of multilateral trade liberalisation.

trade policy reforms in the rest of the world. These effects, along with domestic trade reforms, were treated as exogenous shocks in a national CGE model, which in response to the shocks generated changes in employment by factor type and sector, and changes in factor and product prices. The changes formed inputs to a partly econometric micro-simulation model from which were derived estimates of the effects of the trade reforms on poverty and inequality.

Simulation of the removal of all import taxes and all agricultural subsidies in both Argentina and the rest of the world, while retaining export taxes, resulted in declines in poverty and inequality in Argentina through a reduction in unemployment. When, however, these reforms were confined to agricultural goods, poverty increased and the decline in inequality became negligible. Other simulations ranged from complete global free trade to unilateral, agriculture-only trade reform in Argentina. All had adverse impacts on poverty, especially those that included the removal of export taxes in Argentina. The adverse impacts reflected higher food prices and less favourable or negative effects on employment. In addition, among these other simulations, all but one of those that included the removal of export taxes in Argentina (global free trade), showed small increases in household income inequality.

Gilbert (2008) used a different form of multi-country analysis to that of the the three previous studies, in order to assess the welfare impacts the South Asia Free Trade Agreement (SAFTA). It involved the development of a multi-regional CGE model for South Asia covering Bangladesh, India, Sri Lanka and an aggregate region embodying the remaining countries in South Asia The model, contained 16 production sectors (each producing a joint product for domestic and foreign markets), government, investment and multiple representative households. Consumption of households was based on Stone-Geary utility functions, resulting in linear expenditure systems, with equivalent variations used to measure welfare changes. Household categories varied among regions: ten in Bangladesh, nine in India, and five in Sri Lanka.

Gilbert ran three simulations. The first was a cut in bilateral tariffs in excess of 20 per cent to 20 per cent. Results indicated that this cut would have adverse effects on the poor in Bangladesh, would be pro-poor in India, and have a negligible impact in Sri Lanka. The second simulation was a reduction in preferential tariffs by a half. In this case, the poorest household groups in Bangladesh would gain both absolutely and relative to the richest groups; in India, the poor would also gain absolutely, but inequality was likely to increase slightly; and in Sri Lanka, the rural poor would lose, but all other household groups would gain. The third simulation was a unilateral benchmark in the form of a 10 per cent reduction in all applied tariffs. In terms of direction of change, the results were similar to those of the second simulation.

Focusing on the changes in the total welfare of member countries under the various simulations, Gilbert suggested that the overall welfare effects of trade liberalisation under SAFTA would be positive but small. The reason was that member countries possessed similar export structures and thus only restricted scope for mutually beneficial exchange. Indeed, his evidence indicated that both Bangladesh and India might gain more from unilateral tariff reform.

4.4. CGE MODELLING IN BANGLADESH

Most CGE modeling for Bangladesh has been concerned with taxation policy, trade policy, and agricultural policy. Recently, assessing the poverty and welfare impacts of trade liberalisation using a CGE model has become an increasingly popular practice. This has been due to the greater availability of household survey data, computational facilities and various new softwares. This section provides a brief selective survey of some of the CGE models developed for Bangladesh.

Keyzer (1986) was among the first to conduct CGE simulations for the Bangladesh economy, using part of the Bangladesh Agricultural Model (BAM) constructed by the staff of the Centre for World Food Studies. BAM is an applied general equilibrium model, focused mainly on agriculture and food. There are 17 agricultural sectors, one tradable non-agricultural good sector and one non-tradable non-agricultural service sector, and 10 socioeconomic household groups, classified on the basis of main economic activity and location. The model has a supply component that formulates production and investment plans, and an exchange component that shows what happens when the commodities are brought to market (Ahammad, 1995). Keyzer used the exchange component to undertake three policy simulations: (1) a 50 per cent cut in all tariffs and subsidies and no non-tariff barriers; (2) zero tariffs on import of non- agricultural products; and (3) an adjustment in the excise tax sufficient to keep the trade deficit at its base run level. The policy changes were evaluated in terms of the effects on commodity prices, foreign exchange cost and tax receipts by commodity, national accounting variables, and nutritional status by socio-economic class.

Hossain (1989) developed a multi-sectoral general equilibrium model to assess the effects of the restrictive trade policies on resource allocation and welfare in Bangladesh. Based on the Johansen linearisation technique, his static model of 12 sectors (9 traded and 3 non-traded) was calibrated to the 1976-77 input-output table for Bangladesh. Consisting of one aggregated household and one mobile primary factor, labour, the welfare effects were estimated by means of equivalent variations and compensating variations. Two simulation experiments were conducted: (1) a 20 per cent reduction in quantitative restrictions; and (2) a 20 per cent reduction in all tariffs assuming that quantitative restrictions were non-existent. The results showed that the removal of trade restrictions led to a shift of resources from the import-competing capital-intensive sectors to labour-intensive subsistence crops and export sectors. In terms of welfare effects, the results of the unilateral reductions of tariffs and quantitative restrictions were found to be relatively small. The model's main limitation was its inability to identify clearly the impacts on income distribution. To capture income distribution aspects effectively, the model needed to include more representative households and a large number of factors.

Chowdhury (1990) used a multisectoral general equilibrium model to analyse the impact of various tax policies on resource allocation and income distribution in Bangladesh, while keeping government revenue constant. To assess income distribution effects, a SAM was constructed for the Bangladesh economy for the year 1984-85. Most of the data for the SAM were collected from the base run solution of the macro model of the Bangladesh third five-year plan. The model had seven production sectors, four household groups classified on the basis of income, and a government sector. Household income consisted of primary factor income, remittances from abroad, transfers from government, and the premium received on remittances. The premium on remittances represented the wedge between the official and secondary exchange rates. Chowdhury conducted four sets of experiments for the short run: (1) experiments with excise tax, (2) tariff experiments, (3) experiments with excise tax, tariffs and direct taxes, and 4) experiments with a value-added tax. Simulation results indicated that any tax reform in Bangladesh involving a single tax instrument had little scope for improving efficiency and equity. Chowdhury suggested that a package of tax reforms involving more progressive income taxes and less reliance on indirect taxes would be the best option.

Salma (1992) developed a CGE model to estimate the effects of agricultural price policy reforms in Bangladesh. The CGE model had 25 sectors, one multi-product agricultural sector and the rest single-output manufacturing and services sectors. For the latter sectors, the model followed the ORANI model in which production technology exhibits constant returns to scale and is of a two-level nested form. In contrast, in modelling the agricultural sector, Salma introduced a three-level nested form that allowed greater flexibility in production structure. Institutional aspects of the model included import and export premia, a two-tier foreign exchange system, and a slack labour market with constant nominal wages in the short run and constant real wages in the long run. Two sets of simulation experiments were conducted: first, policy shocks that indirectly contributed to changes in agriculture, for example exchange rate and trade policies; and second, policy shocks that directly affected agricultural prices, such as withdrawal of fertiliser subsidies and food subsidies. Salma's simulation results showed that in both the short run and long run, indirect policies seemed to have much greater impacts on agricultural productivity and outputs than direct policies.

Ahammad (1995) analysed the effects, including welfare implications, of changes in various policies that influence the structure and the growth of industries in Bangladesh. Following the standard ORANI model of the Australian economy, Ahammad (developed a 19-sector neo-classical CGE model that incorporated additional constraints reflecting institutional and policy features of the Bangladesh economy. The model also included a skeleton monetary sector to clear the secondary foreign exchange market. A version of Harberger's (1971) fundamental equation of applied welfare economics was used to evaluate the welfare impacts of policy changes. The simulation experiments included an exogenous inflow of additional foreign aid, devaluation of the official exchange rate, an increase in money supply, an increase in nominal wages, reductions in tariffs, and a reduction in Export Performance Benefit Scheme entitlement rates. All these experiments were conducted under two labour market closures: a Keynesian closure, in which nominal wages were fixed; and a neoclassical closure in which aggregate employment was fixed.

Noman (2001) developed a CGE model for Bangladesh to examine the impact of international price shocks. Based on a trade-focused CGE model described in Dervis et al. (1982), Noman's model included 29 production sectors, 3 factors of production (labour, capital and intermediate inputs), households, government and the rest of the world. It was solved using the General Algebraic Modelling System (GAMS) software. The following simulations were carried out: (1) a 20 per cent rise in international petroleum prices; (2) a 20 per cent rise in international chemical prices; (3) a combination of scenarios 1 & 2; and (4) Scenario 3 combined with full tariff liberalisation. Results showed that the increases in prices of petroleum and chemical products would have severe effects on the economy by reducing production, employment, government revenue, exports and imports. Households' welfare would fall as a result of reduced consumption levels. However, the situation would improve if the price increases were accompanied by full tariff liberalisation.

Mujeri and Khondker (2002) analysed the impacts of trade liberalisation and increased foreign investment on welfare and poverty in Bangladesh. The authors developed astatic CGE model with 26 production sectors, 7 factors of production (6 types of labour and one type of capital) and 7 representative household groups (classified on the basis of location, land ownership, occupation and education level), which was calibrated to the 1995-96 Social Accounting Matrix for Bangladesh. Equivalent variations were used to calculate welfare impacts for household groups, and beta distribution functions were combined with endogenously determined poverty lines to measure changes in poverty. Two sets of simulations were conducted: full tariff liberalisation; and augmentation of the base value of foreign savings to reflect an increased inflow of foreign investment. While the results were generally pro-poor, the gains were relatively small.

Khondker and Raihan (2004) also assessed the poverty and welfare impacts of different policy reforms in Bangladesh, using a CGE model that appears to be essentially the same as the one developed by Mujeri and Khondker (2002). In the later study, three new simulations were undertaken: (1) elimination of tariffs together with revenue-compensating increases in existing production taxes and new taxes on construction; (2) a 25 per cent fall in the volume of ready-made garment exports; and (3) a 50 per cent increase in remittances. The revenue-compensated removal of tariffs produced welfare losses for all household groups. In rural areas, the larger welfare losses accrued to relatively well-off households, whereas the reverse happened in urban areas, where the poorer households suffered more. Poverty also worsened in both rural and urban areas. Similarly, the fall in exports of ready-made garments resulted in a deterioration of welfare and a worsening of poverty in both rural and urban areas, as reduced exports led to a reduction in GDP and falls in household incomes. Finally, the increase in remittances raised welfare for all household groups. In rural areas, however, the poverty profile worsened, and in urban areas the evidence is mixed, although the urban head count index of poverty showed improvement.

Unlike previous studies, Annabi et al. (2006) used a sequential dynamic CGE model to examine the implications of various trade reform scenarios on welfare and poverty in Bangladesh. The model, which took into account accumulation effects as well as efficiency effects, was numerically calibrated to a 1999/2000 SAM of Bangladesh, which included 15 production sectors, four factors of production and nine representative household groups. The household groups were linked to the Bangladesh Household Expenditure Survey for 2000, on the assumption that each household in the survey had the same variation in its income (or consumption) as the group of which it was part. Simulations included a Doha scenario involving removal of export subsidies and cuts in domestic support and tariffs in the rest of the world; complete free trade in the rest of the world; and full domestic trade liberalisation. Results showed that the Doha scenario had minor negative effects on household welfare and overall poverty. The introduction of complete free trade in the rest of the world yielded a similar pattern of effects, but on a larger scale. Domestic trade liberalisation also caused welfare losses and increased poverty in the short run, but welfare increased and poverty fell in the long run as investment brought adjustment in the capital stock.

Khondker et al. (2006) conducted further comparative static CGE investigation of the welfare and poverty impacts of trade liberalisation in Bangladesh. Their first simulation was, full tariff elimination with a 55 per cent increase in existing production taxes and new construction taxes to compensate for loss of government revenue. Its welfare and poverty results broadly confirmed the results of the same simulation by Khondker and Raihan (2004) reported above. Their second simulation was full removal of tariffs with an accompanying revenue-compensating increase in income tax. In this case, there were relatively large welfare losses for richer households and modest welfare gains for poorer households, with the poverty situation improving in both rural and urban areas. The final simulation of Khondker et al. was changes in tariff rates that resembled actual tariff reforms undertaken in Bangladesh, with the foregone revenue offset by new construction taxes. The results showed small gains in welfare for all household groups except large land-owning farm households, a small improvement in the rural poverty situation, and a slight deterioration in the urban poverty situation.

Hoque (2006) developed BAORANI, a large-scale comparative static CGE model for Bangladesh, based on ORANI, a multi sectoral computable general equilibrium model for the Australian economy (Dixon, et al. 1997). However, following Horridge et al.,(1995), Hoque's model included multiple households with a detailed income mapping between agents and institutions. Based on the 2000 Input-Output table and SAM for Bangladesh, his Johansen-type model included 86 industries, 94 commodities, nine representative households and three primary factors of production (land, labour and capital, with labour disaggregated into eight types). Counterfactual simulation experiments were carried out for the complete removal of tariffs and an improvement in investor confidence. Simulation results were presented in terms of changes in macroeconomic variables, sectoral outputs, employment, and real consumption of households.

All of the studies of CGE modelling that have been surveyed in this section were concerned to a greater or lesser extent with the impact of trade liberalisation on the economy of Bangladesh, and a majority of them sought to examine the effects on household welfare. Among this majority, those studies that included only a single representative household, e.g., Hossein (1989) and Ahammad (1995), were obviously unable to offer any insights about the effects of trade liberalisation on poverty and inequality. Of the studies that modelled multiple representative household groups, only Mujeri and Khondker (2002), Khondker and Raihan (2004), Annabi et al. (2005), and Khondker et al. (2006) examined the effects of trade reform on poverty as well as welfare. However, none offered detailed measures of the effects of trade reform on income inequality. Generally, the latter studies suggested that, in the absence of any new tax measures to compensate for the loss of tariff revenue, domestic trade liberalisation would tend to reduce poverty, although in the study by Annabi et al. only in the long run. When revenue-compensating measures accompanied domestic trade liberalisation, however, poverty tended to increase or show little change, except in the case where loss of tariff revenue was offset by an increase in income tax.

Chapter 5

THE BANGLADESH MODEL: THEORETICAL STRUCTURE

5.1. INTRODUCTION

In this chapter a static, multi-factor, multi-household and multi-sectoral computable general equilibrium model, hereafter termed the Bangladesh model, is developed to assess the economic impacts of tariff liberalisation scenarios in Bangladesh. The model follows Horridge et al. (1995)'s IDC-GEM, a SAM-based computable general equilibrium model of the South African economy. IDC-GEM is patterned after ORANI-F (Horridge et al. 1993), which closely follows ORANI, a multisectoral computable general equilibrium model of the Australian economy (Dixon et al. 1997), which uses the Johansen approach of linearising to find the general solution for equilibrium prices and quantities (Johansen, 1960). In this approach, the model is approximated by a series of linear equations relating to percentage changes in the model variables.[1] Like many other CGE models, IDC-GEM uses microeconomic theory to specify the behaviour of producers, consumers, and investors. It is assumed that producers minimise their costs and maximise their profits, and consumers maximise their utility. The demand and supply equations for private sector agents are derived from the optimisation problems. Thus, in similar fashion to the ORANI-G model (Horridge, 2000, 2001a, 2001b, 2004, 2006; Horridge, Parmenter and Pearson, 1998), the theoretical structure of the IDC-GEM model consists of the following equations: (1) producers' demands for intermediate and primary factor inputs; (2) producers' supplies of commodities; (3) households' and other final demands for commodities; (4) zero pure profit conditions; (5) market clearing conditions for primary factors and commodities; and (6) the relationship of basic values to purchasers' prices and production costs.

A distinctive feature of the IDC-GEM model is that it can capture the distributional impacts of government policies. The model has a social accounting matrix (SAM) extension which provides a suitable quantitative framework by which the value added originating in the production process flows down to various factors of production as returns, which in turn flow to various household groups and other institutions as income flows. In addition, in this model, household disposable income is linked to expenditure directly through the consumption function. Thus, the model can estimate income distribution and welfare impacts. However,

---

[1] See Vincent (1985) and Coxhead (1989) for examples of the Johansen method.

the model cannot predict the poverty impact directly, as it does not contain any equation relating to a poverty line. Therefore, one development in the Bangladesh model is to endogenise the poverty lines following Decaluwé et al. (1999), in order to capture the effects of trade reform policy on absolute poverty. Other developments include disaggregation of the labour sector is disaggregated by gender and skill groups and disaggregation of the household sector by location into urban and rural categories.

The main objective of this chapter is to present the theoretical structure of the Bangladesh model. However, since this model closely follows ORANI, which has been documented in detail (see, for example, Dixon et al. (1977; 1997), the derivation of the model equations does not need to be repeated here. Instead, this study uses the template of ORANI-G (Horridge, Parmenter and Pearson (1998), Horridge (2001b), Horridge (2003), Horridge (2004) and Horridge (2006)) to explain the theory of the model in TABLO code, which resembles the algebra.[2] Furthermore, since the Bangladesh model contains multiple households instead of a single household, this study follows the multiple household version of ORANI-G (Horridge, 2004). In TABLO, the equations of the model are defined in percentage change form, which implements the model in GEMPACK.[3] Note that in this chapter, the equations for various problems are formulated in the levels of the variables, whereas the solution of the problems are linear in percentage change form and are presented by a series of TABLO excerpts.[4] The percentage change in a variable and its levels value are distinguished by using lower-case script for percentage change and upper-case script for levels[5].

Section 5.2 introduces the main sets, variables, coefficients and parameters of the model with their notations. Section 5.3 presents the structure of the core CGE model.[6] Section 5.4 discusses income distribution. Section 5.5 presents poverty aspects of the model. Section 6 discusses standard closures. Section 5.7 describes the approach used in solving the model.

5.2. Sets, Variables and Coefficients of the Model

In TABLO, set names appear in upper-case letters and each set is expressed by one index. As an example, the set 'COM' contains all the commodities in the model with the index 'c'. Another example is 'SRC' (domestic and imported sources) expressed by index's' with two (dom, imp) elements. There are some sets that are subsets of other sets. For example, 'MAR', which is a set of margin-type commodities required to facilitate the flows of other commodities from producers and importers to users (Horridge et al. 1993), is basically a

[2] TABLO is the name of the GEMPACK program that processes the file (containing equations of algebra-like syntax) and converts the information on it to a form suitable for running simulations on the model (Harrison and Pearson, 1996).

[3] GEMPACK is a suite of general purpose economic modelling software for calculating solutions of economic models, especially general and partial equilibrium models. It has been developed by the Centre of Policy Studies, Monash University.

[4] The complete description of the theoretical specification of the model around the TABLO frame is available at http://www.monash.edu.au/policy/oranig.htm.

[5] The percentage change in variable X can be defined as $x = 100(\Delta X/X)$. In deriving the percentage-change equations from the non-linear equations, there are three rules (Peter et al. 1996):
the product rule, $X = \beta YZ \rightarrow x = y + z$, where β is a constant,
the power rule, $X = \beta Y^{\alpha} \rightarrow x = \alpha y$, where α and β are constants, and
the sum rule, $X = Y + Z \rightarrow Xx = Yy + Zz$.

[6] This section draws mainly on Horridge (2006) and Dixon et al. (1997).

subset of 'COM', as each element of set MAR is also an element of set COM. Table 5.1 presents the main sets used in the Bangladesh model. There are 94 commodities and 86 industries in the model, which are indexed with 'c' and 'i' under the set names 'COM' and 'IND'. This classification ensures multi-production in the model. A list of the commodity and industry classifications is provided in Appendix Table C 6.1. Labour is disaggregated into four gender and skill-based occupational categories described by the set 'OCC'. The categories are: (1) male low-skilled (Mallowskill); (2) male high-skilled (Malhighskill); (3) female low-skilled (Femlowskill); and (4) female high-skilled (Femhighskill). There are six margin commodities: (1) wholesale trade; (2) retail trade; (3) air transport; (4) water transport; (5) land transport; and (6) rail transport. Household groups (HOUS) are disaggregated into nine categories based on the Bangladesh Social Accounting Matrix 2000: (1) rural landless households (LandlessHH); (2) rural marginal farmer households (MargfarmHH); (3) rural small farmer households (SmallfarmHH); (4) rural large farmer households (LargefarmHH); (5) rural non-agricultural households (NonagriculHH); (6) urban illiterate households (IlliterateHH); (7) urban low-educated households (LoweduHH); (8) urban medium-educated households (MediumeduHH); and (9) urban high-educated households (HigheduHH).[7]

Table 5.1. Main sets of the Bangladesh model

Index	Set name	Description	Typical size
c	COM	Commodities	94
i	IND	Industries	86
s	SRC	Domestic and imported sources	2
m	MAR	Margin commodities	6
o	OCC	Occupations	4
h	HOUS	Household groups	9

In general, in a TABLO input file variables are measured in percentage changes and they appear as lower-case letters.[8] Conventionally, names of variables consist of a letter or letters indicating the type of variable and a main user number. The following are examples of letters indicating the type of variables:

a	technical change
del	ordinary (rather than percentage change)
f	shift variable
p	price, local currency
p_f	price, foreign currency
x	input quantity
t	tax

[7] Details of the classification of the household groups are provided in Chapter 6.

[8] For some variables where ordinary changes are preferred, such as changes in inventories and changes in the ratio of the nominal balance of trade to nominal GDP, their values are reported as the changes in the level values.

The main user numbers (each of the digits 0 to 6 indicates users) are:

1	firms, current production
2	firms, capital creation
3	households
4	exports
5	government
6	inventories
0	all users

Thus x1(c, s, i) implies the percentage changes in the direct demands by producers for source-specific intermediate inputs. Some variables are associated with an underscore character indicating that these variables are an average over the sets of the original variables. As an example, $p1lab\_io$ represents the average nominal wage over IND and OCC. Appendix Table B 5.1 lists the variables contained in the Bangladesh model.

Coefficients are the constants in the linear approximations of the equations. They appear as upper-case characters in the model. They are either supplied directly from the database or computed from the database using a formula statement. Appendix Table B 5.2 presents the list of coefficients and parameters in the Bangladesh model.

Finally, in the model, three or more letters form a descriptor for the variables. As an example, descriptor 'bas' stands for basic (that is, not including margins or taxes), 'cap' for capital, 'imp' for imports (duty paid), 'lab' for labour, 'lnd' for land, 'lux' for linear expenditure system (supernumerary part, 'mar' for margins, 'oct' for other cost tickets, 'prim' for all primary factors (land, labour and capital), 'pur' for purchasers' prices, and 'sub' for linear expenditure system (subsistence part).

5.3. Structure of the Core Model

5.3.1. Structure of Production

The Bangladesh model assumes that each industry can produce several commodities by using domestic and imported intermediate commodities, labour of several types, land, capital and other costs.[9] This multi-product, multi-input specification follows a series of separability assumptions typical of computable general equilibrium (CGE) models. With the separable production function, the decision as to what combination of products to produce is not dependent on the input use decision. Similarly, product prices have no effect on input combinations except through their effect on the level of activity in the industry (Oktaviani, 2000). As an example of input-output separability, following Horridge et al. (1993), the following generalised production function for some industry

$$F\text{ (inputs, outputs)} = 0 \qquad (1)$$

[9] Other costs refer to production taxes net of subsidies, cost of holding liquidity and other miscellaneous production costs incurred in the production process.

can be written as

G (inputs) = X1TOT = H (outputs) (2)

where X1TOT is an index of industry activity level. The structure of this production function for the Bangladesh model is illustrated by the nesting structure shown in Figure 5.1. In the top level of the diagram, the separable function of output is derived from a constant elasticity of transformation aggregation function, while in the bottom part, the input separable function is hierarchically nested in a sequence of nests. It is assumed that product markets and factor markets are competitive so that producers are price takers in both input and output markets. Given constant returns to scale in production, producers are assumed to make optimal input demand decisions by using a cost minimisation decision rule.

At the top level of the nests for the input function, commodity composites made up of intermediate inputs, a primary factor composite and other costs are combined using a Leontief production function. Thus, there is no substitution between intermediate inputs or between intermediates and primary factors and other costs in producing a unit of industry activity. As a result, these input categories – the commodity composites, primary factor composites and other costs – are demanded in direct proportion to the industry activity level. At the second level, the aggregated intermediate input is calculated to obtain the composite intermediate input quantities according to a constant elasticity of substitution (CES) behavioural function. Such aggregation is in turn based on the assumption of imperfect substitutability between imported and domestic commodities (Armington, 1969; Armington, 1970). The primary factor composite is also a CES aggregation of land, capital and composite labour. In addition, the labour composite is a CES aggregation of skilled and unskilled male and female labour.

The following sub-sections provide a brief explanation for each block of equations in the model along with their TABLO excerpts. We begin with the intermediate input branch.

5.3.1.1. Intermediate Input Demand Equations

As stated in section 5.3.1, each industry chooses the cost minimising combination of imported and domestic intermediate inputs of goods subject to the CES production function. The CES specification implies that inputs of the same commodity type are not perfect substitutes for one another (Peter et al. 1996). Here is a very simple example of deriving the percentage change equations of the CES production nest.[10]

Suppose, to determine the composition of intermediate inputs, the costs $\sum_i PiXi$ are minimised subject to the following CES production function:

$$Z = \left(\sum \delta_i X_i^{-\rho} \right)^{-1/\rho} \tag{3}$$

[10] This derivation is adapted from Horridge (2006). For more details on derivation and linearising the resulting level equations, refer to Dixon, et al. (1997, pp. 68-90), Dixon, et al. (1992:, pp. 88-96, 124-126), and Dixon, Bowles and Kendrick (1980).

where Z is output, the X_i's are inputs and δ_i , ρ are positive parameters. Now to optimise the above problem, the first order conditions are

$$P_k = \lambda \partial Z / \partial X_k = \lambda \delta_k X_k^{-(1+\rho)} \left(\sum \delta_i X_i^{-\rho} \right)^{-(1+\rho)/\rho} \tag{4}$$

$$\text{Thus, } P_k / P_i = \delta_k / \delta_i \left(X_i / X_k \right)^{1+\rho} \tag{5}$$

$$\text{or, } X_i^{-\rho} = \left(\delta_i P_k / \delta_k P_i \right)^{-\rho/(\rho+1)} X_k^{-\rho} \tag{6}$$

Substituting the value of X_i into the production function and solving for the following input demand functions:

$$X_k = Z \left(\sum_i \delta_i \left[\delta_k P_i / \delta_i P_k \right]^{\rho/\rho+1} \right)^{\frac{1}{\rho}} \tag{7}$$

$$\text{or } X_k = Z \delta_k^{1/(\rho+1)} \left[P_k / P_{ave} \right]^{-1/(\rho+1)} \tag{8}$$

$$\text{where, } P_{ave} = \left(\sum_i \delta_i^{1/(\rho+1)} P_i^{\rho/\rho+1} \right)^{(\rho+1)/\rho} \tag{9}$$

The percentage form of equation (8) is as follows:

$$x_k = z - \sigma(p_k - p_{ave}) \tag{10}$$

$$\text{where, } P_{ave} = \sum_i S_i P_i \tag{11}$$

and $\sigma = 1/\rho+1$ indicates the elasticity of substitution between imported and domestic goods as inputs into the production of the industry.

$$S_i = \delta_i^{1/(\rho+1)} P_i^{\rho/\rho+1} \Big/ \sum_k \delta_k^{1/(\rho+1)} P_k^{\rho/(\rho+1)} \qquad (12)$$

denotes the weighted average of all intermediate input prices, and the lower case letters such as *x*'s, *p*'s and *z*'s represent the percentage changes in the variables of the corresponding upper case variables. Multiplying both sides of equation (8) by P_k we obtain:

$$S_k = P_k X \Big/ \sum_i P_i X_i \qquad (13)$$

where S_k is the cost share for an intermediate input in the total cost of inputs in an industry.

Equation (10) shows the simple general percentage-change input demand function of a CES nest.[11] Allowing for technological change in the production process and using proper notations for the users and sources in the general input demand functions, the import/domestic composition of intermediate input demand is shown in the following TABLO excerpt no. 1.

Excerpt 1 of TABLO Input File

Industries' choices between domestic and imported goods

(Parameter)(all,c,COM)SIGMA1(c) # *Atkinson Elasticities: Intermediate* #;
Equation E_x1# *source* specific commodity demand #
(all,c,COM)(all,s,SRC)(all,i,IND)x1(c,s,i)-a1(c,s,i)=x1_s(c,i)-SIGMA1(c)*[p1(c,s,i)+
a1(c,s,i)-p1_s(c,i)]; (14)
Equation E_p1_s# *Effective price of commodity composite* #
(all,c,COM)(all,i,IND)p1_s(c,i)=
sum{s,SRC,S1(c,s,i)*[p1(c,s,i)+a1(c,s,i)]}; (15)

Equation (14) shows that the demand for intermediate input, c, from source, s (s = 1 refers to domestic output, whereas s = 2 denotes imports), by industry, i, for current production, x1 (c, s, i) is proportional to demand for the composite, x1_s (c, i), the relative prices of commodities from different sources (effective price from sources relative to the effective cost of the import/domestic composite), and the elasticity of substitution, SIGMA1. If there is no technical change (i.e., a_i's are zero), and no change in the relative prices from alternative sources, then a proportionate change in x1_s (c, i) leads to the same proportionate change in x1 (c, s, i).[12] This reflects the constant returns to scale assumption in production. However, changes in relative prices of domestic and imported goods initiate a substitution in favour of the cheaper source, the magnitude of which depends on the value of the substitution parameter, SIGMA1 (c).

[11] A similar procedure is used for the derivation of labour inputs and primary factor inputs.
[12] For discussion of technical change, see Dixon, et al. (1997, p. 82).

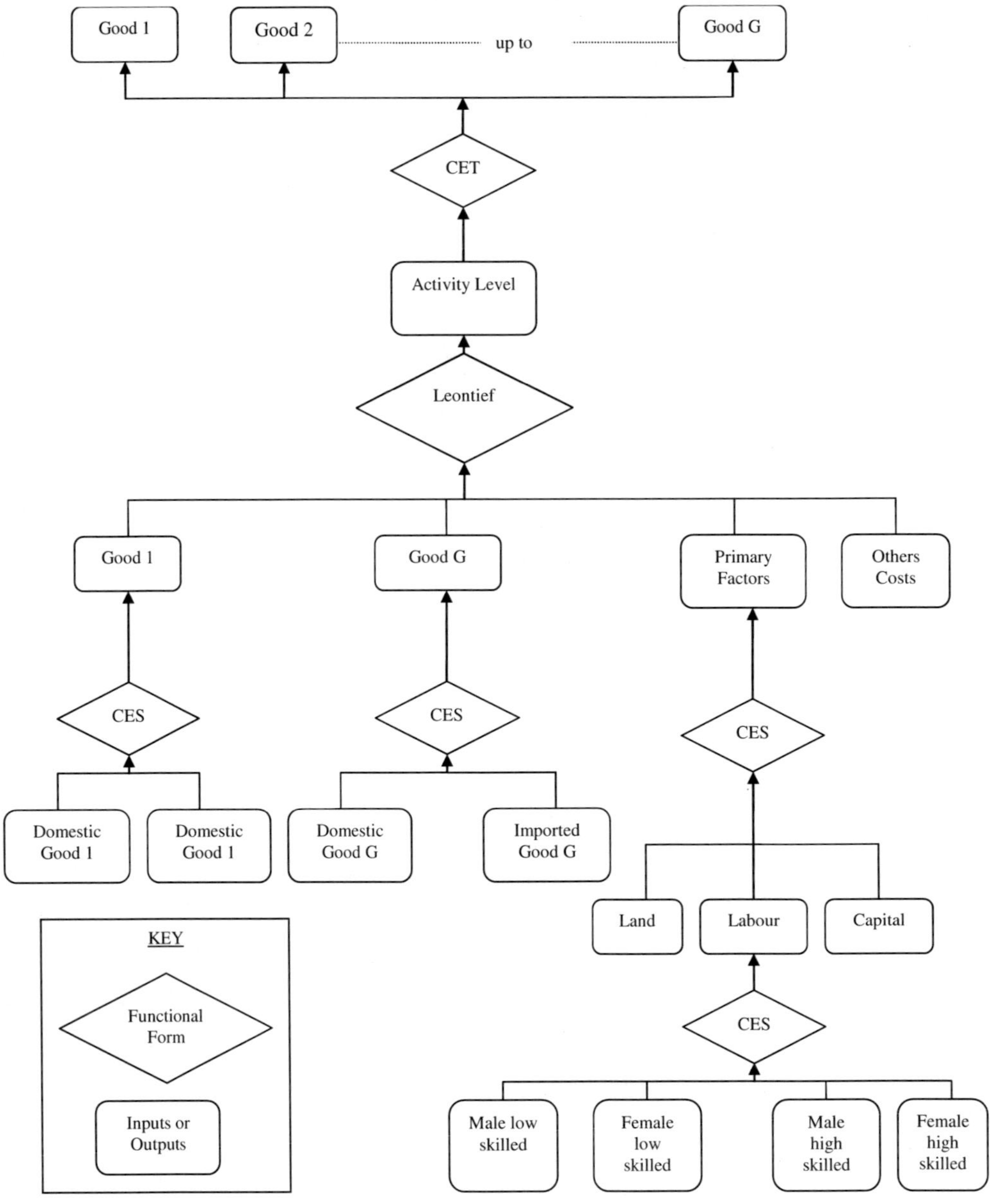

Source: Adapted from Horridge (2003).

Figure 5.1. Structure of production

5.3.1.2. Demand for Primary Factors

In Figure 5.1, at the lowest level nest in the primary-factor branch of the production tree, producers choose a combination of four occupation-specific labour inputs to minimise total labour costs. These labour categories are male low-skilled, male high-skilled, female low-skilled and female high-skilled. The Bangladesh model assumes that producers chose a CES combination to minimise the costs. For each industry *i*, the optimisation problem can be written as follows:

Choose inputs of occupation-specific labour,

$$X1LAB(i,o)$$

to minimise total labour cost,

$$\sum_{o}^{4} P1LAB(i,o) * X1LAB(i,o) \tag{16}$$

subject to,

$$X1LAB\_O(I) = CES\{X1LAB(i,o)\} \tag{17}$$

where $P1LAB(i,o)$ is the price paid by industry for each occupation-specific labour type and $X1LAB\_O(I)$ denotes an effective labour input demanded by industry *i*. Following the derivation of intermediate input demand in section 5.3.1.1, the demand for labour by occupation can be stated in levels as:

$$X1LAB(i,o) = X1LAB\_O(I) * \left(P1LAB(i,o) \Big/ P1LAB\_O(i) \right)^{SIGMA1LAB} \tag{18}$$

where $SIGMA1LAB$ is the parameter for the substitution of various skilled and unskilled labourers and $P1LAB\_O(i)$ is the price of the labour composite to each industry. The solution to this problem in percentage change form is shown in the following TABLO excerpt no. 2.

Excerpt 2 of TABLO Input File

Occupational composition of labour demand

```
Coefficient
(parameter)(all,i,IND)SIGMA1LAB(i)# CES Substitution between skill type #;
(all,i,IND) V1LAB_O(i) # Total labour bill in industry i #;
Read SIGMA1LAB from file BASEDATA header "SLAB";
Equation
E_x1lab# Demand for labour by industry and skill group #
(all,i,IND)(all,o,OCC)x1lab(i,o)
=x1lab_o(i)-SIGMA1LAB(i)*[p1lab(i,o)-p1lab_o(i)];                        (19)
E_p1lab_o# Price to each industry of labour composite #
(all,i,IND)[TINY+V1LAB_O(i)]*p1lab_o(i)=sum{o,OCC,V1LAB(i,o)*p1lab(i,o)};  (20)
E_employ(all,i,IND)ID01[V1LAB_O(i)]*employ(i)=
sum{o,OCC,V1LAB(i,o)*x1lab(i,o)};                                          (21)
E_employ_iV1LAB_IO*employ_i=sum{i,IND,V1LAB_O(i)*employ(i)};               (22)
```

Equation (20) shows that the occupation specific demand for labour is proportional to the demand for the effective composite labour demand and the relative prices of occupational specific labour and an elasticity of substitution, SIGMA1LAB(i). The interpretation of (19) is similar to that of (14). If there is no change in the relative prices of the different types of labour, then the occupational composition of industry $i's$ labour force remains the same. However, with a given level of demand for effective labour, if the wage rate of the labour type o increases relative to a weighted average of the wage rates of all different types of labour, then there will be a substitution of other types of labour for that specific type of labour. This responsiveness of occupational employment in turn depends on the magnitude of $SIGMA1LAB$, the CES between skill types.

At the next level of the of the primary factor branch of the production nest in Figure 5.1, we determine the composition of demand for primary factors. In the Bangladesh model, the primary factors are land, capital and labour. Their derivation follows the same CES pattern as the previous nests. For a given primary input requirement, firms have to form a primary factor composite such that the total primary costs are minimised. Here, it is important to note that whereas in previous section we excluded the technology variables to simplify the exposition, in this section we introduce factor-saving technical changes. In this case, total primary costs are minimised subject to the following production function:

$$X1PRIM(i) = CES\left[\frac{X1LAB\_O(i)}{A1LAB\_O(i)}, \frac{X1CAP(i)}{A1CAP(i)}, \frac{X1LND(i)}{A1LAND(i)}\right] \tag{23}$$

where $X1PRIM(i)$ denotes the industry's overall demand for primary factors and variables $A1LAB\_O(i)$, $A1CAP(i)$ and $A1LND(i)$ denote factor specific technical change variables. The resulting demand equations can be expressed in level form as:

$$\frac{X1LAB\_O(i)}{A1LAB\_O(i)} = X1PRIM(i) * \left(A1LAB\_O(i) * \frac{P1LAB\_O(i)}{P1PRIM(i)}\right)^{SIGMA1PRIM(i)} \tag{24}$$

$$\frac{X1LND(i)}{A1LND(i)} = X1PRIM(i) * \left(A1LND(i) * \frac{P1LND(i)}{P1PRIM(i)}\right)^{SIGMA1PRIM(i)} \tag{25}$$

$$\frac{X1CAP(i)}{A1CAP(i)} = X1PRIM(i) * \left(A1CAP(i) * \frac{P1CAP(i)}{P1PRIM(i)}\right)^{SIGMAPRIM(i)} \tag{26}$$

The following TABLO excerpt 3 shows the equivalent percentage-change demand equations for primary factors. For a given level of technology, the demand function for each factor is proportional to overall factor demand, $x1prim(i)$ and a relative price term (the unit cost of the factor relative to the overall effective cost of primary factor inputs). Changes in the price of a primary factor relative to the average factor price change the demand for that factor. Producers substitute relatively cheaper factors. For example, if the price of labour composite, $p1lab\_o(i)$, increases relative to the effective price of the primary factor composite, $p1prim(i)$, with a given level of primary factor requirement, $x1prim(i)$, the industry will reduce its demand for labour and substitute other factors such as land and capital. The strength of this substitution effect depends on the value of the parameter, $SIGMA1PRIM(i)$, the CES for primary factors. Equation (30) shows that the percentage change in the price of an effective unit of composite primary factor is equal to the weighted average of the percentage changes in the costs of the three groups of primary factors. All the demand equations contain technical change variables which affect quantity demanded and price variables related to primary factors. These technical change variables are usually set exogenously at zero.

Excerpt 3 of TABLO Input File

Primary factor proportions

```
Coefficient (all,i,IND)SIGMA1PRIM(i)# CES Substitution, primary factors #;
Read SIGMA1PRIM from file BASEDATA header"P028";
Equation
E_x1lab_o # Industry demands for effective labour #
(all,i,IND)x1lab_o(i)-a1lab_o(i)=x1prim(i)-SIGMA1PRIM(i)*[p1lab_o(i)+a1lab_o(i)- p1prim(i)];
                                                                                        (27)
E_p1cap # Industry demands for capital #
(all,i,IND)x1cap(i)-a1cap(i)=x1prim(i)-SIGMA1PRIM(i)*[p1cap(i)+a1cap(i)-p1prim(i)];     (28)
E_p1lnd # Industry demands for land #
(all,i,IND)x1lnd(i)-a1lnd(i)=x1prim(i)-SIGMA1PRIM(i)*[p1lnd(i)+a1lnd(i)-p1prim(i)];
                                                                                        (29)
E_p1prim#Effective price term for factor demand equations#
(all,i,IND)V1PRIM(i)*p1prim(i)=V1LAB_O(i)*[p1lab_o(i)+a1lab_o(i)]+
V1CAP(i)*[p1cap(i)+a1cap(i)]+V1LND(i)*[p1lnd(i)+a1lnd(i)];                              (30)
```

5.3.1.3. Demands for Primary Factors and Commodity Composites

At the top-most input demand nest of Figure 5.1 commodity composites, the primary-factor composites and 'other costs' are combined using a Leontief production function to determine the activity level for the industries. This type of production function is similar to a CES production function with the elasticity of substitution set equal to zero. The production function is given by:

$$X1TOT(i) = \frac{1}{A1TOT(i)} xMIN\left[All, c, COM : \frac{X1\_S(c,i)}{A1\_S(c,i)}, \frac{X1PRIM(i)}{A1PRIM(i)}, \frac{X1OCT(i)}{A1OCT(i)}\right] \quad (31)$$

where $X1TOT(i)$ is the activity level or value-added, $A1TOT(i)$ is the Hicks-neutral technological change term,[13] $A1PRIM(i)$ is the all input augmenting technological change and $A1OCT(i)$ is the technological change associated with other cost tickets.

Because of the Leontief specification of the production function, the demand equations for composite primary factors, for intermediate inputs and for other cost tickets are directly proportional to the level of activity in the industry. These are indicated by equations E_x1_s, E_x1prim and E_x1oct in TABLO excerpt no. 4. Equations (32), (33) and (34) show that with technology parameters set exogenously, the effective demand for each of these categories of inputs depends only upon each industry's activity level rather than the relative prices of these inputs.

Excerpt 4 of TABLO Input File

Top nest of industry input demands

Equation E_x1_s # Demands for composite commodities#
(all,c,COM)(all,i,IND)x1_s(c,i)-[a1_s(c,i)+a1tot(i)]=x1tot(i); (32)
Equation E_x1prim *# Demands for primary factor composites #*
(all,i,IND)x1prim(i)-[a1prim(i)+a1tot(i)]=x1tot(i); (33)
Equation E_x1oct *# Demands for other costs tickets #*
(all,i,IND)x1oct(i)-[a1oct(i)+a1tot(i)]=x1tot(i); (34)

5.3.1.4. Output Decisions: From Industry Output to Commodity Outputs

The top level of Figure 5.1 explains the relationship between activity level and outputs of an industry. Following ORANI-G, the Bangladesh model allows some industries to produce a mixture of all the commodities.[14] It is assumed that for a given level of activity and commodity prices, industries will choose their output mix to maximise their revenue. The commodity output combination is formed based on a CET (constant elasticity of transformation) functional form.[15] Thus, the revenue from the output is maximised by the following production function:

$$X1TOT(i) = CET\left[ALL, c, COM : Q1(c,i)\right] \quad (35)$$

Where $Q1(c,i)$ denotes output by commodity and industry and CET is the functional form of a constant elasticity of transformation production possibility frontier.[16] The percentage change form of commodity supply equation that is shown by equation (36) in excerpt 5 of the TABLO input file indicates that each industry's supplies of composite commodities depends upon the industry's overall activity level and the relative prices of the various composite

[13] Hicks-neutral technological change refers to a situation where technological change raises output by a factor of proportionality that is independent of the composition of inputs employed in production (Helpman, 2004: pp. 19-20).

[14] The IDC-GEM model assumes a single product in the production system.

[15] Powell and Gruen (1967) and Powell and Gruen (1968) were the first to introduce CET function into CGE modeling.

[16] The CET form is identical to the CES form except for the restriction on ρ. With CES, ρ is greater than or equal to -1, whereas, with CET, ρ is less than or equal to -1. In the case of CES, the curves are concave from above; in contrast, in the CET case, the curves are concave from below (Dixon, et al. 1992).

commodities it produces. An increase in a commodity price, relative to the average price of all commodities produced induces a transformation in favour of that commodity. Transformation into that commodity is governed by SIGMA1OUT, the CET transformation elasticities between different commodities. Equation (37) shows that the percentage change in composite commodity prices is a revenue-share weighted average of the percentage change in individual commodity prices.

Excerpt 5 of tablo input File

Output mix of commodities

Equation E_q1# *Supplies of commodities by industries #*
(all,c,COM)(all,i,IND)q1(c,i)=x1tot(i)+SIGMA1OUT(i)*[p0com(c)-p1tot(i)]; (36)
E_x1tot# *Average price received by industries #*
(all,i,IND)p1tot(i)=sum{c,COM,[MAKE(c,i)/MAKE_C(i)]*pq1(c,i)}; (37)

5.3.1.5. Input Demands for the Creation of Fixed Capital

In the Bangladesh model, it is assumed that producers of fixed capital goods combine inputs to form units of fixed capital and in so doing minimise their cost subject to technologies. The nesting structure for the production of new units of fixed capital is given in Figure 5.2, where it is shown that the production function for capital goods is a multi-stage production procedure with Leontief technology for combining composite intermediate goods at the top level and the CES technology for combining imported and domestically produced goods at the bottom level. It is also assumed that capital creation requires no primary factor inputs and that these goods are created efficiently and competitively. Thus the model's investment demand equations are derived from the following two-part investor's cost minimising problem. In Figure 5.2, at the bottom level of the nest, the total cost of the domestic-foreign import composite, $X2\_S(c,i)$ is minimised subject to the CES production function:

$$X2\_S(c,i) = CES\left[ALL, s, SRC : \frac{X2(c,s,i)}{A2(c,s,i)}\right] \tag{38}$$

Where $A2(c,s,i)$ denotes the basic technical change parameters for investment.

The resulting demand equation in percentage form is presented in TABLO excerpt no. 6 by equation no. (40), which shows that the demand for source-specific inputs, $x2(c,s,i)$, is a function of total fixed capital units produced, Armington substitution in investment, SIGMA2 (c), and the relative prices of goods from different sources. In the absence of technical change, an increase in the domestic price of a commodity, $p2(c,s,i)$ compared to the weighted average price of imports and domestic commodities, $p2\_s(c,i)$, will decrease the demand for the domestic commodity and increase the demand for the imported commodity. This substitution is governed by SIGMA2 (c), the Armington substitution elasticities for investment. Equation (41) describes the percentage change in the effective price of the commodity composite as the average cost of producing a unit of fixed capital from the two sources. At the top level of Figure 5.2, the total cost of effective units of produced inputs is minimised according to a Leontief production function:

$$X2TOT(i) = \frac{1}{A2TOT(i)} MIN\left[ALL, c, COM : \frac{X2\_S(c,i)}{A2\_S(c,i)} \right] \tag{39}$$

Here, $X2TOT(i)$, the total amount of investment in each industry is assumed exogenous for the above cost minimising problem. The resulting percentage-change demand equation (42) shows that the effective unit of goods *i*, $x2\_s(i)$ is directly proportional to the number of units of fixed capital produced, irrespective of relative input price change.

Excerpt 6 of TABLO Input File

Investment demands

Coefficient
(parameter)(all,c,COM)SIGMA2(c)# *Armington elasticities: Investment#*
Read SIGMA2 from file BASEDATA header*"2ARM"*;
Equation
E_x2# *Source specific commodity demands #*
(all,c,COM)(all,s,SRC)(all,i,IND)
x2(c,s,i)-a2(c,s,i)-x2_s(c,i)=-SIGMA2(c)*[p2(c,s,i)+a2(c,s,i)-p2_s(c,i)]; (40)
E_p2_s#Effective prices of domestic composite #(all,c,COM)(all,i,IND)
p2_s(c,i) = sum{s,SRC, S2(c,s,i)*[p2(c,s,i)+a2(c,s,i)]}; (41)
E_x2_s(all,c,COM)(all,i,IND)x2_s(c,i)-[a2_s(c,i)+a2tot(i)]=x2tot(i); (42)

5.3.1.6. Investment Allocation

The technology for creating fixed capital is described in section 5.3.1.5. This section discusses how the investment level is determined for each industry. In the Bangladesh model, following ORANI and ORANI-G, rate of return theory is used to explain the allocation of investment among industries. In other words, newly created units of capital are distributed between industries on the basis of relative rates of return. To allocate investment across industries, Dixon et al. (1997: pp. 118-122) outlined a number of steps.

It is assumed that the rate of return on fixed capital in industry j is given by

$$R_j(0) = \frac{P^{(1)}{}_{(n+1,2)j}}{\Pi_j} - d_j \tag{43}$$

Where d_j is the rate of depreciation, $P^{(1)}{}_{(n+1,2)j}$ is the rental value of a unit of capital in industry j, and Π_j is the cost of unit of capital in industry j.

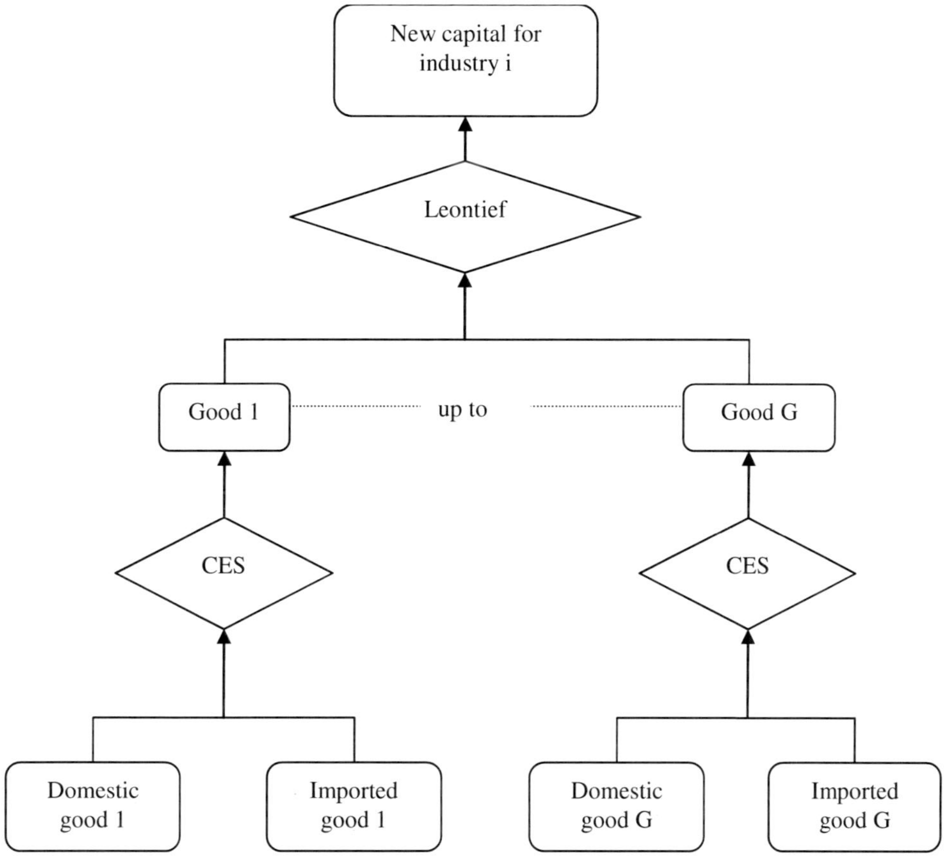

Source: Adapted from Horridge (2003).

Figure 5.2. Structure of investment demand.

It is also assumed that investors expect that industry j 's rate of return schedule in period 1 time will have the following form:

$$R_j(1) = R_j(0)\left(\frac{K_j(1)}{K_j(0)}\right)^{-\beta_j} \tag{44}$$

where β_j is a positive parameter, $K_j(0)$ is the current level of the capital stock in industry j and $K_j(1)$ is the level of capital stock at the end of period 1.

It is further assumed that total private investment expenditure is allocated across industries in such a way so as to equate the expected rates of return. This means that there exists some rate of return Ω such that

$$\left(\frac{K_j(1)}{K_j(0)}\right)^{-\beta_j} R_j(0) = \Omega \;\; j \in J \tag{45}$$

Also, the only variables that determine the capital stock at the end of period 1 are the current capital stock, its rate of depreciation, and the current level of investment, as shown by equation (46).

$$K_j(1) = K_j(0)(1 - d_j) + Y_j \tag{46}$$

Equations (43)-(46) can be represented in percentage change form as follows:

$$r_j(0) = Q_j\left(p^{(1)}{}_{(n+1,2)j} - \pi_j\right) \tag{47}$$

where Q_j is the ratio of gross to net rate of return.

$$\beta_j\left(k_j(1) - k_j(0)\right) + r_j(0) = w \tag{48}$$

$$k_j(1) = k_j(0)(1 - G_j) + y_j G \tag{49}$$

where G_j is the ratio of gross investment to future capital stock in industry j.

On the basis of the above investment theory, investment follows one of three rules for each industry:

First, in the short run, investment is positively related to the profit rate. In excerpt 7 of the TABLO input file, equations (50) and (51) define the percentage change in the gross growth rate of capital and the gross rate of return on capital in industry i respectively. Equation (52) relates the gross growth rate to the net rate of return (relative to the economy-wide rate, *invslack)* for selected industries.[17] This equation implies that industries with higher gross rates of return attract more investment. The variable finv1 (i) allows for exogenous shifts in each industry i.

Secondly, for exogenous investment industries, investment follows national investment, x2tot_i. These are the industries for which the previous investment theory is inappropriate.[18] Equation (53) states that with finv2 (i) exogenous, investment depends on aggregate investment in the economy.

Thirdly' it is assumed that in the long run, the aggregate capital stock adjusts to the previously determined economy-wide rate of return, and the allocation of capital across industries or the industry demand for investment goods is determined by fixed investment/capital ratios. This rule is shown by equation (54). For an industry with fixed finv3 (i), it fixes the gross capital growth rate.

Following ORANI-G, in this model the demand for inventories is fixed.

---

[17] This equation comes from substituting equations (47) and (49) in equation (48). The value 0.33 corresponds to the sensitivity of capital growth to rates of return; G_j and 2.0 corresponds to the ratio of gross to net rate of return, Q_j. These values are from Dixon et al. (1997) and are typical values of these ratios.

[18] They are industries where investment is determined by government policy and not driven by current profits (e.g., education, and public health).

Excerpt 7 of TABLO Input File

```
Equation
E_ggro(all,i,IND)ggro(i)=x2tot(i)-x1cap(i);                              (50)
E_gret(all,i,IND)gret(i)=p1cap(i)-p2tot(i);                              (51)
E_finv1# DPSV investment rule #
(all,i,IND)ggro(i)=finv1(i)+0.33*[2.0*gret(i)-invslack];                 (52)
E_finv2# Alternative rule for exogenous investment industries #;
(all,i,IND)x2tot(i)=x2tot_i+finv2(i);                                    (53)
E_finv3# Alternative long run investment rule #;
(all,i,IND)ggro(i)=finv3(i)+invslack;                                    (54)
```

5.3.1.7. Household Demands

Since the effects of trade liberalisation on income distribution and poverty are the main concerns of this study, the household sector has been disaggregated in the Bangladesh model into nine representative household groups on the basis of rural/urban differences, education levels of heads of households, and households' ownership of land. A neoclassical utility maximisation model that assumes consumers purchase commodities to maximise utility subject to aggregate expenditure constraints explains households' demands.

Figure 5.3 depicts the structure of household consumer demand. It has nearly the same nesting structure as investment demand. The only difference is that in the household demand nest, commodity composites are aggregated by a Klein-Rubin (Stone-Geary) utility function.[19] The Klein-Rubin utility function in turn leads to the linear expenditure system (LES). For each representative household group, total consumption expenditures are determined by a consumption function, equation (135) in section 5.4.2. below.

In Figure 5.3, at the bottom level of the nest, the representative household in each group, h, chooses combinations of domestic and imported commodities to minimise cost subject to a CES utility function. Using a similar derivation to the demand equation for intermediate inputs in section 5.3.1.1, households' demand functions for commodity composites in percentage change form are given by the equations (55) and (56) in TABLO excerpt no. 8. Equation (55) shows that in the absence of changes in taste, the household demand for commodities from a specific source, $x3(c,s,h)$ depends on the household demand for commodity composite, $x3\_s(c,h)$, relative prices of household commodities from different sources and the Armington substitution elasticity for households, SIGMA3(c). Changes in relative commodity prices will affect the household demand for commodities from different sources in the same way they affect demands for intermediate and investment requirements.

Excerpt 8 of TABLO Input File

Import/domestic composition of household demands

```
Coefficient
(parameter) (all,c,COM)SIGMA3(c)# Armington Elasticities: Households #;
```

[19] The Klein-Rubin (Stone-Geary) utility function is often referred to as the Stone-Geary utility function in recognition of the contributions of Stone (1954) and Geary (1949-50) to the formulation of this utility function.

Read SIGMA3 from file BASEDATA header*"3ARM"*;
Equation E_x3# *Source-specific commodity demands #*
(all,c,COM)(all,s,SRC)(all,h,HOUS)
x3(c,s,h)-a3(c,s)=x3_s(c,h)-SIGMA3(c)*[p3(c,s,h)+a3(c,s)-p3_s(c,h)]; (55)
E_p3_s# *Effective price of commodity composite #*(all,c,COM)(all,h,HOUS) p3_s
(c,h) =sum{s,SRC, S3(c,s,h)*[p3(c,s,h)+a3(c,s)]}; (56)

At the top level of the household demand nest, households allocate expenditure between composite commodities according to a Klein-Rubin utility function. The demand equations derived from this utility function consist of the subsistence demand for the good, and the supernumerary expenditure. The expenditure equation obtained from this demand function is a linear function of income and prices (Chung, 1994). Utility per household is given by:

$$UTILITY_h = \frac{1}{Q_h}\prod_c \left(X3\_S(c,h) - X3SUB(c,h)\right)^{S3LUX(c,h)}, h = 1,2,....9 \tag{57}$$

where $X3SUB(c,h)$ and $S3LUX(c,h)$ are behavioral coefficients, Q_h is the number of households of that specific group and $\sum_c S3LUX(c,h) = 1$. $X3SUB(c,h)$ denotes the subsistence level of consumption and $S3LUX(c,h)$ is the proportion of the supernumerary expenditure spent on good c or the marginal budget share of total spending on luxuries (supernumerary).

A representative consumer for a specific household group chooses the commodity composite, $X3\_S(c,h)/Q_h$, to maximise the equation (57) subject to the budget constraint:

$$\sum_c \frac{X3\_S(c,h)}{Q_h} * P3\_S(c,h) = \frac{V3TOTH(h)}{Q_h} \tag{58}$$

Where $V3TOTH(h)$ is the total purchases by a representative household of a given group.

The demand equations that arise from this utility function are:

$$X3\_S(c,h) = X3SUB(c,h) + S3LUX(c,h) * \frac{V3LUX\_C(h)}{P3\_S(c,h)} \tag{59}$$

where

$$V3LUX\_C(h) = V3TOTH(h) - \sum X3SUB(c,h) * P3\_S(c,h) \tag{60}$$

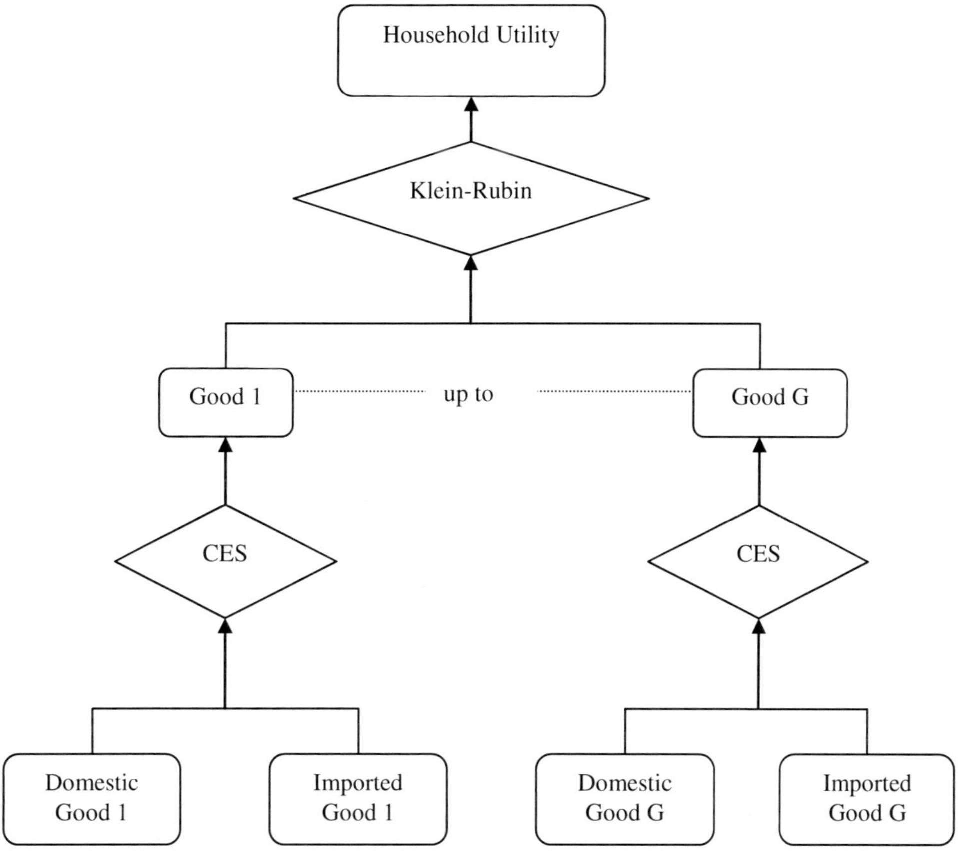

Source: Adapted from Horridge (2003).

Figure 5.3. Structure of consumer demand.

$V3LUX\_C(h)$ represents the supernumerary expenditure, or the amount of total expenditure of the representative consumer of a particular household group that is left over when all of the subsistence requirements have been fulfilled.[20] Equation (60) has the property that expenditure on each good is a linear function of prices $P3\_S(c,h)$ and expenditure $V3TOT(h)$. Thus, in level form the equations can be written as:

$$X3\_S(c,h) = X3SUB(c,h) + X3LUX(c,h) \quad (61)$$

$$X3LUX(c,h) * P3\_S(c,h) = S3LUX(c,h) * V3LUX\_C(h) \quad (62)$$

$$X3SUB(c,h) = Q_h * A3SUB(c,h) \quad (63)$$

The percentage changes of these equations are shown in TABLO excerpt no. 9. Equation (64) shows that the percentage change in subsistence demand for a composite commodity by

[20] Derivation of the demand equations is provided in Appendix B 5.3.

all households in group h is a function of the percentage change in the number of households and the percentage change in the average household subsistence demand. The percentage change in representative household supernumerary demand for a commodity composite, shown by equation (65), is a function of the percentage change in nominal luxury household expenditure and the relative price of the commodity composite. Equation (66) shows the percentage change in the total household demand for the composite good, which is the sum of the percentage changes in subsistence consumption and supernumerary consumption for the good, weighted by their respective shares in total expenditure on commodity, c. Equation (67) is the percentage change form of the utility function (57). The equations described here determine the composition of household demands but not total consumption. Total household consumption is determined by total household disposable income, which is described in sub-section 5.4.2.

Excerpt 9 of TABLO Input File

Household demands for composite commodities

Equation
E_x3sub# *Subsistence demand for composite commodities #*
(all,c,COM)(all,h,HOUS)x3sub(c,h)=qh(h)+a3sub(c,h); (64)
E_x3lux# *Luxury demand for composite commodities #*
(all,c,COM)(all,h,HOUS)x3lux(c,h)+p3_s(c,h)=w3luxh(h)+a3lux(c,h) (65)
E_x3_s# Total household demand for composite commodities #
(all,c,COM)(all,h,HOUS)
x3_s(c,h)=B3LUX(c,h)*x3lux(c,h)+[1-B3LUX(c,h)]*x3sub(c,h); (66)
E_utilityh# *Change in utility disregarding taste change terms #*
(all,h,HOUS)utilityh(h)+qh(h)=sum{c,COM,S3LUX(c,h)*x3lux(c,h)}; (67)

5.3.1.8. Foreign Export Demands

Following ORANI-F and ORANI-G, export commodities are divided into two groups: *traditional* export commodities, mainly agricultural and manufacturing products, which comprise the greater volume of exports; and *non-traditional* exports, mainly service commodities and other commodities.[21] For most commodities in the traditional exports list, exports constitute a large share of total output, whereas for *non-traditional* commodities, shares are small. Demand for a *traditional* export commodity is modelled as a downward sloping foreign export demand function given by:

$$X4(c) = F4Q(c)\left[\frac{P4(c)}{PHI * F4P(c)}\right]^{EXP\_ELAST(c)} \tag{68}$$

where $X4(c)$ is the export volumes of commodity c, $EXP\_ELAST(c)$ is the constant own price elasticity of foreign export demand, which is negative. PHI is the exchange rate, which converts Bangladesh *taka* to foreign currency units, and the shift variables, $F4Q(c)$

[21] In this model the traditional export commodities are jute and jute products, tea, shrimps, leather products, ready-made garments, knitting, toiletries manufactures, fertiliser, insecticides and miscellaneous industrial products.

and $F4P(c)$ allow for horizontal (quantity) and vertical (price) shifts in the export demand curve. Equation (68) states that traditional exports are a negative function of their foreign currency prices.[22] The percentage-change form of this equation is provided in TABLO excerpt no.10 by equation E_x4A.

In case of *non-traditional* export commodities, the above mentioned demand rule seems inappropriate as historically, these commodities comprise only small shares in total output. Typically, export volumes do not necessarily depend on their respective prices in this category. Following ORANI-G, the commodity composition of aggregate *non-traditional* exports is exogenised by treating *non-traditional* exports as a Leontief aggregate (equation E_X4B in excerpt 10). For these types of commodities, exports are assumed to be directly proportional to aggregate *non-traditional* exports. The demand for aggregate *non-traditional* exports is assumed to be inversely related to the average price of non-traditional export commodities by a constant-elasticity demand curve (equation 72).

Excerpt 10 of TABLO Input File

Export demands

Set
TRADEXP# *Traditional Export commodities #*
NTRADEXP# *Non-Traditional export commodities #* = COM-TRADEXP;
EquationE_x4A # *Individual export demand functions #*
(all,c,TRADEXP)x4(c)-f4q(c)=-ABS[EXP_ELAST(c)]*[p4(c)-phi-f4p(c)]; (69)
E_X4B # *Collective export demand functions #*
(all,c,NTRADEXP)x4(c)- f4q(c) = x4_ntrad; (70)
E_p4_ntrad # *Average price of collective exports #*
[TINY+V4NTRADEXP]*p4_ntrad = sum{c, NTRADEXP, V4PUR(c)*p4(c)}; (71)
E_x4_ntrad# *Demand for collective export aggregate #*
X4_ntrad-f4q_ntrad=-ABS [EXP_ELAST_NT]*[p4_ntrad-phi-f4p_ntrad]; (72)

5.3.1.9. Government Consumption Demands

In modelling government consumption demands for both domestic and imported goods, ORANI does not provide any theoretical explanation. Following ORANI-G, the percentage change equations of government demands are provided in TABLO excerpt 11. In equation (73), the shift variables $f5$ and $f5tot$ represent respectively the source-specific commodity shift term and the overall shift term for government demand. With both these shift variables constant, the level and composition of government demand is also determined exogenously. Alternatively, it is possible to treat the government demand endogenously. In this case it is assumed that government consumption expenditure changes in direct proportion to real aggregate household consumption. This can be achieved by treating the shift variable $f5tot2$ (which denotes the ratio of the overall shift term for government demand to real aggregate household expenditure) as exogenous and $f5tot$ as endogenous in equation (74). In the Bangladesh model, the short run closure specifies government consumption demand as exogenous, and the long run closure specifies it as endogenous.

[22] Export prices are defined here as f.o.b prices in foreign currency.

Excerpt 11 of TABLO Input File

Government demands

```
Equation E_x5# Government demands #
(all,c,COM)(all,s,SRC) x5(c,s) = f5(c,s) + f5tot;                          (73)
E_f5tot# Overall Government demands shift #
f5tot= sum {h, HOUS, S3_H(h)*x3toth(h)} + f5tot2;                          (74)
```

5.3.1.10. Trade and Transport Margins

As in both IDC-GEM and ORANI-G, the demands for margins are modelled as proportional to the commodity flows with which the margins are associated.

Excerpt 12 of TABLO Input File

Margin demands

```
Equation
E_x1mar# Margins to producers # (all,c,COM)(all,s,SRC)(all,i,IND)(all,m,MAR)
x1mar(c,s,i,m)=x1(c,s,i)+a1mar(c,s,i,m);                                   (75)
E_x2mar# Margins to investment #
(all,c,COM)(all,s,SRC)(all,i,IND)(all,m,MAR)
x2mar(c,s,i,m)=x2(c,s,i)+a2mar(c,s,i,m);                                   (76)
E_x3mar#Margins to households
(all,c,COM)(all,s,SRC)(all,h,HOUS)(all,m,MAR)
x3mar(c,s,h,m)=x3(c,s,h)+a3mar(c,s,m);                                     (77)
E_x4mar# margins to exports #
(all,c,COM)(all,m,MAR)x4mar(c,m)=x4(c)+a4mar(c,m);                         (78)
E_x5mar# Margins to government #
(all,c,COM)(all,s,SRC)(all,m,MAR)x5mar(c,s,m)=x5(c,s)+a5mar(c,s,m);        (79)
```

5.3.1.11. Zero Pure Profit and the Price System

There are several price sets of commodity prices in the Bangladesh model, for example, basic values, purchasers' prices, f.o.b foreign currency export prices, c.i.f. foreign currency import prices and prices of capital units. Basic values are the prices received by producers. They consist of the cost of raw materials and the cost of the factors of production. Sales taxes and margin costs are not included. For importers, basic prices are c.i.f. import prices paid by importers plus import duties and tariffs. However, they do not include sales taxes and margin costs needed to deliver the products from ports to domestic users. In contrast, purchasers' prices of commodities consist of the basic prices of the goods plus indirect taxes less subsidies and the cost of margin commodities. In this model, this price system is constrained by two assumptions. The first is the zero pure profit condition that is perfect competition exists in all markets. This implies that revenue per unit of output in each industry equals cost per unit of output, a condition that also holds for the distribution of commodities (transporting, etc.). The second condition is that basic prices are uniform across users and producing industries in the case of domestic goods and across importers, in the case of imported goods.

Keeping these assumptions in mind, the basic value of the output of industry j is equal to the total payments of industry j for its inputs:

$$\sum_{i=1}^{g} P_{(i1)}^{(0)} X_{(i1)j}^{(0)} = \sum_{i=1}^{g}\sum_{s=1}^{2} P_{(is)j}^{(1)} X_{(is)j}^{(1)} + \sum_{m=1}^{4} P_{(L,m)j}^{(1)} X_{(L,m)j}^{(1)} + P_{(K)j}^{(1)} X_{(K)j}^{(1)} + P_{(N)j}^{(1)} X_{(N)j}^{(1)} + P_{(oct)j}^{(1)} X_{(oct)j}^{(1)} \quad (80)$$

where $P_{(i1)}^{(0)}$ is the basic price of output of industry j and $X_{(i1)}^{(0)}$ is the production of good $(i1)$ by industry j. $P_{(is)j}^{(1)}$ is the price paid for domestic or imported intermediate inputs i from source s which are used in industry j, and $X_{(is)j}^{(1)}$ denotes intermediate inputs, domestic and imported, used in industry j. $P_{(L,m)j}^{(1)}$, $P_{(K)j}^{(1)}$, $P_{(N)j}^{(1)}$, $P_{(oct)}^{(1)}$ denote respectively the price to industry j of a unit of labour of skill m, rental cost of capital, the price of land to industry j of units of capital and land and the price of other cost tickets in industry j. The percentage-change form of the above zero-profit condition is given by:

$$\sum_{i=1}^{g} p_{(i1)}^{(0)} H_{(i1)}^{(0)} = \sum_{i=1}^{g}\sum_{s=1}^{2} p_{(is)j}^{(1)} H_{(is)j}^{(1)} + \sum p_{(L,m)j}^{(1)} H_{(L,m)j}^{(1)} + p_{(K)j}^{(1)} H_{(K)j}^{(1)} + p_{(N)j}^{(1)} H_{(N)j}^{(1)} + p_{(oct)j}^{(1)} H_{(oct)j}^{(1)} \quad (81)$$

where $H_{(i1)j}^{(0)}$ is the revenue share of industry j accounted for by its sales of commodity ($(i1)$. $H_{(is)j}^{(1)}$, $H_{(L,m)j}^{(1)}$, $H_{(K)j}^{(1)}$, $H_{(N)j}^{(1)}$ and $H_{(oct)j}^{(1)}$ are the shares of industry j's costs accounted for by intermediate inputs (is), by inputs of labour of skill m, by inputs of capital, land and other costs respectively.[23] Equation (81) implies that the revenue–share weighted sum of percentage changes in the basic value of output is equal to the sum of the percentage changes in the industry's input prices weighted by cost-shares.

Similarly, the zero-profit condition for the creation of fixed capital states that the value of new capital equals its cost of production, which is given as:

$$\Pi_j Y_j = \sum\sum P_{(is)j}^{(2)} X_{(is)j}^{(2)} \quad (82)$$

where Π_j is the price of a unit of fixed capital and Y_j is the quantity of fixed capital created in industry j. $P_{(is)j}^{(2)}$ and $X_{(is)j}^{(2)}$ are the price and quantity of good i used as intermediate inputs from all sources in the creation of capital. In percentage-change form,

[23] For a detailed derivation and fuller description refer to Dixon, et al. (1997: pp. 108-117).

$$\pi_j = \sum_{i=1}^{g}\sum_{s=1}^{2} p_{(is)j}^{(2)} H_{(is)j}^{(2)} \quad i = 1, 2, 3, \ldots, g \tag{83}$$

where $H_{(is)j}^{(2)}$ is the share of good i from source s in the costs of creation of one unit of capital for industry j.

For imports, the zero pure profit condition equates the basic price of imported goods with the product of the foreign price of the import, the exchange rate, and the power of the tariff:

$$P_{(i2)}^{(0)} = P_{(i2)}^{(m)} \phi T_{(i2,0)} \quad i = 1, 2, 3, \ldots, g \tag{84}$$

where $P_{(i2)}^{(m)}$ is the foreign currency c.i.f. price of imported units of goods i, ϕ is the exchange rate and $T_{(i2,0)}$ is the power of the tariff.[24]

Similarly, for exports, zero pure profit ensures that the foreign currency f.o.b price, converted to local currency is equal to the basic price of goods, the taxes and margin costs associated with delivering goods to the foreigners from a Bangladesh port. The relation is given by:

$$P_{(i1)}^{(e)} \phi = P_{(i1)}^{(0)} T_{(i1,4)} \sum_{r=1}^{6} A_{(r1)}^{(i1)(4)} P_{(r1)}^{(0)} \tag{85}$$

where $P_{(i1)}^{(e)}$ is the foreign currency f.o.b. price, $P_{(i1)}^{(0)}$ is the basic price of good i, $A_{(r1)}^{(i1)4}$ is the quantity of domestically produced good that is required as margin per unit of export of good, $T_{(i1,4)}$ is the power of export tax. and $P_{(r1)}^{(0)}$ is the price of margins.[25]

The above price equations depict zero pure profit in production, capital creation, importing and exporting. In the model, there are also price equations that show a zero pure profit condition in the distribution of commodities. These are imposed by equating changes in the prices paid by domestic users for all goods with the commodities' changes in basic values plus commodity taxes and the costs of margins. In the TABLO excerpt 13 these conditions are shown by equations E_p1, E_p2, E_p3, E_P4 and E_p5.[26] These are also called purchasers' price equations.

Excerpt 13 of TABLO Input File

Purchasers' prices

Equation E_p1# *Purchasers prices - producers #*
(all,c,COM)(all,s,SRC)(all,i,IND)

---

[24] The power of the tariff is defined as one plus the ad valorem rate of tariff on imports of goods.

[25] In the Bangladesh model there are six margin commodities.

[26] In each equation, the coefficient TINY (a very small number) is added in the left-hand side to avoid the problem of zero-divide or singularity.

[V1PUR(c,s,i)+TINY]*p1(c,s,i)=[V1BAS(c,s,i)+V1TAX(c,s,i)]*[p0(c,s)+t1(c,s,i)]
+ sum{m,MAR, V1MAR(c,s,i,m)*[p0dom(m)+a1mar(c,s,i,m)]}; (86)
Equation E_p2# *Purchasers prices - capital creators* #(all,c,COM)(all,s,SRC)
(all,i,IND)[V2PUR(c,s,i)+TINY]*p2(c,s,i)=[V2BAS(c,s,i)+V2TAX(c,s,i)]*[p0(c,s)+t2(c,s,i)]+sum
{m,MAR,V2MAR(c,s,i,m)*[p0dom(m)+a2mar(c,s,i,m)]}; (87)
Equation E_p3# *Purchasers prices - households* #(all,c,COM)(all,s,
SRC) (all,h,HOUS)[V3PUR(c,s,h)+TINY]*p3(c,s,h)=[V3BASHOU(c,s,h)+V3TAXHOU(c,s,h)]*
[p0(c,s)+t3(c,s)]+ sum{m,MAR, V3MARHOU(c,s,h,m)*[p0dom(m)+a3mar(c,s,m)]}; (88)
Equation E_p4# *Zero pure profits in exporting* #
(all,c,COM)[V4PUR(c)+TINY]*p4(c)=[V4BAS(c)+V4TAX(c)]*[pe(c)+t4(c)]
+ sum{m,MAR, V4MAR(c,m)*[p0dom(m)+a4mar(c,m)]}; (89)
Equation E_p5# *Zero pure profits in distribution to government* #
(all,c,COM) (all,s,SRC)[V5PUR(c,s)+TINY]*p5(c,s)=[V5BAS(c,s)+V5TAX(c,s)]*[p0(c,s)+t5(c,s)
]+sum{m,MAR,V5MAR(c,s,m)*[p0dom(m)+a5mar(c,s,m)]}; (90)

5.3.1.12. Market-clearing Equations

Demand equals supply both for domestically produced commodities and imported commodities. This condition also holds for primary factors of production.

Total demand for domestically produced commodities consists of: (1) demand for intermediate inputs into current production; (2) demand for inputs for fixed capital creation; (3) households' demand for consumption goods; (4) demand for exports; (5) government consumption demand for goods; 6) demand for margin commodities for the delivery of commodities to current production, capital creation, households and government; and (7) demand for margin commodities for the delivery of exports from producers to domestic ports. Similarly, demands for imported commodities are also broken down into intermediate input demand, capital creation demand, households' demand and government demand.[27]

For a locally–consumed domestic commodity, the market clearing equation is given by equation (91), which shows that the change in the aggregate supply of a locally consumed domestic commodity, $x0dom(c)$ is equal to the sum of the changes of all the non-export demands for the commodity. Similarly, equation E_x0imp (92) shows that the change in the aggregate supply of an imported commodity is equal to the sum of the changes in the demands by all local users.

Excerpt 14 of TABLO Input File

Equation E_p0A# *Supply = Demand for domestic commodities*#
#(all,c,COM)0.01*[TINY+DOMSALES(c)]*x0dom(c)=sum{i,IND,V1BAS(c,"dom",i)*x1
(c,"dom",i)+V2BAS(c,"dom",i)*x2(c,"dom",i)}+V3BAS_H(c,"dom")*x3_h(c,"dom") | V4BAS
(c)*x4(c)) +V5BAS(c,"dom")*x5(c,"dom")+ 100*P0LEV(c,"dom")*delx6(c,"dom")
(91)
Equation E_x0imp# *Import volumes* # (all,c,COM)
0.01*[TINY+V0IMP(c)]*x0imp(c) =sum{I,IND,V1BAS(c,"imp",i)+V2BAS(c,"imp",i)
*x2(c,"imp,i)}+V3BAS_H(c,"imp")*x3_h
(c,"imp")+V5BAS(c,"imp")*x5(c,"imp")+ 100*P0LEV(c,"imp")*delx6(c,"imp") (92)
Set LOCUSER# *Non-export users* #
(Interm, Invest, HouseH, GovGE, Stocks,Margins);
E_x1lab_i# *Demand equals supply for labour of each skill* #

[27] No imported goods are directly exported.

(all,o,OCC)V1LAB_I(o)*x1lab_i(o)=sum{i,IND,V1LAB(i,o)*x1lab(i,o)}; (93)
E_p1lab# *Flexible setting of money wages #*
(all,i,IND)(all,o,OCC)p1lab(i,o)=sum{h,HOUS,S3_H(h)*p3toth(h)}+f1lab_io+
f1lab_o(i)+f1lab_i(o)+f1lab(i,o); (94)

The market clearing equation for primary factors is also derived in the model, so that the demand for each factor of production is equal to supply. The market clearing equation for labour is given in excerpt 14 by equation (93), which shows changes in the aggregate demand for occupation-specific labour. Following ORANI and ORANI-G, the Bangladesh model does not contain a theory of labour supply. Instead, there is the choice of treating aggregate employment as exogenous, with market clearing real wages determined endogenously or setting real wage rates exogenously while determining aggregate employment endogenously.

The Bangladesh model adheres to the standard ORANI-G approach in setting all the wage shift variables exogenously in the short run. As a result, all money wages are indexed to the consumer price index (CPI). It is shown in equation (94) that with all $f1lab$ variables exogenous, nominal wages, $p1lab(i,o)$ are proportional to the consumer price index, $p3tot$. It is also assumed that labour is mobile between industries and the supply of each skill type is elastic. In contrast, in a typical long run closure, aggregate employment is set exogenously, while the overall wage shifter, $f1lab\_io$ or the real wage rate, becomes endogenous. However, other wage shifters included in equation (94) are held constant, implying fixed wage relativities.

5.3.1.13. GDP from the Income and Expenditure Sides

In this model, GDP is calculated by both income and expenditure approaches. On the income side, GDP is made up of the nominal aggregation of all factor payments, the value of other costs and all payments of indirect taxes net of subsidies. In level form, this relation can be written as:

$$V0GDPINC = V1PRIM\_I + V1OCT + V0TAX\_CSI \tag{95}$$

where the coefficient V0GDPINC denotes nominal GDP from the income side, V1PRIM_I describes total primary factor payments inclusive of depreciation in the case of capital, and V0TAX_CSI denotes total net indirect tax revenue. In equation (95), V1PRIM_I can be written as the sum of total payments to labour, capital and land and capital as follows:

$$V1PRIM\_I = V1LAB\_IO + V1CAP\_I + V1LND\_I \tag{96}$$

Aggregate net indirect tax revenue, V0TAX_CSI, is made up of intermediate tax revenue (V1TAX_CSI), investment tax revenue (V2TAX_CSI), households' tax revenue (V3TAX_CS), export tax revenue (V4TAX_CS), government tax revenue (V5TAX_CS), tariff revenue (V0TAR_C), other cost ticket payments (V1OCT_I), and production tax/subsidy (V1PTX_I). The linearised form of the formula in equation (95) is given in the excerpt 15 by equation (99).

On the other hand, GDP from the expenditure side consists of total household consumption (V3TOT_H), total fixed investment (V2TOT_I), total government consumption expenditure (V5TOT), total investment in inventories (V6TOT), total export earnings (V4TOT) and the negative value of imports (V0CIF_C). In level form, this relation is given by the following equation:

V0GDPEXP=V3TOT_H + V2TOT_I + V5TOT + V6TOT + V4TOT – V0CIF_C (97)

Equation E_w0gdpexp is the change form of this formula. It divides the nominal percentage change of GDP into price (p0gdpexp) and quantity (x0gdpexp) components. Following ORANI-G and IDC-GEM, for each expenditure component of GDP we define a quantity index and a price index. Equation E_p0gdpexp describes the GDP price index from the expenditure side as a weighted average of changes in local final-demand prices, less the average change in the border price of imports. Using E_p0gdpexp as the GDP price deflator, the change in real GDP is calculated by equation E_x0gdpexp.

Equation (98) is an accounting identity showing in both level and percentage changes forms, that GDP from the expenditure side must equal GDP from the income side:

V0GDPEXP = V0GDPINC and w0gdpexp = w0gdpinc (98)

Excerpt 15 of TABLO Input File

Variable

w0gdpinc # *Nominal GDP from income side #*;
x0gdpexp# *Real GDP from expenditure side #*
p0gdpexp# *GDP price index, expenditure side #*
w0gdpexp# *Nominal GDP from expenditure side #*;
Equation
E_w0gdpincV0GDPINC*w0gdpinc = V1PRIM_I*w1prim_i+100*delV0tax_csi (99)
E_x0gdpexpx0gdpexp=[1/V0GDPEXP]*[V3TOT_H*x3tot_h+V2TOT_I*x2tot_i+
V5TOT*x5tot +V6TOT*x6tot+V4TOT*x4tot-V0CIF_C*x0cif_c]; (100)
E_p0gdpexpp0gdpexp=[1/V0GDPEXP]*[V3TOT_H*sum{h,HOUS,S3_H(h)*p3toth(h)}
+ V2TOT_I*p2tot_i+V5TOT*p5tot+V6TOT*p6tot+V4TOT*p4tot
-V0CIF_C*p0cif_c]; (101)
E_w0gdpexpw0gdpexp = x0gdpexp + p0gdpexp (102)

5.3.1.14. Trade Balance and Other Aggregates

The balance of trade (B) describes the difference between the local currency values of imports (M) and exports (E), which is written as:

B = E - M (103)

Since zero is a feasible base-period value for the balance of trade,[28] the balance of trade is calculated as an ordinary change ($delB$) and to avoid choosing units, this is expressed as a proportion of GDP:

[28] In that case, the percentage change in B would become undefined.

$delB$ = (nominal balance of trade)/ (nominal GDP) (104)

The terms of trade, P0TOFT, are given by the ratio of the export price index (local currency) to the import price index (local currency). The real exchange rate, P0REALDEV, is the ratio of the domestic price level to the foreign price level. Equation (105) in excerpt 16 shows the ordinary change in the balance of trade, equation (106) measures the percentage change in the terms of trade ($p0toft$), and equation (107) measures the percentage change in the real exchange rate, i.e., real devaluation ($p0realdev$). Also in excerpt 16, equations (108) to (110) provide measures of percentage changes in aggregate employment, using wage-bill weights, $employ\_i$; percentage changes in the aggregate capital stock using rental values of capital weights, $x1cap\_i$; and percentage changes in the aggregate land stock, using land rent weights., $x1\ln d\_i$. Equation (111) shows the percentage change in the average real wage.

Excerpt 16 of TABLO Input File

Trade balance index and primary factor aggregates

```
Equation
E_delB100*V0GDPEXP*delB=V4TOT*w4tot-V0CIF_C*w0cif_c-[V4TOT-
V0CIF_C]*w0gdpexp;                                                    (105)
E_p0toftp0toft=p4tot-p0cif_c                                          (106)
E_p0realdevp0realdev=p0cif_c-p0gdpexp                                 (107)
E_employ_i V1LAB_IO*employ_i = sum{i,IND,V1LAB_O(i)*employ(i)};       (108)
E_x1cap_iV1CAP_I*x1cap_i=sum{i,IND,V1CAP(i)*x1cap(i)}                 (109)
E_x1lnd_iID01[V1LND_I]*x1lnd_i = sum{i,IND, V1LND(i)*x1lnd(i)};       (110)
E_realwagerealwage = p1lab_io -sum {h,HOUS,S3_H(h)* p3toth(h)};       (111)
```

5.4. Income Distribution, Saving and Consumption

This section discusses the distributional aspects of the Bangladesh model. It describes the methods used to model the incomes, expenditures and saving patterns of various agents included in the core CGE model in section 5.3. In so doing, this section closely follows IDC-GEM, a SAM based CGE model for the South African economy developed by Horridge, et al. (1995).

There are four categories of income recipients or institutions in the model viz. firms, household groups, government and the rest of the world, and they receive income from various sources. The primary income distribution originates in the value added of the production process and the endowment of factors of production. In addition to factor income, institutions also receive income in the form of transfer payments from other institutions. Institutions dispose of income in some or all of the following ways: consumption, tax payments, other transfer payments and saving.

A simplified representation of the Bangladesh model SAM database is provided in Chapter 6 It captures the mapping of the income payments to factors of production and the subsequent disposal of income by different institutions. The following sub-sections discuss the generation of income of the institutions along with its disposal. As with the core CGE model equations, inclusion of distributional aspects involves defining a set of variables, coefficients and some behavioral equations in several TABLO excerpts.[29]

5.4.1. Gross Operating Surplus

It is assumed that total gross operating surplus (GOS) is derived from aggregate payments to capital (V1CAP_I), aggregate payments to land (V1LND_I), aggregate payments to other cost tickets (V1OCT_I), interest on public debt (WGOVGOS) paid by government,[30] and gross operating surplus from the rest of the world (WROWGOS). Thus, in level form the equation is written as:

VGOS = V1CAP_I + V1LND_I + V1OCT_I +VROWGOS + VGOVGOS (112)

The corresponding percentage change form is given by equation (115) in the TABLO excerpt 17. In equation (115), all terms (variables) on the right-hand side are determined from our core CGE model in section 5.3 except for the variables, $wrowgos$ (Gross operating surplus from the rest of the world) and $wgovgos$ (interest on public debt). Following IDC-GEM, in the Bangladesh model these variables are set to move proportionally with nominal GDP, as shown by the following equations (113) and (114).

E_wgovgos # interest on public debt # wgovgos = w0gdpexp, (113)

E_wrowgos # GOS from rest of the world # wrowgos = w0gdpexp (114)

where $w0gdp\exp$ denotes nominal GDP from the expenditure side.

In apportioning the disposal of total GOS, the first step is to determine total post-tax gross operating surplus (VGOS_POSTTAX) by subtracting corporation tax (VGOSTAX) from total gross operating surplus (VGOS). This relation is given by equation (116) in TABLO excerpt 17. In equation (116), the right-hand side variable, $wgostax$, is corporation tax, which is determined by equation (117) in the same TABLO excerpt. In equation (117), the right hand side variable, $fgostax$, represents the percentage rate of corporation tax.

The post-tax gross operating surplus (VGOS_POSTTAX) is then distributed to different institutions such as household groups, government and the rest of the world. It is assumed that distribution to these institutions is proportionate to post-tax gross operating surplus. Thus, household groups receive gross operating surplus, $wgoshous(h)$, which moves in proportion to post-tax gross operating surplus, $wgos\_posttax$. Similarly, government receipts from gross operating surplus, $wgosgov$ are set to move proportionally with post-tax

[29] For a fuller description of all the equations refer to http://www.monash.edu.au/policy/oranig.htm

[30] In this model we treat the interest on public debt as a transfer payment not to households but to the gross operating surplus of the enterprise sector.

gross operating surplus income. Further, post-tax GOS accruing to the rest of the world, *wgosrow* also moves proportionally with *wgos_posttax*. (See equations (120), (118) and (119) respectively.) Subtracting these transfer payments to households, government and the rest of the world, and the income tax paid by GOS to government from total GOS, we obtain gross retained earnings, *wgossav*, which is given by equation (121) in TABLO excerpt 17.

Excerpt 17 of TABLO Input File

Work out total GOS income and disposal

CoefficientVGOS# *Total GOS #*;
EquationE_wgos# *GOS from income side #*
VGOS*wgos=V1CAP_I*w1cap_i+V1LND_I*w1lnd_i+V1OCT_I*w1oct_i+VROWGOS*
wrowgos +VGOVGOS*wgovgos; (115)
CoefficientVGOS_POSTTAX# *VGOS less VGOSTAX #*
EquationE_wgos_posttax# VGOS less VGOSTAX #
VGOS_POSTTAX*wgos_posttax = VGOS*wgos - VGOSTAX*wgostax; (116)
EquationE_wgostax# *Corporation tax #*
wgostax=fgostax+wgos; (117)
EquationE_wgosgov# *GOS to government #*
wgosgov=wgos_posttax; (118)
EquationE_wgosrow# *GOS to ROW #*
wgosrow=wgos_posttax; (119)
EquationE_wgoshou # GOS to households #
(All,h,HOUS) wgoshou(h) = wgos_posttax; (120)
EquationE_wgossav# *Find VGOSSAVas residual #*
VGOSSAV*wgossav=VGOS*wgos-Sum(h,HOUS,VGOSHOU(h)*wgoshou(h))-
VGOSGOV*wgosgov-VGOSTAX*wgostax-VGOSROW*wgosrow; (121)

5.4.2. Households

In the Bangladesh model the main sources of household income are from labour (V1LABINC_O) from land and capital (VGOSHOU). The coefficient V1LABINC_O, which denotes total wage income of households, is derived by summing all labour income from occupations, V1LABINC (o, h). In Bangladesh, where there is a high prevalence of unincorporated business enterprises, most of the gross operating surplus accruing to households as income from land and capital comes from unincorporated businesses. Besides factor income, households also receive income from government in the form of transfer payments (VGOVHOU), transfers from the rest of the world (VROWHOU) and transfers from other households (VHOUHOU). Thus, the total pre-tax household income for each household group can be defined in level form as:

VHOUSINC (h) = VGOSHOU (h) + V1LABINC_O (h) + VHOUHOU (h) +
VGOVHOU (h) + VROWHOU (h) (122)

The percentage-change form of this equation is provided in the TABLO excerpt 18 by equation (129). It shows that the percentage change in a household group's pre-tax income is a weighted average of the percentage change in the group's total labour income and the percentage changes in the transfers from GOS, government, the rest of the world and other households. Further, the percentage change in the group's total labour income, $wllabinc\_o(h)$, is assumed to be a function of percentage changes in the number of households in the group, $qh(h)$, total wage payments by all industries (classified by occupation), $w1lab\_i(o)$, and the total employment rate, $labslack(o)$, as shown by equation (130). These variables are in turn determined by the following equations:

E_w1lab_i # all-industry labour bills #
(All,o,OCC)(TINY+V1LAB_I(o)*w1lab_i(o)=Sum(i,IND,V1LAB(i,o)
*{p1lab(i,o)+x1lab(i,o)} (123)

where $p1lab(i,o)$ denotes wages by industry and occupation and $x1lab(i,o)$ represents employment by industry and occupation. Both of these variables are determined in our core CGE model in section 5.3.

E_labslack # employment rate # (All, o,OCC) (TINY_V1LAB_I(o))
*w1lab_i(o)= Sum{h,HOUS, V1LABINC(o,h)*w1labinc(o,h)} (124)

E_qh # rule of population growth # (All, h, HOUS) qh (h) = q_h (125)

which shows that the percentage change in the number of households in each household group is a function of percentage change in the total number of households. The transfer from GOS, $wgoshou(h)$ is already determined in the TABLO excerpt 17 by equation (120). The rest of the world's transfers to the household groups, $wrowhou(h)$, and government transfers to households, $wgovhou(h)$ are set to move proportionally with nominal GDP, $w0gdp\exp$. They are written as follows:

E_wgovhou # government transfers to households' #
(All, h, HOUS) wgovhou (h) = w0gdpexp (126)

E_wrowhous # Rest of the world transfers to households'#
(All, h, HOUS) wrowhou (h) = w0gdpexp (127)

In the model, inter-household transfers have been set to move proportionally with post-tax household income of the group making the transfer:

E_whoushous # inter-household transfers # (All, hto, HOUS) (All, hfrom, HOUS)
whouhou (hto, hfrom) = wdispinc (hfrom) (128)

where $wdispinc(hfrom)$ denotes the percentage change in household disposable income.

Excerpt 18 of TABLO Input File

Household pre-tax income

Coefficient (All,h,HOUS) VHOUSINC(h) # *pre-tax h'hold income #*;
Variable(All,h,HOUS) whousinc(h) # *pre-tax h'hold income #*;
Equation E_whousinc# *Pre-tax household income #*
(All,h,HOUS)VHOUSINC(h)*whousinc(h)=VGOSHOU(h)*wgoshou(h)+V1LABINC_O(h)*w1labinc_o(h)+Sum(hfrom,HOUS,VHOUHOU(h,hfrom)*whouhou(h,hfrom))+VGOVHOU(h)*wgovhou(h)+ VROWHOU(h)*wrowhou(h); (129)
Equation E_w1labinc# *Labour income to households'#*
(All,o,OCC)(All,h,HOUS)w1labinc(o,h)=qh(h)+w1lab_i(o)+labslack(o); (130)

Households pay taxes and other transfers to government. After subtracting income tax and transfers from households' total income, we get household disposable income:

VDISPINC (h) = VHOUINC (h)-VHOUGOV (h) (131)

The corresponding percentage change equation is given in TABLO excerpt 19 by equation (133) where variable $housinc\ (h)$, which denotes pre-tax household income, is already determined by equation (129). The other right-hand side variable $whougov(h)$, households' payment of income taxes and transfers to government is given as follows:

E_whougov # households to government: income taxes and transfers #
whougov (h) = whousinc (h) + f_inctaxrate (h) + f_inctaxrate_h (132)

where $f\_inctaxrate(h)$ denotes the income tax shifter by income and $f\_inctaxrate\_h$ is the overall income tax shifter. Normally $f\_inctaxrate\_h$ is considered exogenous and $whousinc\ (h)$ is determined previously from the model, so, equation (132) determines $whougov(h)$.

Households' outlays consist of: 1) total consumption by households ($w3toth(h)$); 2) inter-household transfers ($whouhou(hto,h)$); 3) households' transfers to government ($whougov(h)$); and 4) households' transfers to the rest of the world ($whourow(h)$). After subtracting these outlays from pre-tax household income, we obtain households' saving $whousav(h)$ as a residual. See equation (134) in excerpt 19. In equation (134), the right-hand side variable, $w3toth(h)$ or nominal total household consumption can be linked with households' disposable income by equation (135), where the variable, $f3toth(h)$ denotes the shift term for consumption by household and $f3toth\_h$ denotes the overall shift term for consumption. The other right-hand side variables of equation (134) are already determined except $whourow(h)$, household transfers to rest of the world. This variable is set to move proportionally with post-tax household income $wdispinc(h)$.

Excerpt 19 of TABLO Input File

Apportion household expenditure

Equation E_wdispinc# *Post-tax household income #*
(All,h,HOUS)VDISPINC(h)*wdispinc(h)=VHOUSINC(h)*whousinc(h)-VHOUGOV(h)*whougov(h); (133)
Equation E_whousav# *household saving #*
(All,h,HOUS)VHOUSAV(h)*whousav(h)=VHOUSINC(h)*whousinc(h)-V3TOTh(h)*w3toth(h)
-Sum(hto,HOUS,VHOUHOU(hto,h)*whouhou(hto,h))-VHOUGOV(h)*whougov(h)-VHOUROW(h)*whourow(h); (134)
Equation E_f3tot# *Consumption function #*
(All,h,HOUS)w3toth(h)=f3tot(h)+f3tot_h+wdispinc(h); (135)

5.4.3. Government

Government receives income from net indirect tax revenues on goods and services (sales taxes on producers, investors, households, exports and government, import duties and other cost ticket payments), direct taxes (income taxes from households and corporate taxes from firms), transfers from gross operating surplus and transfers from the rest of the world. In level form, the income equation can be written as:

$$VINGOV = V0TAX\_CSI + VGOSGOV + VGOSTAX + \Sigma\ VHOUGOV(h) + VROWGOV \quad (136)$$

where VINGOV = Government income.

The corresponding linear form equation is provided by equation (139) in TABLO excerpt 20. In equation (139), apart from $wrowgov$, (transfers from the rest of the world), all other right–hand side variables are already determined in our model. For example, variable $w0tax\_csi$, which denotes aggregate revenue from all indirect taxes, is determined in our core CGE model by the following equation:

$$V0TAX\_CSI = V1TAX\_CSI + V2TAX\_CSI + V3TAX\_CSH + V4TAX\_C + V5TAX\_CS + V0TAR\_C + V1OCT\_I \quad (137)$$

In the model, transfers from the rest of the world, $wrowgov$, are set to move in proportion to nominal GDP from expenditure side, $w0gdp\exp$, i.e.:

$$wrowgov = w0gdpexp \quad (138)$$

Following IDC-GEM, government total expenditures (VGOVEXP) are divided into: (1) government current expenditure; and (2) government capital expenditure. Government current expenditure consists of the aggregate nominal value of government consumption demands for goods and services (V5TOT), interest on public debt (VGOVGOS), government transfers to the rest of the world (VGOVROW) and government transfers to households (VGOVHOU). In percentage-change form, the equation for current government expenditure is given in excerpt

20 by equation (140). It shows that the percentage change in government current expenditure as a weighted average of the percentage changes in the various types of government outlays.

Excerpt 20 of TABLO Input File

Government income and expenditures

Equation E_wincgov# *Government income #*
VINCGOV*wincgov=V0TAX_CSI*w0tax_csi+VGOSGOV*wgosgov+VGOSTAX*wgostax-Sum(h,HOUS, VHOUGOV(h)*whougov(h))+VROWGOV*wrowgov; (139)
Equation E_wgovcur# *Current government expenditure #*
VGOVCUR*wgovcur=V5TOT*w5tot+VGOVGOS*wgovgos+VGOVROW*wgovrow+Sum(h,HOUS, VGOVHOU(h)*wgovhou(h)); (140)
Equation E_wgovcap# *Investment government expenditure#*
VGOVCAP*wgovcap=Sum(i,IND,GOVSHRINV(i)*V2TOT(i)*{s2gov(i)+p2tot(i)+x2tot(i)}); (141)
Equation E_wgovsav# *Government saving (Income-Expenditure) #*
VGOVSAV*wgovsav=VINCGOV*wincgov-VGOVEXP*wgovexp; (142)
Equation E_realgovsav# *Real government (Income-expenditure) #*
realgovsav=wgovsav-p0gdpexp; (143)

In equation (140), the variables $wgovgos$ and $wgovhou(h)$ are determined previously by the equations (113) and (126) respectively. The variable $wgovrow$, government transfers to the rest of the world, is assumed to move proportionally with nominal GDP from the expenditure side. The other right-hand side variable $w5tot$, aggregate nominal value of government consumption demands, is determined in the core CGE model by summing the purchasers' value of government purchases of domestically produced and imported goods and services.

Government capital expenditure is undertaken by public sector corporations. In this model, government investment expenditure, VGOCAP, is obtained by multiplying total capital created for industry i, V2TOT (i), with GOVSHRINV (i), the government share of investment by industry i which is written as:

$$\text{VGOCAP} = \sum_i GOVSHRINV(i) * V2TOT(i) \qquad (144)$$

The percentage change form of this equation is given in TABLO excerpt 20 by equation (141), which states that the percentage change in government investment expenditure is a function of the percentage changes in the government share of investment by industry i, $s2gov(i)$, the cost of a unit of capital, $p2tot(i)$, and investment by the using industry, $x2tot(i)$. The model assumes the government share of investment by industry, $s2gov(i)$, is exogenous.

Government saving, $wgovsav$, is calculated as the difference between government income, $wincgov$, and government current expenditure, $wgov\exp$:

VGOVSAV = VINCGOV-VGOVEXP (145)

In percentage change form, the relationship is given in excerpt 20 by equation (142). By deflating the percentage change in nominal government saving, $wgovsav$, by the percentage change in the GDP price deflator, $p0gdp\exp$, we obtain the percentage change in real government saving, which is shown in the TABLO excerpt 20 by equation (143).

5.4.4. Rest of the World

Following the IDC-GEM model, the rest of the world derives income (VINCROW) from households' transfers (VHOUROW (h)), government transfers (VGOVROW), gross operating surplus transfers (VGOSROW), total local currency import costs (V0CIF_C) and wages paid to the rest of the world (VLABROW_O). In level form:

VINCROW = ΣVHOUROW (h) + VGOVROW + V0CIF_C + VGOSROW + VLABROW_O (146)

The percentage change form of the equation is given in TABLO excerpt 21 by equation (147). In equation (147), the right-hand side variables $whourow(h)$, $wgovrow$, $wgosrow$ are determined in sections 5.4.2, 5.4.3 and 5.4.1 respectively. In the model, it is assumed that the wages paid to rest of the world, $wlabrow\_o$, is proportional to total labour bill, $w1lab\_i(o)$. The coefficient, V0CIF_C, total local currency import costs, is obtained by taking the difference between the total basic value of imports (including tariffs) and total tariff revenue.[31]

The rest of the world's expenditure (VROWEXP) is obtained as the sum of the following: total export earnings (V4TOT); transfers to government (VROWGOV), for example, foreign aid; transfers to gross operating surplus (VROWGOS), for example, dividends and interest from abroad; and transfers to households (VROWHOU), for example, remittances from abroad. The percentage change form of this relation is given in excerpt 21 by equation (148) where the variables, $wrowgov$, $wrowgos$ and $wrowhou(h)$ are already determined in the previous sections 5.4.3, 5.4.1 and 5.4.2 by equations (138), (114) and (127) respectively. The coefficient V4TOT, which represents total export earnings, is determined in the core CGE model by summing purchasers' values of export commodities, V4PUR (c). The rest of the world's saving (VROWSAV) is the difference between the ROW's income (VINCROW) and expenditure (VROWEXP). It can be written as:

VROWSAV = VINCROW- VROWEXP.

The percentage change form is given by equation (149).

[31] Due to unavailability of data, and following Hoque (2006), the Bangladesh model assumes that households, government and gross operating surplus transfers to the rest of the world are zero.

Excerpt 21 of TABLO Input File

Find Rest of the world income and expenditure

Equation E_wincrow# *Total ROW income #*

VINCROW*wincrow=Sum(h,HOU,VHOUROW(h)*whourow(h))+VGOVROW*wgovrow+ V0CIF_C*w0cif_c+VGOSROW*wgosrow+VLABROW_O*wlabrow_o; (147)

Equation E_wrowexp# *Total ROW expenditure #*

VROWEXP*wrowexp=V4TOT*w4tot+VROWGOV*wrowgov+VROWGOS*wrowgos +Sum(h,HOUS,VROWHOU(h)*wrowhou(h)); (148)

Equation E_wrowsav# *ROW (Income-Expenditure) #*

VROWSAV*wrowsav=VINCROW*wincrow-VROWEXP*wrowexp; (149)

5.5. Endogenising Poverty Lines

The Bangladesh model follows the approach of Decaluwé et al. (1999) and Decaluwé, Savard and Thorbecke (2006) in endogenising a poverty line within a CGE model. The monetary poverty line is derived from the cost of a basket of goods that reflects basic needs:

$$\text{Monetary poverty line} = \sum W^{p}_{com} P_{qcom} \tag{150}$$

where W^{p}_{com} represents the quantity of a basic-need commodity and P_{qcom} denotes its price. Commodity prices are endogenously determined within the model, and so the nominal value of this basket, i.e., the poverty line, is also determined within the model. As prices rise or fall after shocks, the monetary poverty line also rises or falls.

The Bangladesh model adopts, however, a slightly different procedure to Decaluwé et al. (1999). Instead of endogenising the monetary poverty line itself, the model follows Naranpanawa (2005) by endogenising changes in the monetary poverty line. A price index that reflects changes in the prices of basic–need commodities has been defined in the model. For the base period (2000), the poverty lines for rural and urban areas are those estimated by the BBS Household Income and Expenditure Survey, as reported in Hossain et al. (2005). New poverty lines are then estimated by adjusting the base period poverty lines by the percentage changes in prices generated by the model. Excerpt 22 shows the relevant sets, variables, coefficient and equations for poverty lines for both rural and urban areas.[32] Equation (151), E_pliner, identifies percentage changes in poverty lines for different rural household groups, while equation (152), E_pline_phr, identifies the percentage change in the aggregate poverty line for all rural groups. Equations (153) and (154) identify corresponding changes in poverty lines for urban areas.

Excerpt 22 of TABLO Input File

Incorporation of poverty lines

Set

[32] This part of the TABLO code closely follows Naranpanawa (2005).

PRCOM# *commodities used in computing rural poverty line #* (wheat, potatoCulti, VegCulti,FruitCulti,Milkfat,poultrymeat,Fish,Riceflorbran,EdiNoedoil,SugGuMolass, Teaproduct,Millcloth,Medicines,Electwater);*!prc!*
PRHG# *Household groups used in computing poverty line #* (LandlessHH,MargfarmHH,smallfarmHH,largefarmHH,NonagriculHH,smallfarmHH, largefarmHH,NonagriculHH);*!prh!*
Subset PRHG is subset of HOUS
Subset PRCOM is subset of COM
Variable
(all,prh,PRHG)pliner(prh) # *Poverty line for rural households#*
EquationE_pliner#*Poverty line for rural households'#*
(all,prh,PRHG)V3TOTh(prh)*pliner(prh)=sum{prc,PRCOM,sum{s,SRC,V3PUR (prc,s,prh)
*p3(prc,s,prh)}}; (151)
Coefficient
V3TOT_phr;
Formula
V3TOT_phr=sum{prh,PRHG,V3TOTh(prh)};
Variable
pline_phr;
Equation
E_pline_phr # Aggregate poverty line #
V3TOT_phr*pline_phr=sum{prh,PRHG,V3TOTh(prh)*pliner(prh)}; (152)
Set
PUCOM#*(Commodities used in computing urban poverty line)#*(wheat,potatoCulti,VegCulti,FruitCulti,Milkfat,poultrymeat,Fish,Riceflorbran, EdiNoedoil,SugGuMolass,Teaproduct,Millcloth,Medicines,Electwater);*!puc!*
PUHG#Household groups used in computing poverty line) #
(IlliterateHH,LoweduHH,MediumeduHH);*!puh!*
SubsetPUHG is subset of HOUS
SubsetPUCOM is subset of COM
Variable
(all,puh,PUHG)plineu(puh) # Poverty line for urban households#
Equation
E_plineu(all,puh,PUHG)V3TOTh(puh)*plineu(puh)=sum{puc,PUCOM,sum {s,SRC,V3PUR(puc,s,puh)*p3(puc,s,puh)}}; (153)
Coefficient
V3TOT_phu;
Formula
V3TOT_phu=sum{puh,PUHG,V3TOTh(puh)};
Variable
pline_phu;
Equation
E_pline_phu# *Aggregate poverty line #*
V3TOT_phu*pline_phu=sum{puh,PUHG,V3TOTh(puh)*plineu(puh)}; (154)

5.6. CLOSING AND CHECKING THE MODEL

The Bangladesh model described above has more variables than equations. To close the model, it is necessary to select which variables are to be endogenous and which are to be exogenous. In particular, a solution of the model requires that the number of endogenous variables equals the number of equations. There is no specific rule to make a sensible closure, as it depends on the nature or availability of data, objectives of research and the circumstances of the application. Following Horridge (2001a) and Horridge (2006), Table 5.2 provides a common specification for a standard closure of the Bangladesh model. In making the closure, we identify as endogenous the variables that are explained by equations in the TABLO input file. Variables not explained by equations are considered exogenous. In Table 5.2, the first column shows the various combinations of set indices that have been used in the model, while the second column gives the variable count in the entire model. The third column indicates the number of equations that seems to explain those variables.[33] In the model, there are 117 scalar variables but only 100 equations to explain these variables. Thus, as shown in the fourth column, we have 17 variables that have no matching equations. Termed exogenous variables, these are itemised in the fifth column.

Having undertaken this procedure for each of the dimensions presented in the model, we determine the probable standard closure for the model. For an ORANI-G type model, the following variables are often chosen to be exogenous (Horridge, 2006): technical change variables, mostly beginning with '*a*'; shift variables beginning with '*f*'; industry capital stocks, *x1cap*; land endowments, *x1lnd*; foreign prices, *pf0cif*; inventory to sales ratio, *fx6*; and the exchange rate, *phi,* which acts as a numeraire.[34] Although column 5 defines a valid closure for the Bangladesh model, consideration of our research objectives, suggests a slightly different closure, with some variables being swapped between the endogenous and exogenous lists.[35]

It is usual practice to perform a number of tests to check for any computational errors in the model results. In ORANI-G, these tests are the price homogeneity test and the real homogeneity test. The price homogeneity test checks that there is no money illusion in the model, i.e., a uniform increases in all prices will keep quantity variables unchanged. To implement this test, all exogenous variables are set equal to zero except for *phi,* the exchange rate.[36] The test is satisfied if, with money wages fully indexed, a 1 per cent increase in the exchange rate produces an exactly 1 per cent increase in all domestic prices and nominal flows, with all real endogenous variables unchanged. In contrast, the real homogeneity test checks that there are constant returns to scale in the production functions in the model. The test is satisfied if, keeping all nominal exogenous variables constant, a uniform increase in all real exogenous variables leads to the same proportionate change in all real endogenous variables, leaving relative prices constant.

---

[33] In the TABLO input file, most equations are named after a variable, which makes it easy to identify exogenous variables.

[34] Like other CGE models, price variables in ORANI-G appear as price ratios. Thus, to determine the overall price level/absolute price level, there must be at least one exogenous variable measured in local currency units. This is termed the numeraire.

[35] A detailed description of model closures for the Bangladesh model is provided in Chapter 7.

[36] The consumer price index (p3tot) also can be used as the numeraire.

Along with these homogeneity tests, modellers sometimes use another test to check that a change in GDP on the income side is the same as the change on the expenditure side. Any error in an equation or an unbalanced data set can violate this identity.

The Bangladesh model passed all the above tests.

Table 5.2. Tally of variables and equations of the Bangladesh model (Standard closure)

Dimension	Variable count	Equation count	Exogenous var. count	Unexplained variables
Scalar	117	100	17	Capslack, f1lab_io, f1tax_csi, f2tax_csi, f3tax_cs, f3tot_h, f4p_ntrad, f4q_ntrad, f4tax_ntrad, f4tax_trad, f5tax_cs, f5tot2, fgostax, f_inctaxrate_h, invslack, phi, q_h
IND	39	25	14	a1cap, a1lab_o, a1lnd, a1oct, a1prim, a1tot, a2tot, delPTXRATE, f1lab_o, f1oct, s2gov, x1cap, x1lnd, x2tot
COM	18	13	5	f0tax_s, f4p, f4q, pf0cif, t0imp
OCC	5	4	1	f1lab_i
HOUS	17	15	2	f_inctaxrate, w3luxh
COM*IND	8	6	2	a1_s, a2_s
COM*SRC	11	8	3	a3, f5, fx6
COM*HOUS	7	6	1	a3_s
COM*MAR	2	1	1	a4mar
IND*OCC	3	2	1	f1lab
COM*SRC*IND	10	8	2	a1 a2
COM*SRC*MAR	3	1	2	a3mar, a5mar
COM*SRC*IND*MAR	4	2	2	a1mar, a2mar
EXPMAC	1	1	0	
CONTFAC	1	1	0	
CONTINC	1	1	0	
PRHG	1	1	0	
PUHG	1	1	0	
COM*FANCAT	1	1	0	
COM*DESTPLUS	1	1	0	
OCC*HOUS	1	1	0	
HOUS*HOUS	1	1	0	
COM*SRC*DEST	1	1	0	
COM*SRC*HOUS	3	3	0	
COM*SRC*HOUS*MAR	1	1	0	
Total	258	205	53	

5.7. SOLVING THE BANGLADESH MODEL

This study uses GEMPACK (General Equilibrium Model Package) WinGEM version 9.0 to solve the model developed in the previous sections.[37] Starting from an algebraic representation of the equations of the model, GEMPACK provides software for calculating the solutions of the model.[38] In implementing the model by GEMPACK, the first task is to

[37] WinGEM is the Windows version of GEMPACK.

[38] Detailed discussion about GEMPACK development and use can be found in Pearson (1986) and Codsi and Pearson (1988).

specify the model's equations using the TABLO language contained in the TABLO input file, MODEL.TAB (Figure 5.5). Since the Bangladesh model is a large model containing 86 industries, 94 commodities, 9 households, 4 labour groups and 6 margin commodities, an efficient solution requires the size of the model to be reduced through condensation. Condensation reduces the size of the system of equations by substitution and elimination of variables (Harrison and Pearson, 1996).[39] In Figure 5.5, the MODEL.STI file contains information about the variables for substitution and elimination.

Next, in running the model by the TABLO-generated program method,[40] the GEMPACK program TABLO converts the algebraic expression of the equations into a FORTRAN program specific to the model by using TAB and STI files. MODEL.FOR (Figure 5.5) contains the model-specific code needed for a solution program. TABLO also produces two auxiliary files, MODEL.AXS and MODEL.AXT containing all the information about the model which was present in the TABLO Input file. The FORTRAN program is then compiled and linked to a library of GEMPACK sub-routines to produce an executable program MODEL.EXE, which is used to solve the model.

In the final step, MODEL.EXE computes simulation results in conjunction with two auxiliary files, MODEL.AXS, MODEL.AXT, a data file containing input-output data and behavioural parameters and a command file, MODEL.CMF. In the CMF file there is specification of the exogenous variables, the names of input-output files, detailed solution procedures and the shocks to some exogenous variables.[41] Using these inputs, MODEL.EXE computes a solution file (SL4) where the effects on endogenous variables are shown in the forms of percentage changes from the initial solution. It is expressed in binary format, which is viewed by Windows program ViewSOL. Figure 5.6 provides a diagrammatic representation of how the GEMPACK program computes simulation results.

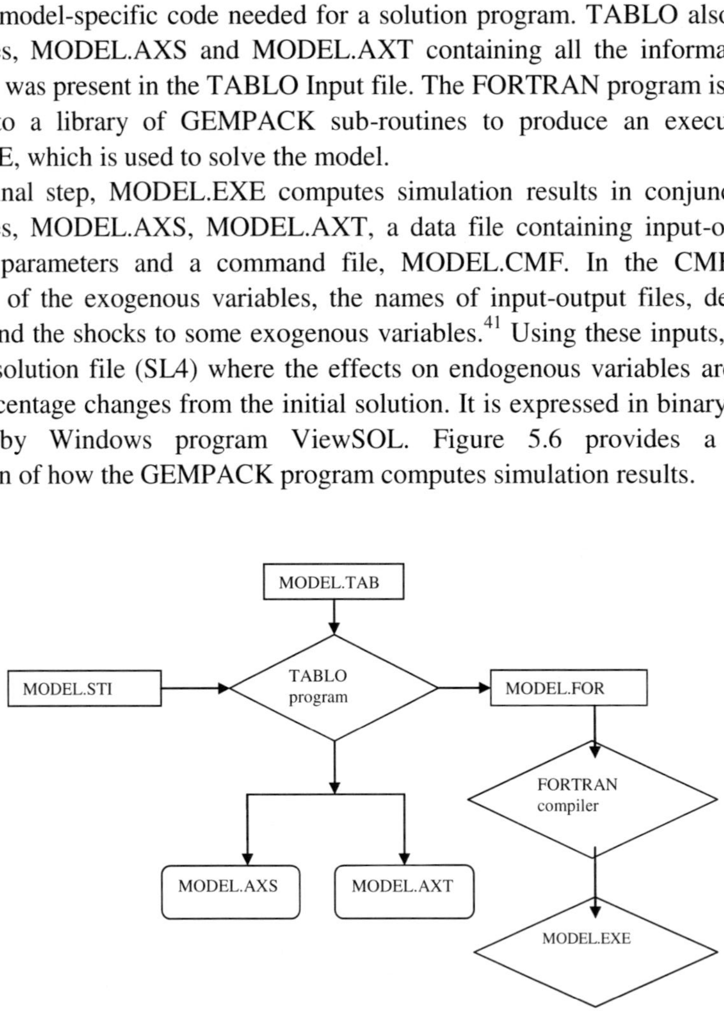

Source: Horridge (2006).

Figure 5.3. From TAB to EXE file.

---

[39] More details about model condensation can be found in Dixon et al. (1997: pp. 207-210).

[40] The TABLO-generated program can result in much quicker simulations for large models, whereas the GEMPACK program GEMSIM is appropriate for small size models.

[41] The shocks are numerical values specifying by how much the exogenous variables will change.

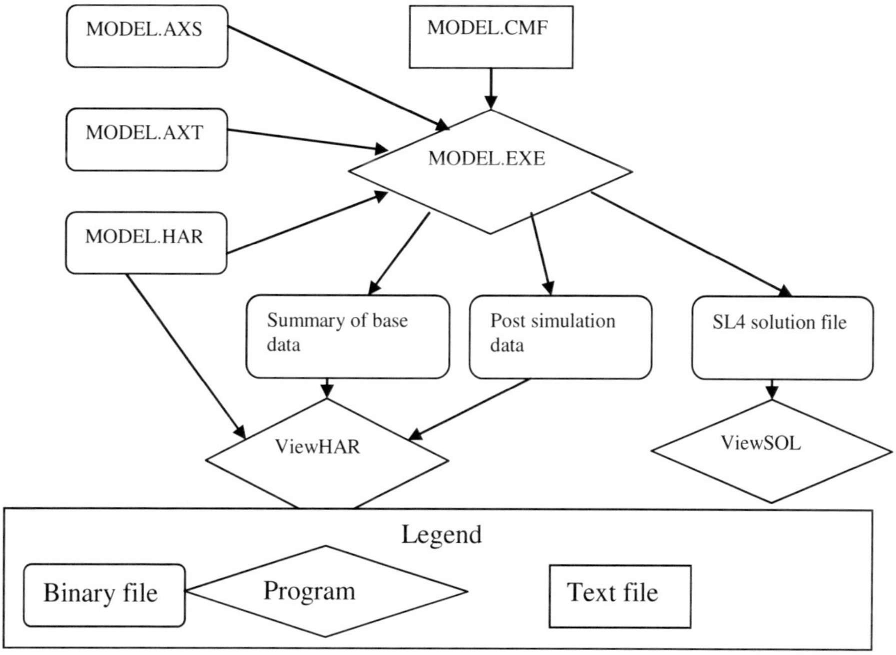

Source: Horridge (2006).

Figure 5.4. From EXE file to model solution.

Chapter 6

THE DATABASE

6.1. INTRODUCTION

This chapter deals with the data requirements of the Bangladesh model and the construction of its database. Section 6.2 outlines the input-output data and elasticity estimates required for the Bangladesh model. Section 6.3 gives a brief description of the sources of the base period data used in the Bangladesh model. Section 6.4 explains the compilation of the model's input-output database. Section 6.5 discusses procedures for assembling elasticity estimates. Section 6.6 describes the compilation of income distribution data, which allows the basic input-output database to be expanded to include the mapping of the factorial income distribution from the structure of production to various household groups. Section 6.7 discusses the sources and distribution of household income.

6.2. BASIC DATA REQUIREMENTS FOR THE MODEL

6.2.1. The Bangladesh Model Input-Output Database

Figure 6.1 (adopted from Horridge (2006)) provides a diagrammatic representation of the model's input output database. The figure divides the database into three parts: an absorption matrix, a production matrix and a trade tax matrix. Column headings in the absorption matrix identify six types of demanders in the economy: producers, divided into I industries; investors, divided into I industries; households, divided into H household groups; an aggregate foreign purchaser of exports; government consumption demands; and changes in inventories. Rows show the sources of purchases made by the agents of each column. For example, the first row in the absorption matrix, sub matrices (V1BAS, V2BAS, ..., V6BAS), shows flows of commodities to the demanders. Each of these sub matrices has CxS rows, which implies that each of the commodity types (c) identified in the model can be obtained (s) locally or imported from overseas. In this model, C is 94 and S is 2. Commodities are absorbed as inputs to current production and fixed investment, consumed by households, exported, consumed by government, and/or are added to or subtracted from inventories.

However, only domestically produced goods appear in the export column. All direct flows are valued at basic prices.[1]

		Absorption Matrix					
		1	2	3	4	5	6
		Producers	Investors	Households	Exports	Government	Change in Inventories
	Size	← I →	← I →	← H →	← 1 →	← 1 →	← 1 →
Basic Flows (domestic)	↑ CxS ↓	V1BAS	V2BAS	V3BAS	V4BAS	V5BAS	V6BAS
Margins	↑ CxSxM ↓	V1MAR	V2MAR	V3MAR	V4MAR	V5MAR	
Taxes	↑ CxS ↓	V1TAX	V2TAX	V3TAX	V4TAX	V5TAX	
Labour	↑ O ↓	V1LAB					
Capital	↑ 1 ↓	V1CAP					
Land	↑ 1 ↓	V1LND					
Other Costs	↑ 1 ↓	V1OCT					
Production Taxes	↑ 1 ↓	V1PTX					

C = Number of Commodities

I = Number of Industries

S = 2: Domestic, Imported

O = Number of Occupation Types

M = Number of Commodities used as Margins

H = Number of Household Types

Note: Export column is for domestic goods only

	Make Matrix	Total
Size	← I →	
↑ C ↓	MAKE	
Total		

	Import Duty
Size	←1→
↑ C ↓	V0TAR

Figure 6.1. The Bangladesh model input-output database.

[1] 'The basic price is the amount receivable by the producer from the purchaser for a unit of a good or service produced as output, minus any tax payable, and plus any subsidy receivable on that unit. It excludes any transport charges invoiced separately by the producers' (United Nations, 1999).

The second row (V1MAR, …., V5MAR) shows the flows of domestically produced commodities used as margins to facilitate the flows of commodities in the matrices V1BAS, V2BAS,……,V6BAS. ORANI-G assumes that all margin flows are domestically produced. In this model, the commodities used as margins are wholesale trade, retail trade, air transport, water transport, land transport and railway transport. Each of the margin matrices corresponds to CxSxM rows, covering the flows of domestically produced commodities used as margins (M) to facilitate the flows of C commodities from S sources. All the margin flows are valued at basic prices. Since inventories (column 6) comprise mainly unsold products, it is assumed that they do not bear margins (Tran, 2007).

The tax matrices in the third row (V1TAX, V2TAX, …, V5TAX) show the taxes on commodities absorbed by producers, investors, households, the government and the export sectors. As with margins, it is assumed that there are no sales taxes on inventories.

Current production needs primary factors (such as land, labour and capital) in addition to intermediate inputs. This model uses three types of primary factors: agricultural land, fixed capital and labour (which is divided into 4 occupational skill types). The V1LAB, V1CAP, and V1LND rows show the primary factors usage for each industry in the first column of the absorption matrix. In particular, matrix V1LAB shows the wages paid to different occupational categories by each industry; V1CAP shows the rental value of each industry's fixed capital; and V1LND shows the rental value of agricultural land used by each industry. As well as purchasing factor inputs, industries have to pay production taxes and other costs tickets (represented in the absorption matrix as V1PTX and V1OCT). Production taxes include output taxes or subsidies that are not user-specific. The other cost category includes various miscellaneous taxes on firms such as municipal taxes, charges and the costs of holding inventories (Horridge, 2006).

The final two matrices are the MAKE (joint production) matrix and the import duty matrix. The joint production matrix (MAKE) shows the value of output of each commodity by each industry. In this model there are 86 industries and 94 commodities.[2] Since, in principle, each industry can produce any of the commodity types, this model does not have a one-to-one correspondence between commodities and industries. As a result, the joint production matrix is not diagonal. The import duty matrix contains the import duty paid on each commodity imported by each industry. Following ORANI-G, it is assumed that tariff rates on imports can vary by commodity but not by user.

Summing all the matrices in the producers' column in the absorption matrix gives the base-period value of output for industries (j) in basic prices. This can also be obtained by adding the value of commodities produced by the industries or by adding the columns of the joint product matrix. In the same way, by adding the usage of commodities (i), i.e., the sum across the ith rows of V1BAS, V2BAS, …, V6BAS (direct use) and the margin matrices V1MAR, V2MAR, ….,V5MAR we can get the value of commodities produced by industries, which will also be equal to the row totals of the joint production matrix. This outcome corresponds to two basic condition of database balancing:

1. The value of output by each industry must equal the total of production costs, i.e., the column sums of the MAKE matrix must equal the corresponding sums in the producers column of Figure 6.1.

[2] The industry and commodity classification of I-O table 2000 for Bangladesh is provided in Appendix Table C 6.1

2. The outputs of domestically produced commodities must equal the total of the demands for them, i.e., the row sums of the MAKE matrix must equal the row sums of the BAS and MAR rows of Figure 6.1. This corresponds to the model's commodity market clearing condition.

6.2.2. Elasticities and Parameters

In addition to input-output data, the following elasticities and other parameters are required to implement the model outlined in Chapter Five:

1. The Armington elasticities of substitution between domestic and imported use of commodities for intermediate inputs (SIGMA1);[3]
2. The Armington elasticities of substitution between the domestic and imported use of commodities for investment (SIGMA2);
3. The Armington elasticities of substitution between the domestic and imported use of commodities by households (SIGMA3);
4. Elasticities of substitution between primary factors (SIGMA1PRIM);
5. Elasticities of substitution between different skill types of labour (SIGMA1LAB);
6. Own-price elasticities of demand for exports (EXP_ELAST; EXP_ELAST_NT);
7. The household expenditure elasticities for each product in the economy (EPS); and,
8. The Frisch parameters (FRISCH).[4]

6.3. Data Sources

6.3.1. The Input-Output Table for Bangladesh for the Year 2000

The Input-Output (I-O) Table 2000 for Bangladesh (GOB, 2003b) forms the main source for the Bangladesh model's absorption matrix.[5] In line with the United Nations *System of National Accounts* (United Nations 1993), the 2000 I-O framework contains non-symmetric Supply and Use tables, in which production activities (industries) are distinguished from commodities.[6] The schematic representation of these tables is provided in Tables 6.1 and 6.2 respectively. The Supply table (Table 6.1) contains a matrix of domestic production broken down into 94 commodities and 86 industries and a vector of imported goods and services. Total supply was first valued at producers' prices and then transferred into purchasers' prices

[3] The concept of Armington elasticity commonly used in CGE analysis derives from Armington (1969), who first emphasised the differentiation of products with respect to their origin and the imperfect substitution in demand between imports and domestic supply.

[4] The Frisch parameter shows the elasticity of the marginal utility of total expenditure with respect to total expenditure.

[5] I-O Table 2000 was prepared by the General Economic Division and the Sustainable Human Development Unit, Planning Commission, Bangladesh.

[6] In the I-O table 2000, one industry can supply more than one commodity and a commodity can be supplied by more than one industry. For example, the livestock rearing industry produces five commodities (meat, milk and fat, draft animals, manure, hides and skin) and the poultry industry produces two commodities (meat and eggs). On the other hand, the commodity 'waste' is produced as a by-product by 12 industries.

by adding a vector of trade and transport margins.[7] This was done to match the figure of total supply with that of total demand in the Use table (Table 6.2).

The Use Table in purchasers' prices (Table 6.2) contains a matrix of intermediate consumption of domestic and imported goods and services covering 94 commodities and 86 industries. There are also columns containing final consumption of households, government final consumption expenditure, gross fixed capital formation, changes in stocks, and exports of goods and services. The value added block includes the following rows (according to industry breakdown): compensation of employees, gross operating surplus (including gross mixed incomes) and indirect taxes. Taxes on imports and taxes on domestic products for 94 commodities are shown in Tables 6.3 and 6.4 respectively. Table 6.3 includes taxes on imports including custom duty, VAT, supplementary duty, advance income tax, license fee, development surcharge, fines and penalties. Table 6.4 includes excise tax, VAT in product stage, VAT on trade items, VAT on services, supplementary duty on manufacturing, and supplementary duty on services.

Table 6.1. Domestic Supply table at purchasers' prices

	Industries1,2,.........,86	Imports	Total supply at producers' prices	Trade and transport margins	Total supply at purchasers' prices
Commodities 1 2 3 . .94	Domestic supply matrix product by industry (producers' value)				
	Total industry output (producers' values)				

Table 6.2. Use Table at purchasers' prices

	Industries 1,2...86	Public consumption	Private consumption	Export goods	Export service	Capital formation	Stock change	Total uses at purchasers price
Products 1 , . . 94	Intermediate part of Use table; products by industry/ imported 94x86							
Input use								
Value added components by industry								
Gross output								

[7] Producers' prices are equal to basic prices plus indirect taxes (less subsidies) on domestic products and import duties and taxes on imports, whereas purchasers' prices are equal to producers' prices plus trade and transport margins.

Table 6.3. Import duties by commodity

Commodity	Import value	Custom duty	VAT	Supp. duty	Advanced Income tax	Licence fee	Dev. surcharge	Fine	Penalty	Total import duty
1 2 3 . . . 94										
Total										

Table 6.4. Domestic taxes by commodity

Commodity 1 2 3 . . . 94	Excise tax	VAT (products)	VAT (trade)	VAT (services)	Supp.duty (manufac. stage)	Supp.duty (services)	Total domestic tax
Total							

6.3.2. Social Accounting Matrix (SAM)

The social accounting matrix (SAM) for Bangladesh for the year 2000 (SHDU 2002) published by the Sustainable Human Development Unit and the General Economic Division (GED) of the Planning Commission of Bangladesh is the main source of data for implementing the income distribution part of the Bangladesh model. The SAM itself draws on the I-0 table 2000 for Bangladesh prepared by the Planning Commission, and on the Labour Force Survey 2000, the Household Income and Expenditure Survey 2000 and National Income Estimates, all prepared by the Bangladesh Bureau of Statistics.

A SAM is a single entry accounting system in which each institutional agent is represented by a column for outgoings and a row for incomings (Round, 1981). It extends beyond the input-output accounts to capture income and expenditure flows between institutions such as households, government, and the rest of the world (Reinert & Ronald-Holst, 1997). The Bangladesh SAM for 2000 classifies the economic transactions of the economy in terms of the following accounts:

1) Production activity accounts for 45 sectors;[8]
2) 6 factors of production (land, capital and four different types of labour);
3) Current account transactions among households, government, corporations and the rest of the world; and

[8] In the Bangladesh SAM 2000, no distinction is made between production activities and commodities.

4) A consolidated capital account that captures the flows of investment and savings by institution and sectors.

Households are divided into nine groups, five groups in rural areas and four groups in urban areas. Rural households are classified according to occupation and ownership of cultivable land as follows:

1. landless households (no cultivable land);
2. marginal farmer households (up to 0.49 acres of land);
3. small farmer households (0.5 to 2.49 acres of land);
4. large farmer households (2.50 acres of land and above); and
5. non-agricultural households.

Urban households are classified according to the education level of the household head as follows:

1. illiterate (no education);
2. low-educated households (class I to class IX);
3. medium-educated households (class X to class XII); and
4. highly-educated households (graduate and above).

The 2000 SAM also classifies the labour force by gender and skill level:

1. male low-skilled;
2. male high-skilled;
3. female low-skilled; and,
4. female high-skilled.

6.3.3. GTAP Database for Bangladesh

In the absence of better information this study uses the estimates of household expenditure elasticities found in the GTAP 6.0 database for Bangladesh (Dimaranan, 2006). However, because of differences in commodity classifications between the GTAP database and the Bangladesh I-O table, a mapping is required between the classifications. In the GTAP 6.0 database there are 57 commodities and 87 regions, but in estimating consumer demand elasticities, commodities were aggregated to 10 commodities. Accordingly, a mapping was performed between the 94 commodities of the I-O table 2000 for Bangladesh and the aggregated 10 commodities of GTAP 6.0.

6.3.4. Household Income and Expenditure Survey 2000 for Bangladesh

To identify poverty impacts, the aggregate results from the present model were linked to data from the Household Income and Expenditure Survey 2000 conducted by the Bangladesh

Bureau of Statistics. The survey included 7440 households comprising 5040 rural households and 2400 urban households.

6.4. Steps in the Compilation of Input-Output Database

The general procedure for transforming the original data into model data is presented in Figure 6.2. Usually, the raw data are supplied in Excel (XLS) format or in plain text (TXT) format, as shown at the top of the figure. There are various ways to convert this raw data from TXT or XLS into the binary Header Array (HAR) file. One method is to move data from the XLS sheet to CSVfiles.[9] Then a text editor (which adds a few lines of descriptive data to the CSV files) is used to make GEMPACK text files. These text data files are especially suitable for a small model whereas for large or complex models, Header Array (HAR) files are more convenient. GEMPACK text files can be converted into HAR files by using either ViewHAR or MODHAR.[10] The next step is to create TABLO files, which perform all the numerical operations needed to turn original data into forms that can be used in the model. However, the tab files do not contain variables or equations. They are mainly read statements, formulae that manipulate the data and written statements that turn the manipulated numbers into the desired format (Harrison & Horridge, 2006).

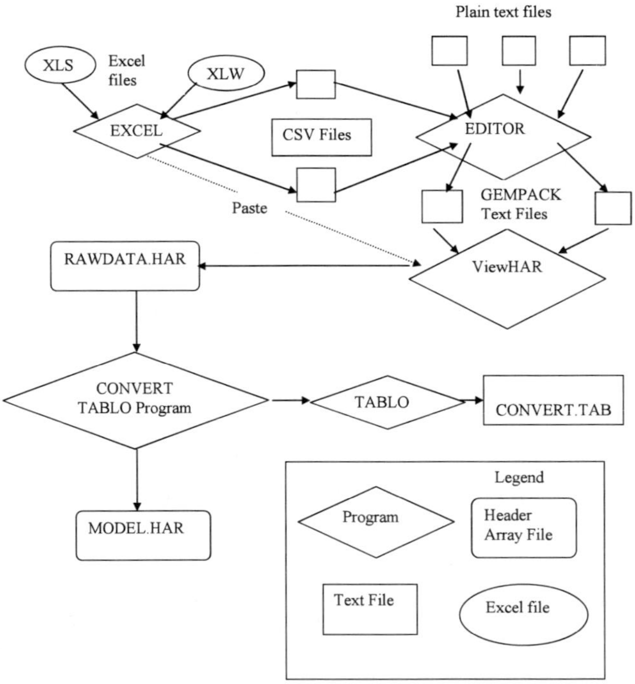

Source: Harrison and Horridge (2006).

Figure 6.2. Overview of data preparation steps.

[9] CSV stands for comma-separated values.

[10] These are utility GEMPACK programs. They are used to process various GEMPACK files, which are binary files and thus cannot be read or modified in a text editor.

Table 6.5. Contents of the RAWDATA.HAR

Header	Size	Coefficient	Long name
MAKE	COM94*IND86	MAKEPD	MAKE matrix at producers' prices
USEP	COM94*USERS	USEPUR	Usage of commodities at purchasers' prices
INTD	COM94*IND86	INTDOM	Intermediate use of domestic products
INTM	COM94*IND86	INTIMP	Intermediate use of imported products
CTAX	COM94*CTAX SET	CTAX	Commodity taxes by commodity and types of tax
FDD	COM94*FDEST	FDD	Final demand
VA	IND86*VASET	VA	Value added by industry and by VA component
VDUT	COM94*MTAX SET	VDUT	Taxes on imports by commodity and types of tax

Source: The Bangladesh model database.

Table 6.6. Contents of the ORANI-G data files

Header	Size	Coefficient	Long name
1BAS	COM*SRC*IND	V1BAS	Intermediate Basic
1MAR	COM*SRC*IND*MAR	V1MAR	Intermediate Margins
1TAX	COM*SRC*IND	V1TAX	Intermediate Tax
1CAP	IND	V1CAP	Capital
1LAB	IND	V1LAB	Labour
1LND	IND	V1LND	Land
1OCT	IND	V1OCT	Other Costs
2BAS	COM*SRC*IND	V2BAS	Investment Basic
2MAR	COM*SRC*IND*MAR	V2MAR	Investment Margins
2TAX	COM*SRC*IND	V2TAX	Investment Tax
3BAS	COM*SRC	V3BAS	Households Basic
3MAR	COM*SRC*MAR	V3MAR	Households margins
3TAX	COM*SRC	V3TAX	Households Tax
4BAS	COM	V4BAS	Exports Basic
4MAR	COM*MAR	V4MAR	Exports Margins
4TAX	V4TAX	V4TAX	Exports Tax
5BAS	COM*SRC	V5BAS	Government Basic
5MAR	COM*SRC*MAR	V5MAR	Government Margins
5TAX	COM*SRC	V5TAX	Government Tax
6BAS	COM*SRC	V6BAS	Stocks
MAKE	COM*IND	MAKE	Multiproduct Matrix
OTAR	COM	VOTAR	Tariff Revenue
1ARM	COM	SIGMA1	Intermediate Armington
2ARM	COM	SIGMA2	Investment Armington
3ARM	COM	SIGMA3	Households Armington
EXNT	1	EXP_ELAST_NT	Non-Traditional Export Elasticity
P018	COM	EXP_ELAST	Traditional Export Elasticity
P021	1	FRISCH	Frisch Parameter
P028	IND	SIGMA1PRIM	Primary Factor Sigma
SCET	IND	SIGMA1OUT	Output Sigma
SLAB	IND	SIGMA1LAB	Labour Sigma
XPEL	COM	EPS	Expenditure Elasticities

Source: Horridge (2006).

The present study followed the procedures described below to convert the I-O table and SAM into the format required by Figure 6.1.

6.4.1. Conversion of HAR Format

First, using the ViewHAR program, the original spreadsheet format of data was converted into binary Header Array (HAR) files, called RAWDATA.HAR (Table 6.5). Then, for each database creation, a separate TABLO input file was written. This converted the RAWDATA.HAR into final MODEL.HAR, similar to the ORANI-G data input format (Table 6.6).

6.4.2. Creating Value-added Matrices

The present model distinguishes six factors of production: male low-skilled labour, male high-skilled labour, female low-skilled labour, female high-skilled labour, capital and land. To allocate the factor payments from the I-O table among these six categories was not straightforward, as the I-O 2000 table for Bangladesh has only one row for 'compensation of employees (COE)' and one row for 'mixed income and operating surplus'. To extract payments to land and capital from mixed income and operating surplus, we followed Hoque (2006) in assuming that for land-using industries, returns to land [V1LND (i)] accounted for 23 per cent of total mixed income and operating surplus. However, for non-extractive industries, the figure was assumed to be zero. From the remainder of mixed income and operating surplus, a fraction was allocated to labour provided by the owners of unincorporated businesses or members of their households who worked in these businesses without receiving an explicit wage or salary. Again following Hoque (2006), the percentages for land-using industries and non-land using industries were fixed at 0.35 and 0.08 respectively.[11] By combining these shares with the compensation of employees' vector in the I-O table, we obtained returns to labour, V1LAB (i). After these adjustments, what was left of mixed income and operating surplus was identified as returns to capital, V1CAP (i). Because of lack of data, we assumed that there was no other cost ticket, OCT (i), in the base year.

The I-O table 2000 for Bangladesh has only one row for compensation of employees with no separate data for different skill levels, whereas the Bangladesh model required information on the wages and salaries paid by each industry to each of the four types of labour. This information was obtained with the aid of SAM 2000 data. Since the sectoral classification in I-O 2000 is different from SAM 2000, it was necessary to undertake a mapping between the 45-sector SAM and the 94-sector I-O table. (See Appendix Table C 6.2.). Applying the mapping, the labour income component of mixed income and operating surplus was allocated among the four types of labour. Applying the mapping, the occupational composition of labour payments from the SAM 2000 was used to allocate the total I-O labour bill (including the labour income component of mixed income and operating surplus) among the four categories of labour in each industry. Applying the mapping, the occupational composition of labour payments from the SAM 2000 was used to allocate the total I-O labour bill (including the labour income component of mixed income and operating surplus) among the four categories of labour in each industry.

---

[11] These figures refer to the percentages of total mixed income and operating surplus after deduction of returns to land.

6.4.3. Conversion from Producers' Prices to Basic Prices and Separating Out Margins

As already noted, the I-O table 2000 for Bangladesh contains a Use table valued at purchasers' prices, USEPUR(c,u), and a Supply matrix valued at producers' prices, MAKEPD(c,i). However, to implement the model, the I-O data matrices needed to be valued at basic prices. The supply matrix, MAKEPD(c,i), was converted to basic prices by deducting commodity taxes from it in the following manner. First, industry shares in commodity output, MAKESHR(c,i), were estimated using MAKEPD(c,i). Second, based on industry shares in commodity output, a tax matrix, MAKETAX(c, i) was formed by distributing total tax on domestic commodities, DTAX(c) to industries. Total tax on commodities, DTAX(c) was formed by adding an index t running over the set CTAX of the domestic tax matrix, CTAX(c,t). Then, the supply matrix at producers' prices, MAKEPD(c,i) was converted to a supply matrix at basic prices, MAKEBASE(c,i) by subtracting MAKETAX(c,i) from MAKEPD(c,i). Production tax, PTX (i), was calculated by summing MAKETAX(c,i) over commodities and by subtracting this from indirect taxes on industry, VA (i, "IndTax").

The model also required separate margin matrices (V1MAR, V2MAR,..., V5MAR) for each commodity. These values were also necessary to convert the Use table at purchaser prices, USEPUR(c,u) to basic prices, USEBAS(c,u). Total supply of margin commodities, MAR_USM(c), was available from the Supply table and the value of direct usage of margin commodities, DIRSALE (m), was available from the Use table. Adding MAKEPD (m,i) over i and subtracting the vector DIRSALE (m) from the resulting vector, we obtained MARSALE (m), which represented the sales of margin commodities for margin purposes. To allocate that amount to each margin commodity, we assumed that each commodity used the same proportion of margin commodities.

In the next step, to allocate margins to different users or to create the margin matrix, MARGIN_S(c,u,m), we relied on Hoque's (2006) assumptions to make a vector of weight, MARFAC (u,m), reflecting the intensity of margin usage by users. Using USEPUR(c,u), MARGIN_S(c,u,m) and MARFAC (u,m), we produced the margin matrix, MARGIN_S(c,u,m), on composite commodities. Finally, by summing MARGIN_S(c,u,m) over m and by deducting the resulting margin matrix from the USE matrix at purchasers' prices, we obtained the USE matrix at producers' prices, USEPD_S(c,u).

6.4.4. Splitting the USEPD Matrix by Sources

All matrices created up to this point include flows for the composite (imported + domestic) commodities. However, the model requires that the domestic and import commodity flow matrices should be separated. A separate matrix of competing imports by commodity and by user would achieve this, but unfortunately the I-O table 2000 for Bangladesh provides only the matrix of imported intermediate inputs, INTIMP(c,i), and a vector of total imports IMP(c). We obtained the values of imports for final demand, FDMPUR_F(c), by subtracting the values for intermediate inputs from the total imports in the

Supply table. This procedure revealed some unusual import flows in the original data.[12] We used the import share, MSHR(c) for these unusual allocations. The value of imports for final demand was then allocated to final users using the import weights assumed in Hoque (2006). Thus we obtained the USE matrix at producers' prices from an imported source, USEPD_0(c, "imp", u). By subtracting the matrix, USEPD_0 (c, "imp",u), from USEPD_0(c,u), the USE matrix of composite commodities at purchasers' prices, we produced USEPD_0(c,"dom",u), which is the USE matrix at producers' prices from domestic sources. Thus we obtained the USE matrix by commodity, sources and user, USEPD_0(c, s, u).

6.4.5. Pro-rate Indirect Tax across Users and Subtract from USE Matrix

As a first step for allocating taxes, matrix USEPD_0 (c,s,u), which was created in section 6.4.4, was used to estimate non-stock users' shares in the total use of commodity USHR(c,s,u). These users' shares were used to allocate taxes on domestic and imported commodities to users. As stated previously, I-O table 2000 has an import duty table and a domestic tax table containing a disaggregation of taxes on imports and domestic products. Combining all non-tariff taxes on imports by commodity we got MTAX(c). Then, multiplying this vector with USHR (c, "imp",u) we obtained TAX(c,"imp",u), and multiplying USHR(c,"dom",u) with DTAX(c) provided us with TAX(c,"dom",u). Thus, we obtained a TAX matrix for all users, TAX(c,s,u). We subtracted the TAX matrix from the USEPD_0(c,s,u) matrix obtained in section 6.4.4 to produce the USE matrix at basic prices, USEBAS(c,s,u).

6.4.6. Estimation of Shares of Investment According to Capital Rentals

The I-O table 2000 for Bangladesh provides capital formation data in a one-column vector, which represents the inputs of each commodity that go into fixed capital formation by all industries. However, to implement the model, a commodity by industry investment matrix was required. To distribute gross fixed capital formation to industries, we needed to know the

fixed investment matrix of the value of inputs of each commodity in the capital stock of each industry. In the absence of readily available published data on investment with respect to different industries in Bangladesh, we followed Oktaviani (2000) in adopting an alternative method in which it was assumed that the share of investment of each industry followed the share of return to capital earned by each industry.

INVSHR (i) = V1CAP (i)/V1CAP_i

where

INVSHR (i) = Investment share in each industry;
V1CAP (i) = value of capital returns in each industry and
V1CAP_i = Total value of capital returns.

[12] For "Animal draft", for example, the import value does not seem to be allocated to any users. For "Wheat" and "Yarn" the values of imports seem too high compared with the total value of final demand.

This investment share matrix was used later in splitting the basic flows, USEBAS(c,s,i). The same investment shares were used to split the margin and tax matrices to V2MAR(c,s,i) and V2TAX(c,s,i).

6.4.7. Creating ORANI-G Basic Flows

The use matrix at basic prices, USEBAS(c,s,u), derived in section 6.4.5 served as the basis for the various basic flows matrices V1BAS to V6BAS (row 1 in Figure 6.1) for various users. The investment share matrix, INVSHR (i) derived in section 6.4.6 was used to estimate an investment basic flows matrix V2BAS(c,s,i). Further, the TAX matrix TAX(c,s,u) created in section 6.4.5 was used to create coefficients for the taxes on basic flows V1TAX, V2TAX,….,V5TAX (row 3 in Figure 6.1). The investment tax matrix, V2TAX, was formed by using the INVSHR matrix. Note that the margin matrix on composite commodity to users, MARGIN_S(c,u,m) was created in section 6.4.3. By using the source splitting share, USEBAS(c,s,u)/[sum{s,SRC,USEBAS(c,s,u),}], a matrix of margins, MARGIN (c,s,u,m) was produced at this stage and used later to create the coefficients for the margin flows V1MAR, V2MAR,…,V5MAR(row 2 in Figure 6.1.

6.4.8. Disaggregation of the Household Sector

We required households' expenditure matrices for domestic and imported goods (V3BASHOUS), their associated margin matrices (V3MARHOUS) and tax matrices (V3TAXHOUS) to compute various expenditure shares for the model. However, the I-O table 2000 for Bangladesh assumes only one aggregate consumer. By applying the mapping between the I-O table and the SAM 2000 for Bangladesh (Appendix Table C 6.2), the total household expenditures reported in the I-O table were disaggregated to the nine household groups of the Bangladesh model. The commodity expenditure shares of the various household groups were calculated from SAM 2000, and then used to split the aggregate consumption expenditure vector into 9 household groups.

6.4.9. Ensuring that Data Written to File Add Up, and Further Adjustments

As stated in section 6.2.1, the initial database should be balanced. The model solution must start from a database that is consistent in levels, for all equations (Horridge, 2006). The conditions to be satisfied are:

- The MAKE matrix's row sums must equal the corresponding row sums of the BAS and MAR rows of the absorption matrix in Figure 6.1. That is, the output of each domestically produced commodity must equal the total of the demands for it;
- The MAKE matrix's column sums must equal the corresponding sums of the producers' column of the absorption matrix in Figure 6.1. That is, the value of output by each industry must equal its total of production costs;

- The average value of the household expenditure elasticities, EPS, should be one.

To check the initial conditions for this model database, two coefficients were used. These were:

DIFFIND (i) = COSTS (i) – MAKE_C (i)
DIFFCOM(c) = SALES(c) – MAKE_I(c)

In principle, their values should be close to zero to ensure balance in the initial database. However, at the first stage, some industry costs did not correspond to the MAKE column sums and for many commodities sales did not correspond to the MAKE row sum. To secure balance in the database, we adjusted capital rentals and changes in inventories. That is, the differences between industry costs and industry sales have been adjusted with V1CAP and STOCKS. This procedure seems plausible as these items were used as balancing items in the Input-output table 2000 compilation. According to United Nations (1999), gross operating surplus (V1CAP) is by definition calculated as residual. It is the difference between industry output and the sum of intermediate input, compensation of employees and net taxes on products and production. Likewise, for the economy as a whole, the net change in inventories can be viewed as the difference between GDP measured from the supply side and the sum of private consumption, private fixed investment, government consumption, government fixed investment and net exports.

6.5. Elasticities and Other Parameters

The elasticity parameters included in the model have been listed in section 6.2.2. Ideally these elasticities should be estimated econometrically using cross-sectional and time series data. However, due to time and data constraints, it was necessary to rely heavily on elasticity values found in other studies of Bangladesh and elsewhere. In some cases, personal judgments or 'guesstimates' have been used.

6.5.1. The Elasticity of Substitution between Domestic and Imported Commodities

The intensity of the elasticity of substitution between home and foreign produced goods is measured by the Armington elasticity, named after Armington (1969). The higher the value of this parameter, the closer is the degree of substitution between domestic and imported commodities, while the lower its value, the weaker is substitutability. In the case of Bangladesh, estimates of the elasticity of substitution between domestic and imported goods are lacking. In their absence, Salma (1992), Ahammad (1995), Noman (2002) and Hoque (2006) borrowed estimates from Chowdhury (1990). In these studies a value of 1.8 was used for the elasticities of primary, semi-processed and light manufacturing commodities on the assumption that these commodities have relatively high substitution possibilities in the domestic market. In the case of capital goods and heavy manufacturing items, the elasticities of substitution between domestic and imported sources were assumed to have relatively low values of 1.2, implying that domestically produced goods within this group are not close substitute for imports. These assumptions are considered plausible, and are used in this study. For other commodities, the study has used the value reported in previous Bangladesh studies cited above by adjusting the classification of various commodities. The elasticity of substitution for various commodities is reported in Appendix Table C 6.3. Because of unavailability of data, and following ORANI (Dixon et al. 1997), this study also assumes that the elasticity of substitution between domestic and imported goods is the same for all users, i.e., intermediate users, investors, and households. In model notation, SIGMA (1) = SIGMA (2) = SIGMA (3).

6.5.2. Elasticity of Substitution between Primary Factors in Each Industry

The elasticity of substitution between primary factors measures the responsiveness of the relative usage of primary factor inputs to changes in relative factor prices (returns.) For Bangladesh, there are a number of estimates of these elasticities, though none is recent. For Bangladesh, Rahman (1973), Demery and Jahangir (1975), Rushdi (1982) and Bairam (1991) estimated factor substitutability between capital and labour, using different methodological frameworks. Rahman (1973) used a constant elasticity of substitution (CES) production function, but did not take into account adjustment costs and time lags in his time series estimation. Taking these into account, Demery and Jahangir (1975) estimated the elasticity of substitution in Bangladesh by sector using pooled cross-sectional and time series data for the period 1962-63 to 1965-66. Their results were an improvement on Rahman's (1973) estimates, despite being based on underlying assumptions that may not have been entirely appropriate for a developing country like Bangladesh. Rushdi (1982) used a trans log cost function to estimate factor substitutability between capital, labour and materials in the manufacturing industries of Bangladesh from data for the period 1969-70 to 1978-79. Bairam (1991) used a variable elasticity of substitution (VES) production function to estimate the elasticity of substitution between labour and capital, using cross-sectional data for forty-seven sectors of the Bangladesh economy in 1977-78. Nevertheless, Salma (1992) and Ahammad (1995) did not use any of these estimates as they were based on old data and various functional forms. Instead, Salma (1992) and Ahammad (1995) assumed a value of 1.00 for all sectors. Following Wittwer (1999) and ORANI (Dixon et al. 1997), the present study has used a default value of 0.5 for the elasticity of substitution between primary factors for all industries. Caddy (1976) obtained this value after time series studies of capital-labour substitution in Australian manufacturing industries.

6.5.3. Substitution Elasticities between Different Occupational Types of Labour

In this model, labour has been classified into four occupational categories based on skill level and gender. In the absence of estimates of the elasticities of substitution between occupational categories, a value of 0.5 has been selected for these elasticities, following

Wittwer (1999) and Horridge et al.(1995). In view of the structural and institutional inflexibilities in the labour market, this relatively low value seems plausible.

6.5.4. Export Demand Elasticities

For Bangladesh, estimates of individual export demand elasticities are rare and dated. In this study, an approximation of a small country assumption has been used for most exports. In particular, it is assumed that with the exception of jute and jute products, price elasticities of demand for exports are high because Bangladesh's export commodities have relatively insignificant shares in world market. Therefore, following ORANI (Dixon et al. 1997), Ahammad (1995), Hoque (2006), Bandara (1989) and Naranpanawa (2005), a value of -20 has been assumed for all traditional export goods and services (except for raw jute and jute goods) and also for all non-traditional exports.

In the case of jute, it was decided (following Salma (1992), Ahammad (1995) and Hoque (2006)) to set the price elasticity of demand for exports at -1.00 for raw jute and -7.00 for jute textiles). These values seem reasonable, considering the importance of Bangladeshi raw jute and jute products in the world market. Bangladesh was the biggest producer and a monopoly exporter of jute goods in the global market until the mid 1970s, and still met 50-60 per cent of the world demand for jute goods and 90 per cent of the world demand for raw jute in the early 2000s (Rahman, 2007).

6.5.5. Household Expenditure Elasticities and Marginal Budget Shares

To implement the commodity demand equations for each of the 9 households, we require estimates of the marginal budget shares for every product that households consume in Bangladesh. The estimation of the marginal budget shares in turn requires data on household expenditure elasticities for Bangladesh. Studies on complete demand system estimation for Bangladeshi households include Mahmud (1979), Pitt (1983), Chowdhury (1982), Kennes (1984), and Golleti (1993). Mahmud (1979) used pooled cross-sectional data from the *Quarterly Survey of Current Economic Conditions* for the years 1964, 1965, 1967 and 1969. Pitt (1983) estimated demand equations for nine commodities using cross-sectional data from the 1973-74 Household Expenditure Survey of Bangladesh. Chowdhury (1982) first estimated expenditure elasticities for 25 commodities employing a simple log-linear functional form. Then, using these expenditure elasticities, he estimated own and cross price elasticities for commodities by applying the Frisch method (Frisch, 1959). Kennes (1984) also estimated elasticities by using the linear expenditure system (LES) and the Almost Ideal Demand System (AIDS) for nine commodities. Golleti (1993) used Tobin's Probit to estimate the food demand system.

In the absence of more recent estimates of expenditure elasticities, we have used values from the GTAP 6.0 data base (Dimaranan 2006). However, since the commodity classification in the GTAP database for Bangladesh differs from that in this study, we needed to match the commodities in this study with the GTAP database on Bangladesh. In addition, the elasticity values were scaled so that their share-weighted sum is equal to one, that is:

$\sum EPS_c.Si^3 = 1$ (Engel aggregation property of demand system)

Where, *Si* is the average budget share of commodity *C* in total household consumption expenditure and EPS is the expenditure elasticity.

By definition, the expenditure elasticity of a good *C* is,

$EPS_c = S3LUX_c / S3_{c\_s}$

where S3LUXc is the marginal budget share; and S3c_*s* is the average budget share for good *C*.

For this study, average budget shares were collected from the input-output table. With known expenditure elasticities and average budget shares, the marginal budget shares for commodities were calculated as $S3LUX_c = EPS_c*S3_{c\_s}$. The expenditure elasticities for this study are provided in Appendix Table C 6.4.

6.5.6. Frisch Parameters

We needed Frisch parameters to calculate the supernumerary expenditure (defined as the excess of total expenditure over subsistence expenditure) for each good. The Frisch parameter is the negative of the ratio between total final household expenditure and household supernumerary expenditure. According to Engel's law, the proportion of income spent on foods falls as income increases. Similarly, we can expect that as income increases, the proportion of income spent on other substantial items will fall. That is, the supernumerary proportion of household consumption should rise as income rises (Tran, 2007). Thus we assume that the Frisch parameter for low income groups will be higher than that for the higher income groups.

Bandara (1989), in his Sri Lankan model, used Frisch parameter values of -6.43, -5.45 and -4.57 for the estate, remaining rural and urban sectors respectively. Wittwer (1999), in his WAYANG model of Indonesia, used the value of -4.00 for the rural landless group, with gradually declining values for other rural groups such as small cultivators, medium cultivators and large cultivators. For the urban groups 1, 2 and 3 in his study, the values were -3.50, -2.75 and -2.00 respectively. For Bangladesh, Arndt, et al. (2002) used the values of -1.6 for urban non-poor households and -4.0 for all other households.

For this study, the following Frisch values have been used for rural households: -4.0 for rural landless households, -3.50 for marginal farmers, -2.75 for small farmers, -2.50 for large farmers and -2.00 for non-agricultural households. For urban households, the Frisch values have been fixed at -3.50 for illiterate households -2.75 for low-educated households, -2.00 for medium-educated households and -1.5 for urban high-educated households.

6.6. Data Compilation for Income Distribution Analysis

Table 6.7 presents a simplified representation of the Bangladesh model SAM database for the year 2000. It provides a comprehensive picture of the economy. Basically, it is an extension of the I-O database with complete income mapping. In addition to information on production structure, it includes information on the distribution of income and the receipts and outlays of institutions. It is worth noting that the main ORANI-G model compiled in sections 6.4 and 6.5 has already determined the values of some cells in the SAM. The income-mapping feature is completed by introducing income-mapping variables, following IDC-GEM (Horridge et al. 1995).[13]

According to standard accounting principles, in a SAM, income in one account is balanced by disposal of incomes in another account, thus for every row there is a corresponding column. In Table 6.7, for each agent, the sum along the row is the agent's total income, while the column total represents current expenditure. The difference between the two indicates is saving. It is a mathematical necessity that, including the rest of the world, the sum of all sectors' net lending/borrowing, i.e., saving minus investment, should be zero. In other words, total saving across institutions equals total investment.

The following discussion is concerned with the procedures for compilation of data for the SAM database.

6.6.1. Production Activities

The first row of Table 6.7 shows the allocation of domestically produced commodities to various destinations, i.e., it shows the amount of output of each industry sold domestically as intermediate inputs (V1BAS), for private consumption by households (V3BAS), for public or government consumption (V5BAS), as capital inputs (V2BAS), as exports (V4BAS) and as net additions to inventories (V6BAS). These figures along with their margins have been calculated in sections 6.4.7 and 6.4.8. On the other hand, the first column shows producers' payments for intermediate commodities and other production costs, e.g., wages. These values have also been calculated in basic data base sections.

6.6.2. Gross Operating Surplus

Gross operating surplus (second row) from the income side, originates from total capital payments (V1CAP_I), total land payments (V1LND_I), total other costs ticket payments (V1OCT_I), interest on public debt (WGOVGOS) paid by government and gross operating surplus from the rest of the world (WROWGOS).[14] From the base data construction in section 6.4, we obtained the values for V1CAP_I, V1LAND_I and V1OCT_I, which give the total value of GOS. On the other hand, the second column shows expenditures of GOS, which take the form of a flow to households (VGOSHOU), corporate taxes to government (VGOSGOV), and transfer payments to the rest of the world (VGOSROW).

---

[13] Income mapping equations have been discussed in section 5.4 of Chapter 5.

[14] Following Hoque (2006), it is assumed that in Bangladesh during 2000, the values of WGOVGOS and WROWGOS were zero.

Table 6.7. A simplified representation of the Bangladesh model SAM database (in Million Taka)

Expenditures											
		1.Firms	2.Gross operating surplus	3.Wages	4.Households	5.Government current expenditure	6.Government Investment	7.Private Investment	8.Stocks	9.Rest of the World	10.Total
	1.Domestic goods	Intermediate inputs 1972185.63	0	0	Final private consumption 1695949.63	Final govt. consumption 105677.02	Final govt. investment 90371.49	Private investment expenditure 390874.50	Changes in inventories -28510.42	Exports 236403.25	4462951.00
	2.Gross operating surplus	1247584.75	0	0	0	0	0	0	0	0	1247584.75
	3.Wages	Labour income 998613.938	0	0	0	0	0	0	0	0	998613.94
Receipts	4.Households	0	Factor income 1131034.88	Wages 998613.94	Transfers 56341.70	Govt. transfers 11871.10	0	0	0	Foreign transfers 9825.10	2207686.75
	5.Government	Taxes on intermediate, import duties 59866.17	Corporation tax 2739.00	0	Income tax 59460.04	0	2561.11	11077.32	5934.55	582.397	142220.58
	6.ImportsCIF	Imports (intermediate) 184700.50	0	0	Household imports 88824.15	Govt. imports 2708.98	Govt. imports 9761.35	Import (investment) 42219.75	101378.75	0	429593.47
	7.Column Total	4462951.00	1133773.875	998614.00	1900575.50	120257.09	102693.95	444171.56	78802.88	246810.73	9488651.00
	8. Income Total	4462951.00	1247584.75	998613.94	2207686.750	142220.58	0	0	0	429593.469	9488650.00
	9. Saving	0	113810.875	0	307111.25	-80730.47	0	-522974.44	0	182782.734	0
	10.Total	13388853 00	3628943.5	2995842.00	6315949.00	302004.28	205387.90	365368.68	157605.75	1105997.62	28465952.00

6.6.3. Labour Income

The third row of Table 6.7 (Wages) shows the labour income paid by industries to various types of labour. The corresponding column shows how this labour income is distributed among households. Because of the presence of unincorporated business in Bangladesh, a significant part of mixed income is included into labour income, as discussed in section 6.4.2.

6.6.4. Households

Household receipts are presented in the fourth row of the SAM, which includes income from gross operating surplus, labour income, transfers from the government and transfers from the rest of the world. In this model, all wage income (V1LAB) has been allocated to households as remuneration for their supply of labour. Returns to land have also been allocated to households, based on Bangladesh SAM 2000 factor share, on the assumption that agricultural households own land. After deducting the rental sha7res and self-employed labour share from the mixed income operating surplus in the I-O table 2000 for Bangladesh, the residual is returns to capital, which has been decomposed into returns to unincorporated capital and corporate capital. It is assumed that households receive all of unincorporated capital incomes. In Bangladesh, most capital income accruing to private individuals derives from informal enterprises. For example, all returns to capital in the agriculture, forestry, construction, trade and transport sectors are assigned to unincorporated capital as most enterprises in these sectors are small. Similarly, the housing sector, which consists of urban and rural house building, is dominated by individuals and small firms, as is the other services sectors, which include the professional services of doctors, lawyers, accountants and consultants (Khondker, 1999). The operating surpluses of these sectors are assumed to accrue to unincorporated capital. The operating surplus originating from the manufacturing sectors consists of returns to unincorporated businesses, government and corporate capital as firms are owned by individuals, government and private or corporate firms (Khondker, 1999).

Because of the high prevalence of mixed income, 90 per cent of the residual operating surplus has been attributed to unincorporated capital income, the same percentage as that used in the 1993-94 SAM for Bangladesh. Besides labour income, land rental income and capital income, households receive transfers from other households, the government and the rest of the world. The income data from these other sources have been taken from the SAM 2000 for Bangladesh.

6.6.5. Government Income

The sixth row of Table 6.7 shows government income originating from indirect taxes on production activities (V0TAX_CSI), income taxes from households (VHOUGOV) and corporation taxes from enterprises (VGOSGOV). Total indirect tax revenue (V0TAX_CSI) includes taxes on intermediate goods (V1TAX_CSI), investment (V2TAX_CSI), consumption (V3TAX_CSI), exports (V4Tax_CS), stocks (V6TOT) and import tariffs

(V0TAR_C). The estimation of indirect tax revenue collected on both domestically produced and imported commodities has been described in the base data construction section, while income taxes from households and corporation taxes from enterprises have been taken from SAM 2000. Total corporation tax collection in 2000 was taka 2,739 million.

6.6.6. Rest of the World Sector

The rest of the world account generates income through payments on imported goods and services (V0CIF_C) and transfer payments from households, government and enterprises. In the absence of data, this survey follows Hoque (2006) in assuming that transfer payments from government (GOVROW), households (HOUROW), and enterprises (GOSROW) are zero. Total payments for imported goods and services (V0CIF_C) includes the cost of insurance and freight incurred by firms, Impcif ("Firms"), households, Impcif ("Households"), Impcif ("Government"), Impcif ("Private investment") and Impcif ("stocks"). These values have already been determined in the base data construction section.

6.6.7. SAM Data Base Balance

By summing the receipts along the rows of Table 6.7 for each agent, we obtain income totals for all agents, which are shown in the eighth row of the table. Similarly, the corresponding columns show total expenditure by each agent (in the seventh row). A balanced database ensures equality of totals by rows to corresponding column totals. The difference between income total and expenditure total is saving for each agent (shown in the ninth row). In this survey, a balance check (VSAMCHECK) ensures that the sum of all saving (including that provided by the rest of the world) is equal to total investment expenditure in the economy.

6.7. Household Income Composition and Distribution

This section describes the sources of income of the various households groups and the distribution of income among the groups in the base year. There are four basic forms of income: labour income, income from capital, land income and income from various transfers. Transfers consists of household transfers (for example, urban households sending money to their rural parents, and rural parents sending money to their urban children for education), government transfers (such as pensions, government old age allowances for the elderly poor, allowances for widowed and distressed women, subsidised education and health services) and Rest of the World transfers (remittances from Bangladeshi workers working abroad).

Table 6.8 shows that both in rural and urban areas, factors of production provide the largest source of income. In rural areas labour provides the major part of factor income for all household categories, except large farmer households. As much as 93.19 per cent of the income of the households with no cultivable land comes from labour and the remainder from various transfers. Marginal farmer households receive 56.83 per cent of their income from labour and 33.18 per cent from capital. Small farmer households (those with land holdings of 0.5 to 2.49 acres of land) receive 52.17 per cent of their income from labour, and 36.19 per cent from land. Large farmer households receive only 16.52 per cent of their income; 59.71 per cent of their income comes from capital and 22.89 per cent from land. Non-agricultural households receive most of their income from labour (56.21 per cent) income and capital (38.02 per cent). Rural non-farm activities include activities outside agriculture such as livestock, fisheries, self-employed subsistence-oriented cottage industries, transport operations, shopkeepers, and petty trading.

Table 6.8. Household income composition (per cent)

Households	Labour	Capital	Land	Intra-house transfers	Govt. transfers	ROW transfers	Total
a)Rural							
Landless HH	93.19	0	0	5.84	0.41	0.57	100
Marginal farmer HH	56.83	33.18	0.71	8.35	0.35	0.58	100
Small farmer HH	52.17	36.19	6.13	4.66	0.11	0.73	100
Large farmer HH	16.52	59.71	22.89	0.53	0.02	0.32	100
Non-agricultural HH	56.21	38.02	1.74	3.01	0.39	0.62	100
b)Urban							
Illiterate HH	60.63	37.33	0	1.60	0.05	0.39	100
Low-educated HH	41.19	53.03	2.28	2.81	0.25	0.43	100
Medium-educated HH	23.93	72.32	2.57	0.34	0.68	0.16	100
High-educated HH	15.39	75.13	4.99	1.07	3.21	0.20	100

Source: Bangladesh model database.

In urban areas, with the exception of the illiterate, household groups receive more of their income from capital than from labour. Lower educated households receive 53.03 per cent of income from capital and 41.19 per cent from labour, with only 2.28 per cent coming from land. Medium-educated households receive 72.32 per cent of income from capital and 23.93 per cent from labour, and high-educated households receive 75.13 per cent from capital and 15.29 per cent from labour. Table 6.9 shows household labour income composition by sex and occupation for each household group. It can be seen that low-skilled labour is the main source of labour income for landless farmers, marginal farmers, small farmers and non-agricultural households in the rural areas and illiterate and low-educated household groups in urban areas. On the other hand, high-skilled labour constitutes the main source of labour income for the medium-educated and high-educated groups in urban areas.

The female labour contribution to the total labour income of households is generally low. The largest contributions of female low-skilled labour are only 17.91 per cent for the illiterate household group in urban areas and 12.02 per cent for the rural landless household group in rural areas. The largest contributions of female high-skilled labour are even smaller: 6.43 per cent for the large farm household group in rural areas and 5.71 per cent for the medium-educated household group in urban areas. In rural areas women are mostly involved in the post harvest work and keeping livestock, poultry and small gardens. In contrast, women in cities are mostly found in domestic and traditional jobs, although from the 1980s manufacturing and services, especially ready-made garment manufacturing, have emerged as increasingly important sources of employment for women.

Table 6.9. Labour income composition by sex and occupation (per cent)

Households	Male low-skilled	Male high-skilled	Female low-skilled	Female high-skilled
a) Rural				
Landless HH	84.94	2.96	12.02	0.07
Marginal farmer HH	86.11	6.44	7.20	0.24
Small farmer HH	67.21	27.91	3.86	1.01
Large farmer HH	34.92	56.49	2.16	6.43
Non-agricultural HH	58.36	32.07	7.94	1.62
b) Urban				
Illiterate HH	79.91	2.05	17.91	0.12
Low-educated HH	76.85	12.35	9.30	1.48
Medium-educated HH	1.58	89.84	2.86	5.71
High-educated HH	0.29	95.87	1.29	2.54

Source: The Bangladesh model database.

Table 6.10 shows the distribution of income among the nine household groups. Although the income data are not adjusted for inter-group differences in consumer price levels, it appears that at least in nominal terms the rural population is on the whole considerably worse off than the urban population. Rural household groups, who together make up 68 per cent of the total population, receive only 51 per cent of total income, while urban household groups, who account for 32 per cent of the population, receive 49 per cent of total income. Among individual groups, urban high-educated households have the highest income per capita, receiving 7.37 per cent of total income but forming only 1.39 per cent of the total population, while rural landless households have the lowest income per capita, receiving only 5.69 per cent of total income, despite comprising 15.62 per cent of the total population. Referring back to Table 6.8, it is also noteworthy that 3.21 per cent of the total income of the urban high-educated group is in the form of government transfers (the highest percentage of any group), while the corresponding share for the rural landless group is only 0.41 per cent.

Table 6.10. Income Distribution among Household Groups

Households	Percentage of total population	Percentage of total household income
a) Rural		
Landless HH	15.62	5.69
Marginal farmer HH	6.82	3.42
Small farmer HH	13.02	8.85
Large farmer HH	5.15	6.93
Non-agricultural HH	27.07	25.89
b) Urban		
Illiterate HH	13.06	11.29
Low-educated HH	10.48	13.81
Medium-educated HH	7.25	16.75
High-educated HH	1.39	7.37
Total	100	100

Source: BBS (2001) and the Bangladesh model data base.

Chapter 7

ELIMINATING TARIFFS: MACROECONOMIC, SECTORAL AND HOUSEHOLD EFFECTS

7.1. INTRODUCTION

In the next two chapters, the Bangladesh model is used to simulate both the short and long run effects of changes in trade policy. After dealing with the issues of simulation design and the closure of the model, the present chapter focuses on the impacts of tariff reform on macroeconomic performance, sectoral output and employment levels, and income and consumption of household groups. The main concerns of this study, the impacts of tariff reform on poverty and income inequality, are the subject of the next chapter.

7.2. SIMULATION DESIGN

Bangladesh has progressively implemented tariff reform policies. Tariff structures have been simplified and tariff rates have been reduced. These reforms have put downward pressure on the tax/GDP ratio because in Bangladesh revenue collected from import duties has comprised a substantial part of total tax revenue.[1] Hence, by itself, the simulation of the effects of a complete removal of tariffs might be considered unrealistic because of a perceived risk that the removal of tariffs would lead to unsustainably large fiscal deficits. To address this problem, the present study also simulates the effects of tariff removal where the resulting loss of revenue is offset by a compensatory consumption tax. The specific simulations are as follows.[2]

Simulation 1: Existing tariffs in all sectors are eliminated completely without any compensatory taxes.

Simulation 2: Existing tariffs are eliminated completely. However, to compensate for the government's revenue loss, an endogenously determined uniform consumption tax (levied at

[1] In Bangladesh, custom duties account for about 50 per cent of total indirect tax revenue and about 25 per cent of total tax revenue (GOB, 2006). The ratio of total tax revenue to GDP ratio averaged 8.22 per cent over the period 2000-05 (see Table 2.3).

[2] In these simulations the complete removal of tariffs is confined to customs duties only.

a rate of 2.7 per cent in the short run and 2.6 per cent in the long run) is imposed to ensure that total indirect tax revenue is unchanged.

7.3. Model Closure

The list of possible exogenous variables or the standard closures has been discussed in Chapter 5. In practice, the choice of closure is governed by two considerations (Horridge, 2006). First, the choice depends on the simulation time scale needed for the economy to adjust to a new equilibrium. It may be short term or long term. The differences between short run and long run are reflected in the assumptions underlying the factor markets. For example, in a short run simulation, sectoral capital stocks are normally treated as fixed or given, because gestation lags are assumed to delay the transformation of investment into additional capital stock. In contrast, in the long run, capital is allowed to grow through investment, and is assumed to be mobile across industries. Cooper et al.(1985), in their econometric experiment found evidence that short run equilibrium is established in about two years, whereas long run equilibrium takes 10 to 20 years, which is long enough to ensure that changes in sectoral capital stocks eliminate differences in sectoral rates of return on capital. Second, the choice of closure should take into account the purposes of a particular simulation. For example, if the modeller wants to find out the aggregate welfare impacts of a trade shock, real aggregate consumption expenditure should be listed in the endogenous variable category.

In this study the model is used for both the short run and long run simulations. Although the standard closure provides a perfectly valid exogenous set for the model, following the ORANI-G type models we have adopted somewhat different closures for our short run and long run simulations. Figures 7.1 and 7.2 depict respectively the sets of assumptions underlying the short run and long run simulations.

7.3.1. Short Run Closure

In Figure 7.1, the exogenous variables are presented in rectangles whereas the endogenous variables are presented in ovals. The arrow signs indicate a plausible direction of causation between variables. The upper part of the figure depicts the supply side of the macro-economy, whereas the lower part depicts the demand side. In the short run, on the supply side, we have exogenised the real wage, *realwage*, (measured in terms of purchasing power over consumer goods and services), the capital stock, *x1cap*, and technology. Given fixed capital stocks (including land) and constant technology (i.e., zero technological change), any changes in industry output levels require changes in labour inputs. The rate of return on capital in each industry adjusts to changes in output, and changes in relative rates of return result in changes in the allocation of the given aggregate investment budget among industries (Dixon, et al. 1997). In the labour market, it is assumed that there is a perfectly elastic supply of labour at a fixed real wage rate. Thus the volume of employment will adjust according to the change in the demand for labour, with workers able to move freely between sectors of the economy in accordance with employment opportunities. Note that the given real wage is maintained by indexing the money wage rate to the consumer price index (CPI). This has been implemented by setting all of the wage shift variables (*f1lab*) as exogenous. On the demand side of the macro-economy, the major expenditure components of real aggregate absorption, namely aggregate real household consumption (*x3toth*), aggregate real fixed investment (*x2tot_i*), aggregate real government consumption (*x5tot*) and the change in aggregate real inventories (*delx6*) are held fixed. This assumption is imposed in the model by putting these variables in the exogenous list. It is implemented by first swapping *x2tot_i* with *invslack* and *x3toth* with *w3luxh* in the standard closure discussed in Chapter 5. Then, to make real government consumption exogenous and to disconnect it from household consumption, we swapped *x5tot* with *f5tot2* (the overall shift term for the ratio of government demand to real household consumption) in the standard closure. The rationale for making real aggregate absorption exogenous is that tariffs are primarily expenditure switching instruments. Tariff policy is designed to affect industrial structure, occupational employment and the balance of trade rather than the level of aggregate demand (Dixon et al. 1997).

Given the supply side determinants of real GDP and fixed aggregate real absorption, the nominal balance of trade as a proportion of nominal GDP (*delB*) is specified as an endogenous swing variable that ensures the GDP identity is maintained. Thus, any shock that leads to a GDP increase (decrease) will result in the balance of trade variable moving towards surplus (deficit).

Foreign prices of imports, number of households, land endowments and, with one exception, all tax rate variables are considered as exogenous in the short run.[3] The nominal exchange rate is fixed and serves as the numeraire, which implies that changes in the domestic price level are evaluated relative to world prices.

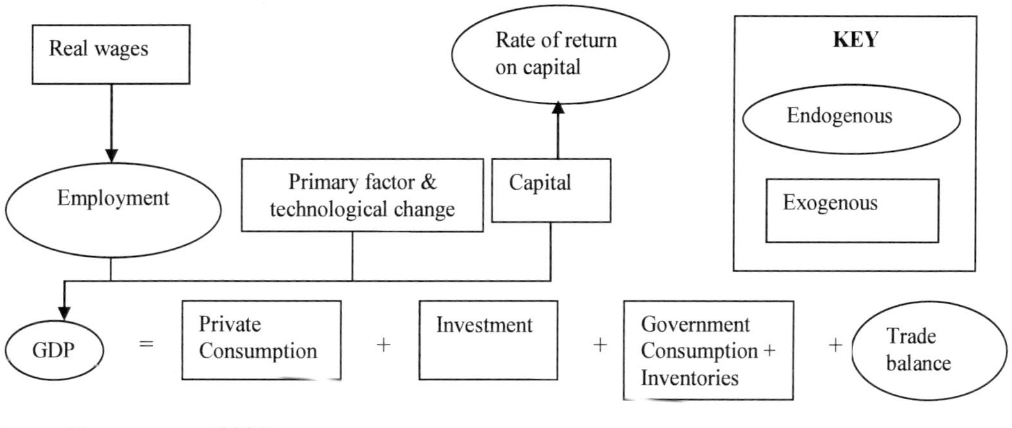

Source: Naranpanawa (2005)

Figure 7.1. The schematic representation of short run closure.

7.3.2. Long Run Closure

In contrast to the short run, it is assumed that in the long run capital stocks adjust so as to maintain fixed rates of returns (*gret*). Given the absence of any link between capital formation

[3] The exception is, f3tax_csi (percentage changes in the powers of all taxes on household consumption), which, in the case of simulation 2, has been treated as an endogenous variable.

and domestic saving, this adjustment implies an open capital market (Horridge, 2006). According to Dixon et al. (1997) a tariff reform might be expected to affect rates of return in the short run, but in the long run adjustments in the level of foreign investment will force domestic rates of return into line with foreign rates of return through changes in domestic capital formation.

In the labour market it is assumed that aggregate employment (*employ_i*) is fixed while the average real wage is determined endogenously.[4] To implement this assumption, the overall wage shifter (*f1lab_io*) has been swapped with the *employ_i* variable. Other wage shift variables (*f1lab*) remain exogenous, reflecting an assumption of fixed wage relativities, which in turn implies that firms do not substitute between labour of different types. Labour, however, is freely mobile between sectors in the economy in response to changes in labour demand.

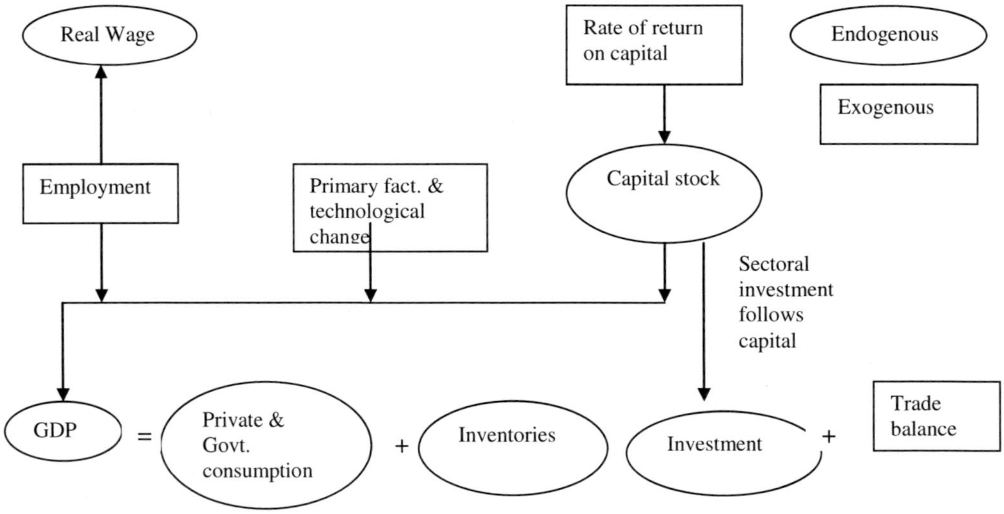

Source: Naranpanawa (2005).

Figure 7.2. The schematic representation of the long run closure.

On the demand side, it is assumed that real private consumption, real government consumption and real investment are determined endogenously, with investment following the capital stock at the sectoral level. It is also assumed that nominal household consumption follows post-tax household income, and real government consumption follows real private consumption. To implement these assumptions, f5tot2 has been swapped with *x5tot,* aggregate real government consumption, as an exogenous variable. With aggregate real absorption endogenous, the change in the nominal balance of trade as a proportion of nominal GDP (*delB*) has been treated as constant. This treatment can be defended on the grounds that, in the long run, the rest of the world might be unwilling to fund an increased trade deficit relative to GDP (Horridge, 2006). As with the short run simulation, production technology, land, foreign prices of imports and the number of households are treated as exogenous in the long run. The nominal exchange rate continues to serve as the numeraire.

---

[4] It is implicitly assumed that in the long run population, labour force participation rates and the natural rate of unemployment determine employment.

In simulation 2, for both the short run and the long run, we offset the loss in government revenue from the elimination of tariffs by imposing a uniform consumption tax, which is determined endogenously. For this purpose, we swapped a tax variable, *f3tax_csi* (percentage changes in the powers of all taxes on household consumption) with *delV0tax_csi* (the change in aggregate revenue from all indirect taxes) in the assignment of exogenous and endogenous variables. This ensures that total indirect tax revenue remains constant.

7.4. Simulation Results

In simulating the effects of a 100 per cent across the board cut in tariffs in Bangladesh, all exogenous variables were set equal to zero except changes in the power of tariffs (*t0imp*), which were set in such a way that the percentage decrease in tariff rates for each good is 100 per cent. In the following sub-sections the results of simulations 1 and 2 under short run and long run closures are presented in terms of macroeconomic effects, sectoral effects, factor market effects and household-level effects.

Table 7.1. Projected effects of a 100 per cent tariff cut in all sectors: Selected macro variables (percentage changes)

	Simulation 1		Simulation 2	
Macro Variables	Short run	Long run	Short run	Long run
Real GDP (Expenditure side)	0.70	0.82	-0.04	0.69
Aggregate Employment	1.47	0	-0.27	0
Aggregate real household consumption	0	0.57	0	-0.31
Aggregate real investment	0	1.12	0	4.33
Real Government consumption	0	0.57	0	-0.31
Consumer price index	-3.61	-1.25	0.27	0.89
Export volume index	9.72	6.35	2.82	5.07
Import volume index (CIF weights)	1.53	2.97	1.74	3.06
Poverty line (Rural areas)	-2.03	-0.55	0.26	0.56
Poverty line (Urban areas)	-1.69	-0.46	0.22	0.47
Terms of trade	-0.57	-0.30	-0.16	-0.24
Average real wage	0	3.24	0	0.74
Export price index	-0.57	-0.30	-0.16	-0.24
Real GDP at factor cost	0.65	0.72	-0.12	0.59
GDP price index (Expenditure side)	-4.03	-1.53	-0.39	0.28
Ordinary change to nominal trade balance GDP ratio (*delB*)	0.004	0	-0.001	0
Real depreciation	4.20	1.55	0.39	-0.28

7.4.1. Macroeconomic Effects

Table 7.1 presents the projected effects of the tariff cut in Bangladesh on a number of key macroeconomic variables including real GDP, aggregate employment, aggregate consumption, the consumer price index, aggregate export and import volumes, real wages, and trade balance as a fraction of GDP *(delB)*. All the variables have been presented as percentage changes except for *delB,* which is reported as an ordinary change. The first column of Table 7.1 identifies the variables; the second and third columns show the short and long run effects of the tariff cuts under simulation 1 (where there are no new taxation measures to compensate for the loss of tariff revenue); and the fourth and fifth columns show the short and long run effects under simulation 2 (where a uniform consumption tax compensates for the loss of tariff revenue).

7.4.1.1. Simulation 1: Effects of a 100 Percent Cut in Tariffs

The short run results for simulation 1 show that real GDP increases by 0.70 per cent and aggregate employment increases by 1.47 per cent, implying a small fall in average labour productivity. This outcome reflects a shift in the composition of aggregate output towards more labour-intensive industries and, at the individual industry level, the assumptions of fixed usages of capital and land, constant returns to scale and constant technology.

With the components of domestic absorption (aggregate real consumption, aggregate real investment and aggregate government spending) held constant, the growth of real GDP implies an improvement in the balance of trade in real terms. This is confirmed by the rate of growth in the volume of exports exceeding the rate of growth of the volume of imports. There is also a small positive change in the nominal balance of trade as a proportion of nominal GDP (0.004, that is 0.4 percentage points). With foreign prices of imports treated as constant (small country assumption), the increase in the import volume index of 1.53 per cent indicates an equivalent percentage increase in nominal import payments. On the other hand, a combination of a 9.72 per cent increase in the export volume index, and a 0.57 per cent fall in the export price index indicates an increase in nominal export receipts in excess of nine per cent. Applied to the database estimates, these changes in nominal imports and exports reveal a reduction of nearly eight per cent in the nominal taka value of the balance of trade deficit.

The improvement in the trade balance reflects an improvement in international competitiveness that is a reduction in domestic costs relative to foreign prices. Tariff cuts reduce domestic costs of production by lowering the domestic prices of imported inputs. They also bring down the domestic prices of imported goods and services, and the prices of locally produced, import-competing goods and services. The result is a fall in the consumer price index (CPI) of 3.61 per cent. Because of the model's assumption of a real wage rate fixed in terms of consumer purchasing power, this fall leads to a corresponding decrease in nominal wages, which in turn leads to lower costs and the expansion of employment and output in export industries. However, with less than infinitely price-elastic export demand schedules, the 9.72 per cent growth in export volumes results in export prices falling by 0.57 per cent. Given fixed world prices of imports, this means an equivalent deterioration in the terms of trade. In addition, trade liberalisation generates substantial real exchange rate depreciation. In the short run, with fixed world prices of imports, the decrease in domestic prices results in a real exchange rate depreciation of 4.20 per cent. This real depreciation provides a general measure of the improvement in international competitiveness.

The long run results for simulation 1 show that, most macroeconomic variables listed in Table 7.1 change in the same direction as in the short run.[5] They change, however, by different magnitudes. For example, the percentage growth in real GDP increases from 0.70 in

[5] The exceptions, of course, are those variables that switch from being exogenous to being endogenous, and vice versa.

the short run to 0.82 in the long run. The difference reflects differences in the assumed closure. In the long run, with no technological change and no growth in aggregate employment or land use, growth of real GDP comes from a 1.40 per cent growth in aggregate capital inputs and the gains in allocative efficiency that occur as a result of inter-industry labour mobility and the adjustment of industry capital stocks to maintain fixed rates of return.

In the long run, on the demand side, real aggregate absorption is determined endogenously. Complete tariff removal leads to an increase in aggregate real household consumption of 0.57 per cent, which can be viewed as a broad indicator of the welfare impact of tariff liberalisation. By assumption, government consumption demand also increases by 0.57 per cent, while aggregate real investment grows by 1.12 per cent. Like real GDP, the volume of imports shows faster growth (2.97 per cent) in the long run than in the short run. This reflects the long run increases recorded by household and government consumption and investment, all of which by assumption show no growth in the short run. Although the long run rate of growth in the volume of exports (6.35 per cent) is slower than its short run rate, it is still noticeably faster than the long run rate of growth in the volume of imports. These outcomes, together with a 0.30 per cent fall in export prices (and equivalent fall in the terms of trade) and a small decline in nominal GDP (as distinct from real GDP), are consistent with the imposed constraint of no change in the nominal balance of trade as a proportion of nominal GDP.

In the long run, the abolition of tariffs induces a 3.24 per cent rise in average real wages through the increased demand for labour that stems from the expansion of labour-intensive industries. The rise in real wages embodies a 1.95 per cent increase in the nominal price of labour and a 1.25 per cent fall in consumer prices. The latter also contributes through a 1.53 per cent fall in the GDP price index, to a real depreciation of 1.55 per cent, which is noticeably smaller than that recorded for the short run.[6]

Finally, in both the short run and in the long run, falls in the commodity prices of the basic need consumption bundles result in declines in the money metric poverty lines for rural and urban areas, with somewhat higher rates of decline for rural areas (Table 7.1). These changes in poverty lines will be used in the simulation of poverty profiles in Chapter 8.

7.4.1.2. Simulation 2: Effects of a 100 Percent Cut in Tariffs with a Uniform Consumption Tax

Columns 4 and 5 of Table 7.1 show the short run and long run macroeconomic results of simulation 2. These results incorporate the effects of endogenously determined consumption taxes of 2.7 per cent in the short run and 2.6 per cent in the long run, introduced to compensate for the revenue loss from the elimination of all tariffs.

It is clear that for the most part the macroeconomic impacts are less pronounced in simulation 2 than simulation 1. Table 7.1 shows that in the short run the combination of tariff cuts and a revenue-compensating consumption tax slightly reduces real GDP by 0.04 per cent and aggregate employment by 0.27 per cent, and slightly increases the consumer price index

[6] With the c.i.f. import price index constant by assumption, equation 107 of the Bangladesh model implies that the percentage real depreciation is equal to the negative of the percentage change in the GDP price index (expenditure side). As shown in Table 7.1, this is indeed the case for simulation 2, but in simulation1there are small discrepancies in both the short run and the long run. A similar outcome occurs in the PEKGEM model, (an ORANI-G model of South Africa, available at http://www.copsmodels.com/oranig.htm), when it is used to simulate the effects of a uniform cut in tariffs.

by 0.27 per cent. Because of indexation, money wages also rise by 0.27 per cent to leave the real wage unchanged in terms of consumer purchasing power. However, this increase in money wages results in a much smaller improvement in international competitiveness than in simulation 1 in the short run, where money wages fall by 3.61 per cent. As measured by the extent of the real depreciation, international competitiveness increases by only 0.39 per cent, compared with the increase of 4.20 per cent in simulation 1 in the short run.

The much smaller improvement in competitiveness in simulation 2 results in a slower growth in the volume of exports (2.82 per cent) and a faster growth in the volume of imports (1.74 per cent). Given the substantial absolute magnitude of the database balance of trade deficit, the result is an increase in the balance of trade deficit measured in constant prices. With aggregate real absorption fixed by assumption, this increase accounts on the demand side for the small fall in real GDP.

The increase in the balance of trade deficit in constant prices is accompanied by an increase in the nominal trade deficit, which also reflects the impact of a 0.16 per cent decline in export prices. (The decline is smaller than the 0.57 per cent decline in the short run version of simulation 1 because of the slower growth in the volume of exports.) The upshot is that, allowing for some decline in nominal GDP (reflecting declines in both real GDP and the GDP price index), the change in the nominal trade balance as a proportion of nominal GDP is slightly negative.

In contrast to the short run version of simulation 2, the long run version shows real GDP increasing by 0.69 per cent. Because of the assumed closure, aggregate employment and rates of return on capital are unchanged, so the increase in real GDP results from a 1.14 per cent growth in the capital stock and improvements in allocative efficiency.

The increase in GDP in the long run might be expected to increase aggregate real household consumption. The imposition of a compensatory consumption tax, however, increases consumer prices directly and thereby reduces the purchasing power of disposable income and hence real consumption. In simulation 2 in the long run, aggregate real household consumption falls by 0.31 per cent. (This decline can be broadly interpreted as a very small aggregate welfare loss.) Real government consumption also falls by 0.31 per cent, as by assumption it follows real household consumption, while aggregate real investment increases by 4.33 per cent.

The long run version of simulation 2 is the only one of the four sets of simulation results reported in Table 7.1 that contains an increase the GDP price index and thus, with a given foreign price level, it is the only one of the four sets of results that does not show a real depreciation. Instead there is a real appreciation of 0.28 per cent. The difference between this real appreciation and the 1.55 per cent real depreciation in the long run version of simulation 1 is consistent with the relatively slow growth in the volume of exports (5.07 per cent compared with 6.35 per cent in the long run version of simulation 1) and the marginally faster growth in the volume of imports (3.06 per cent compared with 2.97 per cent in the long run version of simulation 1). Taken together with a 0.24 per cent fall in export prices and constant import prices, the growth rates for the volume of exports and the volume of imports yield an expansion in the size of the nominal trade deficit that is proportional to the expansion of nominal GDP, thereby satisfying the imposed constraint of no change in the nominal trade balance as a proportion of nominal GDP.

Finally, as with simulation 1, the elimination of tariffs reductions with revenue-compensatory consumption taxes have changed the monetary poverty lines for both rural and urban areas in both the short and long runs. However in this case, because of induced increases in consumer prices, the poverty lines have risen, not fallen, in both rural and urban areas, with larger rises in rural areas.

7.4.2. Sectoral Effects

7.4.2.1. Simulation 1: Effects of a 100 Percent Tariff Cut in Tariffs

A reduction in tariff rates makes imports cheaper, which leads to an increased inflow of imports and reduced demand for domestic goods. As a result, the output of import competing sectors falls. The extent of the fall depends on the import-elasticity of substitution, the import intensity of the sectors and the base line tariffs. Appendix Table D 7.1 presents the pre-liberalisation situation in Bangladesh in 2000 as an aid to explaining the simulated industry results presented in Table 7.2. The first column of Appendix Table D 7.1 lists commodities. The second column shows the share of imports in the local market sales of each commodity (measured as the ratio of the total imports of the commodity to the total value of its domestic production and imports). The third column shows the base period values of the nominal tariff rates, which were obtained from the I-O table 2000 for Bangladesh. The fourth column shows the share of output that was exported. The fifth column lists the industries that produce the commodities. The sixth column roughly classifies the industries as import-competing industries (IC), export-oriented industries (E), export-related industries (ER) and non-traded goods industries. Classification depends on import penetration and export share. Import competing industries are identified as those that sell in domestic markets where the level of import penetration is relatively high. Export-oriented industries are those for which exports constitute a substantial part of total output. Export-related industries do not export directly, but sell a large part of their output to export industries. The remaining industries are identified as non-traded goods industries.

According to Appendix Table D 7.1, in Bangladesh in 2000, the ready-made garments (RMG) and knitting industries were the most export-oriented, with more than 75 per cent of their outputs sold abroad. In addition, the jute and jute fabrication industries sold almost 20 per cent and 56 per cent respectively of their outputs in international markets. Other industries with significant export propensities included tea cultivation, shrimp farming and leather products. In contrast, the chemical products, machinery and cement industries were clearly import-competing industries, facing import shares of nearly 80 per cent, 71 per cent and 67 per cent respectively. Glass products, petroleum refining and transport equipment were also prominent import-competing industries. Export-related industries include the baling industry, which sold the major part of its output to the jute fabrication industry, and the cloth milling industry, which sold the major part of its output to the RMG industry.

Table 7.2. Projected effects of a 100 per cent tariff cut: output and employment by industry (percentage changes)

		Simulation 1				Simulation 2			
		Short run		Long run		Short run		Long run	
Industry	Trade cate-gory	Output	Employment	Output	Employment	Output	Employment	Output	Employment
Paddy	NT	-0.057	-0.096	0.117	-0.38	-0.382	-0.642	-0.41	-0.825
Wheat	IC	-0.225	-0.375	0.213	-0.262	-0.87	-1.443	-0.81	-1.272
Othergrain	NT	-0.201	-0.445	0.365	-0.293	-0.473	-1.044	-0.815	-1.485
JuteCultiv	E	2.278	3.397	-0.261	-0.683	0.097	0.143	-0.675	-1.023
SugcaneCulti	NT	-0.856	-1.836	-1.02	-1.931	-1.262	-2.695	-1.698	-2.523
PotatoCulti	NT	-0.033	-0.08	0.138	-0.624	-0.135	-0.326	-0.218	-0.815
VegCulti	IC	0.333	0.746	-0.92	-1.837	-0.665	-1.47	-1.149	-1.89
PulseCulti	NT	-0.051	-0.121	0.177	-0.572	-0.201	-0.482	0.117	-0.404
OilseedCulti	IC	-0.512	-0.934	-1.969	-2.859	-1.135	-2.06	-2.209	-2.962
FruitCulti	IC	-1.28	-3.786	-1.799	-3.184	-1.531	-4.505	-2.219	-3.427
CottonCulti	IC	0.694	1.955	0.503	-0.258	-0.423	-1.167	-0.06	-0.687
TobaccoCulti	IC	-0.245	-0.494	-0.575	-1.342	-0.979	-1.965	-1.495	-2.225
TeaCulti	E	2.161	4.671	0.48	-0.122	0.252	0.534	-0.069	-0.564
SpiceCulti	IC	-2.301	-5.104	-3.541	-4.99	-2.829	-6.235	-4.008	-5.325
OthcropCulti	NT	0.031	0.07	-0.201	-0.995	-0.484	-1.1	-0.211	-0.778
LivstockRear	NT	0.054	0.125	0.588	-0.05	-0.264	-0.609	1.673	1.505
PoultryRear	NT	-0.187	-0.447	0.313	-0.404	-0.41	-0.975	-0.702	-1.398
ShrimFarming	E	2.683	6.111	2.113	1.819	0.679	1.508	1.421	1.208
Fishing	NT	-0.211	-0.557	0.458	-0.287	-0.29	-0.765	-0.447	-1.144
Forestry	NT	-0.088	-0.26	0.703	-0.038	-0.261	-0.766	2.269	2.227
RiceMilling	NT	-0.057	-0.274	0.041	-1.232	-0.315	-1.494	-0.554	-1.431
GrainMilling	IC	-0.286	-1.466	0.291	-1.01	-0.361	-1.844	-0.42	-1.317
FishProcess	E	0.565	3.261	0.172	-1.151	-0.374	-2.065	-0.928	-1.836
OilIndustry	IC	-0.499	-2.319	-2.65	-3.884	-1.024	-4.674	-3.248	-4.099

		Simulation 1				Simulation 2			
		Short run		Long run		Short run		Long run	
Industry	Trade cate-gory	Output	Employment	Output	Employment	Output	Employment	Output	Employment
SweetenerInd	IC	-0.841	-1.003	-0.996	-1.255	-1.22	-1.454	-1.606	-1.784
TeaProduct	IC	-0.612	-1.017	-0.145	-0.788	-0.61	-1.02	-0.77	-1.213
SaltRefining	IC	-0.011	-0.017	0.513	-0.006	-0.422	-0.621	0.182	-0.177
FoodProcess	IC	-1.051	-2.233	-1.432	-2.28	-1.461	-3.09	-2.087	-2.67
TannFinish	ER	1.516	4.959	1.265	0.153	0.294	0.935	1.648	0.873
LeatherInd	E	1.739	5.242	1.501	0.43	0.34	0.997	1.963	1.216
Baling	ER	7.198	21.699	-0.595	-1.591	1.091	2.95	-0.942	-1.63
JuteFabricat	E	4.927	5.62	-0.515	-0.703	0.743	0.843	-0.721	-0.851
YarnIndustry	IC	0.982	1.385	0.821	0.354	-0.961	-1.344	-0.188	-0.509
ClothMill	ER	2.727	5.348	3.074	2.284	0.422	0.809	1.874	1.333
HandloomClot	NT	-0.375	-0.497	0.253	-0.141	-0.372	-0.493	-0.646	-0.918
DyeingBlech	NT	-0.222	-0.36	0.294	-0.325	-0.404	-0.655	-0.784	-1.209
RMG	E	4.853	8.128	5.37	4.72	0.924	1.509	3.453	3.01
Knitting	E	5.41	9.093	8.809	8.137	1.52	2.492	7.532	7.072
ToiletrieMfg	E	2.448	5.828	10.56	9.555	0.855	1.993	8.612	7.926
CigarettInd	NT	0.108	0.807	0.691	-0.709	0.177	1.333	-0.03	-0.994
BidiIndustry	NT	0.01	0.035	0.458	-0.689	0.042	0.147	-0.117	-0.908
SawPlane	NT	0.075	0.18	0.266	-0.669	-0.324	-0.769	-0.326	-0.97
Furniturind	NT	0.456	1.093	0.56	-0.378	-0.255	-0.606	-0.188	-0.834
PaperInd	IC	-0.64	-2.206	-2.46	-3.579	-1.39	-4.702	-3.242	-4.012
PrintPub	NT	0.432	0.699	-0.17	-0.781	-0.611	-0.983	-0.517	-0.939
PharmaMfg	IC	0.315	0.728	0.512	-0.402	-0.195	-0.447	0.206	-0.426
FertiliseInd	IC	0.649	2.852	3.469	2.193	-0.006	-0.024	0.934	0.07
BasiChemical	IC	0.356	0.776	-0.884	-1.742	-0.752	-1.616	-1.163	-1.757
PetroleumRef	IC	-2.805	-12.506	-7.013	-8.205	-3.823	-16.451	-7.511	-8.334
EarthwareInd	IC	0.05	0.223	-0.775	-2.014	-0.78	-3.404	-1.67	-2.522

Table 7.2. (Continued)

		Simulation 1				Simulation 2			
		Short run		Long run		Short run		Long run	
Industry	Trade category	Output	Employment	Output	Employment	Output	Employment	Output	Employment
ChemicalInd	IC	-0.366	-1.164	-0.279	-1.381	-0.448	-1.423	-0.214	-0.979
GlassInd	IC	-1.996	-3.888	-4.202	-4.966	-3.088	-5.952	-4.282	-4.811
ClayInd	NT	0.116	0.269	0.994	0.07	-0.002	-0.004	3.642	2.984
CementMfg	IC	-2.198	-6.282	-4.938	-5.953	-2.816	-7.955	-3.399	-4.115
BasicMetaMfg	IC	-0.363	-0.723	-0.526	-1.326	-0.993	-1.968	0.529	-0.032
MetalMfg	IC	-0.635	-1.285	-0.59	-1.403	-1.041	-2.096	-0.872	-1.434
MachineEquip	IC	-0.729	-1.083	-3.497	-4.007	-2.828	-4.158	-2.994	-3.35
TranspoEquip	IC	-0.205	-0.792	-0.936	-2.117	-0.931	-3.522	-0.425	-1.249
MiscellaInd	IC	1.554	4.145	5.049	4.01	0.109	0.283	2.269	1.567
Urbanbuild	NT	0.183	0.51	1.152	0.112	0.084	0.234	4.009	3.267
RuralBuild	NT	0.06	0.198	1.068	-0.062	-0.028	-0.092	4.046	3.239
PPlantBuild	NT	-0.011	-0.052	1.155	-0.124	0.003	0.015	4.398	3.482
RuRoadBuild	NT	-0.015	-0.044	1.124	0.059	-0.014	-0.04	4.369	3.607
PoRoadBuild	NT	0.406	0.692	1.114	0.446	0.094	0.16	3.599	3.123
CaDyothBuild	NT	-0.013	-0.022	1.115	0.416	-0.001	-0.001	4.348	3.847
ElectWatGene	NT	0.292	1.294	0.764	-0.486	-0.158	-0.689	-0.218	-1.077
GasExtDist	NT	-0.145	-0.503	0.405	-0.745	-0.45	-1.551	-1.045	-1.831
MinQuarring	NT	-0.164	-0.376	-0.048	-0.817	-0.531	-1.215	0.254	-0.218
WholeTrade	NT	0.622	1.433	1.024	0.111	0.051	0.117	0.607	-0.024
RetailTrade	NT	0.534	1.235	1.01	0.094	0.048	0.111	0.553	-0.08
AirTransport	NT	1.435	2.231	1.104	0.533	0.291	0.45	0.691	0.296
WatTransport	E	2.981	11.627	1.274	0.099	0.747	2.739	0.916	0.103
LanTransport	NT	0.579	1.789	1.073	-0.019	0.055	0.167	0.524	-0.23
RaiTransport	NT	0.629	0.765	1.016	0.729	0.051	0.062	0.571	0.373

		Simulation 1				Simulation 2			
		Short run		Long run		Short run		Long run	
Industry	**Trade cate-gory**	**Output**	**Employment**	**Output**	**Employment**	**Output**	**Employment**	**Output**	**Employment**
OthTransport	NT	1.905	3.717	0.707	-0.067	0.056	0.108	0.165	-0.369
HousingServ	NT	0.027	0.341	0.505	-0.981	-0.123	-1.519	-0.455	-1.476
HealthServ	NT	0.116	0.244	0.551	-0.295	-0.237	-0.497	0.913	0.324
EducatServ	NT	-0.013	-0.015	0.196	-0.062	-0.403	-0.48	-0.795	-0.972
PubAdDefence	E	5.325	6.605	1.221	0.922	1.456	1.79	0.779	0.573
BanInsRestat	NT	0.713	1.128	0.569	-0.021	-0.156	-0.245	0.305	-0.103
ProfesioServ	NT	0.893	2.359	0.667	-0.329	-0.097	-0.253	0.465	-0.225
HotelRest	NT	0.258	0.493	0.479	-0.288	-0.227	-0.433	-0.587	-1.114
Entertainmen	NT	0.057	0.109	0.238	-0.527	-0.421	-0.8	-0.877	-1.402
Communicatio	NT	1.866	3.655	0.506	-0.269	-0.032	-0.062	-0.456	-0.989
OthServices	NT	0.201	0.243	0.096	-0.184	-0.512	-0.619	-0.521	-0.714
InfotechEcom	NT	1.427	2.783	0.551	-0.225	-0.044	-0.085	-0.004	-0.539

The projected short run effects of simulation 1 on industry real output and employment are shown in the third and fourth columns of Table 7.2. Given the short run macroeconomic results for simulation 1, it is not surprising to find that the elimination of tariffs induces expansion in all export-oriented industries. Within the agricultural sector, the three export-oriented industries of jute cultivation, tea cultivation, and shrimp farming, experience the largest percentage growth in terms of both output and employment. In the manufacturing sector, the export-oriented industries of ready-made garments, knitting, jute fabrication, toiletries manufacturing and leather products, and the export-related industries of, baling and cloth milling are the best performers. In the service sector the only industries assessed as export-oriented are water transport, which exported some 12 per cent of its output in 2000, and public administration and defence, which exported about 25 per cent of its output in the same year, most notably, in the form of UN peace-keeping services. (See Appendix Table D 7.1.) These two industries have the highest rates of increase of output and employment in the service sector.

Using the Fan decomposition method, the percentage change of output of the commodity (or commodities) produced by each industry in Table 7.2 can be viewed as the sum of three demand-side effects:

(1) the local market effect, which is measured by the percentage change in the total domestic absorption of the corresponding commodity, irrespective of whether it is locally produced or imported, weighted by the ratio of domestic absorption to output;
(2) the domestic share (or import replacement) effect, which is measured by the negative of the percentage change in imports, weighted by the ratio of imports to output; and
(3) the export effect, which is measured by the percentage change in exports, weighted by the ratio of exports to output.[1]

These three contributions to changes in output are reported for simulation 1 in Appendix Table D 7.2 for both the short run and long run. For example, for the ready-made garments industry in the short run, its output increases by 4.85 per cent (Table 7.2). This is entirely the result of an increase in exports of ready-made garment products by 6.47 per cent (simulation output). Since exports account for about 76 per cent of the total sales of this industry, their contribution to the change in output is 4.92 percentage points (6.47*0.76). In this case, the local market effect and the domestic share (import replacement) effect make small negative contributions to output growth (Appendix Table D 7.2). Likewise in the knitting industry, the 5.41 per cent increase in output is entirely the result of export expansion. With an export share of 0.75 per cent and an increase in exports of 7.31 per cent, the latter contributes 5.48 percentage points (0.75*7.31) to output growth, with the local market and the domestic share (import replacement) effects again making small negative contributions.

On the supply side, a decomposition analysis of average output prices (*p1tot*) using AnalyseGE (Horridge et al. 2003) indicates that decreases in the prices of material inputs (*p1*) and reductions in labour costs (*p1lab*) act as stimuli to the expansion of export-oriented

[1]Fan decomposition was named after MingTai Fan of the Institute of Quantitative and Technical Economics, Beijing (Wittwer and Anderson, 2001).

industries.[2] For example, cheaper fish imports drive the expansion of the fish processing industry, which imports 89 per cent of its fish inputs. Other industries, especially service industries such as, land, air, water and rail transport which use imported petroleum products, and transport equipment intensively, also experience substantial reductions in their input costs.

Notwithstanding cost reductions, the elimination of tariffs leads to reduced output in the great majority of import-competing industries in the short run. The largest percentage declines are in petroleum refining (2.81 per cent), spice cultivation (2.30 per cent), cement manufacturing (2.20 per cent), the glass industry (2.00 per cent), fruit cultivation (1.28 per cent) and food processing (1.05 per cent), Fan decomposition (Appendix Table D 7.2) indicates that in all six industries substitution from domestic goods to cheaper import goods is wholly or mainly responsible for the contraction in their outputs.

These are industries that were protected by relatively high tariff rates on competing imports (Appendix Table D 7.1) and, with the exception of cement manufacturing, they sell mainly to households. Decomposing the change in total imports by commodity and by usage (Appendix Table D 7.3) it is seen that households account for most of the changes in imports that compete with local output. For fruit cultivation, 92 per cent of the increase in competing imports is absorbed by household consumption while for spice cultivation, food processing, petroleum refining and the glass product industry the corresponding figures are 84 per cent, 91 per cent, 60 per cent and 99 per cent respectively.

The various non-traded building and construction industries contained in the model display only very minor short run variations in output and employment, some positive and some negative. The nature of these industries is such that they neither have access to export markets nor face import competition in their domestic markets. Thus, despite the elimination of tariffs reducing operating costs, variations in output can reflect only local market effects, which are basically constrained by the short run closure assumption of a constant level of real aggregate fixed investment. Trade liberalisation brings increases in output and employment in the short run in all but one of the service industries. The exception is education services, where output and employment fall almost imperceptibly, mainly as a result of a fall in demand from the household sector, the principal customer of this industry.

As already observed, the two fastest growing service industries are public administration and defence (where output increased by 5.33 per cent and employment by 6.61 per cent) and water transport (where output increases by 2.98 per cent and employment by 11.63 per cent). Fan decomposition indicates that export growth accounts for 97 per cent of output growth in public administration and defence and 86 per cent in water transport, with local market growth accounting for the remainder in each case. In addition, contrary to their non-traded classifications, the air transport, banking, insurance and real estate, professional services, entertainment, communications, and information technology services industries experience expansions in output that reflect in varying degrees export growth, and in some cases domestic share (import replacement) effects.

On the other hand, positive local market effects account entirely for output growth in the rail and land transport industries, retail and wholesale trades, and warehousing. These effects

[2] AnalyseGE is a software tool of GEMPACK that provides a modeller with 'point and click' access to the model equations, data and simulation results. By movingeasily between these information sources, a modeller can explain the main mechanisms underlying simulation results.

arise at least in part from their inter-industry linkages. Trade liberalisation does not affect the demand for their products directly, as initially they are unprotected, as indeed are all service industries. However, tariff elimination, which results in decreased domestic prices and increased local demand for other products, also leads to increased activity in these service industries.

The projected long run effects of simulation 1 on industry output and employment are shown in the fifth and sixth columns of Table 7.2. In agriculture, the three export-oriented industries of jute cultivation, tea cultivation, and shrimp farming fail to match their short run performances. Jute cultivation experiences falls in both output and employment as a result of increasing costs of production, particularly labour costs. Output in tea cultivation increases by only 0.48 per cent compared with 2.16 per cent in the short run, and employment falls. Only shrimp farming continues to achieve rates of increase in output and employment in excess of two per cent, but these are still less than the corresponding short run rates.

In contrast, in the manufacturing sector, the export-oriented industries of ready-made garments, knitting and toiletries manufacturing exceed their short run rates of growth of output as inter-industry capital mobility compensates for the impact of increased labour costs. In addition, output growth rates jump sharply in the fertiliser and insecticide industry and the miscellaneous industry as a result of faster export growth. However, reflecting less favourable export outcomes, output grows more slowly in the leather products industry and declines absolutely in jute fabrication. Less favourable export outcomes also contribute to slower output growth in the long run in public administration and defence and in water transport, although within the service sector these industries continue to achieve the highest growth rates.

In the long run, as in the short run, the elimination of tariffs results in lower output in the majority of import-competing industries. The largest percentage declines in production occur in petroleum refining (7.01 per cent), cement manufacturing (4.94 per cent), the glass industry (4.20 per cent), spice cultivation (3.54 per cent) and machinery and equipment (3.50 per cent). Employment also declines in these industries. As in the short run, Fan decomposition reveals that for each of these industries, a substitution from domestic to cheaper imported products is wholly or mainly responsible for the contraction in its output (Appendix Table D 7.2).

In contrast to the short run when aggregate real investment is held constant, in the long run it increases endogenously by 1.12 per cent. This expansion imparts a demand-side stimulus through local market effects to the various building and construction industries. As a result, what is essentially the stagnation of these industries in the short run is replaced by their long run achievement of rates of growth of output somewhat in excess of one per cent. Employment also increases in most of these industries. It is not only aggregate real investment that increases endogenously in the long run. So too do the other components of domestic absorption, specifically aggregate real household consumption and real government consumption. The growth in domestic absorption, together with the assumption that the nominal trade balance is a fixed proportion of nominal GDP, ensures that long run rates of growth of output in the great majority of non-traded industries exceed corresponding short run rates. In addition to building and construction, this majority includes paddy, pulses and fishing, the handloom cloth, cigarette and bidi industries, the clay industry, electricity and water, housing services, hotels and restaurants, and entertainment.

7.4.2.2. Simulation 2: Effects of a 100 Percent Cut in Tariffs with a Uniform Consumption Tax

Columns 7 to 10 of Table 7.2 show the industry output and employment effects of complete tariff removal accompanied by a 2.7 per cent consumption tax in the short run and a 2.6 per cent consumption tax in the long run.

In the short run, as we have seen, the introduction of the consumption tax leads to the consumer price index increasing slightly. Because of indexation, money wages also rise, whereas in simulation 1 they fall substantially in the short run. This difference in wage behaviour leads, at the macroeconomic level, to imports growing more rapidly and exports more slowly in simulation 2 than in simulation 1. At the sectoral level, it leads to the output and employment performances of import-competing and export industries being generally weaker in simulation 2 than in simulation 1.

Nearly all of the import-competing industries that experience a short run fall in output in simulation 1 experience a larger short run fall in simulation 2; and among the much smaller number of import-competing industries that experience a short run increase in output in simulation 1, all but one experience a short run fall in simulation 2. The biggest falls in output in simulation 2 are in the same industries as in simulation1: petroleum refining (3.82 per cent), spice cultivation (2.83 per cent), cement manufacturing (2.82 per cent), the glass industry (3.09 per cent), fruit cultivation (1.53 per cent) and food processing (1.46 per cent). A Fan decomposition analysis (Appendix Table D 7.4) reveals that substitution from domestic goods to cheaper import goods is wholly or mainly responsible for the contraction in the outputs of the commodities produced by these industries.

Compared with simulation 1, all export-oriented and export-related industries show much lower short run rates growth of output in simulation 2. For example, under a uniform consumption tax, the ready-made garments, knitting, toiletries manufacturing, jute and jute products, and shrimp farming industries have output growth rates of only 0.92 per cent, 1.52 per cent, 0.86 per cent, 0.10 per cent, 0.74 per cent and 0.68 per cent respectively. The main reason is increased production costs relative to simulation 1. In particular, a decomposition analysis by AnalyseGE reveals that increases in nominal wages exert upward pressure on the basic prices of these export commodities.

Although higher labour costs also occur in the various non-traded building and construction industries, the short run output and employment behaviour of these industries in simulation 2 is essentially the same as short run output and employment behaviour in simulation1; that is, it shows no significant variations from the base period. The reason is also the same as in simulation 1, specifically the closure assumption of a constant level of real aggregate fixed investment. As in most manufacturing and agricultural industries, growth in the service sector is hampered by the consumption tax. The simulation 2 short run rates of growth of output in service industries are generally lower than their simulation 1 counterparts, with more than half the lower rates having negative values. The largest differences are in public administration and defence (1.46 per cent compared with 5.33 per cent) and water transport (0.75 per cent compared with 2.98 per cent), the differences reflecting much smaller improvements in export competitiveness in simulation 2. Nevertheless, these two industries rank among the fastest growing industries in the economy in simulation 2 (as they do in simulation 1), thanks to still substantial, albeit diminished, export growth effects (Appendix Table D 7.4).

Among the other service industries, air transport, banking, insurance and real estate, professional services, entertainment, communications, and information technology services also receive minor benefits from diminished export growth effects (and in some cases from import replacement effects). However, in all cases except air transport, negative local market effects outweigh these benefits, with consequent small falls in output. Output also falls in housing services, health, education, and hotels and restaurants. On the other hand, output still increases through positive local market effects in the rail and land transport industries, retail and wholesale trades, and warehousing, although short run growth rates are tiny in comparison with those in simulation 1.

In the long run, as in the short run, the output and employment performances of export and import-competing industries are for the most part weaker in simulation 2 than in simulation 1. Among export industries, the largest output growth rates are in toiletries manufacturing (8.61 per cent), knitting (7.53 per cent), ready-made garments (3.45 per cent), the leather industry (1.96 per cent) and shrimp farming (1.42 per cent). Although these rates are all much larger than the corresponding short run rates for simulation 2, only that of the leather industry exceeds its long run counterpart in simulation 1.

Similarly, although in simulation 2 there are fewer absolute declines in output among import-competing industries in the long run than in the short run, the number of long run declines in simulation 2 exceeds those in simulation 1. The biggest long run falls in output in simulation 2 are in petroleum refining (7.51 per cent), the glass industry (4.28 per cent), spice cultivation (4.01 per cent), cement manufacturing (3.40 per cent), the edible and non-edible oils industry (3.25 per cent) and the paper industry (3.24 per cent). With the exception of the fall in cement output, all these declines are greater than their counterparts in simulation 1.

Among the industries showing the most rapid long run rates of output growth in simulation 2 are those involved in building and construction and the related clay industry (bricks, tiles, etc.). The growth rates for power plant building (4.40 per cent), rural road building (4.37 per cent), canal, dyke and other building (4.35 per cent), rural building (4.05 per cent), urban building (4.01 per cent), the clay industry (3.64 per cent) and port, road and railway building (3.60 per cent) rank behind only the growth rates for the two fastest growing export industries, toiletries manufacturing and knitting. Their impressive rates of expansion relative to their short run performances reflect, of course, the difference between the endogenously determined 4.33 per cent long run increase in aggregate real investment and the short run assumption of a constant level of aggregate real investment (Table 7.1). Scarcely less striking is the extent to which these long rates of expansion exceed their corresponding long run rates of expansion in simulation 1, where the endogenously determined increase in aggregate real investment is only 1.12 per cent.

Other industries producing non-traded products experience mixed fortunes in terms of output growth. In simulation 2, in line with the difference in real GDP growth rates, service industries with strong inter-industry linkages, such as rail and land transport industries, wholesale trade, warehousing, banking insurance and real estate, and professional services, perform better in the long run than in the short run, although not as well as they do in simulation 1 in the long run. On the other hand, the fishing, rice milling, cigarette manufacturing, gas, housing services, hotel and restaurants, entertainment and communications industries, for which the household sector is the major source of sales, perform worse in the long run than in the short run in simulation 2, and also worse than in the long run in simulation 1. These differences are broadly consistent with differences in aggregate real household consumption behaviour.

7.4.3. Effects on Factor Prices and Employment by Occupational Group

Table 7.3 shows the effects that the elimination of tariffs, both by itself and accompanied by an endogenously determined revenue-compensating consumption tax, has on average nominal factor prices in both the short run and the long run.

Table 7.3. Percentage changes in nominal factor prices

Variable	Simulation 1		Simulation 2	
	Short run	Long run	Short run	Long run
Price of labour	-3.61	1.96	0.27	1.63
Rental price of capital	-1.24	-1.30	-0.77	-0.62
Rental price of land	-3.53	0.99	-1.43	0.67

In the short run in simulation 1, all three nominal factor prices fall in the context of an overall deflation involving a 4.03 per cent decline in the GDP price index (see Table 7.1). The largest proportionate change in factor prices is the 3.61 per cent fall in the average price of labour, which by assumption is indexed to the consumer price index. The next largest is the 3.53 per cent fall in the average rental price of land and the smallest is the 1.24 per cent fall in the average rental price of capital. These figures indicate a fall in the price of labour services relative to the price of capital services and, to a lesser extent, the price of land services. At the aggregate level, this change in relative factor prices reflects the interaction of an increase in aggregate employment with fixed inputs of capital and land.

In the long run in simulation 1, the average nominal price of labour increases by 1.96 per cent, the average nominal rental price of land increases by 0.99 per cent, and the average nominal rental price of capital falls by 1.30 per cent, all in the context of a 1.53 per cent fall in the GDP price index. Given that in the long run both aggregate employment and land use are assumed constant, while the aggregate capital stock grows through investment, it is not surprising to find that the prices of both labour and land services increase relative to the price of capital services; that is, there is a fall in the relative price of capital.

Turning to simulation 2, in the short run in the context of a 0.39 per cent fall in the GDP price index, the nominal price of labour increases by 0.27 per cent (again, the same as the increase in the CPI to which it is indexed). On the other hand, the nominal rental price of capital falls by 0.77 per cent and the nominal rental price of land falls by 1.43 per cent. Thus the price of labour services increases relative to both the prices of capital and land services, an outcome opposite to that found in the short run in simulation 1. In this case, at the aggregate level, the change in relative factor prices in favour of labour reflects the interaction of a decrease in aggregate employment and fixed inputs of capital and land.

Finally, in the long run in simulation 2, where the GDP price index displays an increase of 0.28 per cent, the nominal price of labour increases by 1.63 per cent, the nominal rental price of land increases by 0.67 per cent, and the nominal rental price of capital falls by 0.62 per cent. These prices changes are similar in direction to their counterparts in the long run in simulation 1, but their magnitudes are absolutely smaller and reveal a different pattern of relative price changes. In particular, they show that the prices of both labour and land services increase relative to the price of capital services or, as in the long run in simulation 1, there is a fall in the relative price of capital. As in that case, the present result is consistent with the expansion of the capital stock in the context of constant aggregate employment and land usage.

Table 7.4 shows the effects of the elimination of tariffs on employment in each of the four major occupational groups. In the short run in simulation 1, all groups record positive employment growth. At 2.53 per cent, the female low-skilled group has easily the highest rate of increase, thanks to the rapid expansion of the export-oriented ready-made garment and knitting industries.

Table 7.4. Employment by occupational group (percentage changes)

Occupational group	Simulation 1		Simulation 2	
	Short run	Long run	Short run	Long run
Male low-skilled	1.18	-0.16	-0.37	-0.05
Male high-skilled	1.81	0.02	-0.13	-0.08
Female low-skilled	2.53	0.99	0.01	0.66
Female high-skilled	1.09	0.14	-0.26	-0.31

In the long run in simulation 1, where aggregate employment is constant by assumption, the rates of increase of employment for all four occupational groups fall sharply. The female low-skilled rate of increase is still the highest at 0.99 per cent, but the male and female high-skilled rates are not far above zero, and the rate for the largest group, the male low-skilled category, is now negative. The reason for the decline in male low-skilled employment is that most industries that experience substantial contractions in employment as cheaper capital is substituted for labour are industries that in the base year depended heavily on male low-skilled labour.

In the short run in simulation 2, aggregate employment declines slightly. The decline is primarily a reflection of a fall in employment of male low-skilled workers, but employment also declines for both the male and female high-skilled groups. Only the female low-skilled group records an increase (albeit a tiny one), which is again attributable to expansion in employment in the export-oriented ready-made garment and knitting industries. This expansion becomes larger in the long run in simulation 2, raising the rate of increase of employment in the female low-skilled group to 0.66 per cent. However, with aggregate employment constant, employment again falls in each of the three other occupational groups.

7.4.4. Effects on Household Incomes

Variations in factor remuneration affect the incomes of household groups according to their sources of income. Changes in household disposable (post-tax) income for various scenarios are summarised in Table 7.5. It shows that in the short run under simulation 1, nominal disposable income falls for all household groups. The most substantial decline is experienced by the rural landless household group, whose nominal income falls by 2.26 per cent, while for marginal farmers, small farmers and non-agricultural households, the changes in income are -1.94 per cent, -1.85 per cent, and -1.84 per cent respectively. Large farmer households experience the smallest decrease in their nominal income (-1.51 per cent). Urban household groups also experience declines in their nominal incomes. As with the rural groups, richer households in urban areas – such as medium-educated and high-educated households – experience smaller percentage declines than other urban groups.

Table 7.5. Nominal and real disposable income of households (percentage changes)

	Simulation 1				Simulation 2			
	Short run		Long run		Short run		Long run	
	Nominal	Real	Nominal	Real	Nominal	Real	Nominal	Real
Rural								
Landless HH	-2.26	1.35	1.84	3.05	-0.09	-0.38	1.61	0.73
Marginal farmer HH	-1.94	1.65	1.14	2.33	-0.38	-0.69	1.16	0.26
Small farmer HH	-1.85	1.74	1.05	2.24	-0.40	-0.71	1.09	0.19
Large farmer HH	-1.51	2.05	0.42	1.60	-0.68	-1.02	0.69	-0.23
Non-agricultural HH	-1.84	1.78	1.13	2.37	-0.36	-0.64	1.13	0.26
Urban								
Illiterate	-1.89	1.74	1.24	2.51	-0.35	-0.59	1.22	0.34
Low-educated HH	-1.75	1.87	0.85	2.13	-0.50	-0.74	0.97	0.07
Medium-educated HH	-1.52	2.08	0.55	1.85	-0.60	-0.83	0.76	-0.16
High-educated HH	-1.53	2.11	0.39	1.71	-0.66	-0.87	0.69	-0.24

For each household group, the change in real disposable income has been calculated by adjusting nominal disposable income for the movement in the consumer price index corresponding to that group. The results show that despite all groups experiencing short run declines in nominal income in simulation 1, their corresponding real incomes increase because of proportionately greater falls in consumer prices. These falls do not vary greatly among groups (ranging from 3.56 per cent to 3.64 per cent). As a result, there are no differences between the ranking of declines in nominal income from lowest to highest and the ranking of increases in real income from highest to lowest among groups in rural areas, and only minor differences between the corresponding rankings for urban areas and for rural and urban areas taken together.

In the long run under simulation 1, the percentage changes in income, in both nominal and real terms, are positive for all household groups in both rural and urban areas. However, the types of households that are less favourably affected by the tariff removal in the short run tend to be more favourably affected in the long run, and vice versa.[3] Thus, with respect to nominal income changes, the three household groups that fare worst in the short run, namely the rural landless, marginal farmers and the urban illiterate, fare best in the long run; while the three groups that fare best in the short run, namely large farmers, urban medium-educated households and high-educated households, fare worst in the long run.

These tendencies mainly reflect inter-group differences in the relative importance of various types of income and differences in the behaviour of relative factor prices between the

[3] Agrawal (1989) obtained the same sort of results in her study of the effects of tariff reform on the distribution of income among 40 Australian household groups.

short run and the long run. Referring back to the base year data in Table 6.8, the groups that rely most heavily on labour for their livelihoods are the rural landless, marginal farmers and the urban illiterate, with labour providing respectively 93 per cent, 57 per cent and 61 per cent of their incomes. Hence, given that over the long run, relative factor prices move in favour of labour, these groups fare best in terms of nominal income changes over the long run.

On the other hand, large farmers, urban medium-educated households and high-educated households rely most heavily on capital, which provides respectively 60 per cent, 72 per cent and 75 per cent of their incomes in the base year. Accordingly, given that in the short run relative factor prices move in favour of capital, it is they who fare best in the short run. In simulation 2, all household groups experience smaller short-run proportionate reductions in nominal income than they experience in simulation 1. Unlike simulation 1, however, increases in consumer prices mean that they also all experience short run reductions in real income. In addition, there are some striking changes in rankings. In terms of both nominal and real changes, the rural landless and urban illiterate groups now suffer the smallest short run percentage losses in income, while large farmer households, urban medium-educated households and high-educated households suffer the largest. Given the initial differences in the principal sources of income of the various household groups, the explanation for these ranking reversals appear to lie largely in the different short run pattern of factor price behaviour, in particular a movement in favour of labour.

In the long run in simulation 2, the increases in nominal income for all household groups are broadly similar to the long run results for simulation 1. The changes in real income, however, are substantially smaller and actually negative for large farmer households and urban medium-educated and high-educated households. All groups for whom labour is the major source of income achieve increases in total real income within the context of the 0.74 per cent increase in average real wages across the economy as a whole. On the other hand, the declines in the total real incomes of large farmer households and urban medium-educated and high-educated households reflect a decline in the average rental price of capital services relative to consumer prices.

7.4.5. Household Consumption Effects

Table 7.6 shows the long run changes in aggregate consumption by household group. In the long run in simulation 1, nominal consumption declines for all household groups. When the results are expressed in real terms, however, they change significantly. Falls in consumer price levels are generally larger for urban groups than for rural groups, but each group experiences a fall sufficiently large to more than offset the decline in the nominal value of its consumption. Abstracting from intra-group distributional issues, the resulting increases in real consumption for all household groups imply that the elimination of tariffs has a welfare-enhancing impact on each household group in the long run. Among the groups, urban high-educated households, urban medium-educated households and rural non-agricultural households have the largest percentage increases in real consumption; rural landless households, marginal farmer households and urban illiterate households have the smallest.

There are significant differences in the consumption results when they reflect the effects of a revenue-compensating consumption tax of 2.6 per cent as well as tariff liberalisation. For each household group in the long run in simulation 2, nominal consumption increases while real consumption declines, as the consumer price level for each group increases faster than its nominal consumption expenditure. Thus, again abstracting from intra-group distributional issues, the elimination of tariffs and their replacement with a compensating consumption tax have welfare-reducing impacts on all household groups in the long run. In this case, in what is essentially a reversal of the ranking in simulation 1, the least disadvantaged groups are rural landless households, urban illiterate households and marginal farmer households, while the most disadvantaged are urban high-educated households, urban medium-educated households and rural non-agricultural households.[4]

Table 7.6. Household consumption effects in the long run (percentage changes)

	Nominal consumption		Real consumption	
Household group	Simulation 1	Simulation 2	Simulation 1	Simulation 2
Rural				
Landless HH	-0.88	0.69	0.34	-0.19
Marginal farmer HH	-0.82	0.68	0.38	-0.22
Small farmer HH	-0.72	0.62	0.48	-0.29
Large farmer HH	-0.67	0.60	0.52	-0.32
Non-agricultural HH	-0.56	0.50	0.69	-0.37
Urban				
Illiterate	-0.87	0.67	0.41	-0.21
Low-educated HH	-0.76	0.62	0.52	-0.27
Medium-educated HH	-0.58	0.54	0.73	-0.38
High-educated HH	-0.34	0.41	1.00	-0.51

7.5. Sensitivity Analysis

As stated in Chapter 6, the lack of econometric estimates of the elasticity values required for calibrating the model led to elasticity values being based on estimates from similar studies conducted for Bangladesh or elsewhere. This section seeks to assess how sensitive our simulation results described above are to some of these elasticity values by comparing the results with those obtained using different elasticity values. The analysis is confined to the Armington elasticities between imported goods and domestic goods and the substitution elasticities between primary factor parameters. These elasticities were changed by +50 per cent and -50 per cent from the base elasticities.[5]

7.5.1. Armington Elasticities

The short run results of the sensitivity analysis in Table 7.7 indicate that the magnitudes of the Armington elasticities have only a minor influence on the macroeconomic outcomes of

[4] The fact that household group changes in consumption are not equi-proportionate with the corresponding changes in household group incomes reflects the treatment of the household group consumption shifter, f3tot (h), as endogenous in the Bangladesh model. This treatment follows that of PEKGEM (an ORANI-G model of South Africa, available at http://www.copsmodels.com/oranig.htm)

[5] Base Armington elasticity values are provided in Appendix Table C 6.3. The base elasticity of substitution between primary factors is set at 0.5 for all industries.

the tariff liberalisation shocks. Under simulation 1, 50 per cent higher elasticities of substitution between domestic and foreign products lead to slightly higher growth in real GDP, aggregate employment, the import volume index and the export volume index. The percentage declines in the consumer price index, real exchange rate and the terms of trade are also slightly higher. However, the ordinary change in the nominal trade balance/ nominal GDP ratio is unaffected. In the case of the rural and urban poverty lines, higher substitution elasticities bring slightly larger reductions in their values.

On the other hand, 50 per cent lower Armington elasticity values, which imply less scope for substitution between domestic and imported commodities, have the opposite effects, except in the case of the ordinary change in the nominal trade balance/ nominal GDP ratio, which remains unaffected.

In the case of simulation 2, increasing the values of the Armington elasticities by 50 per cent, leads in the short run to slightly smaller falls in real GDP and aggregate employment, and slightly larger increases in export and import volumes. As expected, when the elasticity values are reduced by 50 per cent, the opposite effects are observed. The ordinary change in the nominal trade balance/ nominal GDP ratio remains, however, insensitive to the changes of elasticity values.

In the long run, in both simulations 1 and 2, changes of the Armington elasticities do not affect the growth of real GDP (as they do in the short run) and have relatively small effects on the simulated changes in other macroeconomic variables (Table 7.8).

Figures 7.3 and 7.4 show for simulation 1 the short run and the long run effects of different Armington elasticity values on the real incomes of different household groups. We would expect larger positive income effects of tariff elimination in cases of higher elasticity values, as trade liberalisation initiates a more efficient allocation of resources over sectors, which in turn leads to higher real incomes. The short run results are consistent with this expectation. For all household groups, complete tariff removal with higher Armington elasticities leads to larger positive income effects and lower elasticities lead to smaller

Table 7.7. Macroeconomic effects of tariff liberalisation for different values of Armington elasticities in the short run (percentage changes)

	Base case		50 % increase		50 % decrease	
Index	Simulation 1	Simulation 2	Simulation 1	Simulation 2	Simulation 1	Simulation 2
Real GDP	0.70	-0.04	0.73	-0.006	0.67	-0.08
Aggregate employment	1.47	-0.27	1.51	-0.24	1.42	-0.32
Consumer price index	-3.61	0.27	-3.81	-0.04	-3.32	0.69
Import volume index	1.53	1.74	1.89	2.22	1.22	1.27
Export volume index	9.72	2.82	10.51	3.87	8.70	1.46
Balance of trade/GDP	0.004	-0.001	0.004	-0.001	0.004	-0.001
Terms of trade	-0.57	-0.16	-0.61	-0.22	-0.51	-0.08
Real depreciation	4.20	0.39	4.41	0.71	3.89	-0.03
Rural poverty line	-2.03	0.26	-2.16	0.07	-1.87	0.51
Urban poverty line	-1.69	0.22	-1.82	0.06	-1.58	0.43

Table 7.8. Macroeconomic effects of tariff liberalisation for different values of Armington elasticities in the long run (percentage changes)

Index	Base case		50 % increase		50 % decrease	
	Simulation 1	Simulation 2	Simulation 1	Simulation 2	Simulation 1	Simulation 2
Real GDP	0.82	0.69	0.82	0.69	0.82	0.69
Average real wage	3.24	0.74	3.26	0.77	3.23	0.70
Consumer price index	-1.25	0.89	-1.36	0.76	-1.12	1.04
Import volume index	2.97	3.06	3.91	4.01	2.15	2.24
Export volume index	6.35	5.07	8.10	6.84	4.53	3.23
Real aggregate consumption	0.57	-0.31	0.62	-0.26	0.52	-0.37
Real aggregate investment	1.12	4.35	1.39	4.09	1.39	4.61
Terms of trade	-0.30	-0.24	-0.21	-0.33	-0.21	-0.15
Real depreciation	1.55	-0.28	1.41	-0.13	1.41	-0.43
Rural poverty line	-0.55	0.56	-0.61	0.48	-0.48	0.64
Urban poverty line	-0.46	0.47	-0.52	0.41	-0.41	0.54

positive income effects. In some cases, however, the differences in magnitudes are difficult to discern in Figure 7.3. These seemingly negligible impacts reflect the interaction of very marginal shifts of factors of production and small variations in the marginal yields of endowments of factors of production among sectors.

In the long run, however, when the Armington elasticities are raised by 50 per cent from their base values, the income effects are positive but less than the base results, whereas for a 50 per cent reduction in elasticities the income effects are positive and mostly greater than the base results (Figure 7.4).[6]

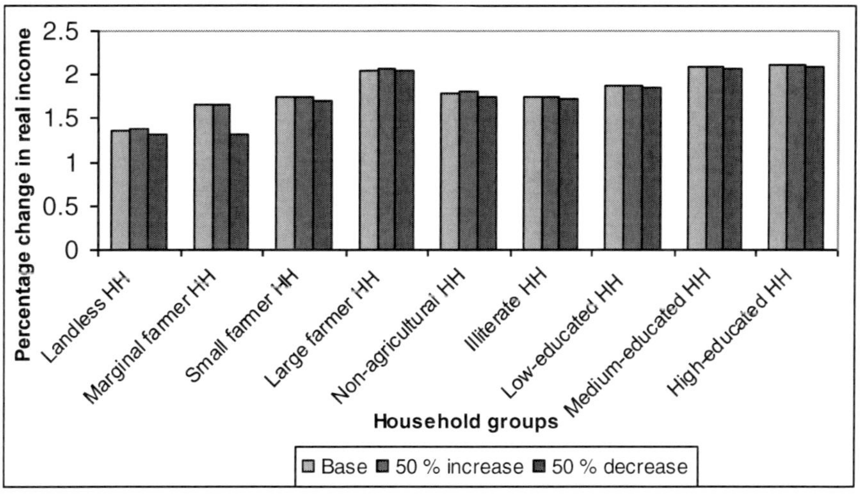

Figure 7.3. Short run effects of complete removal of tariffs on real incomes of household groups for different values of Armington elasticities (Simulation 1).

[6] For simplicity and because of time constraints sensitivity analysis of the effects of changes in Armingtonelasticities on household incomes has not been undertaken for simulation 2. However, the analysis can be made available upon request.

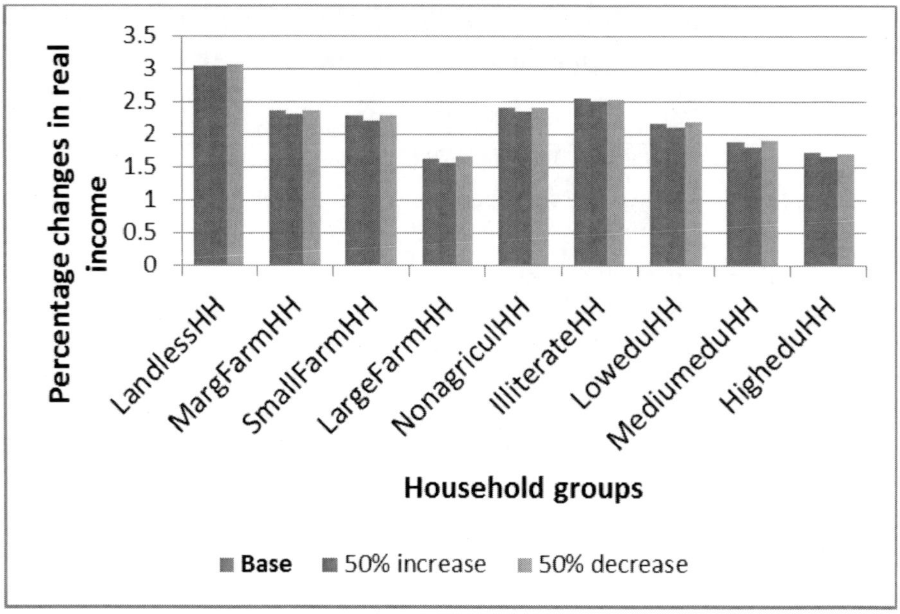

Figure 7.4. Long run effects of complete removal of tariffs on real incomes of household groups for different values of Armington elasticities (Simulation 1)

The general conclusion to be drawn from this sensitivity analysis is that the simulation results are relatively insensitive to changes in Armington elasticities. For nearly all macroeconomic indicators, the qualitative effects of tariff shocks are invariant with respect to the size of elasticities and the quantitative effects of variations in the elasticities are mostly very small. In other words different elasticity values do not result in substantially different effects on household income.

7.5.2. Primary Factor Substitution Elasticities

The short and long run simulation macroeconomic results for different values of primary factor substitution elasticities are reported in Tables 7.9 and 7.10 respectively. In the short run in simulation 1, a 50 per cent increase in the elasticities of substitution between primary factors leads to slightly larger increases in real GDP, aggregate employment and the volume of imports. The most striking change is in the much faster growth of the volume of exports. Greater factor substitutability means that the labour intensive manufacturing industries such as the ready-made garments and knitting sectors experience greater production effects, which increase export growth. The improved export situation in turn improves the balance of trade situation slightly. In the case of the poverty lines, the increase in factor substitution elasticities results in marginally smaller declines.

Table 7.9. Macroeconomic effects of tariff liberalisation for different values of primary factor elasticities in the short run (percentage changes)

Index	Base case		50 % increase		50 % decrease	
	Simulation 1	Simulation 2	Simulation 1	Simulation 2	Simulation 1	Simulation 2
Real GDP	0.70	-0.04	0.97	-0.09	0.41	0.02
Aggregate employment	1.47	-0.27	2.09	-0.42	0.79	-0.13
Consumer price index	-3.61	0.27	-3.49	0.57	-3.92	-0.33
Import volume index	1.53	1.74	1.80	1.95	1.30	1.53
Export volume index	9.72	2.82	12.73	2.47	6.24	2.84
Balance of trade/GDP	0.004	-0.001	0.006	-0.001	0.000	-0.001
Terms of trade	-0.57	-0.16	-0.72	-0.14	-0.38	-0.17
Real depreciation	4.20	0.39	4.10	0.09	4.49	0.99
Rural poverty line	-2.03	0.26	-1.97	0.45	-2.23	-0.12
Urban poverty line	-1.69	0.22	-1.66	0.38	-1.88	-0.09

A 50 per cent decrease in factor substitution elasticities in the short run in simulation 1 has essentially the opposite effects, including slightly smaller increases in real GDP, aggregate employment and the volume of imports, and a much slower growth in the volume of exports.

For simulation 2, where complete tariff removal is accompanied by a compensatory consumption tax, raising factor substitution elasticities by 50 per cent from the base elasticities produces slightly greater negative impacts on real GDP and aggregate employment in the short run. Higher factor substitution elasticities also lead to slightly reduced growth in the volume of exports and slightly larger increases in the consumer price index and poverty lines. However, the ordinary change in the nominal trade balance/ nominal GDP ratio is unaffected.

A lowering of factor substitution elasticities by 50 per cent has the opposite effects on all variables in Table 7.9, except the ordinary change in the nominal trade balance/ nominal GDP ratio, which is again unaffected. Overall, for simulation 2, changes in factor elasticities produced slightly different values in the short run, but for all indicators qualitative effects are invariant.

Table 7.10 shows that in the long run under simulation 1, the higher values for factor substitution elasticities lead to real GDP expanding at a marginally greater rate than in the base case, and a marginally smaller increase in real wages. The effects on the export volume index and the import volume index are also minor, but there is somewhat more substantial growth in real aggregate investment. The poverty lines experience insignificantly larger declines in their values. Directions of change are generally reversed when factor substitution elasticities are reduced. Qualitatively similar outcomes emerge under simulation 2.

Table 7.10. Macroeconomic effects of tariff liberalisation for different values of primary factor elasticities in the long run (percentage changes)

	Base case		50 % increase		50 % decrease	
Index	Simulation 1	Simulation 2	Simulation 1	Simulation 2	Simulation 1	Simulation 2
Real GDP	0.82	0.69	1.10	0.89	0.49	0.44
Average real wage	3.24	0.74	3.10	0.66	3.48	0.85
Consumer price index	-1.25	0.89	-1.25	0.89	-1.27	0.87
Import volume index	2.97	3.06	3.30	3.33	2.72	2.89
Export volume index	6.35	5.07	6.58	5.25	6.06	4.84
Real aggregate consumption	0.57	-0.31	0.57	-0.31	0.58	-0.30
Real aggregate investment	1.12	4.35	2.42	5.30	-0.47	3.14
Terms of trade	-0.30	-0.24	-0.31	-0.25	-0.28	-0.23
Real depreciation	1.55	-0.28	1.51	-0.30	1.62	-0.24
Rural poverty line	-0.55	0.56	-0.56	0.55	-0.54	0.54
Urban poverty line	-0.46	0.47	-0.48	0.47	-0.46	0.45

With respect to the effects on real incomes of household groups, it is expected that the higher (lower) the elasticities of substitution between factors, the more likely it is that the reduction of tariffs will increase (decrease) real income. In simulation 1 in both the short run and the long run, the real incomes of household groups increase more with higher levels of elasticity of substitution and less with lower levels, except for the incomes of the marginal farmer household group in the short and long runs and the landless household group in the long run (Figures 7.5 & 7.6). A 50 per cent reduction in elasticities leads to the marginal farmer group's real income increasing, both in the short run and the long run, by more than it does in the base case). Also in the long run, a 50 per cent increase in elasticities leads to the landless household group's real income increasing by less than in the base case, and a 50 per cent decrease in elasticities leads to it increasing by more than in the base case.[7]

In general, the sensitivity analysis suggests that the model results are slightly more sensitive to variations in factor substitution elasticities than to variations in Armington elasticities, both in the short run and the long run. However, for both sets of elasticities, the great majority of the qualitative impacts of policy shocks on various macroeconomic indicators and household groups' real incomes are invariant to the size of the elasticity and the quantitative effects of variations in the elasticities are mostly very small.

[7] As with the Armington elasticities, sensitivity analysis of the effects of changes in factor substitution elasticities on household incomes has not been provided for simulation 2. However, the analysis can be made available upon request.

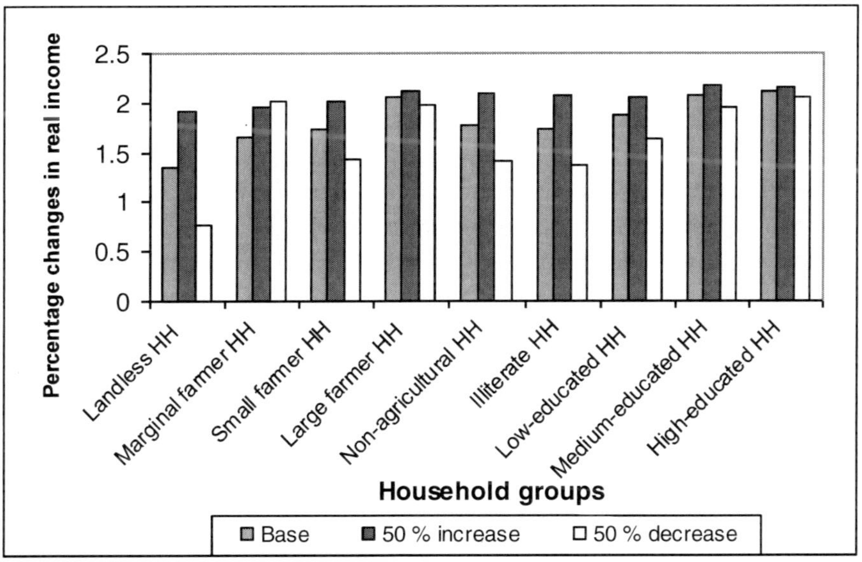

Figure 7.5. Short run effects of complete removal of tariffs on real incomes of household groups for different values of primary factor elasticities (percentage changes) (Simulation 1).

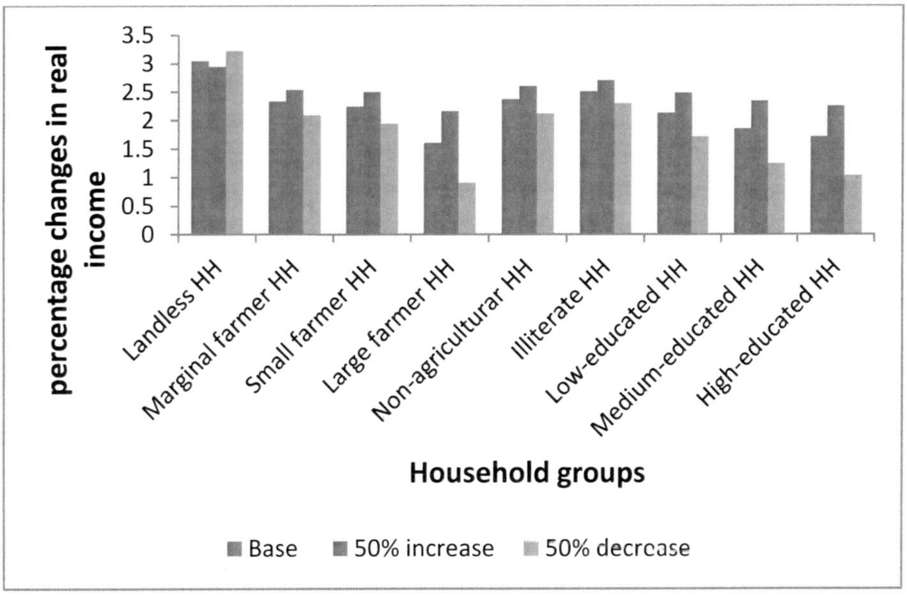

Figure 7.6. Long run effects of complete tariff reduction on real incomes of household groups for different values of primary factor elasticities (percentage changes) (Simulation 1).

CONCLUSION

This chapter has used the Bangladesh model to explore the effects that the elimination of all import tariffs would have on macroeconomic performance, sectoral output and employment levels, and income and consumption of household groups. Two sets of simulations have been undertaken. In simulation 1, tariffs are eliminated without any revenue-compensating changes in other taxes. In simulation 2, tariffs are eliminated, but an endogenously determined consumption tax (levied at a rate of 2.7 per cent in the short run and 2.6 per cent in the long run) is imposed to ensure that total indirect tax revenue is unchanged.

At the macro level, the results of simulation 1 show that, both in the short run and long run, the removal of tariffs leads to real depreciation and hence increases in the volume of exports and real GDP. It also increases aggregate employment in the short run and aggregate real household consumption in the long run. At the sectoral level, output and employment decline in most import-competing industries in both the short run and long run, with the largest falls tending to occur in those industries initially protected by relatively high tariff rates. On the other hand, all export-oriented and export-related industries expand in the short run, and most do so (some at faster rates) over the long run. Among the four occupational categories, female low-skilled employment experiences the biggest percentage increases in both the short run and the long run, because of the rapid growth of the export-oriented ready-made garment and knitting industries.

In simulation 2, the elimination of tariffs coupled with a compensatory consumption tax results in the short run negative growth in real GDP and aggregate employment. In contrast, in the long run, growth in the physical capital stock and capital mobility contribute to an increase in real GDP, although aggregate real household consumption falls slightly. In the short run, real depreciation is much less than in simulation 1 and in the long run there is a small real appreciation. Consequently, both in the short run and the long run, the volume of exports increase less than the figure in simulation 1.

At the sectoral level, the output and employment performances of export and import-competing industries are for the most part weaker in simulation 2 than in simulation 1. The same observation applies to many of the industries producing non-traded products, the most notable exception being the building and construction (and construction-related) group of industries in the long run. In addition, in simulation 2, female low-skilled employment is the only occupational category to experience an increase in employment in the short run and the only category to experience an increase in the long run. Both increases are smaller than the corresponding increases in simulation 1.

With respect to household groups, in simulation 1 real income increases for all groups in both the short run and the long run, with a majority of groups experiencing larger increases in the long run, and all groups experiencing higher levels of real consumption in the long run. In contrast, in simulation 2 real income decreases for all groups in the short run. In the long run a majority of groups achieve gains in real income, but these are smaller than their long run gains in simulation 1, and the remaining groups continue to suffer declines in real income. Despite these differences, all groups experience small long run declines in real consumption.[8]

Sensitivity analysis for key parameters suggests that the simulation results of tariff shocks, with or without accompanying consumption tax, are robust. The qualitative effects on various macroeconomic indicators and on real income are invariant under different elasticity values. In addition, the quantitative effects are relatively insensitive.

---

[8] See footnote above.

Chapter 8

ELIMINATING TARIFFS: EFFECTS ON POVERTY AND INEQUALITY

8.1. INTRODUCTION

The main objective of this chapter is to analyse the effects of the removal of tariffs on poverty and income distribution within the Bangladesh model. As discussed in Chapter 4, in the CGE modelling context there are several approaches to simulating variations in poverty and income distribution. This study adopts a non-parametric representative household approach in which, for each household group, an empirically estimated income distribution function shifts proportionately with the mean income of the group, and in which changes in monetary poverty lines are endogenously determined.

Section 8.2 briefly describes the Kernel density estimation method used to specify income distribution within each household group. Section 8.3 examines various measures of poverty. Section 8.4 discusses the incorporation of poverty analysis into the CGE model. Section 8.5 presents poverty profiles for the base case and simulations 1 and 2. Section 8.6 describes various measures of inequality, and provides estimates of them for the base year and simulations 1 and 2. Section 8.7 performs a sensitivity analysis, and section 8.8 summarises the main findings of the chapter.

8.2. THE NON-PARAMETRIC APPROACH TO INCOME DISTRIBUTION: ESTIMATION WITH THE KERNEL METHOD

In estimating the distribution of income in the *parametric* approach, it is assumed that the income distribution follows a known particular functional form, but with unknown parameters. In this case, modellers need to estimate the unknown parameters of that functional form. In contrast, in the *non-parametric* approach one can estimate the distribution function directly from the given data without any prior assumption about the form of the distribution. There are several ways this can be done. The particular non-parametric method used in this study is kernel density estimation.

Consider sample data organised in the form of a histogram of the relative distribution of households by size of income. The kernel method transforms the histogram into an estimated probability density function by smoothing over the boundaries of the histogram through the use of a kernel weight function (Rosenblatt, 1956; Deaton, 1997; Boccanfuso et al. 2002; Duclos and Araar, 2006). More precisely, suppose x is a random variable with a continuous probability density function $f(x)$. The kernel estimation of the density $f(x)$ or the smoothed histogram can be defined as follows:

$$f(x) = \frac{1}{N}\sum_{i=1}^{N} \frac{1}{h} K\left(\frac{x - x_i}{h}\right)$$

where K is the Kernel function, which is generally symmetric, and unimodal, and h is the bandwidth or smoothing parameter (Boccanfuso et al. 2003).

In the use of this estimator, each observation will provide a 'bump' to the density estimation of $f(x)$ whose shape and width in turn depends upon the shape of K and the size of h respectively. By summing all the 'bumps' the distribution of all data points is obtained. In implementing the kernel estimator, the selection of Kernel and bandwidth is important as these two affect the structure of the distribution. For example, the smaller the value of the bandwidth, the less smooth will be the density estimates. In contrast, if the bandwidth is too large, the estimated density function will be too smooth. In selecting the kernel, the DAD software used in this study adopts the Gaussian kernel type, which possesses nice continuity and differentiability properties (Duclos and Araar, 2006).[1]

8.3. Poverty Measures

In the literature, there are a large number of poverty measures. Among them the most widely used measure is the head count index (H), which is simply the proportion of the total population that falls below the poverty line. It is obtained by dividing the number of people living below the poverty line (q) by the total population (n).

Formally,

$$H = \frac{q}{n}$$

Once the poverty line is known, this index is very simple to compute, but it has major shortcomings. First, while the head count index captures the incidence of poverty among the population, it does not reflect the intensity or depth of poverty suffered by the poor (Chotikapanich, 1994). It cannot capture the extent of the income shortfall of the people who live below the poverty line, thus it violates Sen's (1976) monotonicity axiom for a suitable measure of poverty: namely, other things being equal, a reduction in income of a person below the poverty line must increase the poverty measure. Second, the measure is completely insensitive to the distribution of income among the poor. Thus it also violates Sen's (1976)

[1] DAD or Distributional analysis software (Duclos, Araar and Fortin, 2000) was developed specifically for poverty and inequality estimation. It is freely distributed and available at www.mimap.ecn.ulaval.ca.

transfer axiom, which states that, other things being equal, a pure transfer of income from a person below the poverty line to anyone who is richer must increase the poverty measure.

The second most commonly used measure of poverty is the poverty gap index (PG), which measures the extent to which individuals on average fall below the poverty line. (Individuals above the poverty line are treated as having a zero shortfall.). This index is commonly formulated as:

$$PG = \frac{1}{n}\sum_{i=1}^{q}\left[\frac{z-y_i}{z}\right]$$

where z is the poverty line, q is the number of poor people, n is the total population and y_i is the income of the *i-th* poor individual.

The above index is related to head count index (H) by the following form:

$$PG = I^{*}.H$$

where I is the income gap ratio defined as:

$$I = \frac{z-y_m}{z};\ y_m = \text{mean income of the poor.}$$

In capturing the average depth as well as the incidence of poverty, the poverty gap index satisfies the monotonicity axiom, but not the transfer axiom. The index is insensitive to income inequality among the poor. In other words, it does not capture differences in the severity of poverty.

Sen (1976) proposed a measure that takes into account the severity of poverty, this measure does not satisfy the property of additive decomposability, which requires that aggregate poverty be equal to the population-weighted sum of poverty levels in the various sub-groups of the society.[2] Foster, Greer and Thorbecke (1984) overcame this problem with a generalised measure of poverty that (1) was additively decomposable with population-share weights, (2) satisfied the basic properties proposed by Sen (1976), and (3) was justified by a relative deprivation concept of poverty (Foster et al. 1984). Known as the FGT measure, it consists of a class of additively decomposable poverty measures that simultaneously considers the proportion of the population below the poverty line, the average income (consumption) of the poor and the distribution of income (consumption) among the poor. The mathematical expression is:

$$P_\alpha = \frac{1}{n}\sum_{i=1}^{q}\left(\frac{z-y_i}{z}\right)^{\alpha}$$

[2] Sen's (1976) poverty measure is defined below.

where n is the total population, q is the number of poor people, z is the poverty line, y_i is the income of the *i-th* poor individual and α is a parameter that acts as a measure of poverty aversion. The parameter α can take any positive value or zero. When parameter $\alpha = 0$, P_0 is simply the head count index. When $\alpha = 1$, P_α becomes the poverty gap index. When $\alpha = 2$, P_α measures the severity of poverty, with the weight assigned to a poor individual being greater the further the individual's income is below the poverty line.

In this study, to evaluate the impacts of trade policy simulations on the poverty profiles of the various representative household groups, we use the Foster-Greer-Thorbecke (FGT) approach. However, to test the robustness of the FGT poverty indices, several other poverty indices are also computed.

Watts Index

Watts (1968) proposed a long-overlooked distribution-sensitive poverty measure, which satisfies all the axioms essential for any good measure of poverty (Zheng, 1993).

The index is defined as:

$$W = \frac{1}{N}\sum_{i=1}^{q}\left[\ln(z) - \ln(y_i)\right]$$

where N is the total population, z is the poverty line and y_i is the income of the *i-th* poor individual.

Sen Index

Sen (1976) proposed a poverty measure that was designed to overcome the limitations of the head count index and the poverty gap index by incorporating inequality amongst the poor. Sen's measure of poverty index is:

$$P_s = P_0\left[1 - (1-\gamma_p)\frac{\mu_p}{z}\right]$$

Where P_0 is the head count index, μ_p is the mean income of the poor, and γ_p is the Gini coefficient of inequality among the poor. If inequality among the poor is zero, P_s reduces to the poverty gap measure P_1, whereas if all but one of the poor has nothing, $Ps = P_0$, and the measure becomes the head count ratio (Deaton, 1997).

S-Gini Index

The failure of Sen's poverty measures to satisfy some transfer-sensitivity axioms prompted Kakwani (1980) to develop a generalisation of Sen's poverty index, called the S-Gini poverty index. This measure is expressed as a composite function of the proportion of the population below the poverty line $(F(Z))$, and the normalised Gini welfare indices defined for the poor.

Following Barrett and Donald (2009), the S-Gini poverty index can be written as:

$$P(\partial, z) = F(z) - \frac{1}{z}\partial(\partial - 1)\int_0^1 (1-p)^{\partial - 2} G(pF(z))dp$$

where $1 < \partial < \infty$, ∂ is the inequality aversion parameter which determines the social weight attached to different points in the distribution, z is the poverty line, and $\boldsymbol{p}$ is the income rank of person. For the value of $\partial = 2$, the resulting poverty index is analogous to the standard Gini index of inequality (Duclos and Araar, 2006).

8.4. Incorporating Poverty Analysis into the CGE Model

To estimate the effects of the tariff shock on poverty in each household group, it is first necessary to estimate the effects on the initial income vector for each household group. This is done by adjusting the base year per capita income vector for each household group (obtained from the Bangladesh Household Income and Expenditure Survey 2000) by the post-shock percentage change in the nominal post-tax income of the corresponding household group in the CGE model.[3] Following Decaluwé et al. (1999), this procedure implies that when a policy shock changes the mean income of a household group, its intra-group distribution will shift in the same proportion. In other words, in the absence of information about how the increase or decrease in the total income of the group is distributed among its individual households, it is assumed that the income of each household within the group changes by the same percentage as the mean income of the group, leaving the relative distribution of income unchanged.

The computation of poverty indices requires, of course, a poverty line. This study employs two BBS estimates of poverty lines for the year 2000, one for rural areas and one for urban areas. Their construction involved first the estimation of the cost, at reference year (2000) prices, of a fixed food bundle providing minimal nutritional requirements of 2,122 kilo calorie (kcal.) per day per person. An additional 40 per cent allowance was then made for income needed to satisfy non-food basic needs. The resulting estimates of the poverty lines for 2000 are reported in Hossain et al. (2005) in US dollars, specifically-US \$146 (per person/per year) for rural areas and US \$167 (per person/per year) for urban areas. We converted these figures to domestic currency at the 2000 exchange rate of US \$1= TK 52.14.

[3] Here per capita income vector is defined as the total income of each household within the group divided by the number of members of that household.

Thus, the monetary poverty line for rural areas is TK. 7612.73 and that for urban areas is TK. 8707.71. In order to obtain post-shock poverty indices, these figures were adjusted by the model's simulated percentage changes in monetary (nominal) poverty lines (Table 7.1).

Poverty indices are calculated with the DAD software in combination with Excel. In calculating poverty indices, it is necessary to first organise the data into an ASCII file containing information on sample weights, initial household income and after-simulation household income. This ASCII file is then imported using DAD's data import wizard.

8.5. Estimation of Poverty Indices

8.5.1. Base Year Poverty Profiles

The base case scenario indicates that the incidence of poverty, as measured by the head count index (P_0), is higher in rural areas than in urban areas (Table 8.1). In rural areas, 49.20 per cent of the population is poor, while for urban areas this figure is only 32.56 per cent. In terms of the poverty gap (P_1) index and the squared poverty gap (severity of poverty) index (P_2), poverty is also higher in rural areas than in urban areas.

Within rural areas, the landless household group has the highest proportion of the poor (71.85 per cent), followed by the marginal farmer group (60.66 per cent) and the small farmer household (45.46 per cent). The same rankings are observed for both the poverty gap (P_1) and squared poverty gap (P_2) indices. The landless household group has the highest values of P_1 and P_2 (21.63 per cent and 8.45 per cent respectively); the marginal farmer household group has the second highest values (15.96 and 5.70 per cent respectively); and the small farmer household group the third highest values (10.30 per cent and 3.35 per cent respectively).

In urban areas, the illiterate household group has the highest incidence of poverty (60.11 per cent), with the low-educated household group (24.34 per cent) following a long way behind. Illiterate households also experience the greatest poverty gap and the greatest poverty severity in urban areas, with P_1 and P_2 values of 17.44 per cent and 6.77 per cent respectively. The low-educated household group has the next highest P_1 and P_2 values of 5.32 per cent and 1.61 per cent respectively, but as in the case of P_0, they are far below the corresponding values for the illiterate household group.

The high incidence of income poverty among the rural landless, marginal farmer households and urban illiterate can be explained by the fact that these household groups receive income mainly from labour income and especially from unskilled labour income (Tables 6.8 and 6.9 of Chapter 6). Households in the rural landless group depend heavily for their livelihoods on selling labour in both agricultural and non-agricultural labour markets. The seasonal nature of agricultural employment and limited opportunities for non-farm employment cause the great majority of the group to suffer from chronic or transitory food insecurity (Hossain et al. 2005). In urban areas the illiterate household group is mainly involved in petty trade activities or service activities such as push-carts, rickshaw driving, and shoe cleaning. Most of this group is likely to have migrated from rural areas where they were mostly landless, without other assets, and unable to earn a livelihood.

Table 8.1. Base year estimates of FGT poverty indices (in percentages)

Household groups*	Head count ratio (P_0)	Poverty gap (P_1)	Squared poverty gap (P_2)
Rural (All)	49.20	13.09	4.73
Landless HH	71.85	21.63	8.45
Marginal farmer HH	60.66	15.96	5.70
Small farmer HH	45.46	10.30	3.35
Large farmer HH	20.40	4.36	1.24
Non-agricultural HH	43.45	11.42	4.10
Urban (All)	32.56	8.70	3.21
Illiterate HH	60.11	17.44	6.77
Low-educated HH	24.34	5.32	1.61
Medium-educated HH	5.77	0.97	0.32

* The high–educated household group has not been included in this table as its per capita income is well above the poverty line.

Source: BBS (2001).

8.5.2. Simulated Poverty Profiles

This section reports the effects on poverty of the elimination of all import tariffs (simulation 1) and the elimination of all import tariffs accompanied by the imposition of an endogenously determined uniform consumption tax of 2.7 per cent in the short run and 2.6 per cent in the long run (simulation 2). Tables 8.2 to 8.5 present the simulation results for the three types of FGT poverty indices for the short run and the long run. All results are compared with the corresponding base year estimates. Negative changes in poverty indices indicate reductions in poverty; positive changes indicate increases in poverty.

8.5.2.1. Simulation 1: Effects of a 100 Percent Cut in Tariffs

In simulation 1, the poverty consequences of the removal of tariffs for rural and urban households are somewhat mixed in the short run (Table 8.3). In rural areas, the landless households group experiences an increase in poverty, according to all three poverty indices. All other rural groups, however, experience decreases in poverty, according to all three indices, with the indices for the large farmer group showing the biggest falls. The upshot is that for rural households as a whole, the head count ratio (P_0) falls by 0.28 per cent, the poverty gap index (P_1) falls by 0.23 per cent, and the squared poverty gap index (P_2) falls by 0.21 per cent.

In urban areas, the illiterate household group suffers an increase in poverty in the short run, according to all three indices, while the low-educated household group suffers an increase according to two of the indices, the exception being the head count ratio, which shows no change. On the other hand, all three indicators show a very substantial decline in poverty for the medium-educated household group. For urban households as a whole, the head count ratio (P_0) falls by 0.58 per cent (somewhat more than the corresponding rural figure), but the poverty gap index (P_1) rises by 0.34 per cent, and the squared poverty gap index (P_2) rises by 0.62 per cent.

Comparing the results for all rural households with those for all urban households, the changes in the three poverty indexes are all proportionately very small. Nevertheless, in general terms, they indicate that in the short run trade liberalisation has an unequivocally positive impact in reducing poverty in rural areas, while in urban areas it leads to a combination of some households moving out of a state of poverty and a deterioration of the situation of those who remain poor.

Table 8.2. FGT poverty indices (in percentages) for various policy experiments (short run)

	Simulation 1			Simulation 2		
Household groups	Head count ratio (P_0)	Poverty gap (P_1)	Squared poverty gap (P_2)	Head count ratio (P_0)	Poverty gap (P_1)	Squared poverty gap (P_2)
Rural (All)	49.06	13.06	4.72	49.92	13.38	4.87
Landless HH	71.93	21.75	8.50	72.02	21.80	8.53
Marginal farmer HH	60.41	15.95	5.69	61.75	16.25	5.83
Small farmer HH	45.35	10.24	3.32	46.03	10.53	3.44
Large farmer HH	20.14	4.27	1.20	21.53	4.52	1.30
Non-agricultural HH	43.24	11.35	4.07	43.99	11.62	4.19
Urban (All)	32.37	8.73	3.23	33.08	8.85	3.28
Illiterate HH	60.19	17.53	6.81	61.15	17.69	6.89
Low-educated HH	24.34	5.33	1.62	24.69	5.46	1.67
Medium-educated HH	4.77	0.85	0.28	5.79	1.01	0.33

Source: Simulation results of the Bangladesh model.

Table 8.3. Percentage changes of poverty indices from the base year for various policy experiments (short run)

	Simulation 1			Simulation 2		
Household groups	Head count ratio (P_0)	Poverty gap (P_1)	Squared poverty gap (P_2)	Head count ratio (P_0)	Poverty gap (P_1)	Squared poverty gap (P_2)
Rural (All)	-0.28	-0.23	-0.21	1.46	2.22	2.96
Landless HH	0.11	0.55	0.59	0.24	0.79	1.19
Marginal farmer HH	-0.41	-0.06	-0.18	1.80	1.82	2.28
Small farmer HH	-0.24	-0.58	-0.90	1.25	2.23	2.76
Large farmer HH	-1.27	-2.06	-3.23	5.54	3.67	4.84
Non-agricultural HH	-0.48	-0.53	-0.73	1.28	1.75	2.20
Urban (All)	-0.58	0.34	0.62	1.60	1.72	2.18
Illiterate HH	0.13	0.52	0.59	1.71	1.43	1.77
Low-educated HH	0	0.19	0.62	1.44	2.63	3.73
Medium-educated HH	-17.33	-13.05	-12.22	0.35	3.77	2.33

Sources: Tables 8.1 and 8.2.

The long run results for simulation 1 show more widely spread and much larger reductions in poverty than occur in the short run. The removal of import tariffs leads in the long run to falls in all poverty indicators for all households groups (Table 8.5). In rural areas, the marginal farmer group achieves the largest fall in the head count ratio (4.52 per cent), and the landless group, which in the short run experiences increases in all three poverty indexes, now achieves the largest falls in both the poverty gap index and the squared poverty gap index (5.46 per cent and 7.34 per cent respectively). For rural households as a whole, the head count index decreases by 3.00 per cent; the poverty gap index decreases by 5.27 per cent; and the squared poverty gap index decreases by 6.34 per cent.

In urban areas, the medium-educated household group continues in the long run to register the biggest falls in all three poverty indicators (and indeed the biggest among all urban and rural groups combined). However, compared with the short run, the most striking change among urban household groups is in the poverty situation of the illiterate group. As with the landless group in rural areas, the increases that the illiterate group experiences in all three poverty indexes in the short run are replaced by significant decreases in the long run. For urban households as a whole, the head count index falls by 2.79 per cent; the poverty gap index falls by 4.25 per cent; and the squared poverty gap index falls by 5.30 per cent.

Table 8.4. FGT poverty indices (in percentages) for various policy experiments (long run)

	Simulation 1			Simulation 2		
Household groups	Head count ratio (P_0)	Poverty gap (P_1)	Squared poverty gap (P_2)	Head count ratio (P_0)	Poverty gap (P_1)	Squared poverty gap (P_2)
Rural (All)	47.72	12.40	4.43	48.75	12.84	4.61
Landless HH	70.45	20.45	7.83	71.25	21.11	8.16
Marginal farmer HH	57.92	15.23	5.36	59.18	15.70	5.57
Small farmer HH	44.55	9.75	3.13	45.20	10.12	3.28
Large farmer HH	19.86	4.21	1.18	20.40	4.34	1.23
Non-agricultural HH	43.24	11.35	4.07	43.12	11.24	4.01
Urban (All)	31.65	8.33	3.04	31.99	8.54	3.14
Illiterate HH	58.78	16.73	6.42	59.25	17.13	6.61
Low-educated HH	23.81	5.07	1.52	24.29	5.23	1.58
Medium-educated HH	4.77	0.85	0.28	4.82	0.96	0.32

Source: Simulation results of the Bangladesh model.

Table 8.5. Percentage changes of poverty indices from the base year for various policy experiments (long run)

	Simulation 1			**Simulation 2**		
Household groups	**Head count ratio (P_0)**	**Poverty gap (P_1)**	**Squared poverty gap (P_2)**	**Head count ratio (P_0)**	**Poverty gap (P_1)**	**Squared poverty gap (P_2)**
Rural (All)	-3.00	-5.27	-6.34	-0.91	-1.91	-2.54
Landless HH	-1.95	-5.46	-7.34	-0.84	-2.40	-3.32
Marginal farmer HH	-4.52	-4.57	-5.96	-2.44	-1.63	-2.28
Small farmer HH	-2.00	-5.34	-6.57	-0.57	-1.75	-2.09
Large farmer HH	-2.65	-3.44	-4.84	0	-0.46	-0.81
Non-agricultural HH	-0.48	-0.61	-0.73	-0.76	-1.58	-2.20
Urban (All)	-2.79	-4.25	-5.30	-1.75	-1.84	-2.21
Illiterate HH	-2.21	-4.07	-5.17	-1.45	-1.78	-2.36
Low-educated HH	-2.18	-4.70	-5.59	-0.21	-1.69	-1.86
Medium-educated HH	-17.33	-12.37	-12.50	-16.46	-1.23	0

Sources: Tables 8.1 and 8.4.

The overall results for urban areas are marginally inferior to those for rural areas, but together they indicate that in the long run, within the context of simulation 1, the elimination of all import tariffs reduces the incidence, depth and severity of poverty for the economy as a whole.

8.5.2.2. Simulation 2: Effects of a 100 Percent Cut in Tariffs with a Uniform Consumption Tax

In simulation 2, where the effects of tariff removals on indirect tax revenue are offset by the imposition of a consumption tax, poverty increases for both rural and urban areas in the short run, according to all three poverty indices (Table 8.3). For rural households as a whole, the poverty head count ratio (P_0) increases by 1.46 per cent, the poverty gap index (P_1) by 2.22 per cent, and the squared poverty gap (P_2) index by 2.96 per cent. For urban households as a whole, the corresponding figures are 1.60 per cent, 1.72 per cent and 2.18 per cent.

These results at the rural/urban level reflect increases in all three poverty indexes for all constituent household groups. Among rural households, the large farmer group has the largest percentage increases in all three indices and the landless group has the smallest percentage increases. Among urban households, the illiterate group experiences the largest increase in the head count ratio; the medium-educated group experiences the largest increase in the poverty gap index; and the low-educated group experiences the largest increase in the squared poverty gap index.

The short run poverty outcomes of simulation 2 are consistently more adverse than the mixed short run results of simulation 1. With constant intra-group relative income distributions, the increases in the poverty indices in simulation 2 reflect the combined effects of small declines in the nominal household incomes of all groups and increases in the nominal poverty lines of 0.26 per cent for rural groups and 0.22 per cent for urban groups. On the other hand, the generally better short run poverty results of simulation 1 reflect declines in nominal incomes of all groups that, although larger than the declines of simulation 2, are in most cases smaller than the corresponding falls in the nominal poverty lines of 2.03 per cent for rural groups and 1.69 per cent for urban groups.

The long run results for simulation 2 are close to a complete reversal of the short run results. All measures of poverty decline for both rural and urban areas as a whole and for most constituent household groups (Table 8.5). (Exceptions are the poverty head count index for the rural large farmer group and the squared poverty gap index for the urban medium-educated group, which are unchanged from the base year.).

For the most part, the long run declines in poverty measures in simulation 2 are smaller than their corresponding long run declines in simulation 1. Given constant intra-group relative income distributions, and the minor differences between the simulations in the rates of increase of nominal income at the household group level (Table 7.5), the mainly smaller declines in the simulation 2 poverty indices largely reflect the impact of the consumption tax on the nominal rural and urban poverty lines. In the long run, the nominal rural poverty line increases by 0.56 per cent and the nominal urban poverty line increases by 0.47 per cent in simulation 2, whereas in simulation 1 the rural nominal poverty line decreases by 0.55 per cent and the urban nominal poverty line decreases by 0.46 per cent (Table 7.1).

Table 8.6. Other poverty indices under different policy scenarios (short run)

Households	Sen Index (%)				Watts Index (%)				S-Gini Index (%)			
	Simulation 1		Simulation 2		Simulation 1		Simulation 2		Simulation 1		Simulation 2	
	Before	After	Before	After	Before	After	Before	After	Before	After	Before	After
Landless HH	28.35	28.46	28.35	28.53	27.95	28.11	27.95	28.20	32.55	32.69	32.55	32.76
Marginal farmer HH	21.38	21.30	21.38	21.82	20.06	20.00	20.06	20.45	25.54	25.48	25.54	25.54
Small farmer HH	14.11	14.04	14.11	14.40	12.66	12.57	12.66	12.96	17.66	17.56	17.66	18.00
Large farmer HH	5.76	5.64	5.76	6.06	5.17	5.06	5.17	5.37	8.12	7.97	8.12	8.40
Non-agricultural HH	15.33	15.24	15.33	15.60	14.40	14.32	14.40	14.67	19.58	19.48	19.58	19.88
Illiterate HH	23.19	23.28	23.19	23.60	22.56	22.68	22.56	22.91	27.87	28.19	27.87	28.19
Low-educated HH	7.16	7.17	7.16	7.33	6.41	6.42	6.41	6.58	9.80	9.82	9.80	10.04
Medium-educated HH	1.37	1.28	1.37	1.41	1.24	1.23	1.24	1.28	1.92	1.90	1.92	1.99

Table 8.7. Percentage changes of other poverty indices from the base year (short run)

Households	Sen Index		Watts Index		S-Gini Index	
	Simulation 1	Simulation 2	Simulation 1	Simulation 2	Simulation 1	Simulation 2
	% change	% change	% change	% change	% change	% change
Landless HH	0.57	0.63	0.39	0.89	0.43	0.65
Marginal farmer HH	-0.30	2.06	-0.37	1.94	-0.23	1.49
Small farmer HH	-0.71	2.06	-0.50	2.37	-0.57	1.93
Large farmer HH	-2.13	5.21	-2.08	3.87	-1.85	3.45
Non-agricultural HH	-0.56	1.76	-0.59	1.88	-0.51	1.53
Illiterate HH	0.53	1.77	0.39	1.55	1.15	1.15
Low-educated HH	0.16	2.37	0.14	2.65	0.20	2.45
Medium-educated HH	-0.81	2.92	-6.57	3.25	-1.04	3.65

To complete this section of the study, we use the Watts index, the Sen index and the S-Gini index as checks on the robustness of the poverty results of the FGT poverty measures. The results of the Watts, Sen and S-Gini indices for the base case scenario and simulations 1 and 2 are presented in Tables 8.6 to Table 8.9. The patterns of change they depict are broadly consistent with both the short and long run findings reported above, suggesting that the latter are robust in nature.

Table 8.8. Other poverty indices under different policy scenarios (long run)

Households	Sen Index (%)				Watts Index (%)				S-Gini Index (%)			
	Simulation 1		Simulation 2		Simulation 1		Simulation 2		Simulation 1		Simulation 2	
	Before	After	Before	After	Before	After	Before	After	Before	After	Before	After
Landless HH	28.35	27.03	28.35	27.77	27.95	26.27	27.95	27.20	32.55	31.14	32.55	31.93
Marginal farmer HH	21.38	20.25	21.38	20.89	20.06	19.06	20.06	19.70	25.54	24.56	25.54	25.19
Small farmer HH	14.11	13.49	14.11	13.91	12.66	11.94	12.66	12.42	17.66	16.82	17.66	17.38
Large farmer HH	5.76	5.54	5.76	5.74	5.17	4.97	5.17	5.14	8.12	7.85	8.12	8.08
Non-agricultural HH	15.33	14.64	15.33	15.11	14.40	13.40	14.40	14.16	19.58	18.78	19.58	19.30
Illiterate HH	23.19	22.32	23.19	22.75	22.56	21.56	22.56	22.12	27.87	26.93	27.87	27.46
Low-educated HH	7.16	6.86	7.16	7.06	6.41	6.09	6.41	6.29	9.80	9.37	9.80	9.64
Medium-educated HH	1.37	1.25	1.37	1.28	1.24	1.19	1.24	1.22	1.92	1.84	1.92	1.89

Table 8.9. Percentage changes of other poverty indices from the base (long run)

Households	Sen Index		Watts Index		S-Gini Index	
	Simulation 1	Simulation 2	Simulation 1	Simulation 2	Simulation 1	Simulation 2
	% change	% change	% change	% change	% change	% change
Landless HH	-4.66	-2.05	-6.01	-2.68	-4.33	-1.90
Marginal farmer HH	-5.29	-2.29	-4.98	-1.79	-3.84	-1.37
Small farmer HH	-4.39	-1.42	-5.68	-1.90	-4.76	-1.59
Large farmer HH	-3.82	-0.35	-3.87	-0.58	-3.33	-0.49
Non-agricultural HH	-4.50	-1.44	-6.94	-1.67	-4.09	-1.43
Illiterate HH	-3.75	-1.90	-4.43	-1.95	-3.37	-1.47
Low-educated HH	-4.19	-1.40	-4.99	-1.87	-4.39	-1.63
Medium-educated HH	-8.76	-6.57	-4.03	-1.61	-4.17	-1.56

8.6. INEQUALITY MEASURES

This study uses the following measures to assess the effects that the removal of tariffs, with and without a revenue-compensating consumption tax, have on the inequality of incomes.

Gini Index:

Perhaps the most commonly used measure of inequality is the Gini coefficient. It is based on the Lorenz curve, a cumulative frequency curve which plots the cumulative percentages of total income against the cumulative percentage of individuals ranked from bottom to top. The Gini coefficient is the area between the Lorenz curve and the 45° line of perfect equality expressed as a proportion of the total area under the 45° line. It ranges in value from zero (everyone has the same income) to one (where all income accrues to one person). Following De Silva (2008), it can be written as:

$$\text{Gini index of inequality} = 2\int_0^1 (p - L(p))dp$$

where the implicit assumption is that the distance, $p - L(p)$, from the line of perfect equality of income is weighted equally across percentiles, p.

A familiar single parameter generalisation of the Gini coefficient is the S-Gini index, which is obtained by applying a percentile dependent weight to the distance $p - L(p)$, between the line of perfect equality (45°) and the Lorenz curve. The S-Gini index can be defined as follows:

$$I(\rho) = \int_0^1 (p - L(p))k(p;\ \rho)\,dp.$$

where $k(p;\rho) = \rho(\rho - 1)(1 - p)^{(\rho-2)}$.

When $\rho = 2$, $I(2)$ becomes the standard Gini coefficient.

Atkinson Index:

The Atkinson inequality measure (Atkinson, 1970) is based on an additive social welfare function. It introduces a parameter "epsilon" (ε), which measures society's aversion to inequality or the strength of society's preference for equality. It ranges from zero to infinity. The Atkinson index can be defined as:

$$\text{Atkinson index} = 1 - \frac{1}{\bar{y}}\left(\frac{1}{N}\sum_{i=1}^{N} y_i^{1-\varepsilon}\right)^{1/(1-\varepsilon)} \text{, when } \varepsilon \neq 1$$

$$1 - 1/\bar{y}(\Pi_{i=1}^{N} y_i)^{1/N} \text{, when } \varepsilon = 1$$

where y_i denotes the income of the *i-th* person, N is population size, and $\bar{y}$ is mean income. A zero value of ε implies that the society is indifferent about the distribution of income. The higher above zero is the value of ε, the more society cares about the welfare of lower income groups.

Entropy Index:

Another inequality measure, the generalised entropy family, is able to decompose inequality by population subgroups. It can be defined as follows (Duclos and Araar, 2006):

$$I(\theta)=\begin{cases} \frac{1}{\theta(\theta-1)}\left(\int_0^1 \left(\frac{Q(p)}{\mu}\right)^{\theta} dp-1\right) & \text{if } \theta\neq 0,1 \\ \int_0^1 \ln\left(\frac{\mu}{Q(p)}\right)dp & \text{if } \theta=0 \\ \int_0^1 \frac{Q(p)}{\mu}\ln\left(\frac{Q(p)}{\mu}\right)dp & \text{if } \theta=1 \end{cases}$$

Where μ is the mean income and the parameter θ represents the weight placed on distances between incomes at different parts of the income distribution. The latter can take any real value. The value of $I(\theta)$ varies from 0 to ∞. A zero value of $I(\theta)$ represents an equal distribution whereas a higher value of $I(\theta)$ indicates a higher degree of inequality.

8.6.1. Estimation of Inequality Indices

As with FGT poverty indices, inequality indices have been calculated using the DAD software, where the approach adopts the Kernel non-parametric density estimation method in specifying the probability density function. Calculations were made for the base year and for the simulation household incomes generated by the model. The indices were estimated for the aggregated rural, aggregated urban and total populations of Bangladesh.

8.6.1.1. Base Case Inequality Scenario

Tables 8.10 to Table 8.13 present the S-Gini index numbers (ρ=2.0), Atkinson index numbers ($\varepsilon = 0.5$) and entropy index numbers ($\theta = 0.0$) for the base year (2000), the short runs in both simulations 1 and 2, and the long runs in both simulations 1 and 2. Values of the S-Gini indices for urban and rural areas suggest that in the base year people living in urban areas experienced greater income inequality (0.3660) than people living in rural areas (0.2873).[4] This result is supported by the urban and rural base year values of the Atkinson and Entropy indices.

8.6.1.2. Post Simulation Income Inequality

Tables 8.10 and 8.11 show that in simulation 1 all three measures of inequality increase in the short run for the economy as a whole and for both rural and urban areas, although the percentages changes in the indices are small. These increases in inequality can be traced to increases in the returns to capital and land relative to returns to labour (Table 7.3). With elasticities of substitution between primary factors assigned a value of 0.5, the largest percentage increases in real income in rural areas accrue to large farmer households who depend mainly on their ownership of capital and land to provide income (Table 6.8), and who

[4] The base year Gini figures for both urban and rural areas are lower than the corresponding figures for the year 2000 plotted in Figure 3.5 in Chapter 3. The differences appear to be at least partly attributable to our use of the Kernel non-parametric density estimation method in estimating income distribution.

already receive the highest incomes. On the other hand, the smallest percentage increases in real income in rural areas accrue to landless households who rely almost entirely on their labour to provide income and who already receive the lowest incomes. Likewise in urban areas, the highest percentage increases in real income accrue to high-educated households who receive most of their income from capital, and who already have the highest incomes, while the smallest percentage increases accrue to illiterate households who rely mainly on their labour and who already receive the lowest incomes.

Tables 8.12 and 8.13, however, show that in simulation 1 inequality falls in the long run in the economy as a whole and in both rural and urban areas (and according to all three measures, by more than it rises in the short run). The long run decline reflects an increase in returns to labour relative to returns to capital and land. In contrast to the short run, in both rural and urban areas, it is the poorer households, who rely most heavily on labour for their livelihoods, that experience the largest rates of increase in real income, and it is the richer households, who rely most heavily on ownership of capital and/or land, that experience the smallest rates of increase in real income. This long-term distributional consequence of trade liberalisation is broadly consistent with the Stolper-Samuelson theorem.

In simulation 2, where the removal of tariffs is accompanied by a revenue-compensating consumption tax, inequality decreases in both the short run and long run, with all three indices showing the long run declines to be larger than the short run declines for urban and rural households considered separately as well as for all households (Tables 8.10 to 8.13). Both short and long run declines in inequality are associated with increases in returns to labour relative to returns to capital and land. However, while the increase in the average price of labour relative to the average rental price of capital is larger in the long run than in the short run, the increase relative to the rental price of land was somewhat smaller in the long run than in the short run.

Finally, according to all three indices, the long run falls in inequality in simulation 2 are smaller than the corresponding long run falls in simulation 1. These outcomes are consistent with the long run rise in the price of labour relative to the rental prices of capital and land being smaller in simulation 2 than in simulation 1.

Table 8.10. Inequality measures for different policy simulations (short run)

	S-Gini Index (ρ =2.0)				Atkinson Index (ε =0.5)				Entropy Index (θ =0.0)			
	Simulation 1		Simulation 2		Simulation 1		Simulation 2		Simulation 1		Simulation 2	
Households	Before	After	Before	After	Before	After	Before	After	Before	After	Before	After
All	0.3290	0.3295	0.3290	0.3286	0.0898	0.0901	0.0898	0.0896	0.1749	0.1755	0.1749	0.1745
Rural	0.2873	0.2877	0.2873	0.2871	0.0684	0.0686	0.0684	0.0683	0.1338	0.1342	0.1338	0.1336
Urban	0.3660	0.3665	0.3660	0.3657	0.1085	0.1088	0.1085	0.1083	0.2196	0.2202	0.2196	0.2192

Table 8.11. Percentage changes of inequality indices from the base year (short run)

	S-Gini Index		Atkinson Index		Entropy Index	
	Simulation 1	Simulation 2	Simulation 1	Simulation 2	Simulation 1	Simulation 2
Households	% change	% change	% change	% change	% change	% change
All	0.15	-0.12	0.33	-0.22	0.34	-0.23
Rural	0.14	-0.07	0.29	-0.15	0.30	-0.15
Urban	0.14	-0.08	0.28	-0.18	0.27	-0.18

Table 8.12. Inequality measures for different policy simulations (long run)

	S-Gini Index (ρ =2.0)				Atkinson Index (ε =0.5)				Entropy Index (θ =0.0)			
	Simulation 1		Simulation 2		Simulation 1		Simulation 2		Simulation 1		Simulation 2	
Households	Before	After	Before	After	Before	After	Before	After	Before	After	Before	After
All	0.3290	0.3280	0.3290	0.3283	0.0898	0.0893	0.0898	0.0894	0.1750	0.1740	0.1750	0.1743
Rural	0.2873	0.2867	0.2873	0.2869	0.0684	0.0681	0.0684	0.0682	0.1338	0.1332	0.1338	0.1334
Urban	0.3660	0.3651	0.3660	0.3654	0.1085	0.1080	0.1085	0.1082	0.2196	0.2184	0.2196	0.2189

Table 8.13. Percentage changes of inequality indices from the base year (long run)

	S-Gini Index		Atkinson Index		Entropy Index	
	Simulation 1	Simulation 2	Simulation 1	Simulation 2	Simulation 1	Simulation 2
Households	% change	% change	% change	% change	% change	% change
All	-0.30	-0.21	-0.56	-0.45	-0.57	-0.40
Rural	-0.21	-0.14	-0.44	-0.29	-0.45	-0.30
Urban	-0.25	-0.16	-0.46	-0.28	-0.55	-0.32

8.7. SENSITIVITY ANALYSIS

The purpose of this section is to examine the sensitivity of the poverty and inequality results presented in this chapter to changes in the Armington import elasticities and the primary factor substitution elasticities. The selected changes in the elasticities are +50 per cent and -50 per cent of their base values. To test our simulation 1 results against these changes in model parameters, we ran four new simulations of the complete elimination of tariffs. The first uses Armington elasticities that are 50 per cent lower. The second simulation uses Armington elasticities that are 50 per cent higher. The third and fourth simulations use primary factor substitution elasticities that are 50 per cent lower and 50 per cent higher respectively. These experiments were conducted for both the short run and the long run.[5]

8.7.1. Sensitivity of Poverty to Changes in Armington Elasticities

Armington substitution elasticity indicates the degree of substitutability between domestic and imported products for each sector. Thus, higher values for these elasticities imply greater substitution between imported and domestically produced goods in response to changes in relative prices. Hence imports, exports and real GDP are expected to show larger changes in response to effects of the tariff cuts on domestic prices, thereby amplifying the poverty impact of the tariff cuts. The reverse is true for lower values of elasticities. Figures 8.1 and 8.2 show the short run and long run levels of the head count index (P_0), poverty gap index (P_1) and poverty severity index (P_2) for simulation 1, using the different Armington elasticities.

[5] For simplicity and because of time constraints, sensitivity analysis of the poverty and inequality results in simulation 2 has not been presented here.

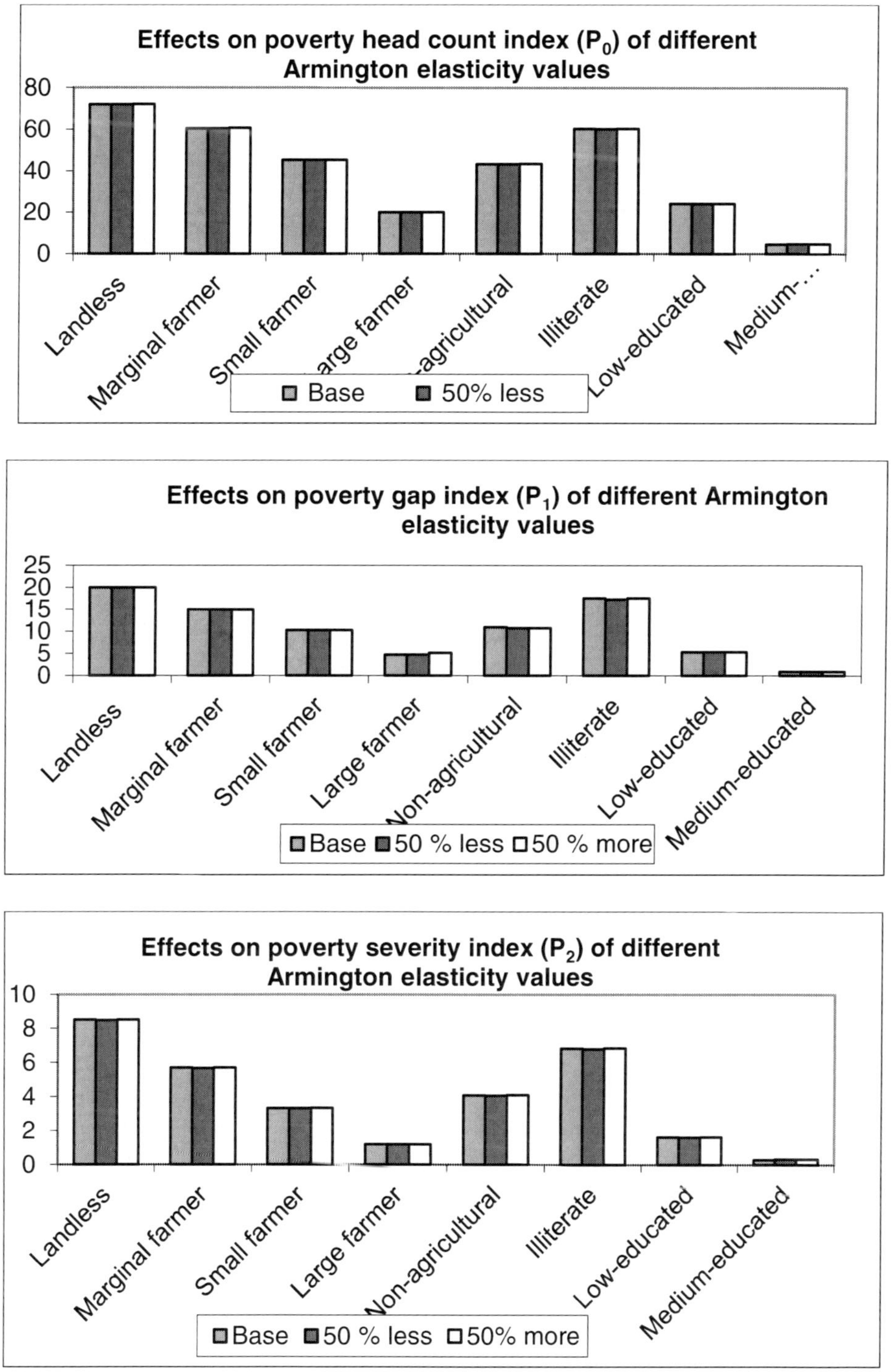

Figure 8.1. Short run poverty effects of complete removal of tariffs under different sets of Armington elasticities.

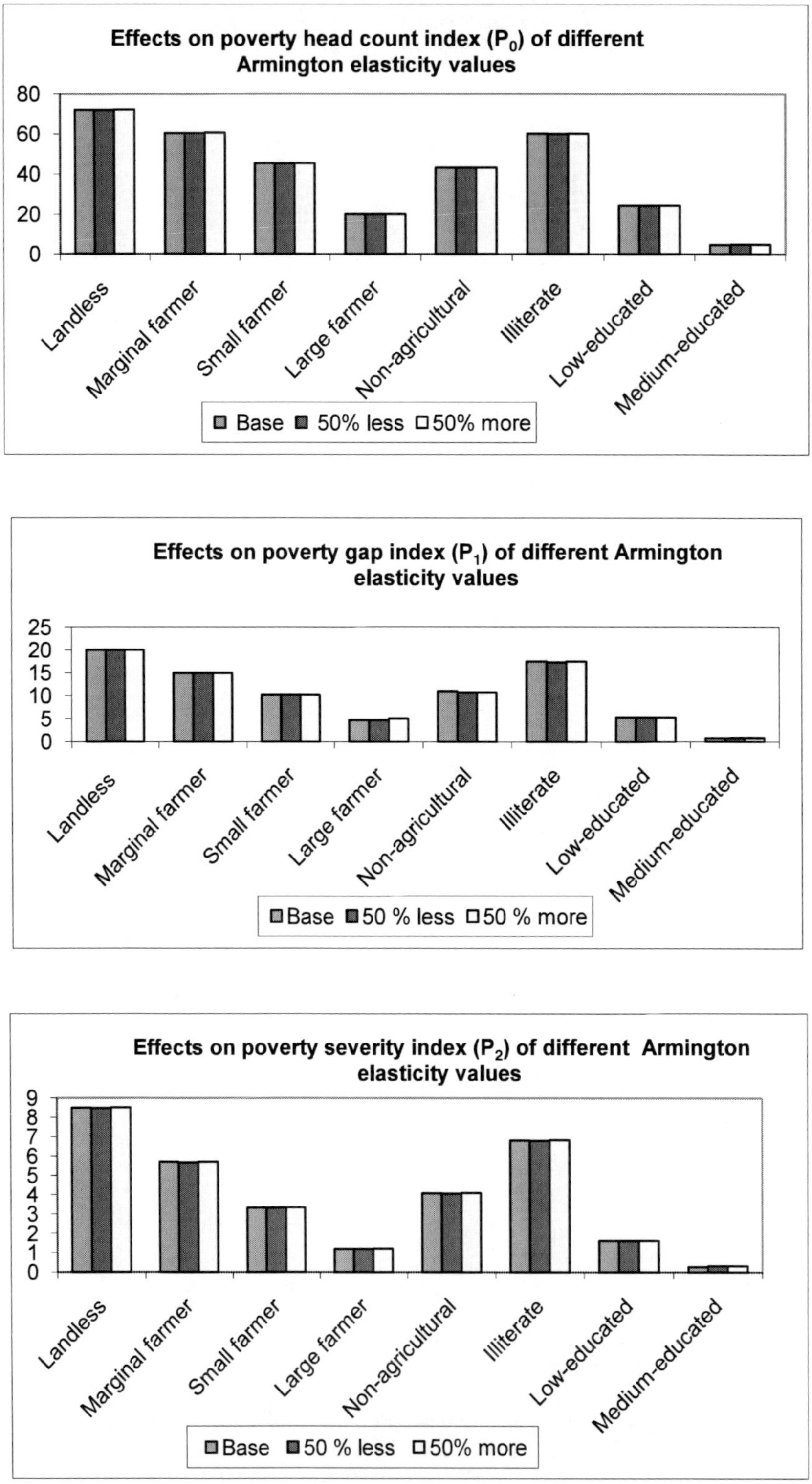

Figure 8.2. Long run poverty effects of complete removal of tariffs under different sets of Armington elasticities.

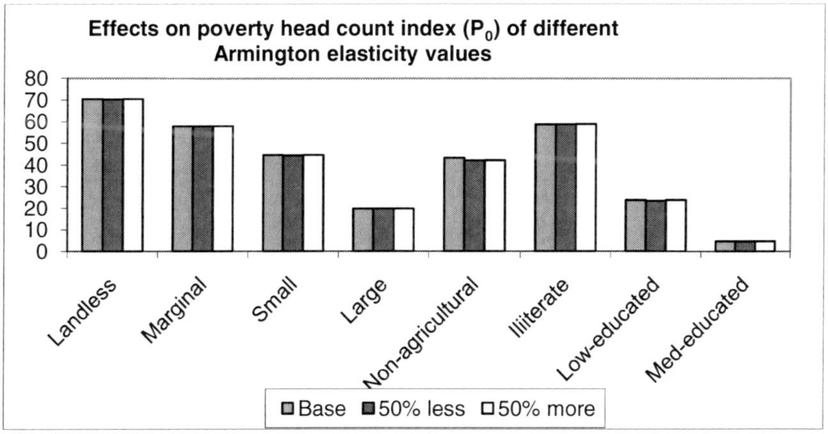

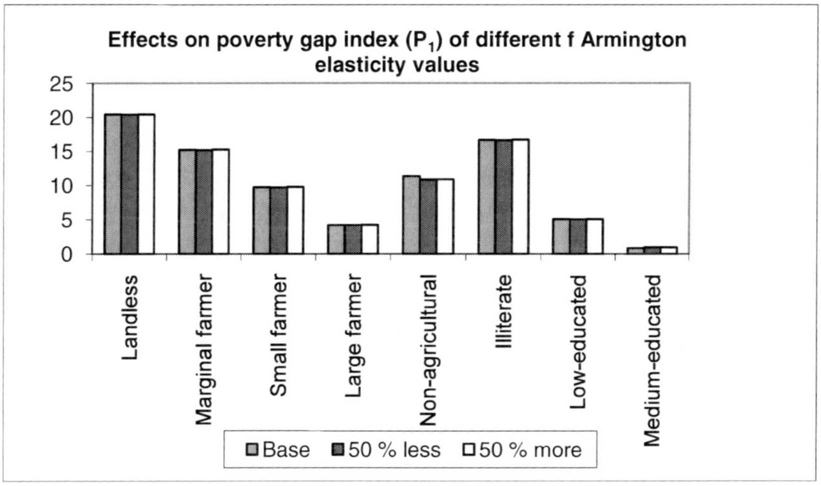

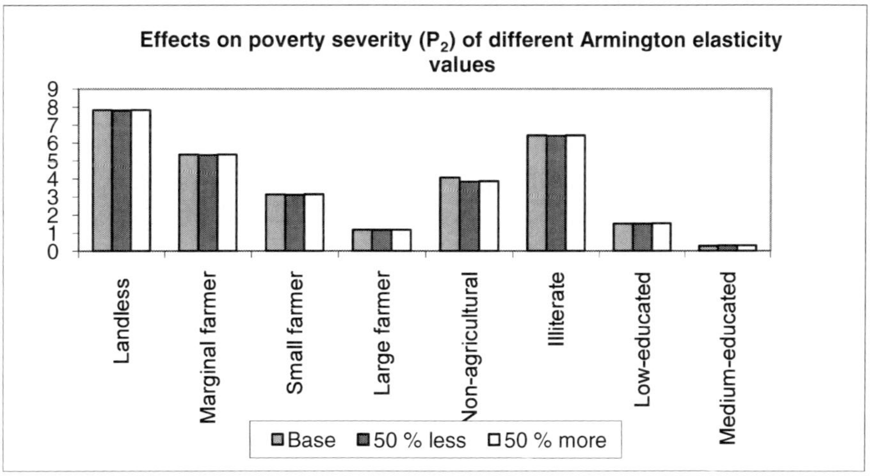

Figure 8.3. Short run poverty effects of complete removal of tariffs under different sets of primary factor elasticities.

For most household groups, variations in the assumed Armington elasticities have little or no effect on their simulated poverty levels. The main reason may be that the imports of the commodities included in the basic needs consumption bundle constitute only a small share of the bundle. All poverty indicators (P_0, P_1 and P_2) are essentially insensitive to the size of the elasticities, so confirming that in this respect the original simulation results are relatively robust.

8.7.2. Sensitivity of Poverty to Changes in Primary Factor Substitution Elasticities

Figures 8.3 and 8.4 present the short run and long run values of the head count index (P_0), poverty gap index (P_1) and poverty severity index (P_2) for simulation 1, using the different assumptions about primary factor substitution elasticities. These figures show that the sensitivity of the poverty of household groups to changes in the primary factor substitution elasticities is slightly larger than its sensitivity to changes in Armington elasticities. Figures 8.3 and 8.4 also reveal, on balance, some tendency for the higher value of primary factor elasticities to result in lower poverty and for the lower elasticity value to result in higher poverty, but only to very small extents. While results vary according to time period (short run and long run) and poverty measure, the more noticeably affected groups include the rural landless, marginal farmer, small farmer and non-agricultural groups in rural areas and the illiterate household group in urban areas. As with the Armington elasticities, however, poverty levels are essentially insensitive to the size of the elasticities, thereby confirming the robustness of the original simulation results.

8.7.3. Income Inequality Sensitivity to Changes in Elasticities

Table 8.14 shows, for simulation 1, the short run and long run values of the S-Gini index ($\underline{\rho} = 2$) or standard Gini coefficient that correspond to the different Armington and primary factor substitution elasticities. Clearly, inequality in the distribution of income among households, as measured by the Gini coefficient, is almost entirely unaffected in both the short run and the long run by the changes in the Armington elasticities.

Inequality is only slightly less insensitive to changes in primary factor substitution elasticities. In the short run, a 50 per cent decrease in the values of these elasticities leads to tiny increases in inequality among urban and rural households considered separately as well as for all households, whereas a 50 per cent increase leads to tiny decreases in inequality. In the long run, outcomes are reversed. A 50 per cent decrease in primary factor substitution elasticity values leads to tiny decreases in inequality, whereas a 50 percent increase in elasticity values leads to tiny increases in inequality.

In general, these results indicate that the original Gini coefficient results are robust with respect to the sizes of both the Armington and primary factor substitution elasticities.

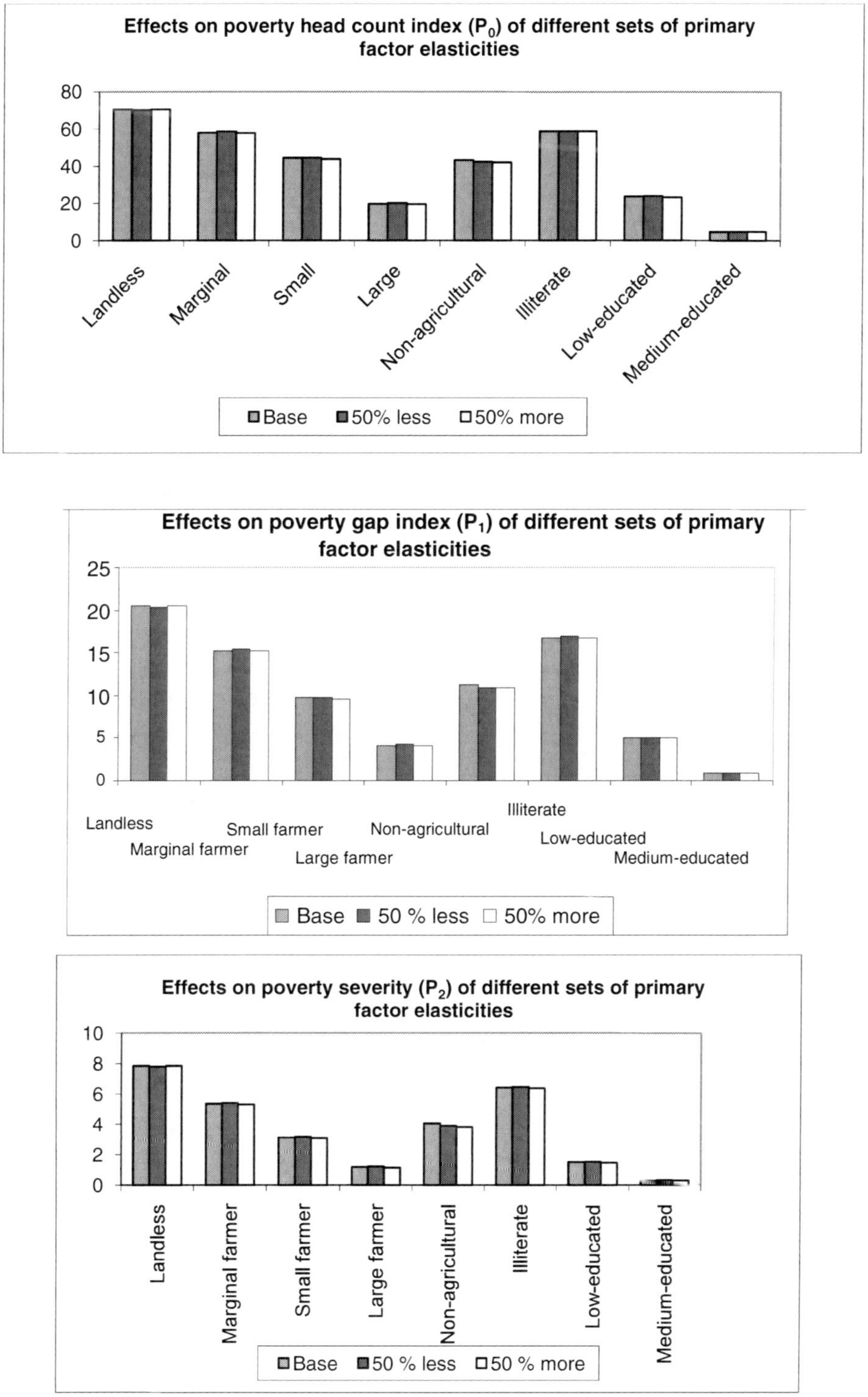

Figure 8.4. Long run poverty effects of complete removal of tariffs under different sets of primary factor elasticities.

Table 8.14. Income inequality sensitivity to changes in elasticities (simulation 1)

	S-Gini index (Short run)			S-Gini index (Long run)		
Armington elasticity	All	Rural	Urban	All	Rural	Urban
50% less*	0.3295	0.2877	0.3664	0.3280	0.2866	0.3651
Base	0.3295	0.2877	0.3665	0.3280	0.2867	0.3651
50 % more*	0.3295	0.2877	0.3664	0.3279	0.2866	0.3650
Primary factor substitution elasticity						
50 % less*	0.3299	0.2879	0.3668	0.3273	0.2862	0.3645
Base	0.3295	0.2877	0.3665	0.3280	0.2867	0.3651
50% more*	0.3291	0.2874	0.3661	0.3284	0.2869	0.3654

* from base elasticities

Source: calculated from simulation results.

8.8. Main Findings

This chapter links the macro CGE results obtained in Chapter 7 with household survey data to analyse the impact of trade reform on poverty and income inequality in Bangladesh. The analysis was undertaken within the framework of two simulations: (1) the complete removal of tariffs without a revenue-compensating consumption tax; and (2) the complete removal of tariffs with an endogenously determined revenue-compensating consumption tax.

The following are the main findings with respect to simulation 1.

1. In the short run, all three FGT measures of poverty decline for rural households as a whole, whereas for urban households as a whole there are mixed results. The incidence of poverty declines, but the poverty gap and the severity of poverty indices increase.
2. In the long run, poverty falls in terms of all three FGT measures for both rural households as a whole and urban households as a whole.
3. In the short run, all three measures of inequality (the Gini index, the Atkinson index and the entropy index) increase for rural households, urban households and all households.
4. In the long run, all three measures of inequality decline for rural households, urban households and all households.

The following are the main findings with respect to simulation 2.

5. In the short run, according to all three FGT measures, poverty increases for rural households as whole and for urban households as a whole.
6. In the long run, poverty falls in terms of all three FGT measures for both rural households as whole and urban households as a whole. In each case, the declines in the FGT indices are smaller than the corresponding long run declines in simulation 1.
7. In the short run, all three measures of inequality decline for rural households, urban households and all households.

8. In the long run also, all three measures of inequality decline for rural households, urban households and all households. In each case, the declines are larger than the short run declines, but smaller than the corresponding long run declines in simulation 1.

Chapter 9

CONCLUSION

9.1. INTRODUCTION

This chapter completes the study. Section 9.2 presents a general overview of the research. Section 9.3 provides a summary of the main findings. Section 9.4 discusses some implications of these findings. Section 9.5 outlines the limitations of the study and Section 9.6 suggests areas for further research.

9.2. OVERVIEW OF THE STUDY

The central concern of this study has been to identify the impact that the unilateral elimination of all import tariffs would have on poverty and inequality in Bangladesh. In tracing this impact, the study has also explored the effects that trade liberalisation would have on macroeconomic performance, on output and employment in individual industries, on employment by skill category, and on the household income and consumption of various socio-economic groups.

A static, multi-sectoral, multi-household CGE model, termed the Bangladesh Model, was developed to investigate these issues. The model provides an analytical framework that includes endogenised poverty lines and a complete income mapping from the production sectors to the various household groups and institutions in the economy. The model has been used to simulate the short run and long run effects of:

1. the unilateral removal of all tariffs in Bangladesh without any policy action to compensate for the loss of tariff revenue (Simulation 1);
2. the unilateral removal of all tariffs accompanied by an endogenously determined uniform consumption tax (levied at a rate of 2.7 per cent in the short run and 2.6 per cent in the long run), which ensures that total indirect tax revenue is unchanged (Simulation 2).

Chapter 1 presented an outline of the research problem, a statement of the research objectives, and a brief description of the method of analysis. Chapter 2 produced a review of Bangladesh trade liberalisation policies and macroeconomic performance in recent decades.

Chapter 3 described poverty, inequality and labour market developments in Bangladesh over the same period. Chapter 4 provided a review of relevant literature. Chapter 5 developed the Bangladesh Model, following IDC-GEM, a SAM based CGE model for the South African economy (Horridge et al. 1995). Chapter 6 explained the compilation of data for the Bangladesh model. In Chapter 7 the model was used to simulate the effects of the removal of tariffs on key macroeconomic variables, industry level variables and household level variables. Chapter 8 presented the simulated effects on poverty and income inequality in the Bangladesh economy.

9.3. Summary of Results

The macroeconomic results of the simulations presented in Chapter 7 reveal that in the short run, the elimination of tariffs without a revenue-compensating consumption tax (simulation 1) leads to increases in real GDP and aggregate employment, accompanied by a fall in the consumer price level and a substantial depreciation of the real exchange rate. The volume of exports grows faster than the volume of imports and with only a small decline in the terms of trade, the nominal balance of trade (expressed as a proportion of nominal GDP) moves towards surplus.

In the long run, with the same policy package, the percentage increase in real GDP is slightly higher than in the short run. In addition, there are increases in aggregate real household consumption, real government consumption and aggregate real investment (all of which were held constant in the short run). As a result, the volume of imports grows faster than in the short run, while the opposite holds for the volume of exports. Real wages (which were also held constant in the short run) rise substantially in the long run, as money wages increase and the consumer price level falls, although by less than in the short run.

The imposition of a uniform consumption tax to neutralise the loss of indirect tax revenue from an across-the-board tariff elimination (simulation 2) leads in the short run to falls in real GDP and aggregate employment, and a small increase in the consumer price level. In comparison with the short run in simulation 1, there is a smaller improvement in international competitiveness, which results in the volume of exports growing more slowly and the volume of imports growing more rapidly. Expressed as a proportion of nominal GDP, the nominal trade balance deteriorates slightly.

In the long run in simulation 2, real GDP growth is positive (although smaller than in the long run in simulation 1), while the increase in consumer prices is higher than in the short run. Notwithstanding the increase in real GDP and a modest rise in average real wages, aggregate real household consumption falls slightly. This suggests that tariff removal with a consumption tax is likely to play a small negative role in terms of aggregate welfare.

The industry results reveal that in simulation 1 in the short run the elimination of tariffs without a compensatory consumption tax induces expansion of output and employment in existing export-oriented industries through reducing costs of material inputs and labour. These industries include jute cultivation, tea cultivation and shrimp farming in the agricultural sector; ready-made garments, knitting, jute fabrication, toiletries manufacturing and leather products in the manufacturing sector; and water transport and public administration and defense in the service sector. On the other hand, despite cost reductions, tariff elimination without a compensatory consumption tax leads to reduced output and employment in the great majority of previously protected import-competing industries, as they face increased competition from imported goods. The biggest proportionate falls in output are in petroleum refining, spice cultivation, cement manufacturing the glass industry, fruit cultivation and food processing. These are industries that were initially protected by relatively high tariff rates on competing imports.

Most export-oriented and export related industries expand in the long run in simulation 1, but those in the agricultural and service sectors fail to match their short run performances. On the other hand, in the manufacturing sector, the export-oriented industries of ready-made garments, knitting and toiletries manufacturing exceed their short run rates of growth of output. In addition, the expansion of aggregate domestic absorption, taken in conjunction with the assumption that the nominal trade balance is a constant proportion of nominal GDP, results in most non-traded industries experiencing a rate of growth of output that is larger in the long short than in the short run.

When a uniform compensatory consumption tax is associated with complete tariff removal (simulation 2), import-competing industries experience larger short run falls in output than they do in simulation 1. Export-oriented and export-related industries show much lower short run rates growth of output, and the short run performances of non-traded service industries are also generally inferior to their performances in simulation 1. The common explanatory factor is the effect of the consumption tax in increasing the consumer price index. The rise in the CPI increases nominal money wages and thus production costs, whereas in the absence of the consumption tax, the CPI falls substantially, leading to falls in money wages and production costs.

In simulation 2 in the long run, relatively rapid growth in aggregate real investment boosts the expansion of output in the building and construction industries. In addition, export industries such as ready-made garments, knitting, toiletries manufacturing, shrimp farming and leather products experience faster growth than in the short run. On the other hand, of this group, only the leather industry exceeds its long run growth rate in simulation 1. Likewise, although in simulation 2 import-competing industries show fewer contractions of output in the long run than in the short run, the number of long run contractions is greater than in simulation 1.

Among the four occupational categories of employment (male low-skilled, male high-skilled, female low-skilled, and female high-skilled) female low-skilled employment is proportionately the largest beneficiary of the removal of tariffs in all simulation scenarios, and indeed the only beneficiary in the two simulation 2 scenarios.

In simulation 1 in the short run, when aggregate employment expands, female low-skilled employment has the highest rate of increase among the four categories. In simulation 1 in the long run, when aggregate employment is constant by assumption, its rate of increase is much lower, but still the highest among the three categories still showing positive growth (Male low-skilled employment falls absolutely). In simulation 2 in the short run, when aggregate employment declines, female low-skilled employment is the only category to register an increase, albeit one of negligible magnitude. It is also the only category to register an increase in simulation 2 in the long run, when aggregate employment is again constant by assumption. These results are largely a reflection of the high concentration of low skilled women workers in the ready-made garments and knitting industries and the positive response of these export-oriented industries to the economy-wide removal of tariff protection.

With respect to income changes among household groups, in simulation 1 all groups experience increases in real income in both the short run and the long run. Percentage gains are greater in the long run for all groups except large farmer households in rural areas and medium and high-educated households in urban areas. In simulation 2, all household groups suffer falls in real income in the short run, but in the long run most groups gain, the exceptions being once more large farmer households in rural areas and medium and high-educated households in urban areas. For the groups that do gain, their percentage increases in real income are smaller than those they achieve in the long run in simulation 1.

Results provided in Chapter 8 reveal that in simulation 1 in the short run the three FGT poverty indices decrease marginally for rural groups as a whole, despite increases in the indices for the landless household group. For urban groups as a whole, a decrease in the overall head count index and increases in the poverty gap and the squared poverty gap indices imply that fewer people experience poverty but the average depth and severity of poverty increase. Long run results are more clear-cut. The removal of tariffs without a revenue-compensating consumption tax leads to significant reductions in all three FGT poverty indices for rural households as a whole and for urban households as a whole.

In simulation 2, all three poverty measures increases in the short run for rural households as a whole and for urban households as a whole. On the other hand, in the long run all three poverty measures decrease for both rural households as a whole and for urban households as a whole. These declines are smaller than the corresponding long run declines in simulation 1.

Three measures of inequality have been used to assess the effects of the removal of tariffs on inequality: the Gini index, the Atkinson index and the entropy index. Results for simulation 1 reveal that in the short run, according to all three indices, the removal of tariffs without a revenue-compensating consumption tax increases inequality slightly among households in both rural and urban areas, as well as in the economy as a whole. In the long run, however, the three indices show declines in inequality, a result broadly consistent with Stolper-Samuelson theory.

In simulation 2, where the removal of tariffs is combined with a revenue-compensating consumption tax, inequality falls among rural, urban and all households in both the short run and the long run, again according to all three indices. The long run declines in the indices, although larger than their short run declines, are themselves smaller than the long run declines in simulation 1.

Comparisons of the poverty and inequality results of this study with those of other CGE studies of trade liberalisation reveal both consistencies and contradictions. The simulation 1 results indicating that poverty reduction is at best small in the short run but significant in the long run are broadly consistent with the short run findings of Mujeri and Khondker (2002) for Bangladesh and the short and long run findings of Naranpanawa (2005) for Sri Lanka. In addition, the simulation 1 results indicating a short run increase in inequality are the same in terms of direction of change as those of Vos and de Jong (2003) for Ecuador and Naranpanawa (2005) for Sri Lanka. On the other hand, the simulation 1 results point to a long run decline in inequality, whereas Naranpanawa's (2005) long run results point to an increase in inequality among all households, albeit a smaller increase than that indicated by his short run results.

The simulation 2 results show that poverty increases in the short run and decreases in the long run. The short run increase is broadly consistent with short run increases found in a range of studies that employ some form of replacement taxation to compensate for the loss of tariff revenue. They include Khondker and Raihan (2004) and Annabi et al. (2006) for Bangladesh, Annabi et al. (2005) for Senegal, and Emini et al. (2006) for Cameroon. (However, Bibi and Chatti's (2006) short run findings for Tunisia and the majority of the short run findings for Pakistan in Siddiqui et al. (2008) show favourable poverty outcomes.)

The long run decrease in poverty in simulation 2 is similar to the long run findings of Annabi et al. (2006) for Bangladesh, Annabi et al. (2005) for Senegal, Bibi and Chatti (2006) for Tunisia and Siddiqui et al. (2008) for Pakistan.

Finally, simulation 2 shows inequality declining in both the short run and the long run. These results contrast with the short and long run increases found by Annabi et al. (2005) for Senegal. The short run decline also contrasts with the short run increases in inequality found by Emini et al. (2006) for Cameroon.

9.4. Policy Implications

Although an across-the-board complete elimination of tariffs reduction may not be politically feasible, this study offers some useful policy insights. It results suggest that in the long run, the efficiency of resource allocation would be improved and poverty and inequality reduced by the Bangladesh government pursuing further trade liberalisation efforts. Yet Bangladesh has already implemented extensive liberalisation measures, with top tariff rates now at low levels and trade related quantitative restrictions nearly eliminated. In this situation, further trade liberalisation needs careful assessment of its likely benefits and adjustment costs, including those relating to government revenue. Further restructuring of the import policy regime might result in a substantial reduction in government revenues (Hossain, 2003; Raihan, 2008). Policy-makers would need to be careful in identifying avenues for possible expansion of the tax base, and in choosing an appropriate revenue replacement tax scheme. In view of the simulations involving a compensatory consumption tax, it is possible that the use of this tax to replace lost tariff revenue would not be a politically acceptable option in Bangladesh because of its apparent adverse short-run effects on total employment, the real incomes of all household groups and poverty, and because even in the long run its use appears to lead to a decline in aggregate real consumption.

Looking at the simulated effects on output and employment at the industry level, it appears that the removal of trade barriers would commit the Bangladesh economy to a development path involving a greater degree of specialisation in export industries such as ready-made garments and knitting where it presently possesses a strong comparative advantage. In recent times exports of ready-made garments and knitting exports have accounted for about 75 per cent of total export earnings and 81 per cent of exports of manufactures. The further narrowing of the export base would, however, increase the already high vulnerability of the economy to external shocks. In this regard, the abolition of the Multi-Fibre Agreement (MFA) from January 2005 in accordance with the provisions of the World Trade Organization (WTO) Agreement on Textile and Clothing (ATC) has provided Bangladesh with a great challenge. The ready-made garment sector now faces increased competition from export industries in countries such as China, India, Pakistan, Sri Lanka, Indonesia, Vietnam and Thailand, with possible negative consequences for household consumption and welfare (Arndt et al. 2002; Mlachila and Yongzheng, 2004). Although

Bangladesh achieved increases in both export value and market share in the USA market after the abolition of MFA quotas (Ahmed, 2009), this may prove to be only a short term phenomenon.

Partly because of the vulnerability arising from a high degree of commodity concentration in exports and partly because of the importance of increased agricultural productivity for pro-poor economic growth in a country like Bangladesh (Datt and Ravallion 1998), it is important that policy makers do not neglect the agricultural sectors that lose or gain little from tariff liberalisation. Despite its diminishing contribution to GDP, agriculture remains the main source of food supplies and continues to absorb a large proportion of unskilled labour. Thus there is still a need to improve strategies for providing agricultural credit, promoting technology-based modern agriculture, extending land reform, removing barriers to investment in agriculture, and (as agricultural activities are still highly exposed to major production shocks such as floods and droughts) implementing rehabilitation programs.

The simulation results support the prediction of the Stolper-Samuelson theorem that in the long run in the removal of tariffs leads to an increase real wages in a labour-abundant country. The results also show that in terms of increased employment opportunities female low-skilled labour is the principal beneficiary, indeed the sole beneficiary in simulation 2. This is essentially a reflection of the expansion of the export-oriented ready-made garment and knitting industries. Increased employment for women in these industries brings changing life styles as well as improved living standards. From a gender perspective on poverty, such outcomes would be particularly welcome. In the Bangladesh context, however, where total employment is not expanding rapidly and there is still a large male/female wage gap, they might be a source of social tensions.

Finally, the adverse short run poverty impacts of the removal of tariffs, particularly in simulation 2, suggest a need to soften these transitory effects. Targeted poverty reduction strategies and safety net programs could be considered as policy options to protect poor households during trade liberalisation. Possible measures include skill-enhancing programs focused on the more vulnerable household groups (which would, of course, also bring longer run benefits) and the expansion of existing schemes such as the Food for Works Program, old-age allowances, Vulnerable Group feeding programs and micro-credit schemes. Even though the latter programs have been in place for quite some time, their progress has been slow. To date, their coverage has been too limited to make a substantial impact on poverty levels.

9.5. Limitations of the Research

The present study has four major limitations.

First, the values of the elasticity parameters used in the study have not been estimated econometrically from time series and cross-sectional data for Bangladesh. Instead, the values have been borrowed from other related studies. Although we have established the robustness of the simulation results with respect to elasticity values, it is still necessary to interpret the results with caution.

Second, in the absence of more recent information, the model used to simulate the effects of the removal of tariffs was based on data from the Input-Output Table 2000, SAM 2000 and

HIES of 2000 for Bangladesh. However, it is apparent that since 2000 there have been considerable changes in economic structure, performance and policy in Bangladesh. These developments can be expected to have reduced somewhat the usefulness of this study's analysis of the impacts of trade reform policies.

Third, the study has used a comparative static model in which the simulation results show only the difference between two alternative states (with and without the policy change). The model fails to show the adjustment path to the new equilibrium state, even though by using alternative closures it is possible to differentiate between long run and short run equilibrium outcomes. In other words, it does not track variables continuously over time.

Fourth, in simulating the poverty and inequality impacts of the removal of tariffs, the present study has adopted a representative household approach in which it is assumed that when the mean income of a household group changes, the income of each household within the group changes by the same percentage. This abstraction from possible variations in the relative dispersions of intra-group incomes may have resulted in biased estimates of the poverty and inequality impacts of trade liberalisation. A better way to predict the poverty and inequality impacts of trade liberalisation would be to follow a micro-simulation approach that takes into account individual heterogeneities through econometrically estimated household behavioural equations. However, this type of model needs data at the household level, which at the time of the study were not yet available for Bangladesh.

9.6. Areas for Further Research

A number of extensions can be suggested for further research into the impact of trade liberalisation on poverty and inequality in Bangladesh.

To overcome the limitation of a comparative static framework that captures the economic impact of trade liberalisation at only a single point in time, either short run or long run, the model could be extended to incorporate a dynamic structure that that explicitly traces each variable through time. A dynamic CGE model would allow the tracking of the impacts of trade reform on capital accumulation and thus the growth path of the economy, and it would enable the identification of the changing income and expenditure patterns of households, thereby providing a more complete picture of poverty and inequality effects.

In addition, the broad rural/urban approach to the analysis of the impact of trade reform on poverty and inequality need to be extended geographically to take into account regional disparities. A regionally disaggregated computable general equilibrium model would be useful in providing detailed spatial analysis of the impact of trade policy, which would in turn help in designing regionally targeted policies to ameliorate adverse effects of policy reform.

Another area for further research is the analysis of the gender dimension of poverty and inequality. According to Fontana and Rodgers (2005), taking gender inequality into consideration in CGE models could significantly improve our knowledge of the mechanisms through which macroeconomic policy affects poverty and how men and women experience poverty differently.

Although the present model includes an aggregate treatment of the labour market, it lacks a micro analysis of industry and occupational labour markets. A more detailed treatment of labour markets, including regional markets, could contribute to a deeper understanding of the effects of trade liberalisation on poverty and inequality, including the role played by rural-urban migration.

In the present study, no allowance was made for the deployment of instruments of welfare adjustment when tracing the effects of eliminating tariffs. A further modification would be to include some 'safety net' policy options, specifically designed to provide some protection for the poorest groups in the population. In addition, given the desirability of offsetting the loss of tariff revenue or, more broadly, ensuring that trade liberalisation is budget-neutral, it would be useful to explore the effects of a range of fiscal alternatives to a compensatory consumption tax.

Finally, when the data become available, the development of a CGE-micro simulation top-down model that captures individual heterogeneity in sources of income, consumption preferences and endowment of human capital would provide a much more comprehensive analysis of the effects of trade liberalisation poverty and inequality in Bangladesh.

APPENDICES

APPENDIX A

Table A 2.1. Effective protection rates (EPRs) in 40 sectors in Bangladesh (percentages)

	Effective rates of protection							
Sector Name	1992/93	1993/94	1994/95	1995/96	1996/97	1997/98	1998/99	1999/00
01. Rice	-8.0	0.9	2.4	-5.8	-5.7	-5.4	-5.3	-4.7
02. Wheat	-3.9	8.5	11.0	2.0	2.2	2.6	2.8	0.2
03. Coarse Grains	-4.9	-4.1	-0.8	-0.2	-0.2	0.1	0.1	0.4
04. Jute	64.4	67.2	30.6	31.8	32.0	32.4	32.5	26.8
05. Sugar Cane	68.4	71.3	14.2	14.8	15.0	15.2	15.2	15.8
06. Cotton	4.8	5.4	-2.0	-1.7	-1.7	-1.5	-1.5	-1.4
07. Tobacco	12.5	-0.9	10.2	11.8	12.1	11.1	11.3	12.2
08. Potato	58.9	60.4	48.8	36.7	35.7	26.9	24.5	23.1
09. Other Vegetable	71.7	43.6	44.5	32.1	32.2	32.1	32.1	26.9
10. Pulses	19.9	18.1	17.4	16.9	17.0	18.2	11.3	8.3
11. Oil Seeds	53.8	42.7	35.6	24.6	24.7	22.8	22.8	19.7
12. Fruits	58.2	60.5	44.9	40.2	39.9	38.1	36.3	33.1
13. Tea	82.7	85.1	66.0	48.7	48.8	46.4	43.4	41.0
14. Other Crops	64.9	40.4	41.5	28.3	28.6	28.1	27.2	22.5
15. Livestock	74.3	54.0	42.0	33.2	32.8	28.8	28.0	24.8
16. Fish	78.4	45.3	45.1	28.4	28.5	27.9	28.0	23.2
17. Forestry	38.8	32.7	23.9	22.7	22.9	19.7	19.2	16.9
18. Other Fruits	489.2	327.4	88.5	88.3	86.0	76.7	68.3	66.9
19. Edible Oil	74.8	46.5	39.6	55.6	53.7	41.4	35.3	35.0
20. Sugar and Gur	96.3	42.3	52.3	51.1	51.4	40.0	38.5	31.1
21. Salt	51.4	61.6	43.5	37.2	34.6	30.7	29.1	29.6
22. Yarn	69.0	57.4	60.9	51.7	35.0	34.2	33.7	30.5
23. Cloth: Mill	189.7	147.5	131.6	98.0	110.2	86.2	78.2	72.7
24. Cloth: Handloom	157.7	128.5	114.6	87.6	94.9	75.5	68.8	64.6
25.Readymade Garments	237.2	130.0	84.1	53.7	57.4	65.4	60.5	58.9
26. Jute Textile	98.2	93.5	81.0	55.7	56.0	48.4	44.1	43.5
27. Paper	68.3	74.1	48.8	25.4	22.7	12.7	11.3	15.5
28. Leather and Leather Products	98.6	87.3	42.3	20.7	15.8	8.8	5.90	6.5
29. Chemical Fertilizer	-5.6	-2.2	-5.0	-3.6	-3.0	0.4	0.5	0.6

Table A 2.1. (Continued)

	Effective rates of protection							
Sector Name	1992/93	1993/94	1994/95	1995/96	1996/97	1997/98	1998/99	1999/00
30. Pharmaceutical	1.5	-2.2	-2.5	-2.6	-1.4	0.7	0.6	-1.7
31. Chemical	30.3	15.4	14.9	12.5	13.8	15.2	16.1	9.7
32. Petroleum Products	40.2	32.8	45.7	35.5	35.7	32.3	31.2	27.3
33. Cement	56.0	30.6	21.4	18.5	19.1	19.0	20.3	21.2
34. Steel and Basic Metal	40.9	27.2	27.4	25.1	24.6	25.0	25.1	19.5
35. Metal Products	52.7	43.3	25.1	25.8	27.0	18.2	17.3	15.4
36. Machinery	47.5	28.9	15.1	12.6	12.3	9.3	9.6	5.2
37. Transport Equipment	69.9	49.1	41.9	38.0	22.8	21.8	19.8	17.9
38.Wood and Wood Products	124.0	81.0	48.1	47.3	47.3	32.9	32.9	31.8
39. Tobacco Products	133.6	69.9	89.7	85.0	86.7	81.9	74.7	68.5
Other Industries	72.7	65.1	38.5	37.3	29.6	21.9	21.0	19.9
a) Average ERP	75.7	56.7	40.6	33.0	32.4	28.6	26.8	24.5
b)Standard Deviation (SD)	84.4	57.0	31.2	25.7	26.9	23.0	20.9	20.0
c)Coefficient of Variation	111.5	100.6	76.9	77.7	82.6	80.4	78.2	81.6

Source World Bank (1999a).

APPENDIX B

Table B 5.1. List of variables in the Bangladesh model

Variable	Set	Description
(Change)		
delV1TAX(c,s,i)	COMxSRCxIND	*Intermediate tax revenue*
delV2TAX(c,s,i)	COMxSRCxIND	*Investment tax revenue*
delV3TAXHOU(c,s,h)	COMxSRCxHOUS	*Household tax revenue*
delV4TAX(c)	COM	*Export tax revenue*
delV5TAX(c,s)	COMxSRC	*Government tax revenue*
delV1PTX(i)	IND	*Ordinary change in production tax revenue*
delV0TAR(c)	COM	*Ordinary change in tariff revenue*
delV1PRIM(i)	IND	*Ordinary change in cost of primary factors*
delV1CST(i)	IND	*Change in ex-tax cost of production*
delV1TOT(i)	IND	*Change in tax-inc cost of production*
delPTXRATE(i)	IND	*Change in rate of production tax*
delV6(c,s)	COMxSRC	*Value of inventories*
delx6(c,s)	COMxSRC	*Inventories demands*
Delsgovsav	1	*Government (income - expenditure)/GDP*
delSale(c,s,d)	COMxSRCxDEST	*Sales aggregates*
delV1tax_csi	1	*Aggregate revenue from indirect taxes on intermediate*
delV2tax_csi	1	*Aggregate revenue from indirect taxes on investment*

Variable	Set	Description
delV3tax_csh	1	*Aggregate revenue from indirect taxes on households*
delV4tax_c	1	*Aggregate revenue from indirect taxes on export*
delV5tax_cs	1	*Aggregate revenue from indirect taxes on government*
delV0tar_c	1	*Aggregate tariff revenue*
delV1PTX_i	1	*Ordinary change in all-industry production tax revenue*
delV0tax_csi	1	*Aggregate revenue from all indirect taxes*
delB		*(Balance of Trade)/GDP*
Scalar variables		
p3tot_h	1	*Consumer Price Index*
x3tot_h	1	*Real Household Consumption*
w3tot_h	1	*Nominal Total Household Consumption*
f1lab_io	1	*Overall Wage Shifter*
w1lab_io	1	*Aggregate Payments to Labour*
f1tax_csi	1	*Uniform % Change in Powers of Taxes on Intermediate Usage*
f2tax_csi	1	*Uniform % Change in Powers of Taxes on Investment*
f3tax_cs	1	*Uniform % Change in Powers of Taxes on Household Usage*
f4tax_ntrad	1	*Uniform % change in powers of taxes on nontraditional exports*
f4tax_trad		*Uniform % change in powers of taxes on traditional exports*
f5tax_cs	1	*Uniform % Change in Powers of Taxes on "Other" Usage*
x4_ntrad	1	*Quantity, collective export aggregate*
f4p_ntrad	1	*Upward demand shift, collective export aggregate*
f4q_ntrad	1	*Right demand shift, collective export*
p4_ntrad		*Price, collective export aggregate*
f3tot_h	1	*Overall Shift Term For Consumption*
f5tot	1	*Overall Shift Term For "Other" Demands*
f5tot2	1	*Ratio between f5tot and x3tot*
p0cif_c	1	*Imports Price Index, CIF, Taka*
p0gdpexp	1	*GDP Price Index, Expenditure Side*
p0imp_c	1	*Duty - paid Imports Price Index, Rand*
x1prim_i	1	*Aggregate Output: Primary Factor Cost Weights*
p0realdev	1	*Real Devaluation*
p0toft	1	*Terms of Trade*
pLabEff		*Effective price of labour, inc. labour-saving technical change*
pLabEff_p1prim		*PLabEff / p1prim_i*
pLabEff_p3tot		*PLabEff / p3tot*
p3tot_p0GNE		*P3tot / p0GNE*
p0GNE_p0GDPExp		*P0GNE / p0GDPExp*
p0GDPExp_p1prim		*P0GDPExp / p1prim_i*
pCap_p1prim		*PCap / p1prim_i*
pCap_p2tot		*PCap_i / p2tot*
p2tot_p0GNE		*P2tot_i / p0GNE*
p1prim_i	1	*Primary Factor Cost Deflator*

Table B 5.1. (Continued)

Variable	Set	Description
w1prim_i	1	*Aggregate Primary Factor Payments*
employ_i	1	*Aggregate Employment - Wage Bill Weights*
Realwage		*Average real wage*
x1cap_i	1	*Aggregate Capital Stock, Rental Weights*
x1lnd_i		*Aggregate land stock, Rental Weights*
p1cap_i	1	*Average Capital Rental*
p2tot_i	1	*Aggregate Investment Price Index*
Phi	1	*Exchange Rate, Taka/$world*
p4tot	1	*Exports Price Index*
p5tot	1	*"Other" Demands Price Index*
p6tot	1	*Inventories Price Index*
x0gne	1	*Real GNE*
p0gne	1	*GNE price index*
w0gne	1	*Nominal GNE*
Xgdpfac	1	*Real GDP at factor cost (inputs) = x1prim_i*
x0gdpinc (change)	1	*Real GDP from the income side*
p1lab_io	1	*Average nominal wage*
p1lnd_i	1	*Average land rental*
x0gdpfac (change)	1	*Real GDP at factor cost*
contBOT	1	*Contribution of BOT to real expenditure-side GDP*
w0cif_c	1	*CIF Taka Value of Imports*
w0gdpexp	1	*Nominal GDP from Expenditure Side*
w0gdpinc	1	*Nominal GDP from Income Side*
w0imp_c	1	*Value of Imports plus Duty*
w0tax_csi	1	*Aggregate Revenue from All Indirect Taxes*
w1cap_i	1	*Aggregate Payments to Capital*
w1lnd_i	1	*Aggregate Payments to Land*
w1oct_i	1	*Aggregate Other Cost Ticket Payments*
w2tot_i	1	*Aggregate Nominal Investment*
w4tot	1	*Taka Border Value of exports*
w5tot	1	*Aggregate Nominal Value of "Other" Demands*
w6tot	1	*Aggregate Nominal Value of Inventories*
Invslack		*Investment slack variable for exogenising aggregate investment Economy–wide rate of return*
f2tot	1	*Ratio, investment/consumption*
Capslack	1	*Slack variable to allow fixing aggregate capital*
x0cif_c	1	*Import Volume Index, CIF Weights*
x0gdpexp	1	*Real GDP from Expenditure Side*
x0imp_c	1	*Import Volume Index, Duty - Paid Weights*
x2tot_i	1	*Aggregate Real Investment Expenditure*
x4tot	1	*Export Volume Index*
x5tot	1	*Aggregate Real "Other" Demands*
x6tot	1	*Aggregate Real Inventories*
q_h	1	*Total Number of Households*
Wgosgov	1	*GOS income to government + GOS transfers to government*
Wgosrow	1	*GOS income to ROW + GOS transfers to ROW*
Wgostax	1	*Corporation tax*
Wgovgos	1	*Interest on public debt*
Wgovrow	1	*GOV transfers to ROW*

Variable	Set	Description
Wrowgos	1	*GOS from ROW*
Wrowgov	1	*Transfers from ROW to government*
Wgossav	1	*Retained earnings*
Wgos	1	*Total GOS*
Wgos_posttax	1	*VGOS less VGOSTAX*
Fgostax	1	*Ad valorem rate of corporation tax*
Wgoshou_h	1	*Total GOS to households*
Whousinc_h	1	*Total pre-tax household income*
Wdispinc_h	1	*Total post-tax household income*
avetax_h	1	*Average tax factor : wdispwagerate-avewagerate*
f_inctaxrate_h	1	*Income tax shifter: overall*
f_gosinctax	1	*fgostax - f_inctaxrate_h*
Wincgov	1	*Government income*
Wgovcur	1	*Current government expenditure*
Wgovcap	1	*Investment government expenditure*
Wgovexp	1	*Total government expenditure*
Wgovsav	1	*Government (income - expenditure)*
Realgovsav	1	*Real government (income - expenditure)*
Wprivcap	1	*Investment private expenditure*
Wrowexp	1	*Total ROW expenditure*
Wincrow	1	*Total ROW income*
Wrowsav	1	*ROW (income - expenditure)*
pline_phr	1	*Aggregate poverty line*
pline_phu	1	*Aggregate poverty line*
Wsamcheck	1	*Global (income - expenditure)*
Vector variables		
x4(c)	COM	*Export*
t4(c)	COM	*Power of Export Tax*
p4(c)	COM	*Exports Taka*
x1cap(i)	IND	*Current Capital Stock*
p1cap(i)	IND	*Rental Price of Capital*
a1cap(i)	IND	*Capital Augmenting Technical Change*
x1lnd(i)	IND	*Use of Land*
p1lnd(i)	IND	*Rental Price of Land*
a1lnd(i)	IND	*Land Augmenting Technical Change*
x1oct(i)	IND	*Demand for "Other Cost" Tickets*
p1oct(i)	IND	*Price of "Other Cost" Tickets*
a1oct(i)	IND	*"Other Cost" Ticket Augmenting Technical Change*
f1oct(i)	IND	*Shifts in Price of "Other Cost" Tickets*
Ggro(i)	IND	*Gross growth rate of capital = Investment/capital*
Gret(i)	IND	*Gross rate of return = Rental/[Price of new capital]*
p1mat(i)	IND	*Intermediate cost price index*
p1var(i)	IND	*Short-run variable cost price index*
pliner(prh)		*Poverty line for rural Households*
plineu(puh)		*Poverty line for urban. Households*
Finv1(i)	IND	*Shifter to enforce DPSV investment rule*
Finv2(i)	IND	*Shifter for "exogenous" investment rule*
Finv3(i)	IND	*Shifter for long run investment rule*
fgret(i)	IND	*Shifter to lock together industry rates of return*

Table B 5.1. (Continued)

Variable	Set	Description
t0imp(c)	COM	*Power of Tariffs*
p0imp(c)	COM	*Basic price of imported goods = p0(c,"imp")*
pe(c)		*Basic price of exportables*
p0dom(c)		*Basic price of domestic goods = p0(c,"dom")*
x0loc(c)	COM	*Real percent change in LOCSALES (dom+imp)*
p0com(c)	COM	*General output price of locally-produced commodity*
x0com(c)	COM	*Output of commodities*
qh(h)	HOUS	*Number of Households*
Utilityh(h)	HOUS	*Utility per Household*
w3luxh(h)	HOUS	*Nominal Supernumerary Expenditure*
w3tot(h)	HOUS	*Nominal Household Consumption*
f3tot(h)	HOUS	*Shift Term For Consumption*
p3tot(h)	HOUS	*Consumer Price Index*
x3tot(h)	HOUS	*Real Household Consumption*
f0tax_s(c)		*General Sales Tax Shifter*
f4p(c)	COM	*Price (upward) Shift in Export Demand Schedule*
f4q(c)	COM	*Quantity (right) Shift in Export Demands*
pf0cif(c)	COM	*C.I.F. Foreign Currency Import Prices*
x0dom(c)	COM	*Total Supplies of Domestic Goods*
x0imp(c)	COM	*Total Supplies of Imported Goods*
a1prim(i)	IND	*All Factor Augmenting Technical Change*
a1tot(i)	IND	*All Input Augmenting Technical Change*
a2tot(i)	IND	*Neutral Technical Change - Investment*
employ(i)		*Employment by industry*
p1prim(i)	IND	*Effective Price of Primary Factor Composite*
p1tot(i)	IND	*Average Input/Output Price*
p2tot(i)	IND	*Costs of Units of Capital*
a1lab_o(i)	IND	*Labour-Augmenting Technical Change*
f1lab_o(i)	IND	*Industry Specific Wage Shifter*
p1lab_o(i)	IND	*Price of Labour Composite (B)*
p1lab_i(o)	OCC	*Average wage of occupation*
x1lab_o(i)	IND	*Effective Labour Input*
x1lab_i(o)	OCC	*Employment by occupation*
f1lab_i(o)	OCC	*Occupation - Specific Wage Shifter*
x1prim(i)	IND	*Primary Factor Composite*
x1tot(i)	IND	*Activity Level or Value - Added*
x2tot(i)	IND	*Investment by Using Industry*
p1cst(i)		*Index of production costs (for AnalyseGE)*
t0imp(c)		*Power of tariff*
Wgoshou(h)	HOUS	*GOS to households*
Wgovhou(h)	HOUS	*Government transfers to households*
Whougov(h)	HOUS	*Income tax + households transfers to government*
Whourow(h)	HOUS	*Household transfers to ROW*
Wrowhou(h)	HOUS	*ROW transfers to households*
w1labinc_o(h)	HOUS	*Total wages to households(h)*
whousinc(h)	HOUS	*Pre-tax household income*
wdispinc(h)	HOUS	*Post-tax household income*
f_inctaxrate(h)	HOUS	*Income tax shifter: by income*
Whousav(h)	HOUS	*Household saving*

Variable	Set	Description
f3tot(h)	HOUS	*Shift term for consumption (ratio, Consumption/GDP)*
w1lab_i(o)	OCC	*Total labour bills(o)*
labslack(o)	OCC	*Employment rate*
s2gov(i)	IND	*Government share of investment by industry*
contGDPexp(e)		*Contributions to real expenditure-side GDP*
contGDPinc(c)		*Income-side real GDP decomposition*
contGDPfac(c)		*Contributions to real GDP at factor cost:x0gdpfac*
Matrix variables		
x1(c,s,i)	COMxSRCxIND	*Intermediate basic demands*
x2(c,s,i)	COMxSRCxIND	*Investment basic demands*
x3(c,s,h)	COMxSRCxHOUS	*Household basic demands*
x5(c,s)	COMxSRC	*Government basic demands*
a3(c,s)	COMxSRC	*Household basic taste change*
x3_s(c,h)	COMxHOUS	*Household use of imp/dom composite*
a1(c,s,i)	CONxSRCxIND	*Intermediate basic technical change*
q1(c,i)	COMxIND	*Output by commodity and industry*
p0(c,s)	COMxSRC	*Basic price of commodity c, source s*
pq1(c,i)	COMxIND	*Price of commodity c produced by industry i*
f5(c,s)	COMxSRC	*Other Demand Shift*
x1mar(c,s,i,m)	COMxSRCxINDx MAR	*Intermediate margin demand*
x2mar(c,s,i,m)	COMxSRCxINDx MAR	*Investment margin demands*
x3mar(c,s,m,h)	COMxSRCxMARx HOUS	*Household margin demands*
x4mar(c,m)	COMxMAR	*Export margin demands*
x5mar(c,s,m)	COMxSRCxMAR	*Government margin demands*
a1mar(c,s,i,m)	COMxSRCxINDx MAR	*Intermediate margin technical change*
a2mar(c,s,i,m)	COMxSRCxINDx MAR	*Investment margin technical change*
a3mar(c,s,m)	COMxSRCxMAR	*Household margin technical change*
a4mar(c,m)	COMxSRC	*Export margin technical change*
a5mar(c,s,m)	COMxSRCxMAR	*Government margin technical change*
t1(c,s,i)	COMxSRCxIND	*Power of tax on intermediate*
t2(c,s,i)	COMxSRCxIND	*Power of tax on investment*
t3(c,s)	COMxSRC	*Power of tax on household*
t5(c,s)	COMxSRC	*Power of tax on government*
p1(c,s,i)	COMxSRCxIND	*Purchaser's price, intermediate*
p2(c,s,i)	COMxSRCxIND	*Purchaser's price, investment*
p3(c,s,h)	COMxSRCxHOUS	*Purchaser's price, household*
p5(c,s)	COMxSRC	*Purchaser's price, government*
fx6(c,s) (Change)		*Shifter on rule for stocks*
x1lab(i,o)	INDxOCC	*Employment by industry and occupation*
p1lab(i,o)	INDxOCC	*Wages by industry and occupation*
f1lab(I,o)	INDxOCC	*Wage shift variable*
x1_s(c,i)	COMxIND	*Intermediate use of imp/dom composite*
x2_s(c,i)	COMxIND	*Investment use of imp/dom composite*
x3lux(c,h)	COMxHOUS	*Household - supernumerary demands*
x3sub(c,h)	COMxHOUS	*Household - subsistence demands*

Table B 5.1. (Continued)

Variable	Set	Description
a3lux(c,h)	COMxHOUS	*Taste change, supernumerary demands*
a3sub(c,h)	COMxHOUS	*Taste change, subsistence demands*
p1_s(c,i)	COMxIND	*Price, intermediate imp/dom composite*
p2_s(c,i)	COMxIND	*Price, investment imp/dom composite*
p3_s(c,h)	COMxHOUS	*Price, household imp/dom composite*
a3_s(c,h)	COMxHOUS	*Taste change, household imp/dom composite*
a2(c,s,i)	COMxSRCxIND	*Investment basic technical change*
a1_s(c,i)	COMxIND	*Technical change, intermediate imp/dom composite*
a2_s(c,i)	COMxIND	*Technical change, investment imp/dom composite*
Fandecomp(c,f)	COM	*Fan decomposition*
SalesDecomp(c,d)	COMxDEST	*Sales decomposition*
Whouhou(hto,hfrom)	HOUSxHOUS	*intra-household transfers*
w1labinc(o,h)	OCCxHOUS	*Labour income from OCC to House*

Table B 5.2. List of coefficients and parameters in the Bangladesh model

Coefficients	Set	Description
V1BAS(c,s,i)	COMxSRCxIND	*Intermediate basic flows*
V2BAS(c,s,i)	COMxSRCxIND	*Investment basic flows*
V3BASHOU(c,s,h)	COMxSRCxHOUS	*Household basic flows*
V4BAS(c)	COM	*Export basic flows*
V5BAS(c,s)	COMxSRC	*Government basic flows*
V6BAS(c,s)	COMxSRC	*Inventories basic flows*
V1MAR(c,s,i,m)	COMxSRCxINDxMAR	*Intermediate margins*
V2MAR(c,s,i,m)	COMxSRCxINDxMAR	*Investment margins*
V3MARHOU(c,s,h,m)	COMxSRCxHOUSxMAR	*Household margins*
V4MAR(c,m)	COMxMAR	*Export margins*
V5MAR(c,s,m)	COMxSRCxMAR	*Government margins*
V1TAX(c,s,i)	COMxSRCxIND	*Taxes on intermediate*
V2TAX(c,s,i)	COMxSRCxIND	*Taxes on investment*
V3TAXHOU(c,s,h)	COMxSRCxHOUS	*Taxes on households*
V4TAX(c)	COM	*Taxes on export*
V5TAX(c,s)	COMxSRC	*Taxes on government*
V1LAB(i,o)	INDxOCC	*Wage bill matrix*
V1CAP(i)	IND	*Capital rentals*
V1LND(i)	IND	*Land rentals*
V1PTX(i)	IND	*Production tax*
V1OCT(i)	IND	*Other cost tickets*
V0TAR(c)	COM	*Tariff revenue*
V1PUR(c,s,i)	COMxSRCxIND	*Intermediate purchase. value*
V2PUR(c,s,i)	COMxSRCxIND	*Investment purchase. value*
V3PUR(c,s,h)	COMxSRCxHOUS	*Households purchase. value*
V4PUR(c)	COM	*Export purchase. value*
V5PUR(c,s)	COMxSRC	*Government purchase. value*
SIGMA1LAB(i)	IND	*CES substitution between skill types*
V1LAB_O(i)	IND	*Total labour bill in industry i*
SIGMA1PRIM(i)	IND	*CES substitution, primary factors*
V1PRIM(i)	IND	*Total factor input to industry i*
SIGMA1(c)	COM	*Armington elasticities: Intermediate*

Coefficients	Set	Description
V1PUR_S(c,i)	COMxIND	*Dom+imp intermediate purchase. value*
S1(c,s,i)	COMxSRCxIND	*Intermediate source shares*
V1MAT(i)	IND	*Total intermediate cost for industry i*
V1VAR(i)	IND	*Short-run variable cost for industry i*
V1CST(i)	IND	*Total cost of industry i*
V1TOT(i)	IND	*Total industry cost plus tax*
PTXRATE(i)	IND	*Rate of production tax*
SIGMA1OUT(i)	IND	*CET transformation elasticities*
MAKE(c,i)	COMxIND	*Multiproduction matrix*
MAKE_C(i)	IND	*All production by industry i*
MAKE_I(c)	COM	*Total production of commodities*
EXPSHR(c)	COM	*Share going to exports*
TAU(c)	COM	*1/Elast. of transformation, exportable/locally used*
SIGMA2(c)	COM	*Armington elasticities: Investment*
V2PUR_S(c,i)	COMxIND	*Dom+imp investment purchase. value*
S2(c,s,i)	COMxSRCxIND	*Investment source shares*
V2TOT(i)	IND	*Total capital created for industry i*
SIGMA3(c)	COM	*Armington elasticities: households*
V3PUR_S(c,h)	COMxHOUS	*Dom+imp households purchase. value*
S3(c,s,h)	COMxSRCxHOUS	*Household source shares*
V3TOTh(h)	HOUS	*Total purchases by households*
V3TOT_H		*Total purchases by households*
S3_S(c,h)	COMxHOUS	*Household average budget shares*
FRISCH(h)	HOUS	*Frisch LES 'parameter'= - (total/luxury)*
EPS(c,h)	COMxHOUS	*Household expenditure elasticities*
S3_H(h)	HOUS	*Household shares*
B3LUX(c,h)	COMxHOUS	*Ratio(supernumerary /total expenditure)*
S3LUX(c,h)	COMxHOUS	*Marginal household budget shares*
EXP_ELAST(c)	COM	*Export demand elasticities*
EXP_ELAST_NT		*Collective export demand elasticity*
V4NTRADEXP		*Total collective export earnings*
MARSALES(c)	COM	*Total usage for margins purposes*
SALE(c,s,d)	COMxSRCxDEST	*Sales aggregates*
V0IMP(c)	COM	*Total basic-value imports of good c*
SALES(c)	COM	*Total sales of domestic commodities*
DOMSALES(c)	COM	*Total sales to local market*
V1TAX_CSI		*Total intermediate tax revenue*
V2TAX_CSI		*Total investment tax revenue*
V3TAX_CSH		*Total households tax revenue*
V4TAX_C		*Total export tax revenue*
V5TAX_CS		*Total government tax revenue*
V0TAR_C		*Total tariff revenue*
V1CAP_I		*Total payments to capital*
V1LAB_IO		*Total payments to labour*
V1LND_I		*Total payments to land*
V1PTX_I		*Total production tax/subsidy*
V1OCT_I		*Total other cost ticket payments*
V1PRIM_I		*Total primary factor payments*
V0GDPINC		*Nominal GDP from income side*
V0TAX_CSI		*Total indirect tax revenue*

Table B 5.2. (Continued)

Coefficients	Set	Description
V0CIF(c)	COM	*Total ex-duty imports of good c*
V0IMP_C		*Total basic-value imports (includes tariffs)*
V2TOT_I		*Total investment usage*
V4TOT		*Total export earnings*
V5TOT		*Total value of government demands*
V6TOT		*Total value of inventories*
V0GNE		*GNE from expenditure side*
V0GDPEXP		*GDP from expenditure side*
V1LAB_I(o)	OCC	*Total wages, occupation o*
LOCSALES(c)	COM	*Total local sales of dom + imp good c*
V1LABINC(o,h)	OCCxHOUS	*Labour income from occupation to household*
V1LABINC_O(h)	HOUS	*Total wage income to households*
VGOSSAV		*Gross retained earnings*
VGOSGOV		*GOS income to government + GOS transfers to government*
VGOSROW		*GOS income to ROW + GOS transfers to ROW*
VGOSTAX		*Corporation tax*
VGOVGOS		*Interest on public debt*
VGOVROW		*GOV transfers to ROW*
VROWGOS		*GOS from ROW*
VROWGOV		*Transfers from ROW to government*
VGOSHOU(h)	HOUS	*GOS to households*
VGOVHOU(h)	HOUS	*Government transfers to households*
VHOUGOV(h)	HOUS	*Income tax + household transfers to government*
VHOUROW(h)	HOUS	*Household transfers to ROW*
VROWHOU(h)	HOUS	*ROW transfers to households*
VHOUHOU(hto,hfrom)	HOUSxHOUS	*Intra-household transfers*
GOVSHRINV(i)	IND	*Government share of investment by industry*
VGOS		*Total GOS*
VGOS_POSTTAX		*VGOS less VGOSTAX*
GOSTAXRATE		*Ad valorem GOS Tax*
VGOSHOU_H		*Total GOS to households*
VHOUSINC(h)	HOUS	*Pre-tax household income*
VDISPINC(h)	HOUS	*Post-tax household income*
VHOUSAV(h)	HOUS	*Household saving*
VINCGOV		*Government income*
VGOVCUR		*Current government expenditure*
VGOVCAP		*Investment government expenditure*
VGOVEXP		*Total government expenditure*
VGOVSAV		*Government (income - expenditure)*
VPRIVCAP		*Investment private expenditure*
VROWEXP		*Total ROW expenditure*
VINCROW		*Total ROW income*
VROWSAV		*ROW (income - expenditure)*
VSAMCHECK		*Global (income - expenditure)*
INCTAXRATE(h)	HOUS	*Tax rates*
INITVGDPfac		*Initial factor cost GDP at current prices*
EXPGDP(e)	EXPMAC	*Expenditure Aggregates*
INCGDP(i)	INCMAC	*Income Aggregates*
TAX(t)	TAXMAC	*Tax Aggregates*

Coefficients	Set	Description
IMPSHR(c)	COM	*Share of imports in local market*
TARFRATE(c)	COM	*Ad valorem tariff rate*
PRVSHRINV(i)	IND	*Private share of investment by industry*
DOMINV(i)	IND	*Investment use of domestic goods*
DOMUSE(u)	USER	*Total domestic use*
IMPUSE(c,u)	COMxUSER	*Imports at basic prices*
IMPDUTY(u)	USER	*Duty paid, by user*
IMPCIF(u)	USER	*Imports CIF*
V2TAX_CS(i)	IND	*Total investment tax*
SAM(i,j)	CASHDESTxSPENDER	*Social accounting matrix*
INCTOT(i)	CASHDEST	*Total income*
EXPTOT(j)	SPENDER	*Expenditure totals*
V3TOT_phr		*Aggregate monetary poverty line for rural areas*
V3TOT_phu		*Aggregate monetary Poverty line for urban areas*
BPOVLINE		*Base year poverty line*

B 5.3. Derivation of consumer demand for a composite commodity[1]

The Stone-Geary utility function is

$$\text{utility per household} = \frac{1}{Q}\prod_{c}\{X3\_S(c) - X3SUB(c)\}^{S3LUX(c)} \quad (1)$$

where $X3SUB$ and $S3LUX$ are behavioural coefficients; Q is the number of households and $\sum_{c} S3LUX(c)=1$. The household's problem is to choose $X3\_S(c)/Q$ to maximise utility subject to the budget constraint:

$$\sum_{c} X3\_S(c)/Q * P3\_S(c) = V3TOT/Q \quad (2)$$

The Lagrangian function is

$$L = \frac{1}{Q}\prod_{c}\{X3\_S(c) - X3SUB(c)\}^{S3LUX(c)} - \lambda[V3TOT/Q - \frac{\sum X3\_S(c)}{Q} * P3\_S(c)] \quad (3)$$

The first order condition is,

[1] This section is mainly taken from Horridge, et al. (1993).

$$\partial L \big/ \partial(X3\_S(c)/Q) = \prod_c S3LUX(c)\{\frac{X3\_S(c)}{Q} - X3SUB(c)\}^{S3LUX(c)-1} - \lambda P3\_S(c) \tag{4}$$

$$= S3LUX(c).U.\{X3\_S(c) - X3SUB(c)\}^{-1} - \lambda P3\_S(c)$$

$$\lambda P3\_S(c) = S3LUX(c).U.\{\frac{X3\_S(c)}{Q} - X3SUB(c)\}^{-1} \tag{5}$$

Manipulating the above equation we obtain,

$$P3\_S(c).X3\_S(c) - p3\_S(c).X3SUB(c) = S3LUX(c).Q.\frac{U}{\lambda} \tag{6}$$

Now summing over c and by using equation (2) we obtain,

$$\frac{Q.U}{\lambda}.\sum_c S3LUX(c) = V3TOT - \sum_c P3\_S(c).X3SUB(c) \tag{7}$$

Substituting this result back into equation (6) we get the following Linear Expenditure System (LES) which shows that expenditure on each good is a linear function of prices (P3_S) and expenditure (V3TOT).

$$P3\_S(c).X3\_S(c) = P3\_S(c).X3SUB(c) - V3TOT - \sum_c P3\_S(c).X3SUB(c) \tag{8}$$

By definition, $V3TOT - \sum_c X3SUB(c).P3\_S(c) = V3LUX\_C$ (9)

i.e., households' 'supernumerary' expenditures ($V3LUX\_C$) are determined after subsistence expenditures are deducted from total expenditure ($V3TOT$).

Substituting equation (9) in equation (8) we obtain the following demand equation

$$X3\_S(c) = X3SUB(c) + S3LUX(c).V3LUX\_C / P3\_S(c) \tag{10}$$

APPENDIX C

Table C 6.1. Commodity and industry classification in the Bangladesh model

No.	I-O table industries	Model industry code	I-O table commodities	Model commodity code
1	Paddy Cultivation	Paddy	Paddy	Paddy
2	Wheat Cultivation	Wheat	Wheat	Wheat
3	Other Grain Cultivation	Othergrain	Other Grains	Othergrain
4	Jute Cultivation	JuteCultiv	Jute	JuteCultiv
5	Sugarcane Cultivation	SugcaneCulti	Sugarcane	SugcaneCulti
6	Potato Cultivation	PotatoCulti	Potato	PotatoCulti
7	Vegetable Cultivation	VegCulti	Vegetables	VegCulti
8	Pulses Cultivation	PulseCulti	Pulses	PulseCulti
9	Oilseed Cultivation	OilseedCulti	Oilseeds	OilseedCulti
10	Fruit Cultivation	FruitCulti	Fruits	FruitCulti
11	Cotton Cultivation	CottonCulti	Cotton	CottonCulti
12	Tobacco Cultivation	TobaccoCulti	Tobacco	TobaccoCulti
13	Tea Cultivation	TeaCulti	Tea	TeaCulti
14	Spice Cultivation	SpiceCulti	Major Spices	SpiceCulti
15	Other Crop Cultivation	OthcropCulti	Other Crops	OthcropCulti
16	Livestock Rearing	LivstockRear	Meat	Meat
17	Poultry Rearing	PoultryRear	Milk and Fat	MilkFat
18	Shrimp Farming	ShrimFarming	Animal draft	Animaldraft
19	Fishing	Fishing	Manure	Manure
20	Forestry	Forestry	Hides and Skins	HidesSkins
21	Rice Millling	RiceMilling	Poultry Meat	PoultryMeat
22	Grain Milling	GrainMilling	Poultry Eggs	PoutryEggs
23	Fish Process	FishProcess	Shrimp	Shrimp
24	Oil Industry	OilIndustry	Fish	Fish
25	Sweetener Industry	SweetenerInd	Forestry	Forestry
26	Tea Product	TeaProduct	Riceflour Bran	RiceflourBran
27	Salt Refining	SaltRefining	Flour Bran Feed	FlourBrafeed
28	Food Process	FoodProcess	Fish and Seafood	FishSeafood
29	Tanning and Finishing	TannFishing	Edible-Nonedible Oil	EdiNoedOil
30	Leather Industry	LeatherInd	Sugar Gur Molasses	SugGuMolass
31	Baling	Baling	Tea Product	TeaProduct
32	Jute Fabrication	JuteFabricat	Salt	Salt
33	Yarn Industry	YarnIndustry	Processed Food	ProcessFood
34	Cloth Milling	ClothMill	Tanning and Leather	TaningLethr
35	Handloom Cloth	HandloomClot	Leather Product	LethrProdt
36	Dyeing and Bleaching	DyeingBlech	Baling	Baling
37	RMG	RMG	Jute Product	JuteProduct
38	Knitting	Knitting	Yarn	Yarn
39	Toiletries Mfg.	ToiletrieMfg	Mill Cloth	MillCloth
40	Cigarette Industry	CigarettInd	Handloom Cloth	HandlmCloth
41	Bidi Industry	BidiIndustry	Dyed Bleach Yarn Fabrics	DyeingBlech
42	Saw and Plane	SawPlane	Ready Made Garments	RMG
43	Furniture Industry	Furniturind	Knitted RMG and Hosiery	Knitting

Table C 6.1. (Continued)

No.	I-O table industries	Model industry code	I-O table commodities	Model commodity code
44	Paper Industry	PaperInd	Toiletries	ToiletrieMfg
45	Printing and Publishing	PrintPub	Cigarettes	CigarettInd
46	Pharmacuticals Mfg.	PharmaMfg	Bidi	BidiIndustry
47	Fertiliser Industry	FertiliseInd	Basic Wood Product	BasicWProdt
48	Basic Chemical	BasiChemical	Wooden Furniture	WoodnFur
49	Petroleum Ref.	PetroleumRef	Pulp Paper and Board	PulpPaBoard
50	Earthware Industry	EarthwareInd	Printing and Publishing	PrintPub
51	Chemical Industry	ChemicalInd	Medicines	Medicines
52	Glass Industry	GlassInd	Fertilizer, Insecticides	fertilizerInsec
53	Clay Industry	ClayInd	Chemicals	Chemicals
54	Cement Mfg.	CementMfg	Petroleum Product	PetroProduct
55	Basic Metal Mfg.	BasicMetaMfg	China Pottery	Chinapottery
56	Metal Mfg.	MetalMfg	Chemical Products	ChemProdt
57	Machinery and Equipments	MachineEquip	Glass Products	GlassProdt
58	Transport Equipments	TranspoEquip	Bricks, Tiles and Clay Products	BricTCProdt
59	Miscellaneous Industry	MiscellaInd	Cement	Cement
60	Urban Building	Urbanbuild	Iron Steel Basic	IronStBasic
61	Rural Building	RuralBuild	Fabricated Metal Products	FabMetProdt
62	Power Plant Building	PPlantBuild	Machinery	Machinery
63	Rural Road Building	RuRoadBuild	Transport Equipment	TransEquipment
64	Port Road Railway Building	PoRoadBuild	Miscellaneous Industry Products	MiscellaInd
65	Canal Dyke Other Buildings	CaDyothBuild	Urban Buildings	UrbanBuild
66	Electricity and Water Generation	ElectWatGene	Rural Buildings	RuralBuild
67	Gas Extraction and Distribution	GasExtDist	Building Maintenance	BldgMantence
68	Mining and Quarrying	MinQuarring	Plants for construction	PlantConst
69	Wholesale Trade	WholeTrade	Rural Roads	RuRoads
70	Retail Trade	RetailTrade	Ports, Airports Railways	PortAirRlwy
71	Air Transport	AirTransport	Canal, Dyke, Other Buildings	CaDyothBuild
72	Water Transport	WatTransport	Infrastructure Maintenance	InfrastrMtn
73	Land Transport	LanTransport	Electricity and Water	ElectWater
74	Railway Transport	RaiTransport	Gas Extraction and Distribution	GasExtDist
75	Other Transport	OthTransport	Mining and Quarring	MinQuarring
76	Housing Service	HousingServ	Trade Wholesale	WholeTrade
77	Health Service	HealthServ	Trade Retail	RetailTrade
78	Education Service	EducatServ	Air Transport	AirTransport
79	Public Administration and Defense	PubAdDefence	Water Transport	WatTransport
80	Bank Insurance and Real Estate	BanInsRestat	Land Transport	LanTransport
81	Professional Service	ProfessioServ	Railway Transport	RailTransport
82	Hotel and Restaurant,	HotelRest	Warehousing	Warehousing
83	Entertainment	Entertainmen	Housing Service	HousingServ
84	Communication	Communicatio	Health Services	HeathServ
85	Other Services	OthServices	Education Services	EducatServ

No.	I-O table industries	Model industry code	I-O table commodities	Model commodity code
86	Information Technology and ECom	InfotechEcom	Public Administration and Defense	PubAdDefence
87			Bank Insurance	BanInsurance
88			Professional Services	ProfesioServ
89			Hotels and Restaurants	HotelRest
90			Entertainments	Entertainmen
91			Communications	Communica
92			Other Services	Othservices
93			Information Technology and Services	InfTechServ
94			Waste	Waste

Table C 6.2. Sectoral mapping of I-O Table 2000 and SAM 2000 for Bangladesh

Industry in model	2000 SAM Industry	Commodity in model	2000 SAM Commodity
Paddy	Paddy	Paddy	Paddy
Wheat	Grains	Wheat	Grains
Othergrain	Grains	Othergrain	Grains
JuteCultiv	Jute	JuteCultiv	Jute
SugcaneCulti	CommCrop	SugcaneCulti	CommCrop
PotatoCulti	OthCrop	PotatoCulti	OthCrop
VegCulti	OthCrop	VegCulti	OthCrop
PulseCulti	OthCrop	PulseCulti	OthCrop
OilseedCulti	OthCrop	OilseedCulti	OthCrop
FruitCulti	OthCrop	FruitCulti	OthCrop
CottonCulti	CommCrop	CottonCulti	CommCrop
TobaccoCulti	CommCrop	TobaccoCulti	CommCrop
TeaCulti	Tea	TeaCulti	Tea
SpiceCulti	OtherFood	SpiceCulti	OthCrop
OthcropCulti	OtherFood	OthcropCulti	OthCrop
LivstockRear	Livestock	Meat	Livestock
PoultryRear	Poultry	MilkFat	Livestock
ShrimFarming	OtherFish	Animaldraft	Livestock
Fishing	OtherFish	Manure	Livestock
Forestry	Forestry	HidesSkins	Livestock
RiceMilling	RiceMill	PoultryMeat	Poultry
GrainMilling	AtaMill	PoutryEggs	Poultry
FishProcess	OtherFood	Shrimp	OtherFish
OilIndustry	OtherFood	Fish	OtherFish
SweetenerInd	OtherFood	Forestry	Forestry
TeaProduct	TeaProd	RiceflorBran	RiceMill
SaltRefining	OtherFood	FlourBrafeed	AtaMill
FoodProcess	OtherFood	FishSeafood	OtherFood

Table C 6.2. (Continued)

Industry in model	2000 SAM Industry	Commodity in model	2000 SAM Commodity
TannFishing	OtherFood	EdiNoedOil	OtherFood
LeatherInd	LeatherProd	SugGuMolass	OtherFood
Baling	JuteText	TeaProduct	TeaProd
JuteFabricat	JuteText	Salt	OtherFood
YarnIndustry	Yarn	ProcessFood	OtherFood
ClothMill	MillCloth	TaningLethr	LeatherProd
HandloomClot	Clothing	LethrProdt	LeatherProd
DyeingBlech	Clothing	Baling	JuteText
RMG	ReadymadeGar	JuteProduct	JuteText
Knitting	ReadymadeGar	Yarn	Yarn
ToiletrieMfg	Chemical	MillCloth	MillCloth
CigarettInd	TobbaProd	HandlmCloth	Clothing
BidiIndustry	TobbaProd	DyeingBlech	Clothing
SawPlane	WoodProd	RMG	ReadymadeGar
Furniturind	WoodProd	Knitting	ReadymadeGar
PaperInd	PrintPub	ToiletrieMfg	Chemical
PrintPub	PrintPub	CigarettInd	TobbaProd
PharmaMfg	Chemical	BidiIndustry	TobbaProd
FertiliseInd	Fertiliser	BasicWProdt	ForestProd
BasiChemical	Chemical	WoodnFur	ForestProd
PetroleumRef	PetroProd	PulpPaBoard	MiscIndus
EarthwareInd	ClayProd	PrintPub	PrintPub
ChemicalInd	Chemical	Medicines	Chemical
GlassInd	MiscIndus	FertzerInsec	Fertiliser
ClayInd	ClayProd	Chemicals	Chemical
CementMfg	Cement	PetroProduct	PetroProd
BasicMetaMfg	IronSteelBas	Chinapottery	ClayProd
MetalMfg	IronSteelBas	ChemProdt	Chemical
MachineEquip	Machinery	GlassProdt	MiscIndus
TranspoEquip	TransSer	BricTCProdt	ClayProd
MiscellaInd	MiscIndus	Cement	Cement
Urbanbuild	UrbBuild	IronStBasic	IronSteelBas
RuralBuild	RuBuild	FabMetProdt	IronSteelBas
PPlantBuild	Construction	Machinery	Machinery
RuRoadBuild	Construction	TransEquipmt	Machinery
PoRoadBuild	Construction	MiscellaInd	MiscIndus
CaDyothBuild	Construction	UrbanBuild	UrbBuild
ElectWatGene	Utility	RuralBuild	RuBuild
GasExtDist	Utility	BldgMantence	Construction
MinQuarring	utility	PlantConst	Construction
WholeTrade	TradSer	RuRoads	Construction
RetailTrade	TradSer	PortAirRlwy	Construction
AirTransport	TransSer	CaDyothBuild	Construction
WatTransport	TransSer	InfrastrMtn	Construction
LanTransport	TransSer	ElectWater	Utility
RaiTransport	TransSer	GasExtDist	Utility
OthTransport	TransSer	MinQuarring	Utility
HousingServ	Housing	WholeTrade	TradSer
HealthServ	Health	RetailTrade	TradSer
EducatServ	Education	AirTransport	TransSer

Industry in model	2000 SAM Industry	Commodity in model	2000 SAM Commodity
PubAdDefence	PubAdm	WatTransport	TransSer
BanInsRestat	OthServ	LanTransport	TransSer
ProfesioServ	OthServ	RaiTransport	TransSer
HotelRest	HotetRest	Warehousing	TransSer
Entertainmen	OthServ	HousingServ	Housing
Communicatio	Communicat	HeathServ	Health
OthServices	OthServ	EducatServ	Education
InfotechEcom	InfoTechnSer	PubAdDefence	PubAdm
		BanInsurance	OthServ
		ProfesioServ	OthServ
		HotelRest	HotetRest
		Entertainmen	OthServ
		Communica	Communicat
		Othservices	OthServ
		InfTechServ	InfoTechnSer
		Waste	OthServ

Table C 6.3. Elasticities of substitution between domestic and imported commodities

Commodities	Elasticity values	Commodities	Elasticity values
1 Paddy	1.8	48 WoodnFur	1.3
2 Wheat	1.8	49 PulpPaBoard	1.3
3 Othergrain	1.8	50 PrintPub	1.3
4 JuteCultiv	1.61	51 Medicines	1.2
5 SugcaneCulti	1.8	52 FertzerInsec	1.2
6 PotatoCulti	1.8	53 Chemicals	1.2
7 VegCulti	1.8	54 PetroProduct	1.2
8 PulseCulti	1.8	55 Chinapottery	1.3
9 OilseedCulti	1.8	56 ChemProdt	1.2
10 FruitCulti	1.8	57 GlassProdt	1.2
11 CottonCulti	1.61	58 BricTCProdt	1.2
12 TobaccoCulti	1.61	59 Cement	1.2
13 TeaCulti	1.61	60 IronStBasic	1.2
14 SpiceCulti	1.8	61 FabMetProdt	1.2
15 OthcropCulti	1.8	62 Machinery	1.2
16 Meat	1.8	63 TransEquipmt	1.2
17 MilkFat	1.8	64 MiscellaInd	1.2
18 Animaldraft	1.8	65 UrbanBuild	1.2
19 Manure	1.8	66 RuralBuild	1.2
20 HidesSkins	1.8	67 BldgMantence	1.2
21 PoultryMeat	1.8	68 PlantConst	1.2
22 PoutryEggs	1.8	69 RuRoads	1.2
23 Shrimp	1.8	70 PortAirRlwy	1.2
24 Fish	1.8	71 CaDyothBuild	1.2
25 Forestry	1.61	72 InfrastrMtn	1.2
26 RiceflorBran	1.8	73 ElectWater	1.2
27 FlourBrafeed	1.8	74 GasExtDist	1.2

Table C 6.3. (Continued)

Commodities	Elasticity values	Commodities	Elasticity values
28 FishSeafood	1.8	75 MinQuarring	1.2
29 EdiNoedOil	1.8	76 WholeTrade	1.2
30 SugGuMolass	1.8	77 RetailTrade	1.2
31 TeaProduct	1.8	78 AirTransport	1.2
32 Salt	1.8	79 WatTransport	1.2
33 ProcessFood	1.61	80 LanTransport	1.2
34 TaningLethr	1.3	81 RaiTransport	1.2
35 LethrProdt	1.3	82 Warehousing	1.2
36 Baling	1.3	83 HousingServ	1.2
37 JuteProduct	1.3	84 HeathServ	1.2
38 Yarn	1.3	85 EducatServ	1.2
39 MillCloth	1.3	86 PubAdDefence	1.2
40 HandlmCloth	1.3	87 BanInsurance	1.2
41 DyeingBlech	1.3	88 ProfesioServ	1.2
42 RMG	1.3	89 HotelRest	1.2
43 Knitting	1.3	90 Entertainmen	1.2
44 ToiletrieMfg	1.2	91 Communica	1.2
45 CigarettInd	1.61	92 Othservices	1.2
46 BidiIndustry	1.61	93 InfTechServ	1.2
47 BasicWProdt	1.3	94 Waste	1.2

Table C 6.4. Household expenditure elasticities

Commodities	Landless	Marg-farmer	Small-farmer	Large-farmer	Non-agricul	Illi-terate	Low-edu	Medium-edu	High-edu
1 Paddy	0.449	0.449	0.448	0.445	0.444	0.444	0.439	0.433	0.429
2 Wheat	0.449	0.449	0.448	0.445	0.444	0.444	0.439	0.433	0.429
3 Othergrain	0.449	0.449	0.448	0.445	0.444	0.444	0.439	0.433	0.429
4 JuteCultiv	1.044	1.044	1.041	1.034	1.034	1.032	1.021	1.006	0.998
5 SugcaneCulti	0.449	0.449	0.448	0.445	0.444	0.444	0.439	0.433	0.429
6 PotatoCulti	0.449	0.449	0.448	0.445	0.444	0.444	0.439	0.433	0.429
7 VegCulti	0.449	0.449	0.448	0.445	0.444	0.444	0.439	0.433	0.429
8 PulseCulti	0.449	0.449	0.448	0.445	0.444	0.444	0.439	0.433	0.429
9 OilseedCulti	0.449	0.449	0.448	0.445	0.444	0.444	0.439	0.433	0.429
10 FruitCulti	0.449	0.449	0.448	0.445	0.444	0.444	0.439	0.433	0.429
11 CottonCulti	1.044	1.044	1.041	1.034	1.034	1.032	1.021	1.006	0.998
12 TobaccoCulti	0.449	0.449	0.448	0.445	0.444	0.444	0.439	0.433	0.429
13 TeaCulti	0.449	0.449	0.448	0.445	0.444	0.444	0.439	0.433	0.429
14 SpiceCulti	0.449	0.449	0.448	0.445	0.444	0.444	0.439	0.433	0.429
15 OthcropCulti	0.449	0.449	0.448	0.445	0.444	0.444	0.439	0.433	0.429
16 Meat	1.327	1.326	1.323	1.314	1.314	1.312	1.298	1.279	1.269
17 MilkFat	1.327	1.326	1.323	1.314	1.314	1.312	1.298	1.279	1.269
18 Animaldraft	1.327	1.326	1.323	1.314	1.314	1.312	1.298	1.279	1.269
19 Manure	1.327	1.326	1.323	1.314	1.314	1.312	1.298	1.279	1.269
20 HidesSkins	1.044	1.044	1.041	1.034	1.034	1.032	1.021	1.006	0.998
21 PoultryMeat	1.327	1.326	1.323	1.314	1.314	1.312	1.298	1.279	1.269
22 PoutryEggs	1.327	1.326	1.323	1.314	1.314	1.312	1.298	1.279	1.269
23 Shrimp	1.327	1.326	1.323	1.314	1.314	1.312	1.298	1.279	1.269
24 Fish	1.327	1.326	1.323	1.314	1.314	1.312	1.298	1.279	1.269

Commodities	Landless	Marg-farmer	Small-farmer	Large-farmer	Non-agricul	Illi-terate	Low-edu	Medium-edu	High-edu
25 Forestry	1.337	1.336	1.333	1.324	1.324	1.321	1.308	1.289	1.278
26 RiceflorBran	0.82	0.819	0.817	0.812	0.812	0.81	0.802	0.79	0.784
27 FlourBrafeed	0.82	0.819	0.817	0.812	0.812	0.81	0.802	0.79	0.784
28 FishSeafood	1.327	1.326	1.323	1.314	1.314	1.312	1.298	1.279	1.269
29 EdiNoedOil	0.82	0.819	0.817	0.812	0.812	0.81	0.802	0.79	0.784
30 SugGuMolass	0.82	0.819	0.817	0.812	0.812	0.81	0.802	0.79	0.784
31 TeaProduct	0.82	0.819	0.817	0.812	0.812	0.81	0.802	0.79	0.784
32 Salt	0.82	0.819	0.817	0.812	0.812	0.81	0.802	0.79	0.784
33 ProcessFood	0.82	0.819	0.817	0.812	0.812	0.81	0.802	0.79	0.784
34 TaningLethr	1.044	1.044	1.041	1.034	1.034	1.032	1.021	1.006	0.998
35 LethrProdt	1.044	1.044	1.041	1.034	1.034	1.032	1.021	1.006	0.998
36 Baling	1.044	1.044	1.041	1.034	1.034	1.032	1.021	1.006	0.998
37 JuteProduct	1.044	1.044	1.041	1.034	1.034	1.032	1.021	1.006	0.998
38 Yarn	1.044	1.044	1.041	1.034	1.034	1.032	1.021	1.006	0.998
39 MillCloth	1.044	1.044	1.041	1.034	1.034	1.032	1.021	1.006	0.998
40 HandlmCloth	1.044	1.044	1.041	1.034	1.034	1.032	1.021	1.006	0.998
41 DyeingBlech	1.044	1.044	1.041	1.034	1.034	1.032	1.021	1.006	0.998
42 RMG	1.044	1.044	1.041	1.034	1.034	1.032	1.021	1.006	0.998
43 Knitting	1.044	1.044	1.041	1.034	1.034	1.032	1.021	1.006	0.998
44 ToiletrieMfg	1.337	1.336	1.333	1.324	1.324	1.321	1.308	1.289	1.278
45 CigarettInd	0.82	0.819	0.817	0.812	0.812	0.81	0.802	0.79	0.784
46 BidiIndustry	0.82	0.819	0.817	0.812	0.812	0.81	0.802	0.79	0.784
47 BasicWProdt	1.337	1.336	1.333	1.324	1.324	1.321	1.308	1.289	1.278
48 WoodnFur	1.337	1.336	1.333	1.324	1.324	1.321	1.308	1.289	1.278
49 PulpPaBoard	1.337	1.336	1.333	1.324	1.324	1.321	1.308	1.289	1.278
50 PrintPub	1.337	1.336	1.333	1.324	1.324	1.321	1.308	1.289	1.278
51 Medicines	1.337	1.336	1.333	1.324	1.324	1.321	1.308	1.289	1.278
52 FertzerInsec	1.337	1.336	1.333	1.324	1.324	1.321	1.308	1.289	1.278
53 Chemicals	1.337	1.336	1.333	1.324	1.324	1.321	1.308	1.289	1.278
54 PetroProduct	1.337	1.336	1.333	1.324	1.324	1.321	1.308	1.289	1.278
55 Chinapottery	1.337	1.336	1.333	1.324	1.324	1.321	1.308	1.289	1.278
56 ChemProdt	1.337	1.336	1.333	1.324	1.324	1.321	1.308	1.289	1.278
57 GlassProdt	1.337	1.336	1.333	1.324	1.324	1.321	1.308	1.289	1.278
58 BricTCProdt	1.337	1.336	1.333	1.324	1.324	1.321	1.308	1.289	1.278
59 Cement	1.337	1.336	1.333	1.324	1.324	1.321	1.308	1.289	1.278
60 IronStBasic	1.337	1.336	1.333	1.324	1.324	1.321	1.308	1.289	1.278
61 FabMetProdt	1.337	1.336	1.333	1.324	1.324	1.321	1.308	1.289	1.278
62 Machinery	1.337	1.336	1.333	1.324	1.324	1.321	1.308	1.289	1.278
63 TransEquipmt	1.337	1.336	1.333	1.324	1.324	1.321	1.308	1.289	1.278
64 MiscellaInd	1.337	1.336	1.333	1.324	1.324	1.321	1.308	1.289	1.278
65 UrbanBuild	1.366	1.365	1.362	1.353	1.353	1.35	1.336	1.317	1.306
66 RuralBuild	1.366	1.365	1.362	1.353	1.353	1.35	1.336	1.317	1.306
67 BldgMantence	1.366	1.365	1.362	1.353	1.353	1.35	1.336	1.317	1.306
68 PlantConst	1.366	1.365	1.362	1.353	1.353	1.35	1.336	1.317	1.306
69 RuRoads	1.366	1.365	1.362	1.353	1.353	1.35	1.336	1.317	1.306
70 PortAirRlwy	1.366	1.365	1.362	1.353	1.353	1.35	1.336	1.317	1.306
71 CaDyothBuild	1.366	1.365	1.362	1.353	1.353	1.35	1.336	1.317	1.306
72 InfrastrMtn	1.366	1.365	1.362	1.353	1.353	1.35	1.336	1.317	1.306

Table C 6.4. (Continued)

Commodities	Landless	Marg-farmer	Small-farmer	Large-farmer	Non-agricul	Illi-terate	Low-edu	Medium-edu	High-edu
73 ElectWater	1.366	1.365	1.362	1.353	1.353	1.35	1.336	1.317	1.306
74 GasExtDist	1.366	1.365	1.362	1.353	1.353	1.35	1.336	1.317	1.306
75 MinQuarring	1.337	1.336	1.333	1.324	1.324	1.321	1.308	1.289	1.278
76 WholeTrade	1.073	1.073	1.07	1.063	1.063	1.061	1.05	1.035	1.026
77 RetailTrade	1.073	1.073	1.07	1.063	1.063	1.061	1.05	1.035	1.026
78 AirTransport	1.347	1.346	1.343	1.334	1.333	1.331	1.317	1.298	1.287
79 WatTransport	1.347	1.346	1.343	1.334	1.333	1.331	1.317	1.298	1.287
80 LanTransport	1.347	1.346	1.343	1.334	1.333	1.331	1.317	1.298	1.287
81 RaiTransport	1.347	1.346	1.343	1.334	1.333	1.331	1.317	1.298	1.287
82 Warehousing	1.347	1.346	1.343	1.334	1.333	1.331	1.317	1.298	1.287
83 HousingServ	1.034	1.034	1.031	1.024	1.024	1.022	1.012	0.997	0.989
84 HeathServ	1.034	1.034	1.031	1.024	1.024	1.022	1.012	0.997	0.989
85 EducatServ	1.034	1.034	1.031	1.024	1.024	1.022	1.012	0.997	0.989
86 PubAdDefence	1.034	1.034	1.031	1.024	1.024	1.022	1.012	0.997	0.989
87 BanInsurance	1.366	1.365	1.362	1.353	1.353	1.35	1.336	1.317	1.306
88 ProfesioServ	1.2	1.2	1.197	1.189	1.188	1.186	1.174	1.157	1.147
89 HotelRest	1.073	1.073	1.07	1.063	1.063	1.061	1.05	1.035	1.026
90 Entertainmen	1.034	1.034	1.031	1.024	1.024	1.022	1.012	0.997	0.989
91 Communica	1.347	1.346	1.343	1.334	1.333	1.331	1.317	1.298	1.287
92 Othservices	1.034	1.034	1.031	1.024	1.024	1.022	1.012	0.997	0.989
93 InfTechServ	1.034	1.034	1.031	1.024	1.024	1.022	1.012	0.997	0.989
94 Waste	1.034	1.034	1.031	1.024	1.024	1.022	1.012	0.997	0.989
Total	102.6	102.5	102.3	101.62	101.59	101.40	100.3	98.896	98.08

APPENDIX D

Table D 7.1. Base case tariff rates, import share and export share (expressed as ratios)

Commodity	Import share	Tariff rate	Export share	Industry	Trade category
Paddy	0	0	0	Paddy	NT
Wheat	0.342	0.032	0	Wheat	IC
Othergrain	0.007	0	0	Othergrain	NT
JuteCultiv	0	0	0.1966	JuteCultiv	E
SugcaneCulti	0	0	0	SugcaneCulti	NT
PotatoCulti	0.003	0.05	0	PotatoCulti	NT
VegCulti	0.275	0.038	0.0324	VegCulti	IC
PulseCulti	0	0	0	PulseCulti	NT
OilseedCulti	0.303	0.047	0	OilseedCulti	IC
FruitCulti	0.069	0.211	0	FruitCulti	IC
CottonCulti	0.658	0	0	CottonCulti	IC
TobaccoCulti	0.174	0.107	0.0283	TobaccoCulti	IC
TeaCulti	0	0	0.4493	TeaCulti	E
SpiceCulti	0.115	0.232	0	SpiceCulti	IC
OthcropCulti	0.104	0.027	0.003	OthcropCulti	NT

Commodity	Import share	Tariff rate	Export share	Industry	Trade category
Meat	0.026	0	0	LivstockRear	NT
MilkFat	0.509	0.316	0	LivstockRear	IC
Animaldraft	0.016	0.003	0	LivstockRear	NT
Manure	0.016	0	0	LivstockRear	NT
HidesSkins	0.022	0.006	0	LivstockRear	ER
PoultryMeat	0.01	0	0	PoultryRear	NT
PoultryEggs	0.004	0.101	0	PoultryRear	NT
Shrimp	0	0	0.3487	ShrimFarming	E
Fish	0	0.114	0	Fishing	NT
Forestry	0.001	0.08	0	Forestry	NT
RiceflorBran	0.018	0.016	0	RiceMilling	NT
FlourBrafeed	0.012	0.118	0	GrainMilling	IC
FishSeafood	0.034	0.162	0.0955	FishProcess	E
EdiNoedOil	0.508	0.059	0	OilIndustry	IC
SugGuMolass	0.055	0.182	0	SweetenerInd	IC
TeaProduct	0.012	0.205	0	TeaProduct	IC
Salt	0.028	0.114	0	SaltRefining	IC
ProcessFood	0.11	0.172	0	FoodProcess	IC
TaningLethr	0	0.016	0	TannFishing	ER
LethrProdt	0.008	0.144	0.3465	LeatherInd	E
Baling	0	0	0	Baling	ER
JuteProduct	0	0.097	0.5611	JuteFabricat	E
Yarn	0.317	0.034	0	YarnIndustry	IC
MillCloth	0.29	0.019	0	ClothMill	ER
HandlmCloth	0	0	0	HandloomClot	NT
DyeingBlech	0.029	0	0	DyeingBlech	NT
RMG	0.389	0.004	0.7585	RMG	E
Knitting	0.063	0.078	0.7529	Knitting	E
ToiletrieMfg	0.209	0.121	0.2532	ToiletrieMfg	E
CigarettInd	0.009	0.02	0	CigarettInd	NT
BidiIndustry	0	0	0	BidiIndustry	NT
BasicWProdt	0.028	0.176	0	SawPlane	NT
WoodnFur	0.008	0.233	0	Furniturind	NT
PulpPaBoard	0.423	0.073	0	PaperInd	IC
PrintPub	0.128	0.031	0	PrintPub	NT
Medicines	0.258	0.012	0	PharmaMfg	IC
FertzerInsec	0.45	0.009	0.224	FertiliseInd	IC
Chemicals	0.795	0.085	0	BasiChemical	IC
PetroProduct	0.611	0.244	0.0198	PetroleumRef	IC
Chinapottery	0.091	0.268	0.064	EarthwareInd	IC
ChemProdt	0.521	0.048	0	ChemicalInd	IC
GlassProdt	0.647	0.167	0	GlassInd	IC
BricTCProdt	0.022	0.076	0	ClayInd	NT

Table D 7.1. (Continued)

Commodity	Import share	Tariff rate	Export share	Industry	Trade category
Cement	0.674	0.166	0	CementMfg	IC
IronStBasic	0.357	0.053	0	BasicMetaMfg	IC
FabMetProdt	0.288	0.153	0	MetalMfg	IC
Machinery	0.711	0.059	0.0266	MachineEquip	IC
TransEquipmt	0.478	0.089	0	TranspoEquip	IC
MiscellaInd	0.504	0.067	0.4618	MiscellaInd	IC
UrbanBuild	0	0	0	Urbanbuild	NT
RuralBuild	0	0	0	RuralBuild	NT
BldgMantence	0	0	0	RuralBuild	NT
PlantConst	0	0	0	PPlantBuild	NT
RuRoads	0	0	0	RuRoadBuild	NT
PortAirRlwy	0	0	0	PoRoadBuild	NT
CaDyothBuild	0	0	0	CaDyothBuild	NT
InfrastrMtn	0	0	0	CaDyothBuild	NT
ElectWater	0	0	0	ElectWatGene	NT
GasExtDist	0.022	0.073	0	GasExtDist	NT
MinQuarring	0.1	0.08	0	MinQuarring	NT
WholeTrade	0	0	0	WholeTrade	NT
RetailTrade	0	0	0	RetailTrade	NT
AirTransport	0	0	0.0411	AirTransport	NT
WatTransport	0	0	0.1242	WatTransport	E
LanTransport	0	0	0	LanTransport	NT
RaiTransport	0	0	0	RaiTransport	NT
Warehousing	0	0	0	OthTransport	NT
HousingServ	0	0	0	HousingServ	NT
HealthServ	0	0	0	HealthServ	NT
EducatServ	0	0	0	EducatServ	NT
PubAdDefence	0.041	0	0.2513	PubAdDefence	E
BanInsurance	0.02	0	0.0146	BanInsRestat	NT
ProfesioServ	0.014	0	0.0208	ProfesioServ	NT
HotelRest	0	0	0	HotelRest	NT
Entertainmen	0.0003	0	0.001	Entertainmen	NT
Communica	0.021	0	0.1276	Communicatio	NT
Othservices	0	0	0	OthServices	NT
InfTechServ	0.016	0	0.0356	InfotechEcom	NT
Waste	0.717	0.07	0		NT

Table D 7.2. Fan decomposition (simulation 1) (per cent)

	Short run				Long run			
Commodity	Output growth	Local market effect	Domestic share effect	Export effect	Output growth	Local market effect	Domestic share effect	Export effect
1 Paddy	-0.0568	-0.0568	0	0	0.117	0.117	0	0
2 Wheat	-0.2253	-0.2627	0.0375	0	0.213	0.312	-0.099	0
3 Othergrain	-0.2013	-0.2154	0.0141	0	0.365	0.363	0.002	0
4 JuteCultiv	2.2785	1.8776	0	0.4009	-0.261	-0.227	0	-0.034
5 SugcaneCulti	-0.8556	-0.8556	0	0	-1.02	-1.02	0	0
6 PotatoCulti	-0.0329	-0.0283	-0.0046	0	0.138	0.156	-0.018	0
7 VegCulti	0.3332	-0.0756	-0.2596	0.6684	-0.92	0.15	-1.169	0.1
8 PulseCulti	-0.0506	-0.0506	0	0	0.177	0.177	0	0
9 OilseedCulti	-0.5122	-0.37	-0.1423	0	-1.969	-1.563	-0.406	0
10 FruitCulti	-1.2799	0.11	-1.3901	0.0002	-1.799	0.06	-1.859	0
11 CottonCulti	0.6945	0.3079	0.3866	0	0.503	0.25	0.253	0
12 TobaccoCulti	-0.2446	-0.106	-0.7232	0.5847	-0.575	0.252	-0.914	0.087
13 TeaCulti	2.1614	-0.3946	0	2.556	0.48	-0.085	0	0.565
14 SpiceCulti	-2.3006	-0.1044	-2.1961	0	-3.541	-0.439	-3.102	0
15 OthcropCulti	0.0306	-0.0646	0.0326	0.0626	-0.201	0.102	-0.313	0.009
16 Meat	0.0159	-0.0784	0.0943	0	0.842	0.848	-0.007	0
17 MilkFat	-3.8463	5.7594	-9.6056	0	-3.995	6.892	-10.887	0
18 Animaldraft	-0.0559	-0.1438	0.0879	0	0.25	0.235	0.015	0
19 Manure	-0.0615	-0.1373	0.0758	0	-0.441	-0.476	0.035	0
20 HidesSkins	1.4811	1.4584	0.0227	0	1.284	1.324	-0.04	0
21 PoultryMeat	-0.169	-0.2201	0.051	0	0.327	0.319	0.008	0
22 PoutryEggs	-0.2072	-0.1706	-0.0367	0	0.298	0.352	-0.055	0
23 Shrimp	2.6833	0.2192	0	2.4641	2.113	0.54	0	1.573
24 Fish	-0.2106	-0.2091	-0.0015	0	0.458	0.46	-0.002	0
25 Forestry	-0.0885	-0.0855	-0.003	0	0.703	0.708	-0.006	0

Table D 7.2. (Continued)

	Short run				Long run			
Commodity	Output growth	Local market effect	Domestic share effect	Export effect	Output growth	Local market effect	Domestic share effect	Export effect
26 RiceflorBran	-0.0571	-0.1059	0.0487	0	0.041	0.079	-0.039	0
27 FlourBrafeed	-0.2859	-0.1834	-0.1025	0	0.291	0.422	-0.131	0
28 FishSeafood	0.6189	-0.5162	-0.8337	1.9688	0.172	0.733	-0.855	0.294
29 EdiNoedOil	-0.4986	0.0215	-0.5201	0	-2.65	0.162	-2.812	0
30 SugGuMolass	-0.8414	0.0581	-0.8996	0	-0.996	0.177	-1.174	0
31 TeaProduct	-0.6125	-0.3397	-0.2728	0	-0.145	0.163	-0.308	0
32 Salt	-0.0113	-0.0082	-0.0031	0	0.513	0.505	0.009	0
33 ProcessFood	-1.0779	0.3419	-1.4198	0	-1.418	0.485	-1.903	0
34 TaningLethr	1.5161	1.5163	-0.0002	0	1.265	1.266	0	0
35 LethrProdt	1.7389	-0.8299	-0.071	2.6398	1.501	0.104	-0.07	1.468
36 Baling	7.1983	7.1983	0	0	-0.595	-0.595	0	0
37 JuteProduct	4.9274	-0.5017	-0.0012	5.4303	-0.515	0.013	-0.001	-0.527
38 Yarn	0.9823	1.3196	-0.3374	0	0.821	1.813	-0.992	0
39 MillCloth	2.7018	2.352	0.3497	0	3.031	2.634	0.397	0
40 HandlmCloth	-0.3755	-0.3755	0	0	0.253	0.253	0	0
41 DyeingBlech	-0.3315	-0.3967	0.0651	0	0.309	0.305	0.003	0
42 RMG	4.854	-0.017	-0.0324	4.9034	5.371	0.048	-0.04	5.363
43 Knitting	5.41	-0.0393	-0.0507	5.5	8.809	0.07	-0.059	8.798
44 ToiletrieMfg	2.4478	0.0551	-1.2437	3.6364	10.56	2.234	-1.027	9.354
45 CigarettInd	0.1079	0.0812	0.0267	0	0.691	0.685	0.005	0
46 BidiIndustry	0.0101	0.0101	0	0	0.458	0.458	0	0
47 BasicWProdt	0.1047	0.1285	-0.0238	0	0.317	0.344	-0.027	0
48 WoodnFur	0.4555	0.4691	-0.0136	0	0.559	0.574	-0.016	0
49 PulpPaBoard	-0.6403	0.1442	-0.7845	0	-2.46	-0.115	-2.345	0
50 PrintPub	0.4487	0.4651	-0.0164	0	-0.148	0.179	-0.327	0
51 Medicines	0.3149	-0.0993	0.4141	0	0.512	0.538	-0.026	0
52 FertzerInsec	0.6486	-0.0856	-0.3649	1.0991	3.469	-0.042	-0.088	3.599
53 Chemicals	-0.5219	0.0824	-0.6043	0	-1.038	0.218	-1.257	0

	Short run				Long run			
Commodity	Output growth	Local market effect	Domestic share effect	Export effect	Output growth	Local market effect	Domestic share effect	Export effect
54 PetroProduct	-2.8049	1.1731	-4.3865	0.4084	-7.013	0.548	-7.622	0.061
55 Chinapottery	0.0497	0.2919	-1.5632	1.3211	-0.775	0.74	-1.712	0.197
56 ChemProdt	-0.1106	-0.1065	-0.0041	0	-0.059	0.09	-0.149	0
57 GlassProdt	-1.9923	4.0718	-6.0641	0	-4.182	4.944	-9.125	0
58 BricTCProdt	0.116	0.1248	-0.0088	0	0.995	1	-0.006	0
59 Cement	-2.1979	-0.2598	-1.9381	0	-4.938	-0.287	-4.651	0
60 IronStBasic	-0.3625	-0.2117	-0.1508	0	-0.526	-0.233	-0.293	0
61 FabMetProdt	-0.6411	0.8074	-1.4485	0	-0.633	1.331	-1.964	0
62 Machinery	-0.724	0.2296	-1.5026	0.5491	-3.488	0.793	-4.363	0.082
63 TransEquipmt	-0.2052	0.2999	-0.505	0	-0.936	0.648	-1.583	0
64 MiscellaInd	1.5561	0.4631	-1.3366	2.4296	5.049	0.526	-1.147	5.671
65 UrbanBuild	0	0	0	0	1.123	1.123	0	0
66 RuralBuild	-0.0003	-0.0003	0	0	1.122	1.122	0	0
67 BldgMantence	0.819	0.819	0	0	0.843	0.843	0	0
68 PlantConst	0	0	0	0	1.123	1.123	0	0
69 RuRoads	0	0	0	0	1.123	1.123	0	0
70 PortAirRlwy	0.4348	0.4348	0	0	1.133	1.133	0	0
71 CaDyothBuild	0	0	0	0	1.123	1.123	0	0
72 InfrastrMtn	0	0	0	0	1.123	1.123	0	0
73 ElectWater	0.2917	0.2917	0	0	0.764	0.764	0	0
74 GasExtDist	-0.1449	-0.0952	-0.0497	0	0.405	0.491	-0.086	0
75 MinQuarring	-0.1636	0.0188	-0.1824	0	-0.048	0.316	-0.365	0
76 WholeTrade	0.6215	0.6215	0	0	1.024	1.024	0	0
77 RetailTrade	0.5338	0.5338	0	0	1.01	1.01	0	0
78 AirTransport	1.4355	0.5886	0	0.8468	1.104	0.977	0	0.126
79 WatTransport	2.9812	0.4199	0	2.5613	1.274	0.892	0	0.382

Table D 7.2. (Continued)

	Short run				Long run			
Commodity	Output growth	Local market effect	Domestic share effect	Export effect	Output growth	Local market effect	Domestic share effect	Export effect
80 LanTransport	0.5787	0.5787	0	0	1.073	1.073	0	0
81 RaiTransport	0.6287	0.6287	0	0	1.016	1.016	0	0
82 Warehousing	1.9052	1.9052	0	0	0.707	0.707	0	0
83 HousingServ	0.0272	0.0272	0	0	0.505	0.505	0	0
84 HealthServ	0.1157	0.1157	0	0	0.551	0.551	0	0
85 EducatServ	-0.0127	-0.0127	0	0	0.196	0.196	0	0
86 PubAdDefence	5.3249	0.1611	-0.019	5.1829	1.221	0.452	-0.004	0.773
87 BanInsurance	0.713	0.368	0.0437	0.3014	0.569	0.523	0.001	0.045
88 ProfesioServ	0.8927	0.4396	0.0246	0.4285	0.667	0.598	0.005	0.064
89 HotelRest	0.2582	0.2582	0	0	0.479	0.479	0	0
90 Entertainmen	0.0571	0.0344	0.0013	0.0214	0.238	0.235	0	0.003
91 Communica	1.8664	-0.7499	-0.0149	2.6312	0.506	0.116	-0.003	0.393
92 Othservices	0.2009	0.2009	0	0	0.096	0.096	0	0
93 InfTechServ	1.4269	0.6615	0.0311	0.7343	0.551	0.438	0.003	0.11
94 Waste	-0.4698	1.0125	-1.4823	0	-0.846	2.249	-3.095	0

Table D 7.3. Short run changes in imports by usage (simulation 1) (in Million Taka)

Commodity	1 Interm	2 Invest	3 HouseH	4 Export	5 GovGE	6 Stocks	7 Margins	Total
1 Paddy	0.00	0.00	0.00	0.00	0.00	0.00	0.00	0.00
2 Wheat	-56.47	0.00	0.00	0.00	0.00	0.00	0.00	-56.47
3 Othergrain	-0.21	0.00	0.00	0.00	0.00	0.00	0.00	-0.21
4 JuteCultiv	0.00	0.00	0.00	0.00	0.00	0.00	0.00	0.00
5 SugcaneCulti	0.00	0.00	0.00	0.00	0.00	0.00	0.00	0.00
6 PotatoCulti	0.21	0.00	0.88	0.00	0.00	0.00	0.00	1.08
7 VegCulti	7.64	0.00	51.38	0.00	0.00	0.00	0.00	59.02
8 PulseCulti	0.00	0.00	0.00	0.00	0.00	0.00	0.00	0.00
9 OilseedCulti	-2.87	0.00	0.00	0.00	0.00	0.00	0.00	-2.87

Commodity	1 Interm	2 Invest	3 HouseH	4 Export	5 GovGE	6 Stocks	7 Margins	Total
10 FruitCulti	40.02	0.00	445.67	0.00	0.00	0.00	0.00	485.69
11 CottonCulti	21.63	0.00	0.00	0.00	0.00	0.00	0.00	21.63
12 TobaccoCulti	23.28	0.00	8.55	0.00	0.00	0.00	0.00	31.83
13 TeaCulti	0.00	0.00	0.00	0.00	0.00	0.00	0.00	0.00
14 SpiceCulti	21.01	0.00	106.65	0.00	0.00	0.00	0.00	127.66
15 OthcropCulti	-3.45	0.00	-9.78	0.00	0.00	0.00	0.00	-13.22
16 Meat	-94.91	-25.59	-4.25	0.00	0.00	0.00	0.00	-124.74
17 MilkFat	14.34	0.00	638.74	0.00	0.00	0.00	0.00	653.08
18 Animaldraft	-49.36	0.00	0.00	0.00	0.00	0.00	0.00	-49.36
19 Manure	-7.04	0.00	0.00	0.00	0.00	0.00	0.00	-7.04
20 HidesSkins	2.08	0.00	0.00	0.00	0.00	0.00	0.00	2.08
21 PoultryMeat	-0.75	0.00	-9.88	0.00	0.00	0.00	0.00	-10.63
22 PoutryEggs	0.75	0.00	5.95	0.00	0.00	0.00	0.00	6.70
23 Shrimp	0.00	0.00	0.00	0.00	0.00	0.00	0.00	0.00
24 Fish	0.33	0.00	3.09	0.00	0.00	0.00	0.00	3.42
25 Forestry	0.91	0.96	0.42	0.00	0.00	0.00	0.00	2.29
26 RiceflorBran	-12.71	0.00	-171.17	0.00	0.00	0.00	0.00	-183.88
27 FlourBrafeed	33.50	0.00	7.96	0.00	0.00	0.00	0.00	41.45
28 FishSeafood	11.42	0.00	159.41	0.00	0.00	0.00	0.00	170.83
29 EdiNoedOil	47.28	0.00	144.53	0.00	0.00	0.00	0.00	191.82
30 SugGuMolass	8.03	0.00	426.09	0.00	0.00	0.00	0.00	434.11
31 TeaProduct	1.12	0.00	10.55	0.00	0.00	0.00	0.00	11.67
32 Salt	0.07	0.00	0.00	0.00	0.00	0.00	0.00	0.07
33 ProcessFood	33.88	0.00	361.76	0.00	0.00	0.00	0.00	395.64
34 TaningLethr	0.20	0.00	0.00	0.00	0.00	0.00	0.00	0.20
35 LethrProdt	1.72	0.00	24.16	0.00	0.00	0.00	0.00	25.88
36 Baling	0.00	0.00	0.00	0.00	0.00	0.00	0.00	0.00
37 JuteProduct	0.03	0.00	0.29	0.00	0.00	0.00	0.00	0.32

Table D 7.3. (Continued)

Commodity	1 Interm	2 Invest	3 HouseH	4 Export	5 GovGE	6 Stocks	7 Margins	Total
38 Yarn	263.23	0.00	0.00	0.00	0.00	0.00	0.00	263.23
39 MillCloth	186.33	0.00	0.00	0.00	0.00	0.00	0.00	186.33
40 HandlmCloth	0.00	0.00	0.00	0.00	0.00	0.00	0.00	0.00
41 DyeingBlech	-4.04	0.00	0.00	0.00	0.00	0.00	0.00	-4.04
42 RMG	41.95	0.00	-24.45	0.00	0.00	0.00	0.00	17.50
43 Knitting	6.57	0.00	4.05	0.00	0.00	0.00	0.00	10.62
44 ToiletrieMfg	17.69	0.00	97.28	0.00	0.00	0.00	0.00	114.96
45 CigarettInd	-0.17	0.00	-2.32	0.00	0.00	0.00	0.00	-2.49
46 BidiIndustry	0.00	0.00	0.00	0.00	0.00	0.00	0.00	0.00
47 BasicWProdt	0.88	0.00	0.00	0.00	0.00	0.00	0.00	0.88
48 WoodnFur	0.22	0.00	1.85	0.00	0.00	0.00	0.00	2.06
49 PulpPaBoard	116.66	0.00	36.70	0.00	0.00	0.00	0.00	153.36
50 PrintPub	5.89	0.00	0.00	0.00	0.00	0.00	0.00	5.89
51 Medicines	0.52	0.00	-61.90	0.00	0.00	0.00	0.00	-61.38
52 FertzerInsec	44.54	0.00	-1.90	0.00	0.00	0.00	0.00	42.64
53 Chemicals	59.41	0.00	0.00	0.00	0.00	0.00	0.00	59.41
54 PetroProduct	723.39	0.00	1097.06	0.00	0.00	0.00	0.00	1820.45
55 Chinapottery	50.37	0.00	88.21	0.00	0.00	0.00	0.00	138.58
56 ChemProdt	-10.62	0.00	-4.10	0.00	0.00	0.00	0.00	-14.72
57 GlassProdt	1.22	0.00	187.84	0.00	0.00	0.00	0.00	189.06
58 BricTCProdt	0.88	0.00	0.00	0.00	0.00	0.00	0.00	0.88
59 Cement	93.40	0.00	0.00	0.00	0.00	0.00	0.00	93.40
60 IronStBasic	18.46	0.00	0.00	0.00	0.00	0.00	0.00	18.46
61 FabMetProdt	27.12	0.00	606.60	0.00	0.00	0.00	0.00	633.72
62 Machinery	429.38	127.54	47.94	0.00	0.00	0.00	0.00	604.86
63 TransEquipmt	41.74	162.04	0.00	0.00	0.00	0.00	0.00	203.78
64 MiscellaInd	461.80	0.00	3.52	0.00	0.00	0.00	0.00	465.32
65 UrbanBuild	0.00	0.00	0.00	0.00	0.00	0.00	0.00	0.00
66 RuralBuild	0.00	0.00	0.00	0.00	0.00	0.00	0.00	0.00
67 BldgMantence	0.00	0.00	0.00	0.00	0.00	0.00	0.00	0.00
68 PlantConst	0.00	0.00	0.00	0.00	0.00	0.00	0.00	0.00

Commodity	1 Interm	2 Invest	3 HouseH	4 Export	5 GovGE	6 Stocks	7 Margins	Total
69 RuRoads	0.00	0.00	0.00	0.00	0.00	0.00	0.00	0.00
70 PortAirRlwy	0.00	0.00	0.00	0.00	0.00	0.00	0.00	0.00
71 CaDyothBuild	0.00	0.00	0.00	0.00	0.00	0.00	0.00	0.00
72 InfrastrMtn	0.00	0.00	0.00	0.00	0.00	0.00	0.00	0.00
73 ElectWater	0.00	0.00	0.00	0.00	0.00	0.00	0.00	0.00
74 GasExtDist	0.00	0.00	0.84	0.00	0.00	0.00	0.00	0.84
75 MinQuarring	32.63	0.00	26.17	0.00	0.00	0.00	0.00	58.80
76 WholeTrade	0.00	0.00	0.00	0.00	0.00	0.00	0.00	0.00
77 RetailTrade	0.00	0.00	0.00	0.00	0.00	0.00	0.00	0.00
78 AirTransport	0.00	0.00	0.00	0.00	0.00	0.00	0.00	0.00
79 WatTransport	0.00	0.00	0.00	0.00	0.00	0.00	0.00	0.00
80 LanTransport	0.00	0.00	0.00	0.00	0.00	0.00	0.00	0.00
81 RaiTransport	0.00	0.00	0.00	0.00	0.00	0.00	0.00	0.00
82 Warehousing	0.00	0.00	0.00	0.00	0.00	0.00	0.00	0.00
83 HousingServ	0.00	0.00	0.00	0.00	0.00	0.00	0.00	0.00
84 HealthServ	0.00	0.00	0.00	0.00	0.00	0.00	0.00	0.00
85 EducatServ	0.00	0.00	0.00	0.00	0.00	0.00	0.00	0.00
86 PubAdDefence	32.08	0.00	-3.91	0.00	0.00	0.00	0.00	28.17
87 BanInsurance	0.74	0.00	-23.16	0.00	0.00	0.00	0.00	-22.42
88 ProfesioServ	-1.44	0.00	-30.30	0.00	0.00	0.00	0.00	-31.74
89 HotelRest	0.00	0.00	0.00	0.00	0.00	0.00	0.00	0.00
90 Entertainmen	0.00	0.00	-0.19	0.00	0.00	0.00	0.00	-0.19
91 Communica	3.00	0.00	-3.26	0.00	0.00	0.00	0.00	-0.26
92 Othservices	0.00	0.00	0.00	0.00	0.00	0.00	0.00	0.00
93 InfTechServ	0.00	0.00	-0.85	0.00	0.00	0.00	0.00	-0.84
94 Waste	0.25	0.00	11.60	0.00	0.00	0.00	0.00	11.86

Table D 7.4. Ranked Fan decomposition (simulation 2) (per cent)

	Short run					Long run			
Commodity	Local market effect	Domestic share effect	Export effect	Output growth	Commodity	Local market effect	Domestic share effect	Export effect	Output growth
1 MilkFat	5.94	-10.47	0.00	-4.53	1 PetroProduct	-0.03	-7.54	0.07	-7.51
2 PetroProduct	0.69	-4.63	0.12	-3.82	2 GlassProdt	4.00	-8.27	0.00	-4.26
3 GlassProdt	4.23	-7.31	0.00	-3.08	3 MilkFat	6.01	-10.05	0.00	-4.04
4 SpiceCulti	-0.29	-2.53	0.00	-2.83	4 SpiceCulti	-0.92	-3.09	0.00	-4.01
5 Machinery	-0.14	-2.85	0.16	-2.83	5 Cement	1.07	-4.47	0.00	-3.40
6 Cement	-0.39	-2.42	0.00	-2.82	6 EdiNoedOil	-0.50	-2.75	0.00	-3.25
7 FruitCulti	0.08	-1.61	0.00	-1.53	7 PulpPaBoard	-0.84	-2.40	0.00	-3.24
8 Waste	1.25	-2.74	0.00	-1.49	8 Machinery	1.93	-5.01	0.09	-2.99
9 ProcessFood	0.23	-1.69	0.00	-1.46	9 FruitCulti	-0.35	-1.87	0.00	-2.22
10 PulpPaBoard	-0.28	-1.11	0.00	-1.39	10 OilseedCulti	-1.90	-0.31	0.00	-2.21
11 SugcaneCulti	-1.26	0.00	0.00	-1.26	11 ProcessFood	-0.18	-1.90	0.00	-2.08
12 Chemicals	-0.16	-1.10	0.00	-1.26	12 SugcaneCulti	-1.70	0.00	0.00	-1.70
13 SugGuMolass	-0.15	-1.07	0.00	-1.22	13 Chinapottery	-0.18	-1.71	0.21	-1.67
14 OilseedCulti	-0.80	-0.34	0.00	-1.14	14 SugGuMolass	-0.44	-1.16	0.00	-1.61
15 FabMetProdt	0.77	-1.83	0.00	-1.07	15 TobaccoCulti	-0.61	-0.98	0.09	-1.49
16 EdiNoedOil	-0.01	-1.02	0.00	-1.02	16 Waste	1.26	-2.74	0.00	-1.48
17 IronStBasic	-0.63	-0.36	0.00	-0.99	17 Chemicals	0.17	-1.33	0.00	-1.16
18 TobaccoCulti	-0.28	-0.87	0.17	-0.98	18 VegCulti	-0.19	-1.07	0.11	-1.15
19 Yarn	-0.16	-0.80	0.00	-0.96	19 GasExtDist	-0.96	-0.09	0.00	-1.04
20 TransEquipmt	-0.10	-0.83	0.00	-0.93	20 Baling	-0.94	0.00	0.00	-0.94
21 Wheat	-0.64	-0.23	0.00	-0.87	21 FishSeafood	-0.40	-0.85	0.32	-0.92
22 Chinapottery	0.40	-1.57	0.38	-0.78	22 FabMetProdt	0.92	-1.83	0.00	-0.91
23 VegCulti	-0.06	-0.79	0.19	-0.66	23 Entertainmen	-0.88	0.00	0.00	-0.88
24 Manure	-0.67	0.03	0.00	-0.64	24 Othergrain	-0.81	0.00	0.00	-0.81
25 TeaProduct	-0.31	-0.30	0.00	-0.61	25 Wheat	-0.53	-0.28	0.00	-0.81
26 PrintPub	-0.35	-0.24	0.00	-0.59	26 EducatServ	-0.80	0.00	0.00	-0.80

	Short run					Long run			
Commodity	Local market effect	Domestic share effect	Export effect	Output growth	Commodity	Local market effect	Domestic share effect	Export effect	Output growth
27 MinQuarring	-0.22	-0.32	0.00	-0.53	27 DyeingBlech	-0.77	0.00	0.00	-0.77
28 Othservices	-0.51	0.00	0.00	-0.51	28 TeaProduct	-0.46	-0.31	0.00	-0.77
29 OthcropCulti	-0.27	-0.23	0.02	-0.48	29 JuteProduct	-0.46	0.00	-0.26	-0.72
30 Othergrain	-0.48	0.00	0.00	-0.47	30 PoutryEggs	-0.66	-0.05	0.00	-0.72
31 GasExtDist	-0.38	-0.07	0.00	-0.45	31 PoultryMeat	-0.70	0.01	0.00	-0.69
32 PoutryEggs	-0.38	-0.05	0.00	-0.43	32 Manure	-0.75	0.07	0.00	-0.68
33 CottonCulti	-0.24	-0.19	0.00	-0.42	33 JuteCultiv	-0.66	0.00	-0.01	-0.68
34 DyeingBlech	-0.44	0.01	0.00	-0.42	34 HandlmCloth	-0.65	0.00	0.00	-0.65
35 Salt	-0.41	-0.01	0.00	-0.42	35 HotelRest	-0.59	0.00	0.00	-0.59
36 Entertainmen	-0.43	0.00	0.01	-0.42	36 RiceflorBran	-0.52	-0.04	0.00	-0.55
37 EducatServ	-0.40	0.00	0.00	-0.40	37 Othservices	-0.52	0.00	0.00	-0.52
38 PoultryMeat	-0.41	0.02	0.00	-0.39	38 PrintPub	-0.15	-0.34	0.00	-0.49
39 Paddy	-0.38	0.00	0.00	-0.38	39 Communica	-0.88	0.00	0.43	-0.46
40 HandlmCloth	-0.37	0.00	0.00	-0.37	40 HousingServ	-0.46	0.00	0.00	-0.46
41 FlourBrafeed	-0.24	-0.12	0.00	-0.36	41 Fish	-0.45	0.00	0.00	-0.45
42 FishSeafood	-0.12	-0.81	0.57	-0.36	42 TransEquipmt	2.20	-2.62	0.00	-0.43
43 Animaldraft	-0.35	0.02	0.00	-0.33	43 FlourBrafeed	-0.29	-0.13	0.00	-0.42
44 RiceflorBran	-0.30	-0.02	0.00	-0.32	44 Paddy	-0.41	0.00	0.00	-0.41
45 Fish	-0.29	0.00	0.00	-0.29	45 BasicWProdt	-0.23	-0.03	0.00	-0.26
46 BasicWProdt	-0.25	-0.03	0.00	-0.28	46 ElectWater	-0.22	0.00	0.00	-0.22
47 Forestry	-0.26	0.00	0.00	-0.26	47 PotatoCulti	-0.20	-0.02	0.00	-0.22
48 WoodnFur	-0.24	-0.02	0.00	-0.26	48 OthcropCulti	0.05	-0.28	0.01	-0.21
49 HealthServ	-0.24	0.00	0.00	-0.24	49 Yarn	0.84	-1.03	0.00	-0.19
50 HotelRest	-0.23	0.00	0.00	-0.23	50 WoodnFur	-0.17	-0.02	0.00	-0.19

Table D 7.4. (Continued)

Short run					Long run				
Commodity	Local market effect	Domestic share effect	Export effect	Output growth	Commodity	Local market effect	Domestic share effect	Export effect	Output growth
51 PulseCulti	-0.20	0.00	0.00	-0.20	51 Animaldraft	-0.22	0.09	0.00	-0.13
52 Medicines	-0.21	0.02	0.00	-0.19	52 BidiIndustry	-0.12	0.00	0.00	-0.12
53 ElectWater	-0.16	0.00	0.00	-0.16	53 TeaCulti	-0.56	0.00	0.49	-0.07
54 BanInsurance	-0.25	0.01	0.09	-0.16	54 CottonCulti	-0.03	-0.03	0.00	-0.06
55 Meat	-0.17	0.02	0.00	-0.15	55 CigarettInd	-0.03	0.00	0.00	-0.03
56 ChemProdt	-0.01	-0.13	0.00	-0.14	56 InfTechServ	-0.13	0.00	0.12	0.00
57 PotatoCulti	-0.12	-0.02	0.00	-0.13	57 ChemProdt	0.10	-0.09	0.00	0.00
58 HousingServ	-0.12	0.00	0.00	-0.12	58 PulseCulti	0.12	0.00	0.00	0.12
59 ProfesioServ	-0.23	0.01	0.12	-0.10	59 Warehousing	0.16	0.00	0.00	0.16
60 InfTechServ	-0.27	0.01	0.21	-0.04	60 Salt	0.18	0.00	0.00	0.18
61 Communica	-0.79	0.00	0.76	-0.03	61 Medicines	0.09	0.11	0.00	0.21
62 FertzerInsec	-0.40	-0.36	0.76	-0.01	62 MinQuarring	0.58	-0.33	0.00	0.25
63 BricTCProdt	0.01	-0.02	0.00	0.00	63 BanInsurance	0.24	0.01	0.05	0.30
64 RuralBuild	0.00	0.00	0.00	0.00	64 ProfesioServ	0.39	0.01	0.07	0.47
65 RuRoads	0.00	0.00	0.00	0.00	65 LanTransport	0.52	0.00	0.00	0.52
66 CaDyothBuild	0.00	0.00	0.00	0.00	66 IronStBasic	0.59	-0.06	0.00	0.53
67 InfrastrMtn	0.00	0.00	0.00	0.00	67 RetailTrade	0.55	0.00	0.00	0.55
68 PlantConst	0.00	0.00	0.00	0.00	68 RaiTransport	0.57	0.00	0.00	0.57
69 UrbanBuild	0.00	0.00	0.00	0.00	69 WholeTrade	0.61	0.00	0.00	0.61
70 BldgMantence	0.02	0.00	0.00	0.02	70 AirTransport	0.55	0.00	0.14	0.69
71 BidiIndustry	0.04	0.00	0.00	0.04	71 PubAdDefence	-0.06	0.00	0.84	0.78
72 RetailTrade	0.05	0.00	0.00	0.05	72 HeathServ	0.91	0.00	0.00	0.91
73 WholeTrade	0.05	0.00	0.00	0.05	73 WatTransport	0.50	0.00	0.41	0.92
74 RaiTransport	0.05	0.00	0.00	0.05	74 FertzerInsec	-0.49	-0.31	1.73	0.93
75 LanTransport	0.05	0.00	0.00	0.05	75 Shrimp	-0.10	0.00	1.52	1.42
76 Warehousing	0.06	0.00	0.00	0.06	76 TaningLethr	1.65	0.00	0.00	1.65

Short run					Long run				
Commodity	Local market effect	Domestic share effect	Export effect	Output growth	Commodity	Local market effect	Domestic share effect	Export effect	Output growth
77 JuteCultiv	0.03	0.00	0.07	0.10	77 BldgMantence	1.65	0.00	0.00	1.65
78 PortAirRlwy	0.10	0.00	0.00	0.10	78 MillCloth	1.61	0.23	0.00	1.83
79 MiscellaInd	-0.13	-1.56	1.80	0.11	79 HidesSkins	1.90	-0.02	0.00	1.88
80 CigarettInd	0.17	0.01	0.00	0.18	80 LethrProdt	-0.40	-0.07	2.43	1.96
81 HidesSkins	0.23	-0.01	0.00	0.22	81 Forestry	2.28	-0.01	0.00	2.27
82 TeaCulti	-0.44	0.00	0.69	0.25	82 MiscellaInd	0.35	-1.28	3.20	2.27
83 AirTransport	0.05	0.00	0.25	0.29	83 Meat	2.76	-0.04	0.00	2.72
84 TaningLethr	0.29	0.00	0.00	0.29	84 RMG	0.00	-0.02	3.47	3.45
85 LethrProdt	-0.43	-0.07	0.84	0.34	85 PortAirRlwy	3.57	0.00	0.00	3.57
86 MillCloth	0.39	0.02	0.00	0.41	86 BricTCProdt	3.62	0.02	0.00	3.64
87 Shrimp	-0.16	0.00	0.84	0.68	87 RuralBuild	4.33	0.00	0.00	4.33
88 JuteProduct	-0.40	0.00	1.15	0.74	88 RuRoads	4.33	0.00	0.00	4.33
89 WatTransport	0.00	0.00	0.74	0.75	89 UrbanBuild	4.33	0.00	0.00	4.33
90 ToiletrieMfg	0.27	-1.31	1.90	0.86	90 PlantConst	4.33	0.00	0.00	4.33
91 RMG	-0.01	-0.01	0.95	0.92	91 CaDyothBuild	4.33	0.00	0.00	4.33
92 Baling	1.09	0.00	0.00	1.09	92 InfrastrMtn	4.33	0.00	0.00	4.33
93 PubAdDefence	-0.04	-0.01	1.50	1.46	93 Knitting	0.02	-0.06	7.57	7.53
94 Knitting	-0.02	-0.04	1.57	1.52	94 ToiletrieMfg	1.40	-1.05	8.26	8.61

Table D 7.5. Base year total wage payments by industry and occupational group (in Million Taka)

Industry	Male low-skilled	Male high-skilled	Female low-skilled	Female high-skilled	Total
1 Paddy	101181.20	8136.84	5982.85	1082.91	116383.80
2 Wheat	1869.90	150.37	110.57	20.01	2150.86
3 Othergrain	297.16	23.90	17.57	3.18	341.81
4 JuteCultiv	9118.94	733.33	539.20	97.60	10489.07
5 SugcaneCulti	4879.65	392.41	288.53	52.23	5612.83
6 PotatoCulti	3924.27	315.58	232.04	42.00	4513.90
7 VegCulti	6814.30	548.00	402.93	72.93	7838.16
8 PulseCulti	5222.16	419.96	308.79	55.89	6006.79
9 OilseedCulti	379.58	30.53	22.44	4.06	436.62
10 FruitCulti	4479.60	360.24	264.88	47.94	5152.66
11 CottonCulti	1027.39	82.62	60.75	11.00	1181.75
12 TobaccoCulti	597.70	48.07	35.34	6.40	687.50
13 TeaCulti	654.32	52.62	38.69	7.00	752.63
14 SpiceCulti	1111.56	250.28	71.13	0.54	1433.52
15 OthcropCulti	3362.48	757.09	215.18	1.64	4336.39
16 LivstockRear	18740.82	1507.11	1108.15	200.58	21556.65
17 PoultryRear	3987.48	320.67	235.78	42.68	4586.61
18 ShrimFarming	9881.96	596.88	124.24	0.00	10603.08
19 Fishing	25380.71	1533.02	319.10	0.00	27232.84
20 Forestry	6608.91	3935.37	700.66	0.00	11244.94
21 RiceMilling	5426.64	1221.86	1289.75	9.85	7948.10
22 GrainMilling	1017.23	229.04	65.10	0.50	1311.87
23 FishProcess	823.69	185.46	52.71	0.40	1062.26
24 OilIndustry	1343.58	302.52	85.98	0.66	1732.73
25 SweetenerInd	10302.89	2319.79	659.32	5.04	13287.03
26 TeaProduct	574.16	129.28	95.20	0.73	799.36
27 SaltRefining	453.22	102.05	29.00	0.22	584.49
28 FoodProcess	3664.51	825.10	234.50	1.79	4725.91
29 TannFishing	1383.91	311.60	88.56	0.68	1784.75
30 LeatherInd	1465.09	1123.75	36.98	15.85	2641.67

Industry	Male low-skilled	Male high-skilled	Female low-skilled	Female high-skilled	Total
31 Baling	233.67	50.69	2.64	0.23	287.24
32 JuteFabricat	6996.31	1517.77	79.18	6.82	8600.08
33 YarnIndustry	4284.98	929.58	97.98	8.44	5320.98
34 ClothMill	6404.92	1389.48	377.71	32.53	8204.63
35 HandloomClot	7457.12	1617.74	1248.50	107.51	10430.87
36 DyeingBlech	1204.30	261.26	201.63	17.36	1684.55
37 RMG	6240.90	1944.28	14776.90	424.16	23386.24
38 Knitting	1880.54	585.86	4452.66	127.81	7046.87
39 ToiletrieMfg	746.84	1276.78	9.22	97.29	2130.13
40 CigarettInd	86.26	4.41	12.36	0.00	103.03
41 BidiIndustry	81.58	4.17	11.69	0.00	97.45
42 SawPlane	394.64	54.42	23.63	0.00	472.69
43 Furniturind	2459.04	339.12	147.27	0.00	2945.44
44 PaperInd	595.32	882.58	9.45	20.72	1508.06
45 PrintPub	872.36	1293.29	13.84	30.36	2209.85
46 PharmaMfg	1183.24	2022.84	14.61	154.13	3374.83
47 FertiliseInd	1074.91	1837.64	10.51	110.85	3033.91
48 BasiChemical	209.85	358.75	2.59	27.34	598.53
49 PetroleumRef	233.18	726.10	0.01	0.09	959.38
50 EarthwareInd	423.00	302.88	13.35	1.47	740.69
51 ChemicalInd	491.50	840.26	6.07	64.02	1401.85
52 GlassInd	318.42	53.16	19.67	2.16	393.41
53 ClayInd	650.06	465.47	20.51	2.25	1138.30
54 CementMfg	640.82	458.85	20.22	2.22	1122.12
55 BasicMetaMfg	4061.02	581.12	0.05	0.00	4642.19
56 MetalMfg	5734.94	820.66	0.07	0.00	6555.67
57 MachineEquip	8328.17	1390.50	511.51	0.00	10230.18
58 TranspoEquip	2976.71	492.42	11.96	4.04	3485.13

Table D 7.5. (Continued)

Industry	Male low-skilled	Male high-skilled	Female low-skilled	Female high-skilled	Total
59 MiscellaInd	6019.88	1005.10	371.88	40.80	7437.66
60 Urbanbuild	12363.70	2549.63	802.43	0.00	15715.77
61 RuralBuild	37837.67	7802.86	2455.76	0.00	48096.29
62 PPlantBuild	1510.85	311.57	98.06	0.00	1920.48
63 RuRoadBuild	2186.50	450.90	141.91	0.00	2779.31
64 PoRoadBuild	8058.00	1661.72	522.98	0.00	10242.70
65 CaDyothBuild	1040.35	214.54	67.52	0.00	1322.41
66 ElectWatGene	2344.53	1676.27	195.46	0.00	4216.25
67 GasExtDist	129.10	92.31	10.76	0.00	232.17
68 MinQuarring	2893.92	2069.07	241.26	0.00	5204.26
69 WholeTrade	30724.09	11530.17	1206.66	127.67	43588.59
70 RetailTrade	62589.88	23488.80	2458.15	260.09	88796.93
71 AirTransport	10139.60	1677.33	40.73	13.76	11871.43
72 WatTransport	6701.81	1108.64	26.92	9.09	7846.46
73 LanTransport	27379.97	4529.30	110.00	37.15	32056.42
74 RaiTransport	1655.16	273.80	6.65	2.25	1937.86
75 OthTransport	22199.24	3672.28	89.18	30.12	25990.83
76 HousingServ	6735.31	6798.51	0.00	418.57	13952.39
77 HealthServ	4652.24	13999.48	2533.51	3227.33	24412.56
78 EducatServ	2243.95	29596.54	560.78	6827.69	39228.95
79 PubAdDefence	15768.98	39159.83	844.44	1156.36	56929.60
80 BanInsRestat	9800.82	13780.70	8461.34	0.00	32042.86
81 ProfesioServ	17001.40	23905.25	14677.82	0.00	55584.46
82 HotelRest	5797.46	330.77	397.10	93.08	6618.42
83 Entertainmen	1594.25	2241.64	1376.37	0.00	5212.26
84 Communicatio	612.94	4956.71	116.03	502.82	6188.50
85 OthServices	17525.69	24642.44	15130.45	0.00	57298.58
86 InfotechEcom	137.39	1189.66	0.00	37.78	1364.84
Total	619884.3125	274163.2813	88755.8672	15810.6328	998614.1

Source: Bangladesh model database.

REFERENCES

ADB and Government of Japan (2004). *Economic Growth and Poverty Reduction in Bangladesh*. Dhaka: copublished by the Asian Development Bank Bangladesh Resident Mission and the Embassy of Japan in Bangladesh.

Adelman, I. & Morris, C. T. (1973). *Economic Growth and Social Equity in Developing Countries*. Standford, California: Standford University Press.

Adelman, I. & Robinson, S. (1978). *Income Distribution in Developing Countries: A Case Study of Korea*. Oxford: Oxford University Press.

Adelman, I. & Robinson, S. (1989). Income distribution and development. In H. Chenery & T. N. Srinivasan (Eds.), *Handbook of Development Economics*. Amsterdam: Elsevier Science Publishers B.V.

Agrawal, N. (1989). Tariff reform and the distribution of household incomes. Preliminary Working Paper No. IP-42, IMPACT Research Centre and Industries Assistance Commission, Melbourne.

Ahammad, H. (1995). *Foreign Exchange and Trade Policy Issues in a Developing Economy: The Case of Bangladesh*. Aldershot: Avebury.

Ahluwalia, M. (1976). Income distribution and development : some stylized facts. *American Economic Review, 66*(2), 128-135.

Ahmed, N. (2001). *Trade Liberalization in Bangladesh: An Investigation into Trends*. Dhaka: University Press Limited.

Ahmed, N. (2005). External sector: performance and prospects. Dhaka: Bangladesh Institute of Development Studies (BIDS), Seminar on National Budget for 2005-06 and PRSP (May).

Ahmed, N. (2009). Sustaining ready-made garment exports from Bangladesh. *Journal of Contemporary Asia*, 39(4), 597-618.

Ahmed, S. (2006). The political economy of development experience in Bangladesh. In S. Ahmed & W. Mahmud (Eds.), *Growth and Poverty: The Development Experience of Bangladesh*. Dhaka: University Press Limited.

Aka, B. F. (2004). Fiscal adjustment, poverty, inequality and welfare in Cote d'Ivoire: a computational general equilibrium model analysis. Available at http://www.csae.ox.ac.uk/conferences/2004-GPRaHDiA/papers/2m-Aka-CSAE2004.pdf. Accessed September 2008.

Alam, M. (1995). *Trade and Financial Liberalisation in Bangladesh*. Dhaka: Desh Prakasan.

Annabi, N., Cisse, F., Cockburn, J. & Decaluwe, B. (2005). Trade liberalisation, growth and poverty in Senegal: A dynamic microsimulation CGE model analysis. CIRPEE Working Paper No. 05-12.

Annabi, N., Khondker, B., Raihan, S., Cockburn, J. & Decaluwé, B. (2006). Implications of WTO agreements and unilateral trade policy reforms for poverty in Bangladesh: Short versus long-run impacts. In T. W. Hertel & L. A. Winters (Eds.), *Poverty and The WTO: Impacts of the Doha Development Agenda*. Washington, DC: a copublication of the World Bank and Palgrave Macmillan.

Armington, P. S. (1969). A theory of demand for products distinguished by place of production. *IMF Staff Papers,* 16, 159-178.

Armington, P. S. (1970). Adjustment of trade balances: Some experiments with a model of trade among many countries. *IMF Staff Papers,* 17, 488-523.

Atkinson, A. B. (1970). On the measurement of inequality. *Journal of Economic Theory,* 2(3), 244-263.

Arndt, C., Dorosh, P., Fontana, M., Zohir, S., El-Said, M. & Lungren, C. (2002). Opportunities and challenges in agriculture and garments: a general equilibrium analysis of the Bangladesh economy. TMD Discussion Paper No. 107, Trade and Macroeconomics Division, International Food Policy Research Institute.

Bairam, E. (1991). Capital-labour substitution in sectors of a less developed economy: The case of Bangladesh. *Bangladesh Development Studies,* 21(4), 87-91.

Bandara, J. S. (1989). A multi sectoral general equilibrium model of the Sri Lankan economy with an application to the analysis of the effects of external shocks. Unpublished Ph.D dissertation, La Trobe University, Melbourne.

Bandara, J. S. (1991). Computable general equilibrium models for development policy analysis in LDCs. *Journal of Economic Surveys,* 5(1), 3-69.

Bangladesh Bank, *Economic Trends* (various issues).

Bannister, G. J. & Thugge, K. (2001). International trade and poverty alleviation. International Monetary Fund Working Paper No. WP/01/54.

Barrett, G. F. & Donald, S. G. (2009). Statistical inference with generalised Gini indices of inequality, poverty, and welfare. *Journal of Business & Economics Statistics,* 27(1), 1-16.

Bautista, R. M. & Thomas, M. (1997). Income effects of alternative trade policy adjustments on Phillippine rural households: A general equilibrium analysis. TMD Discussion Paper No. 22, Trade and Macroeconomics Division, International Food Policy Research Institute.

Bayes, A. & Muhammad, A. (1998). *Bangladesh at 25: An Analytical Discourse on Development*. Dhaka: University Press Limited.

BBS, *Statistical Yearbook of Bangladesh* (various issues). Dhaka: Bangladesh Bureau of Statistics.

BBS (1988). *Report of the Bangladesh Household Expenditure Survey 1985-86*. Dhaka: Bangladesh Bureau of Statistics (BBS).

BBS (2001). *Report on Household Income and Expenditure Survey-2000*. Dhaka: Bangladesh Bureau of Statistics.

BBS (2004a). *Bangladesh Statistical Yearbook*, Dhaka: Bangladesh Bureau of Statistics.

BBS (2004b). *Report of the Labour Force survey, Bangladesh 2003*. Dhaka, Bnagladesh: Bangladesh Bureau of Statistics.

BBS (2006). *Preliminary Report on Household Income and Expenditure Survey-2005*. Dhaka: Bangladesh Bureau of Statistics.

Bhagwati, J. (1959). Protection, real wages, and real incomes. *Economic Journal, 69*(276), 733-748.

Bhagwati, J. N. (1988). Export-promoting trade strategies:issues and evidence. *The World Bank Research Observer, 3*(1), 27-57.

Bhuyan, A. R. & Rashid, M. A. (1993). *Trade Regimes and Industrial Growth: A Case Study of Bangladesh*. Dhaka: Bureau of Economic Research, University of Dhaka.

Bibi, S. & Chatti, R. (2006). Trade liberalisation and the dynamics of poverty in Tunisia: A layered microsimulation analysis. MPIA Working Paper 2006-07, Poverty and Economic Policy (PEP) research network.

Boccanfuso, D., Decaluwé, B. & Savard, L. (2003). Poverty, income distribution and CGE modeling: Does the functional form of distribution matter? Cahiers de recherche 03-32, CIRPEE.

BOI (2005). *FDI in Bangladesh during 2004: The 4th FDI Inflow Survey*. Dhaka: Board of Investment.

Bourguignon, F., de Melo, J.& Suwa, A. (1991). Distributional effects of adjustment policies: simulations for two archetype economics.World Bank Policy Research Working Paper Series,No. 674.

Bourguignon, F., Pereira da Silva, L. & Stern, N. (2006). Evaluating the poverty impact of economic policies: some analytical challenges. In A. Mody & C. Pattiloo (Eds.), *Macroeconomic Policies and Poverty Reduction*. London: Routledge.

Bourguignon, F., Robilliard, A.-S. & Robinson, S. (2003). Representative versus real households in the macro-economic modelling of inequality. DELTA Working Papers 2003-05, DELTA (Ecole normale superieure).

Bussolo, M. & Lay, J. (2003). Globalisation and poverty changes in Columbia. OECD Development Centre Working Paper No. 226.

Bussolo, M. & Round, J. J. (2002). Redistribution and Poverty: Experience with a CGE model for Ghana. Paper presented at the XIII International Conference on Input-Output Techniques, 21-25 August. Macerata, Italy.

Caddy, V. (1976). Empirical estimation of the elasticities of substitution: A review. IMPACT Preliminary Working Paper No. OP-09, mimeo, pp. 43.

Case, A. (1998). Income distribution and expenditure patterns in South Africa. Available at http://www.princeton.edu/rpds/papers/pdfs/IncomcDistribution.pdf. Accessed January, 2008.

Chen, S. & Ravallion, M. (2004). Welfare impacts of China's accession to the World Trade Organization. *World Bank Economic Review*, 18(1), 29-57.

Chia N. C., Wahba, S. and Whalley, J. (1994). Poverty-reduction targeting programs: a general equilibrium approach. *Journal of African Economies*, 3(2), 309-338.

Chipman, J. S. (1969). Factor price equalization and the Stolper-Samuelson theorem. *International Economic Review,* 10(3), 399-406.

Chotikapanich, D. (1994). *Techniques for Measuring Income Inequality:an application to Thailand*, Avebury: Ashgate Publishing.

Chowdhury, A. (2000). Politics, society and financial sector reform in Bangladesh. World Institute for Development Economics Research Working Papers, No. 191.

Chowdhury, A. R. (2001). The impact of financial reform on private savings in Bangladesh. World Institute for Development Economics Research Discussion Paper No. 2001/78.

Chowdhury, O. H. (1982). Complete consumer model: A preliminary estimate for Bangladesh. *Bangladesh Development Studies,* 10(1), 91-104.

Chowdhury, O. H. (1990). Tax policy analysis in Bangladesh: a computable general equilibrium approach. Unpublished Ph.D dissertation, University of the Philippines, Diliman, Quezon City.

Chowdhury, O. H. (2005). Domestic resource generation and public expenditure. Dhaka: Bangladesh Institute of Development Studies (BIDS), Seminar on National Budget for 2005-06 and PRSP (May).

Chung, J. W. (1994). *Utility and Production Functions: Theory and Applications*. Cambridge: Blackwell.

Cicowiez, M., Diaz-Bonilla, C. & Diaz-Bonilla, E. (2009). The impact of trade liberalisation on poverty and inequality in Argentina. Agricultural Distortions Working Paper105, World Bank.

Cloutier, M., Cockburn, J., Decaluwé, B., Raihan, S. & Khondker, B. H. (2008). Welfare, Poverty and Distribution Effects of Trade Liberalisation: A Review of the CGE Literature. In J. Cockburn, B. Decaluwé & V. Robichaud (Eds.), *Trade Liberalization and Poverty: A CGE Analysis of the 1990s Experience in Africa and Asia*: Poverty and Economic Policy (PEP) Research Network.

Cockburn, J. (2002). Trade liberalisation and poverty in Nepal: A computable general equilibrium micro simulation analysis. CSAE Working Paper WPS/2002-11.

Codsi, G. & Pearson, K. R. (1988). GEMPACK: General-purpose software for applied general equilibrium and other economic modellers. *Computer Science in Economics and Management,* 1(3), 189-207.

Cogneau, D. & Robilliard, A. (2000). Growth, distribution and poverty in Madagascar: learning from a microsimulation model in a general equilibrium framework.TMD Discussion Paper No. 61, Trade and Macroeconomics Division, International Food Policy Research Institute.

Collier, P. & Dollar, D. (2001). Can the world cut poverty in half? How policy reform and effective aid can meet international development goals. *World Development,* 29(11), 1787-1802.

Cooper, R., McLaren, K. & Powell, A. (1985). Macroeconomic closure in applied general equilibrium modelling: experiences from ORANI and agenda for further research. In J. Piggot & J. Whalley (Eds.), *New Development in Applied General Equilibrium Analysis*. New York: Cambridge University Press.

Corden, W. M. (1997). *Trade Policy and Economic Welfare*. New York: Oxford University Press.

Cornia, G. A. (2003). The impact of liberalisation and globalisation on income inequality in developing and transitional economies. CESifo Working Paper, No. 843.

Cororaton, C. B., Cockburn, J. & Corong, E. (2006). Doha scenarios, trade reforms, and poverty in the Philippines: a CGE analysis. In T. W. Hertel & L. A. Winters (Eds.), *Poverty and the WTO: Impacts of the Doha Development Agenda*. Washington DC: a copublication of the World Bank and Palgrave Macmillan.

Coxhead, I. A. (1989). Technical change in agriculture, income distribution and economic policy: the Philippines. Unpublished PhD dissertation, Australian National University, Canberra.

Croser, J. (2002). Impacts of trade policy reform on income distribution and poverty in Indonesia. ACIAR Indonesia Research Project Working Paper No. 02.01.

Datt, G. & Ravallion, M. (1998). Farm productivity and rural poverty in India. *Journal of Development Studies,* 34(4), 62-85.

Davies, J. B. (2004). Microsimulation, CGE and macro modelling for transition and developing economies. World Institute for Development Economics Research Discussion Paper No. 2004/08.

de Janvry, A., Sadoulet, E. & Fargeix, A. (1991). Politically feasible and equitable adjustment: some alternatives for Ecuador. *World Development,* 19(11), 1577-1594.

De Silva, I. (2008). Micro-level determinants of poverty reduction in Sri Lanka: A multivariate approach. *International Journal of Social Economics,* 35(3), 140-158.

Deardorff, A. V. & Stern, R. M. (Eds.) (1994). *The Stolper-Samuelson Theorem: A Golden Jubilee*. Ann Arbor:University of Michigan Press.

Deaton, A. (1997). *The Analysis of Household Surveys: A Microeconometric Approach to Development Policy*. Baltimore: Johns Hopkins University Press.

Decaluwé, B., Party, A., Savard, L. & Thorbecke, E. (1999). Poverty analysis within a general equilibrium framework. Working Paper 9909, CRÉFA99-06. Laval University.

Decaluwé, B., Savard, L. & Thorbecke, E. (2006). General equilibrium approach for poverty analysis: With an application to Cameroon. *African Development Review,* 17(2), 213-243.

Demery, L. & Jahangir, H. (1975). Adjustment dynamics and the elasticity of substitution: the case of manufacturing activity in Bangladesh. *Bangladesh Development Studies,* 2(3), 725-731.

Dervis, K., Melo, J. D. & Robinson, S. (1982). *General Equilibrium Models for Development Policy*. Cambridge,: Cambridge University Press.

Dimaranan, V. B., (Ed.) (2006). Global Trade, Assistance, and Production: The GTAP 6 Data Base, Center for Global Trade Analysis, Purdue University, Indiana.

Dixon, P. B., Bowles, S. & Kendrick, D. (1980). *Notes and Problems in Microeconomic Theory*. Amsterdam: North-Holland Publishing Company.

Dixon, P. B., Parmenter, B. R., Ryland G. J. & Sutton, J. (1977). ORANI, *A General Equilibrium Model of the Australian Economy: Current Specification and Illustrations of Use for Policy Analysis*. Vol. 2 of First Progress Report of the IMPACT Project. Canberra: Australian Government Publishing Service.

Dixon, P. B., Parmenter, B. R., Powell, A. A. & Wilcoxen, P. J. (1992). *Notes and Problems in Applied General Equilibrium Economics*. Amsterdam: North-Holland Publishing Company.

Dixon, P. B., Parmenter, B. R., Sutton, J. & Vincent, D. P. (1997).*ORANI: A Multisectoral Model of the Australian Economy*. Amsterdam: North-Holland Publishing Company.

Dollar, D. & Kraay, A. (2001). Trade, growth, and poverty. World Bank Policy Research Working Paper, No. 2615.

Dollar, D. & Kraay, A. (2002). Growth is good for the poor. *Journal of Economic Growth,* 7(3), 195-225.

Dorosh, P., Nssah, B. E. & Samba-Mamadou, O. (1994). Terms of trade and the real exchange rate in the CFA zone: implications for income distribution in Niger. Working

Paper No. 57, Cornell Food and Nutrition Policy Program Cornell University, Ithaka, NY.

Dorosh, P. A. & Sahn, D. E. (2000). A general equilibrium analysis of the effect of macroeconomic adjustment on poverty in Africa. *Journal of Policy Modeling*, 22(6), 753-776.

Duclos, J.-Y & Araar, A. (2006). Poverty and equity: measurement, policy and estimation with DAD. Available at: http://www.ecn.ulaval.ca/~jyves/publications/pedag.pdf Accessed June 2009.

Duclos, J.-Y., Araar, A. & Fortin, C. (2000). DAD: A software for distributive analysis/ Analyse distributive. MIMAP, International Research Centre, Government of Canada and CREFA, Laval University. Available at www.mimap.ecn.ulaval.ca.

Either, W. J. (1974). Some of the theorems of international trade with many goods and factors. *Journal of International Economics,* 4(2), 199-206.

Emini, C. A., Cockburn, J. & Decaluwé, B. (2006). The poverty impacts of the Doha Round in Cameroon: the role of tax policy. In T. W. Hertel & L. A. Winters (Eds.), *Poverty and the WTO: Impacts of the Doha Development Agenda*. New York: A copublication of Palgrave Macmillan and the World Bank.

Ferreira-Filho, J. B. & Horridge, M. (2005). The Doha Round, poverty and regional inequality in Brazil. World Bank Policy Research Working Paper No. 3701.

Fontana, M. & Rodgers, Y. V. d. M. (2005). Gender dimensions in the analysis of macro-poverty linkages. *Development Policy Review*, 23(3), 333-349.

Foster, J., Greer, J. & Thorbecke, E. (1984). A class of decomposable poverty measures. *Econometrica,* 52(3), 761-766.

Frisch, R. (1959). A complete scheme for computing all direct and cross price elasticities in a model with many sectors. *Econometrica,* 27(2), 177-196.

Geary, R. C. (1949-50). A Note on 'a constant utility index of the cost of living'. *Review of Economic Studies*, 18(1), 65-66.

Gilbert, J. (2008). Trade policy, poverty, and income distribution in CGE models: An application to SAFTA. Department of Economics and Finance Working Paper No. 2008-02, Utah State University.

GOB (1998). *The Fifth Five Year Plan*. Dhaka: Planning Commission, Government of the People's Republic of Bangladesh.

GOB (2003a). *Bangladesh Economic Review 2003*. Economic Adviser's Wing, Finance Division, Ministry of Finance, Government of the People's Republic of Bangladesh.

GOB (2003b). *Supplementary Document, Input-output Table 2000 for Bangladesh*. Dhaka: SHD Unit, Planning Commission.

GOB (2005). *Bangladesh Economic Review 2005*. Economic Adviser's Wing, Finance Division, Ministry of Finance, Government of the People's Republic of Bangladesh.

GOB (2006). *Bangladesh Economic Review 2006*. Economic Adviser's Wing, Finance Division, Ministry of Finance, Government of the People's Republic of Bangladesh.

Golleti, F. (1993). Food consumption parameters in Bangladesh. Bangladesh Food Policy Project Manuscript No 29, International Food Policy Research Institute, Dhaka, Bangladesh.

Gunter, B. G. & van der Hoeven, R. (2004). The social dimension of globalisation: a review of the literature. *International Labour Review,* 14*3*(1-2), 7-43.

Harberger, A. C. (1971). Three basic postulates for applied welfare economics: an interpretative essay, *Journal of Economic Literature*, 9(3): 785-797.

Harris, R. L. (1999). The distributional impact of macroeconomic shocks in Mexico: threshold effects in a multi-region CGE model. TMD Discussion Paper No. 44, Trade and Macroeconomics Division, International Food Policy Research Institute.

Harrison, J. & Horridge, M. (2006). Preparing data files for a CGE model using GEMPACK. Material prepared for the constructing of a CGE database program, 10-11 July, 2006, Monash University, Australia.

Harrison, W. J. & Pearson, K. R. (1996). Computing solutions for large general equilibrium models using GEMPACK. *Computational Economics*, 9(2), 83-127.

Helpman, E. (2004). *The Mystery of Economic Growth*. Cambridge: Harvard University Press.

Herault, N. (2007). Trade liberalisation, poverty and inequality in South Africa: A computable general equilibrium microsimulation analysis. *Economic Record,* 83(262), 317-328.

Hertel, T. W. (Ed.) (1997), *Global Trade Analysis: Modeling and Applications*. Cambridge: Cambridge University Press.

Hertel, T. W. & Ivanic, M. (2006). World market impacts of multilateral trade reforms. In T. W. Hertel & L. A. Winters (Eds.), *Poverty and the WTO: Impacts of the Doha Development Agenda*. Washington DC, a copublication of the World Bank and Palgrave Macmillan.

Hertel, T. W. & Reimer, J. (2004). Predicting the poverty impacts of trade reform.World Bank Policy Research Working Paper No. 3444.

Hoque, S. (2006). A computable general equilibrium model of Bangladesh for analysis of policy reforms. Unpublished Ph.D dissertation, Monash University, Melbourne.

Horridge, J. M. (2000). ORANI-G: A general equilibrium model of the Australian economy. Preliminary Working Paper No. OP-93,Centre of Policy Studies and the Impact Project, Monash University. Available at http://www.monash.edu.au/policy. Accessed April 2006.

Horridge, J. M. (2001a). MINIMAL: A simplified general equilibrium model. Centre of Policy Studies and the Impact Project, Monash University. Available at http://www.monash.edu.au/policy. Accessed April 2006.

Horridge, J. M. (2001b). ORANI-G: A generic single-country computable general equilibrium model. Edition prepared for the practical GE Modelling course, Centre of Policy Studies and the Impact Project, Monash University. Available at http://www.monash.edu.au/policy. Accessed April 2006.

Horridge, J. M. (2003). ORANI-G: A generic single-country computable general equilibrium model. Edition Prepared for the Practical GE Modelling Course, Centre of Policy Studies and the Impact Project, Monash University. Available at http://www. monash.edu.au/policy/oranig.htm. Accessed April 2006.

Horridge, J. M. (2004). Multiple households version of ORANIGO3. Centre of Policy Studies and the Impact Project, Monash University. Available at http://www. monash.edu.au/policy, Accessed April 2006.

Horridge, J. M. (2006). ORANI-G: A generic single-country computable general equilibrium model. Edition prepared for Practical GE Modelling Courses, Centre for Policy Studies and the Impact Project, Monash University. Available at www.ufjf.br/poseconomia/files/2012/05/**oranig**06.doc. Accessed May 2006.

Horridge, J. M., Harrison, W. J., & Pearson, K. R. (2003). Using analyseGE to examine an ORANI-G tariff cut simulation. Centre of Policy Studies and Impact Project, Monash University, Australia.

Horridge, J. M., Parmenter, B. R., Cameron, M., Joubert, R., Suleman, A. & de Jong, D. (1995). The macroeconomic, industrial, distributional and regional effects of government spending programs in South Africa.Working Paper No.G-109, Centre of Policy Studies, Monash University.

Horridge, J. M., Parmenter, B. R. & Pearson, K. R. (1993). ORANI-F: A general equilibrium model of the Australian economy. *Economic and Financial Computing,* 3(2), 71-140.

Horridge, J. M., Parmenter, B. R., & Pearson, K. R. (1998). ORANI-G: A general equilibrium model of the Australian economy, Edition prepared for course in practical GE Modelling. Centre for Policy Studies and the Impact Project, Monash University,. Available at http://www.monash.edu.au/policy Accessed April 2006.

Hossain, A. (1995). *Inflation, Economic Growth and the Balance of Payments in Bangladesh.* Delhi: Oxford University Press.

Hossain, A. (2000). *Exchange Rates, Capital Flows and International Trade: The Case of Bangladesh.* Dhaka: The University Press Limited.

Hossain, A. (2006). Overview of the Bangladesh economy. In A. Hossain, F. Khan & T. Akram (Eds.), *Economic Analyses of Contemporary Issues In Bangladesh.* Dhaka: The University Press Limited.

Hossain, M. (2003). Promoting rural non-farm economy of Bangladesh. CPD-IRRI Policy Brief -3, available at http://www.cpd-bangladesh.org/publications/cpdiri/cpdiri_3.pdf. Accessed April 2006.

Hossain, M., Naher, F. & Shahabuddin, Q. (2005). Food security and nutrition in Bangladesh: progress and determinants. *Journal of Agricultural and Development Economics*, 2(2), 103-132.

Hossain, M., & Sen, B. (1992). Rural poverty in Bangladesh: trends and determinants. *Asian Development Review,* 10(1), 1-34.

Hossain, Z. (1989). Analysis of the restrictive trade policies in Bangladesh: an applied general equilibrium approach. Unpublished Ph.D dissertation, University of The Philippines, Diliman, Quezon City.

Ianchovichina, E., Nicita, A. & Soloaga, I. (2002). Trade reform and poverty: the case of Mexico. *The World Economy,* 25(7), 945-972.

IMF, *International Financial Statistics* (various issues).

Johansen, L. (1960). *A Multi-Sectoral Study of Economic Growth.* Amsterdam: North-Holland Publishing Company.

Jones, R. W. (1965). The structure of simple general equilibrium models. *Journal of Political Economy,* 73(6), 557-572.

Jones, R. W. & Scheinkman, J. (1977). The relevance of the two-sector production model in trade theory. *Journal of Political Economy*, 85(5), 909-935.

Kakwani, N. (1980). On a class of poverty measures. *Econometrica*, 48(2), 437-446.

Kemal, A. R., Siddiqui, R. & Siddiqui, R. (2001). Tariff reduction and income distribution: a CGE-based analysis for urban and rural households in Pakistan. MIMAP Technical Paper Series, No. 11, Pakistan Institute of Development Economics.

Kennes, W. (1984). Food demand systems for Bangladesh. Staff Working Paper SOW-84-15, Centre for World Food Studies, Amsterdam.

Keyzer, M. A. (1986). Short-run impact of trade liberalization measures on the economy of Bangladesh: exercises in comparative statics for the year 1977. In T. N. Srinivasan & J. Whalley (Eds.), *General Equilibrium Trade Policy Modeling*. Cambridge, Massachusetts: MIT Press.

Khan, A. R. (1990). Poverty in Bangladesh: a consequence of and a constraint on growth. *Bangladesh Development Studies,* 18(3), 19-33.

Khan, A. R. (2006). Rising inequality in Bangladesh: an analysis of sources and policies for containment. In S. Ahmed & W. Mahmud (Eds.), *Growth and Poverty: The Development Experience of Bangladesh.* Dhaka: The University Press Limited.

Khan, A. R., & Hossain, M. (1989). *The Strategy of Development in Bangladesh.* London: Macmillan.

Khan, H. A. (2004). Using macroeconomic CGE models for assessing poverty impact of structural adjustment policies. Asian Development Bank Institute Discussion Paper No. 12.

Khondker, B. H. (1999). A manual for social accounting matrix (SAM) construction. MAP Technical Paper Series, No. 10. Centre on Integrated Rural Development for Asia and the Pacific.

Khondker, B. H., Mujeri, M. & Raihan, S. (2006). Welfare and poverty impacts of tariff reforms in Bangladesh: A general equilibrium approach. MPIA Working Paper 2006-05, Poverty and Economic Policy (PEP) research network.

Khondker, B. H. & Raihan, S. (2004). Welfare and poverty impacts of policy reforms in Bangladesh: A general equilibrium approach. Paper presented at the the Northwest Universities Development Consortium Conference (NEUDC), HEC Montreal, Canada, 1-3 October.

Khundker, N., Mahmud, M., Sen, B., & Ahmed, M. N. (1994). Urban poverty in Bangladesh: Trends, determinants and policy issues. *Asian Development Review, 12*(1), 1-31.

Krueger, A. O. (1978). *Liberalization Attempts and Consequences.* Cambridge, MA: Ballinger Pub.Co. for NBER.

Lambert, S., Schneider, H. & Suwa, A. (1991). Adjustment and equity in Cote d'Ivoire: 1980-86. *World Development,* 19(11), 1563-1576.

Levinsohn, J., Steven, B. & Friedman, J. (1999). Impacts of the Indonesian economic crisis: price changes and the poor. Paper presented at the Conference on Poverty and the International Economy, organised by World Bank and Swedish Parliamentary Commission on Global Development.

Lofgren, H., Robinson, S. & El-Said, M. (2003). Poverty and inequality analysis in a general equilibrium framework: the representative household approach. In F. Bourguignon & L. A. P. da Silva (Eds.), *The Impact of Economic Policies on Poverty and Income Distribution: Evaluation Techniques and Tools*: A copublication of the World Bank and Oxford University Press.

Mahmud, W. (1979). Foodgrain demand elasticities of rural households in Bangladesh: an analysis of pooled cross-section data. *Bangladesh Development Studies,* 7(1), 59-70.

Mahmud, W., Ahmed, S. & Mahajan, S. (2008). Economic reforms, growth and governance: the political economy aspects of Bangladesh's development surprise. Commission on Growth and Development Working Paper No. 22. Washington DC: World Bank.

McCulloch, N., Winters, L. A. & Cirera, X. (2001). *Trade Liberalisation and Poverty: A Handbook*. London: Centre for Economic Policy Research.

Metzler, L. A. (1949). Tariffs, the terms of trade, and the distribution of national income. *Journal of Political Economy,* 57(1), 1-29.

Minot, N. & Goletti, M. (2000). Rice market liberalisation and poverty in Viet Nam. IFPRI Research Report No. 114, Washington, DC.

Mlachila, M. & Yongzheng, Y. (2004). The end of textiles quotas: a case study of the impact on Bangladesh. IMF Working Paper No 108, International Monetary Fund, Washington, DC.

Morrison, C. (1991). Adjustment, income and poverty in Morocco. *World Development,* 19 (11), 1633-1651.

Mujeri, M. & Khondker, B. (2002). Poverty implications of trade liberalization in Bangladesh: A general equilibrium approach. Available at http://unpan1.un.org/intradoc/groups/public/documents/apcity/unpan015815.pdf. Accessed September 2008.

Mujeri, M. K. (2004). Bangladesh decent work statistical indicators: A fact-finding study. Decent Work Pilot Progarm, National Policy Group, International Labour Organisation, available at http://www.ilo.org/public/english/bureau/dwpp/countries/bangladesh/. Accessed August 2007.

Naranpanawa, R. M. A. K. B. (2005). Trade liberalisation and poverty in a computable general equilibrium (CGE) model: the Sri Lankan case. Unpublished Ph.D dissertation, Griffith University, Queensland.

Nicita, A. (2004). Who benefited from trade liberalisation in Mexico? Measuring the effects on household welfare. World Bank Policy Research Working Paper No. 3265.

Noman, A. N. K. (2001). External shocks to a liberalised economy: simulations with a CGE model of Bangladesh. *Bank Parikrama,* 26(3 & 4), 33-55.

Noman, A. N. K. (2002). The impact of foreign trade policies and external shocks on the agricultural sector of Bangladesh. *Farming and Rural Systems Economics*, Vol. 45. Weikersheim: Margraf Verlag.

Oktaviani, R. (2000). The impact of APEC trade liberalisation on the Indonesian economy and its agricultural sector. Unpublished Ph.D dissertation, University of Sydney.

Osmani, S. R. (1990). Structural change and poverty in Bangladesh: the case of a false turning point. *Bangladesh Development Studies,* 18(3), 55-74.

Osmani, S. R. (2005). The impact of globalization on poverty in Bangladesh. Working Paper No. 65, Policy Integration Department, National Policy Group, International Labour Office, Geneva.

Osmani, S. R., Mahmud, W., Sen, B., Dagdeviren, H. & Seth, A. (2003). *The Macroeconomics of Poverty Reduction: the Case Study of Bangladesh*., Dhaka:United Nations Development Programme.

Oxfam (2002). *Rigged Rules and Double Standards: Trade, Globalisation, and the Fight against Poverty*. Oxford: Oxfam International.

Paukert, F. (1973). Income distribution at different levels of development: a survey of evidence. *International Labour Review,* 108 (2 & 3), 97-125.

Pearson, K. R. (1986). Automating the computation of solutions of large economic models. *Economic Modelling,* 5(4), 385-395.

PEKGEM An ORANI-G model of South Africa, available at http://www .copsmodels.com/oranig.htm. Accessed August 2008.

Peter, W. M., Horridge, M., Meagher, G. A., Naqvi, F. & Parmenter, B. R. (1996). The theoretical structure of MONASH-MRF. Preliminary Working Paper No. OP-85, Centre of Policy Studies, Monash University.

Pitt, M. (1983). Food preferences and nutrition in rural Bangladesh. *Reveiw of Economics and Statistics*, 65(1), 105-114.

Porto, G. G. (2003). Trade reforms, market access, and poverty in Argentina. Policy Research Working Paper No. 3135, Development Economics Research Group, World Bank, Washington, DC.

Powell, A. A. & Gruen, F. H. (1967). The estimation of production frontiers: The Australian livestock/cereals complex. *Australian Journal of Agricultural Economics,* 11(June), 63-81.

Powell, A. A. & Gruen, F. H. (1968). The constant elasticity of transformation frontier and linear supply system. *International Economic Review*, 9(October), 315-328.

Pradhan, B. K. & Sahoo, A. (2006). Impact of trade liberalization on household welfare and poverty in India. MPIA Working Paper 2006-01, Poverty and Economic Policy (PEP) Network Project.

Rahman, A. N. M. A. (1973). Elasticities of substitution in manufacturing industries in Bangladesh: An international comparison. *Bangladesh Development Studies,* 1(2), 173-185.

Rahman, M. (2007). Policy and prospect of jute and allied fibers with special reference to Bangladesh. Available at www.jute.org/Documents_Seminar_Workshop_Meeting/Paper%20by%20Secretary%20 MOTJ,%20Ban_myn.doc. Accessed September 2008.

Rahman, R. I. & Islam, K. M. N. (2003). Employment poverty linkages: Bangladesh. *Issues in Employment and Poverty.* Discussion Paper No. 10, Recovery and Reconstruction Department, International Labour Office, Geneva.

Raihan, S. (2008). Trade liberalisation, growth employment and poverty in Bangladesh.

Retrieved 16th November 2008 from http://www.gtap.agecon.purdue.edu/ resources/ download/3941.pdf.

Rajan, R. S. & Bird, G. (2002). Trade liberalisation and poverty: Where do we stand? Discussion Paper No. 0230, Centre for International Economic Studies, University of Adelaide.

Rashid, M. A. (2000). Impact of trade policy reforms on industrial capacity and employment in Bangladesh. Report prepared for Structural Adjustment Participatory Review Initiative (SAPRI) and presented at the Second National Forum on 13-15 March, 2001, Dhaka, Bangladesh.

Ravallion, M. & Sen, B. (1996). When method matters: Monitoring poverty in Bangladesh. *Economic Development and Cultural Change,* 44(4), 761-792.

Reimer, J. (2002). Estimating the poverty impacts of trade liberalisation. World Bank Policy Research Working Paper No. 2790.

Reinert, K. A. & Ronald-Holst, D. W. (1997). Social Accounting Matrices. In J. F. Francois & K. A. Reinert (Eds.), *Applied Methods for Trade Policy Analysis: A Handbook.* Cambridge: Cambridge University

Robilliard, A., Bourguignon, F., & Robinson, S. (2001). Crisis and income distribution: A micro-macro model for Indonesia. Available athttp://siteresources.worldbank.org/

INTPSIA/Resources/490023-1171549810534/14988_Indonesia_Crisis.pdf. Accessed September 2008.

Robilliard, A. & Robinson, S. (2005). The social impact of a WTO agreement in Indonesia. World Bank Policy Research Working Paper No. 3747.

Rosenblatt, M. (1956). Remarks on some non-parametric estimates of a density function. *Annals of Mathematical Statistics,* 27(3), 832-837.

Round, J. I. (1981). Income distribution within a social accounting matrix: A review of some experiences in Malaysia and other L.D.C.'s. Development Economics Research Centre, University of Warwick, Discussion Paper no 3.

Roy, D. K. (1996). Poverty alleviation and trade policy reform in Bangladesh: some selected issues. *Bangladesh Development Studies,* 26(1&2).

Rushdi, A. A. (1982). Factor substitutability in the manufacturing industries of Bangladesh: An application of the translog cost model. *Bangladesh Development Studies,* 10(2), 85-106.

Salma, U. (1992). Agricultural price policy in Bangladesh: general equilibrium effects on growth and income distribution. Unpublished Ph.D dissertation, Australian National University.

Savard, L. (2003). Poverty and income distribution in a CGE-household micro-simulation model: top-down /bottom up approach. CIRPEE Working Paper No. 03-43.

Savard, L. (2005). Poverty and inequality analysis within a CGE framework: a comparative analysis of the representative agent and microsimulation approaches. *Development Policy Review,* 23(3), 313-331.

Sen, B., Mujeri, K. & Shahabuddin, Q. (2004). Operationalizing pro-poor growth: Bangladesh as a case study. Available at http://siteresources. worldbank.org/ INTPGI/Resources/342674-1115051237044/oppgbangladesh(Nov).pdf. Accessed August 2007.

Sen, B., & Hulme, D. (2006). *Chronic Poverty in Bangladesh: Tales of Ascent, Descent, Marginality and Persistence.* Dhaka: Bangladesh Institute of Development Studies (BIDS) and Chronic Poverty Research Centre (CPRC), University of Manchester, Manchester, UK.

SHDU (2002). Social Accounting Matrix 2000 for Bangladesh (SHD-SAM 2000): A Social Accounting Matrix for Sustainable Human Development. Sustainable Human Development Unit, Planning Commission, Government of Bangladesh.

Siddiqui, R., Kemal, A. R., Siddiqui, R. & Kemal, M. A. (2008). Tariff reduction, fiscal adjustment and poverty in Pakistan: A CGE-based analysis. In J. Cockburn, B. Decaluwé & V. Robichaud (Eds.), *Trade Liberalisation and Poverty: A CGE Analysis of the 1990s Experience in Africa and Asia.* Quebec: Poverty & Economic Policy Research Network 2008. Available at www.pep-net.org/NEW-PEP/PDFFiles/TradeLiberalization&Poverty-final.pdf. Accessed February 2009.

Stifel, D. C. & Thorbecke, E. (2003). A dual-dual CGE model of an archetype African economy: trade reforms, migration and poverty. *Journal of Policy Modeling,* 25(3), 207-235.

Stolper, W. F. & Samuelson, P. A. (1941). Protection and real wages. *Review of Economic Studies,* 9(1), 58-73.

Stone, R. (1954). Linear expenditure systems and demand analysis: An application to the pattern of British demand. *Economic Journal*, 64(255), 511-527.

Thorbecke, E. (1991). Adjustment, growth and income distribution in Indonesia. *World Development,* 19(11), 1595-1614.

Thorbecke, E. (1997). A dual-dual framework to analyze the process of development. Paper Prepared for a Conference in Memory of John C. H. Fei on the economics and political economy of development at the turn of the century, Taipei.

Tran, H. N. (2007). Monash-VN: Development of a Dynamic CGE Model for the Vietnamese Economy and Analysis of Structural Changes During 1996-2003. Unpublished Ph.D dissertation, Monash University.

UNDP (2006). *Human Development Report 2006.* Oxford University Press for the United Nations Development Program.

United Nations (1993). *System of National Accounts.*United Nations publications sales no. E.94. New York: United Nations.

United Nations (1999). *Handbook of Input-Output Table Compilation and Analysis.*Vol. F, No.74. New York.

Vincent, D. P. (1985).Exchange rate devaluation, monetary policy and wages: A general equilibrium analysis for Chile. *Economic Modelling,* 2(1), 17-32.

Vos, R. & de Jong, N. D. (2003). Trade liberalization and poverty in Ecuador: A CGE macro-microsimulation analysis. *Economic Systems Research,* 15(2), 211-232.

Watts, H. (1968).An economic definition of poverty. In D.P. Moynihan (Ed.), *On Understanding Poverty: Perspectives from the Social Sciences.* New York: Basic Books.

Winters, L. A. (2000). Trade, trade policy and poverty: what are the links? Centre for Economic Policy Research (CEPR) Discussion Paper No. 2382.

Winters, L. A. (2002). Trade liberalisation and poverty: what are the links? *World Economy, 25*(9), 143-171.

Winters, L. A., McCulloch, N. & McKay, A. (2004). Trade liberalization and poverty: the evidence so far. *Journal of Economic Literature*, 42(1), 72-115.

Wittwer, G. (1999). WAYANG: *A general equilibrium model adapted for the Indonesian economy.* ACIAR Indonesia Working Paper 99.10 CIES, University of Adelaide.

Wittwer, G & Anderson, K. (2001). Impact of trade reform on the Australian wine industry: a CGE analysis. Discussion Paper No. 9908, Centre for International Economic Studies, Adelaide University.

Wodon, Q. T. (1997). Food and energy intake and cost of basic needs: measuring poverty in Bangladesh. *Journal of Development Studies*, 34(2), 66-101.

Wodon, Q. T. (1999). Microdeterminants of consumption, poverty, growth, and inequality in Bangladesh. Policy Research Working Paper No. 2076, Poverty Reduction and Economic Management Sector Unit, South Asia Region,World Bank.

World Bank (1995). Bangladesh:recent economic developments and priority reform agenda for rapid growth. Report No. 13875-BD, Country Operation Division, South Asia Region, World Bank.

World Bank (1998). Bangladesh: from counting the poor to making the poor count. Report No. 17534-BD, Poverty Reduction and Economic Management Network, South Asia Region, World Bank.

World Bank (1999a). Bangladesh trade liberalization: its pace and impacts. Report No. 19591-BD, Poverty Reduction and Economic Management Unit, South Asia Region.

World Bank (1999b). Foreign direct investment in Bangladesh: Issues of long-run sustainability. Available at http://www-wds.worldbank.org/servlet/ WDSContentServer/

WDSP/IB/2000/02/03/000094946_00011505355643/Rendered/PDF/multi_page.pdf. Accessed February, 2007.

World Bank (2002). *Poverty in Bangladesh: Building on Progress*. Report No. 24299-BD, Poverty Reduction and Economic Management Sector Unit, South Asia Region, World Bank.

World Bank (2004). *Global Economic Prospects 2004:Realizing the Development Promise of the Doha Agenda*. Washington, DC: World Bank.

World Bank (2006a). Country Assistance Strategy for the Peoples Republic of Bangladesh for the Period FY06-09. Report No. 53193, Bangladesh Country Management Unit, South Asia Region, World Bank.

World Bank (2006b). India-Bangladesh Bilateral Trade and Potential Free Trade Agreement. Bangladesh Development Series Paper No. 13, Poverty Reduction and Economic Management Unit, World Bank Office, Dhaka..

World Bank (2007). *World Development Indicators 2007*. Washington DC: World Bank Publications.

World Bank (2012), *World Development Indicators 2012*. Washington DC: World Bank.

WTO (2006). 2.

Younus, S. & Chowdhury, M. N. (2006). An analysis of Bangladesh's transition to flexible exchange rate regime. Working Paper Series, No. WP 0706, Policy Unit Analysis, Research Department, Bangladesh Bank.

Zhai, F. & Hertel, T. W. (2006). Impacts of the DDA on China: the role of labour markets and complementary education reforms. In T. W. Hertel & L. A. Winters (Eds.), *Poverty and The WTO: Impacts of the Doha Development Agenda*. Washington DC:a copublication of the World Bank and Palgrave Macmillan.

Zheng, B. (1993). An axiomatic characterization of the Watts poverty index. *Economics Letters,* 42(1), 81-86.

INDEX

A

absorption matrix, 99, 101, 102, 111
aggregate absorption (*see also* domestic absorption), 125, 129
agricultural credit, 182
agricultural land, 101
agriculture, 10, 16, 20, 21, 28, 29, 35, 39, 44, 45, 52, 53, 54, 118, 120, 138, 182, 222, 225
air transport, 59, 101, 137, 140
allocative efficiency, 1, 129, 130
AnalyseGE, 136, 137, 139, 190
anti-export bias ratio, 18, 19
Argentina, 41, 51, 52, 224, 231
Armington elasticities, xii, xvi, 70, 102, 145, 146, 147, 148, 150, 168, 169, 170, 172, 192, 193
Asian financial crisis, 40
Asia-Pacific Trade Agreement (APTA), 3
Atkinson index, vii, 6, 165, 166, 174, 180

B

balance of trade (*see also* trade balance), 22, 59, 83, 84, 125, 126, 128, 129, 130, 148, 178
baling, 131, 136
Bangkok Agreement (*see also* Asia-Pacific Trade Agreement (APTA), 3
Bangladesh Agricultural Model, 53
Bangladesh Bureau of Statistics, xix, 4, 20, 25, 26, 104, 106, 222, 223
Bangladesh model, xi, xii, xv, xvii, 6, 57, 58, 59, 60, 61, 64, 66, 68, 69, 70, 73, 77, 78, 80, 82, 84, 85, 86, 91, 92, 94, 95, 96, 99, 100, 102, 104, 107, 108, 111, 115, 117, 120, 121, 123, 129, 145, 151, 153, 160, 161, 178, 186, 192, 197, 220
banking, insurance and real estate, 137, 140
basic price, 78, 79, 80, 100, 101, 103, 109, 110, 111, 139, 195
basic values (*see* basic price), 57, 78, 80
Bay of Bengal Initiative for Multi-Sectoral Technical and Economic Cooperation, 3
Brazil, 51, 226
budget deficit, 4, 18
building and construction, 137, 138, 139, 140, 152, 179

C

Cameroon, 181, 225, 226
canal, dyke and other building, 140
capital, 15, 16, 17, 22, 37, 38, 39, 46, 47, 48, 49, 50, 53, 54, 55, 56, 60, 61, 66, 67, 69, 70, 71, 72, 78, 79, 80, 81, 82, 84, 85, 86, 89, 90, 94, 101, 104, 105, 108, 110, 112, 113, 116, 118, 119, 120, 124, 125, 126, 128, 129, 130, 138, 141, 142, 144, 152, 166,167, 183, 184, 188, 189, 193
capital stock, 47, 55, 71, 72, 84, 94, 110, 124, 125, 126, 129, 130, 141, 142, 152
CBN method (*see also* Cost of basic needs method), 26
CBN poverty lines, 26
cement manufacturing, 137, 138, 139, 140, 179
CGE model(s) (see computablr general equilibrium model(s)), 6, 43, 44, 45, 46, 47, 48, 48, 49, 50, 51, 52, 53, 54, 55, 56, 57, 58, 59, 60, 84, 85, 87, 89, 90, 91, 178, 227
CGE-IMH analysis, 47
chemical products, 54, 131
China, 2, 3, 47, 51, 181, 198, 223, 234
classical theory of international trade, 37
clay industry, 138, 140
closure, xi, xvi, 6, 54, 77, 82, 94, 95, 123, 124, 125, 126, 129, 130, 137, 139, 224
cloth milling, 131, 136

Columbia, 49, 223
commodity concentration in exports (*see also* commodity composition of exports), 182
communications, 137, 140
comparative advantage, 181
compensation of employees, 103, 108, 112
computable general equilibrium model(s) 6, 37, 42, 56, 57, 183
constant returns to scale, 38, 51, 54, 61, 63, 94, 128
consumer price index, 82, 94, 124, 127, 128, 129, 139, 141, 143, 146, 149, 179
consumer price level, 121, 144, 145, 178
consumption, vii, xii, 3, 6, 20, 25, 26, 27, 30, 40, 41, 43, 45, 46, 48, 50, 54, 55, 56, 57, 73, 74, 76, 77, 81, 82, 84, 88, 103, 111, 112, 115, 116, 117, 118, 123, 124, 125, 126, 127, 128, 129, 130, 137, 138, 139, 141, 144, 145, 147, 149, 150, 151, 152, 155, 159, 162, 164, 167, 172, 174, 177, 178, 179, 180, 181, 184, 188, 191, 226, 233
consumption function, 57, 73
consumption tax, vii, 6, 46, 123, 127, 128, 129, 130, 139, 141, 144, 149, 152, 159, 162, 164, 167, 174, 177, 178, 179, 180, 181, 184
Cost of basic needs method (CBM Method), 27
cost-of-living analysis, 39
Cote d'Ivoire, 42, 45
cross-country regression analysis, 39, 40
current account, 4, 17, 22

D

DAD software, 154, 158, 166
DCI method (*see* Direct Caloric Intake Method), 25
depreciation, 10, 70, 72, 82, 127, 128, 130, 146, 147, 149, 150, 178
depth of poverty, vii, 154
devaluation, 10, 54, 233
development economics, ix, 37, 38
Direct Caloric Intake Method (DCI method), 25
direct taxes, 17, 49, 54, 89
disposable income (*see* household disposable income), xii, 43, 88, 130, 142, 143
Doha Development Agenda, 48, 222, 224, 226, 227, 234
Doha Round, 1, 45, 51, 226
domestic absorption, 128, 136, 138, 179
domestic share, 136, 137
droughts, 182
dynamic CGE model, 48, 55, 183

E

economic growth, 4, 5, 21, 30, 33, 36, 39, 40, 182
Ecuador, 42, 49, 180, 225, 233
edible and non-edible oils, 140
education services, 137
effective rates of protection, 13
elasticity of substitution, 61, 62, 63, 66, 67, 112, 113, 131, 145, 150, 225
elasticity of substitution between primary factors, 113, 145
electricity and water, 138
employment, vii, xi, xii, 5, 6, 25, 28, 33, 34, 35, 36, 38, 39, 40, 47, 48, 49, 52, 54, 56, 66, 82, 84, 87, 120, 123, 124, 126, 127, 128, 129, 130, 132, 136, 137, 138, 139, 140, 141, 142, 146, 148, 149, 151, 152, 158, 177, 178, 179, 181, 182, 231
endogenous variables, 94, 96, 124, 127
entertainment, 137, 138, 140
entropy index, vii, 166, 174, 180
exchange controls, 4, 9
exchange rate, xi, 4, 10, 16, 17, 19, 39, 54, 76, 80, 84, 94, 125, 126, 128, 157, 234
exchange rates, xi, 4, 17, 19, 54
exogenous variables, 50, 94, 96, 124, 127
export credit guarantee facilities, 4, 15
export demand elasticities, 114
export effect, 136
export incentives, 4
export orientation ratio, 18, 21
Export Performance Benefit Scheme, 14, 54
export price index, 84, 128
export promotion policies, 9, 14, 15
export volume index, 128, 146, 149
export-oriented industries, 15, 131, 136, 137, 138, 178, 179
export-related industries, 131, 136, 139, 152, 179
exports, xv, 4, 5, 10, 14, 15, 16, 18, 19, 21, 22, 38, 45, 48, 54, 55, 60, 76, 77, 78, 80, 81, 83, 89, 99, 102, 103, 112, 114, 116, 118, 128, 129, 130, 131, 136, 139, 148, 149, 152, 168, 178, 181, 187, 188, 193, 221

F

factorial income distribution, 99
factors of production, 37, 38, 41, 42, 44, 46, 48, 54, 55, 57, 78, 84, 104, 108, 119, 147
Fan decomposition, xvii, 136, 137, 138, 139, 192, 207, 214
female low-skilled employment, 152, 179
fertiliser and insecticide industry, 138

financial liberalisation, 4
financial reform, 15, 224
financial sector reform policies, 15
fiscal deficits, 123
fish processing, 137
fishing, 138, 140
fixed capital, 69, 70, 79, 81, 101, 103, 110, 124
fixed investment, 72, 82, 99, 110, 112, 125, 137, 139
flexible beta distribution, 43
floods, 26, 182
Food for Work Program, 182
Food Energy Intake Method (FEI method), 26
food processing, 137, 139, 179
foreign direct investment, 23, 39
foreign exchange market, 9, 54
Free Trade Agreement for the Americas, 49
Frisch parameters, 102, 115
fruit cultivation, 137, 139, 179
functional distribution of income, 1, 38, 42

G

gas, 23, 140
Gaussian kernel, 154
GDP price index, 83, 127, 129, 130, 141
GEMPACK, 58, 95, 96, 106, 137, 224, 227
gender dimension of poverty and inequality, 183
General Algebraic Modelling System (GAMS), 54
Gini index, vii, 6, 50, 157, 163, 165, 166, 172, 174, 180
glass, 137, 138, 139, 140, 179
Global Trade Analysis Project (GTAP), xix, 47, 51
globalisation, 1, 2, 25, 224, 226
government consumption, 77, 81, 82, 89, 90, 99, 112, 116, 125, 126, 129, 130, 138, 178
gross operating surplus, 85, 86, 89, 91, 103, 112, 116, 118

H

handloom cloth, 138
head count index, vii, 27, 48, 55, 154, 155, 156, 158, 161, 162, 168, 172, 180
head count ratio, 6, 25, 26, 50, 156, 159, 160, 162
high-educated households, 59, 115, 120, 121, 143, 144, 145, 167, 180
hotels and restaurants, 138, 140
household disposable income, 57, 76, 87, 88
household expenditure elasticities, 102, 105, 112, 114
household income, vii, 3, 5, 6, 30, 31, 41, 42, 44, 46, 48, 49, 52, 55, 86, 87, 88, 89, 99, 121, 126, 147, 148, 150, 158, 162, 166, 177, 189, 190, 194, 221
household income composition, 119, 120
Household Income and Expenditure Survey, xix, 27, 92, 104, 105, 157, 222, 223
household income distribution (*see* income distribution), 5, 31
housing services, 138, 140

I

IDC-GEM, 6, 57, 68, 78, 83, 84, 85, 89, 91, 116, 178
illiterate households, 59, 115, 144, 145, 167
import duties, xv, 11, 12, 78, 89, 103, 117, 123
import duty matrix, 101
import liberalisation, 9, 16
import licensing, 4, 16
import penetration, 18, 20, 131
import penetration ratio, 18, 20
import price index, 84, 129
import replacement effect, 140
import volume index, 128, 146, 149
import-competing industries, 131, 137, 138, 139, 140, 152, 179
imports, xvii, 4, 5, 10, 11, 13, 14, 17, 18, 19, 22, 38, 39, 44, 45, 54, 60, 63, 69, 80, 83, 91, 101, 102, 103, 107, 109, 110, 113, 117, 125, 126, 128, 129, 130, 131, 136, 137, 139, 148, 149, 168, 172, 178, 179, 193, 194, 195, 210
income distribution, 6, 31, 37, 38, 40, 42, 43, 44, 46, 47, 48, 49, 51, 53, 57, 58, 73, 84, 99, 104, 153, 162, 166, 223, 225, 226, 228, 231, 232, 233
income inequality, 6, 25, 30, 31, 36, 37, 40, 42, 51, 56, 123, 155, 166, 174, 178, 224
income mapping, 56, 116, 177
income tax exemptions, 4
indexation, 130, 139
India, 3, 23, 44, 52, 181, 225, 231, 234
indirect tax revenue, 17, 82, 89, 118, 123, 124, 127, 152, 162, 177, 178, 193
indirect taxes, 17, 44, 54, 78, 82, 89, 103, 109, 118, 127, 186, 187
Indonesia, 41, 42, 48, 115, 181, 225, 231, 232, 233
industry, xii, xvii, 6, 10, 13, 14, 20, 21, 35, 38, 44, 45, 59, 60, 61, 62, 63, 64, 65, 66, 67, 68, 70, 71, 72, 78, 79, 80, 87, 90, 94, 101, 102, 103, 107, 108, 109, 110, 111, 112, 116, 124, 128, 129, 131, 132, 136, 137, 138, 139, 140, 178, 179, 181, 183, 187, 189, 190, 191, 192, 193, 194, 195, 197, 198, 218, 233
inequality, vii, xiii, xv, 2, 3, 5, 6, 24, 25, 31, 33, 36, 37, 39, 42, 43, 44, 45, 46, 47, 48, 49, 50, 51, 52,

56, 153, 154, 156, 157, 164, 165, 166, 167, 168, 172, 174, 175, 177, 178, 180, 181, 183, 184, 221, 222, 223, 224, 226, 227, 229, 232, 233
inflation, 4, 10, 16, 23
information technology services, 137, 140
input-output database, xv, 99, 100
input-output table, 53, 115
interest on public debt, 85, 89, 116
interest rates, 4, 9, 15, 16
intermediate inputs, 54, 60, 61, 68, 73, 79, 81, 101, 102, 109, 116
international competitiveness, 128, 130, 178
International Monetary Fund (IMF), 9
intra-group incomes, 45, 183
inventories, 59, 60, 72, 83, 99, 101, 112, 116, 117, 125, 186, 194
investment, xv, 3, 10, 15, 23, 24, 39, 52, 53, 55, 69, 70, 71, 72, 73, 78, 82, 83, 90, 102, 105, 110, 111, 112, 116, 117, 118, 119, 124, 126, 127, 128, 129, 130, 138, 140, 141, 147, 149, 150, 178, 179, 182, 186, 188, 189, 191, 192, 193, 194, 195, 233
iterative top-down/bottom-up approach, 46

J

Johansen approach, 57
jute cultivation, 136, 138, 178
jute fabrication, 131, 136, 138, 178
jute goods, 10, 114

K

kernel density estimation (*see also* kernel non-parametric approach), 153
kernel non-parametric approach, 160
Klein-Rubin utility function, 73, 74
knitting, 76, 131, 136, 138, 139, 140, 142, 148, 152, 178, 179, 181, 182

L

labour demand, 65, 66, 126
labour force, xi, 21, 25, 28, 33, 34, 50, 66, 105, 126
labour force by gender and skill level, 105
labour force status, xi, 28
labour income, 41, 86, 87, 108, 118, 119, 120, 158
labour income composition, 120
labour market, 5, 6, 25, 33, 36, 39, 48, 49, 50, 54, 114, 124, 126, 158, 178, 183, 234
labour mobility, 129
land, xv, 17, 29, 37, 38, 46, 55, 56, 59, 60, 61, 66, 67, 73, 79, 82, 84, 85, 86, 94, 101, 104, 105, 108, 116, 118, 119, 120, 124, 125, 126, 128, 129, 137, 141, 142, 166, 167, 182, 188, 193
land ownership, 29, 55
land reform, 182
landless households, 59, 105, 115, 121, 144, 145, 159, 167
large farmer households, 59, 105, 119, 144, 166, 180
Laspeyres cost-of-living index, 41
leather products, 22, 76, 131, 136, 138, 178, 179
linear expenditure system, 40, 50, 52, 60, 73, 114
local market effect, 136, 137, 138, 140
log-normal distribution, 43
Lorenz curve, 165
low-educated households, 59, 105, 115
lower poverty line, 26, 27

M

machinery and equipment, 138
macroeconomic effects, 127
macroeconomic indicators, 5, 148, 150, 152
macroeconomic performance, vii, 5, 6, 9, 123, 151, 177
Madagascar, 46, 224
MAKE matrix, 101, 102, 107, 111
male low-skilled employment, 142
marginal budget shares, 114, 115
marginal farmer households, 59, 105, 144, 145, 158
medium-educated households, 59, 105, 115, 143, 144, 145
Mexico, 41, 42, 47, 227, 228, 230
micro-credit schemes, 182
micro-macro synthesis, 39, 47
micro-simulation, 43, 45, 46, 47, 48, 49, 50, 51, 52, 183, 232
Millennium Development Goals, xix, 1, 2
miscellaneous industry, 138
mixed income, 103, 108, 118
money supply, 10, 54
money wages, 82, 94, 130, 139, 178, 179
monotonicity axiom, 154, 155
multi-country analysis, 52
Multi-Fibre Agreement, 181

N

Nepal, 3, 46, 224
non-agricultural households, 59, 105, 115, 120, 143, 144, 145
non-traded goods industries, 131

non-traditional exports, 22, 76, 77, 114
numeraire, 94, 125, 126

O

old-age allowances, 182
openness, 18, 19, 40
ORANI, xii, 6, 54, 56, 57, 58, 68, 70, 72, 76, 77, 78, 82, 83, 94, 101, 107, 108, 111, 113, 114, 116, 124, 129, 145, 224, 225, 227, 228, 230
ORANI-F, 6, 57, 76, 228
ORANI-G, xii, 57, 58, 68, 70, 72, 76, 77, 78, 82, 83, 94, 101, 107, 108, 111, 116, 124, 129, 145, 227, 228, 230

P

paddy, 138
Pakistan, 4, 9, 15, 23, 42, 181, 228, 232
paper industry, 140
parametric representative household approach, 6, 45, 153
para-tariffs, 11
Pareto distribution, 43
petroleum refining, 131, 137, 138, 139, 140, 179
Philippines, 42, 45, 50, 224, 225, 228
population, xi, 2, 3, 4, 10, 20, 25, 26, 27, 28, 29, 33, 34, 38, 87, 121, 126, 154, 155, 156, 157, 158, 165, 184
port, road and railway building, 140
poverty, vii, ix, xi, xii, xiii, xv, xvi, 1, 2, 3, 4, 5, 6, 24, 25, 26, 27, 28, 29, 30, 33, 36, 37, 38, 39, 40, 41, 42, 43, 44, 45, 46, 47, 48, 49, 50, 51, 52, 53, 55, 56, 58, 73, 92, 93, 105, 123, 129, 130, 146, 147, 148, 149, 150, 153, 154, 155, 156, 157, 158, 159, 160, 161, 162, 163, 164, 166, 168, 169, 170, 171, 172, 173, 174, 177, 178, 180, 181, 182, 183, 184, 189, 195, 221, 222, 223, 224, 225, 226, 227, 228, 229, 230, 231, 232, 233, 234
poverty gap index, vii, 6, 43, 155, 156, 159, 161, 162, 168, 172
poverty incidence, 25, 26, 42, 43, 44
poverty line, xi, 4, 6, 25, 26, 27, 42, 44, 45, 55, 58, 92, 93, 129, 130, 146, 147, 148, 149, 150, 153, 154, 155, 156, 157, 159, 162, 177, 189, 195
poverty profile, 25, 55, 129, 153, 156
Poverty Reduction Strategy Paper, xix, 2
power of tariff, 127
power plant building, 140
price homogeneity test, 94
price of labour, 67, 129, 141, 167, 187
primary factors, 38, 56, 57, 60, 61, 66, 67, 68, 81, 82, 101, 102, 113, 148, 166, 186, 192
privatisation, 4
production function, 60, 61, 62, 66, 67, 68, 69, 70, 94, 113
production matrix, 99, 101
professional services, iv, 118, 137, 140
protectionist trade policy, 4, 10
public administration and defence, 136, 137, 138, 139
pulses, 138
purchasing power parity, xi, 2, 3, 30

Q

quantitative restrictions, 1, 4, 10, 13, 53, 181

R

rail and land transport, 137, 140
rate of return on capital, 72, 124
raw jute, 10, 114
ready-made garments, 15, 20, 22, 35, 55, 76, 131, 136, 138, 139, 140, 148, 178, 179, 181
real depreciation, 128, 129, 130, 152
real devaluation, 84
real exchange rate, 16, 84, 128, 146, 178, 225
real GDP, 4, 10, 20, 49, 83, 125, 127, 128, 129, 130, 140, 146, 148, 149, 152, 168, 178, 191
real GDP per head, 10, 20
real homogeneity test, 94
real wages, 1, 25, 33, 35, 36, 39, 54, 82, 127, 129, 144, 149, 178, 182, 223, 232
reconstruction and rehabilitation, 10
regionally disaggregated computable general equilibrium model, 183
rental price of capital, 141, 144, 167
rental price of land, 141, 167
representative household approach, 6, 43, 45, 46, 47, 48, 49, 50, 183, 229
retail and wholesale trade, 137, 140
rural building, 140
rural households, 28, 41, 45, 93, 106, 115, 159, 160, 161, 162, 167, 172, 174, 175, 180, 222, 228, 229
rural road building, 140
rural-urban migration, 184

S

safety net, 182, 184
SAM database, xii, 84, 115, 116, 117

saving, xv, 23, 66, 84, 88, 89, 90, 91, 116, 119, 126, 187, 190, 194
sectoral distribution of employment, 35
Sen index, 163
Senegal, 45, 47, 181, 222
sensitivity analysis, 145, 147, 148, 150, 153, 168
sequential top-down/layered micro-simulation approach, 47
service industries, 137, 138, 139, 140, 179
services sector, 21, 54, 118
severity of poverty, vii, 155, 156, 158, 162, 174, 180
S-Gini poverty index, 157
shrimp farming, 131, 136, 138, 139, 140, 178, 179
simulation design, 123
size distribution of income, 38, 42
small farmer households, 59, 105
social accounting matrix (SAM), 6, 57, 104, 229
South African economy, 57, 84, 178
South African households, 49
South Asian Free Trade Area (SAFTA), 3
South Asian Preferential Trade Agreement (SAPTA), 3
spatial equilibrium model, 41
Special Bonded Warehouse Facility, 14
spice cultivation, 137, 138, 139, 140, 179
squared poverty gap index, vii, 6, 159, 161, 162
Sri Lanka, 3, 23, 45, 52, 115, 180, 181, 222, 225, 230
Stolper-Samuelson theorem, 1, 38, 167, 182, 223
Stone-Geary utility function, 52, 73, 195
structural adjustment, 1, 3, 9, 17, 229
structural adjustment programs, 3, 9
structural change, 20, 21, 22, 25
subsidies, 14, 19, 41, 51, 52, 53, 54, 55, 60, 78, 82, 101, 103

T

TABLO, 58, 59, 61, 63, 65, 66, 67, 68, 69, 70, 72, 73, 75, 76, 77, 78, 80, 81, 83, 84, 85, 86, 87, 88, 89, 90, 91, 92, 94, 96, 106, 108
tariff liberalisation, xii, 6, 54, 55, 57, 129, 144, 146, 147, 149, 150, 182
tariff reform, 10, 40, 52, 56, 123, 126, 143, 229
tariff revenue, vii, 6, 45, 56, 82, 91, 128, 177, 181, 184, 186, 187, 193
tariffs, vii, xv, xvi, 4, 5, 6, 10, 11, 13, 39, 40, 41, 44, 46, 47, 49, 50, 51, 52, 53, 54, 55, 56, 78, 91, 118, 123, 125, 127, 129, 130, 131, 136, 137, 138, 141, 142, 144, 145, 147, 148, 150, 151, 152, 153, 159, 160, 162, 164, 167, 168, 169, 170, 171, 173, 174, 177, 178, 179, 180, 181, 182, 183, 184, 194
tax holidays, 4, 10, 15
tea cultivation, 131, 136, 138, 178
terms of trade, 39, 84, 128, 129, 146, 178, 230
toiletries manufacturing, 136, 138, 139, 140, 178, 179
trade and transport margins, 103
trade balance, 22, 127, 128, 130, 138, 146, 149, 178, 179, 222
trade liberalisation, 1, 2, 3, 5, 6, 9, 10, 17, 20, 25, 27, 33, 36, 37, 39, 40, 41, 42, 43, 44, 45, 46, 47, 48, 49, 51, 52, 53, 55, 56, 73, 128, 146, 160, 167, 177, 180, 181, 182, 183, 184, 224, 230, 231
trade openness, 9
trade policy reform (*see also* trade liberalisation), 4, 5, 9, 18, 52, 222, 225, 231, 232
trade tax matrix, 99
trade-GDP ratio, 18
traditional exports, 76, 77, 187
transfer axiom, 155
transfer payments, 84, 86, 116, 119
transfers, 39, 45, 49, 53, 86, 87, 88, 89, 90, 91, 117, 118, 119, 120, 121, 188, 190, 192, 194
transport equipment, 131, 137
Tunisia, 181, 223
Tunisian economy, 48

U

UN peace-keeping services, 136
underemployment, 34
unemployment, 34, 52, 126
unincorporated businesses, 86, 108, 118
upper poverty line, xi, xv, 26, 27, 28, 29, 36
urban building, 140
urban households, 28, 47, 93, 106, 115, 119, 159, 160, 161, 162, 174, 175, 180

V

Vietnam, 41, 42, 181
Vulnerable Group feeding programs, 182

W

Wage Earner's Scheme, 16
warehousing, 137, 140
water transport, 59, 101, 136, 137, 138, 139, 178
Watts index, 163
welfare, 1, 5, 25, 37, 39, 40, 41, 42, 44, 45, 47, 48, 52, 53, 54, 55, 56, 57, 124, 129, 130, 144, 145, 157, 165, 178, 181, 184, 221, 222, 227, 230, 231
within-group variation of inequality, 45

World Bank, xx, 1, 2, 3, 4, 9, 11, 12, 13, 14, 15, 17, 18, 19, 23, 25, 26, 27, 28, 29, 30, 51, 186, 222, 223, 224, 225, 226, 227, 229, 230, 231, 232, 233, 234
World Economic Forum, 1
World Trade Organization (WTO), 1, 181